THE COMMON LAW
AND ENGLISH JURISPRUDENCE
1760–1850

The Common Law
and English Jurisprudence
1760–1850

MICHAEL LOBBAN

CLARENDON PRESS · OXFORD

1991

Oxford University Press, Walton Street, Oxford OX2 6DP

Oxford New York Toronto
Delhi Bombay Calcutta Madras Karachi
Petaling Jaya Singapore Hong Kong Tokyo
Nairobi Dar es Salaam Cape Town
Melbourne Auckland
and associated companies in
Berlin Ibadan

Oxford is a trade mark of Oxford University Press

Published in the United States
by Oxford University Press, New York

British Library Cataloguing in Publication Data
data available

Library of Congress Cataloging in Publication Data
Lobban, Michael.
The common law and English jurisprudence, 1760–1850/Michael Lobban.
Based on the author's thesis (Corpus Christi College, Cambridge).
Includes bibliographical references and index.
1. Common law—Great Britain—History. 2. Law—Great Britain—
History and criticism. 3. Jurisprudence—History. I. Title.
KD671.L6   1991   349.42—dc20   [344.2]   91–52
ISBN 0–19–825293–5

Typeset by Joshua Associates Limited, Oxford
Printed in Great Britain by
Bookcraft Ltd
Midsomer Norton
Avon

Preface

No work of this type can be completed without incurring a great number of debts of gratitude, and it gives me great pleasure to have this opportunity to acknowledge the help and advice of a number of people without whose support and encouragement this project would not have seen the light of day. My greatest debt is to V. A. C. Gatrell, who supervised the thesis on which this book is based, and whose inspired teaching first awakened my interest in the history of legal matters in the eighteenth and nineteenth centuries. I have greatly enjoyed his good will and intellectual companionship since my undergraduate days. I have also benefited greatly from the comments of several other people who read parts of the work, and supplied me with useful comment and criticism. In particular, Nigel Simmonds' generous and incisive criticism encouraged me to think about many jurisprudential arguments in new light. David Sugarman also read parts of the original thesis, and provided me with very valuable advice and ideas not only on particular points, but on the approach to writing legal history as a whole. Tim Hochstrasser's comments and conversation, over a number of years, have always been enlightening and insightful and I have learned much from his perspectives. I am grateful also to my examiners, Professors J. H. Burns and Peter Stein, who made a number of helpful suggestions and encouraged me to develop the arguments in the thesis, and to Professor Brian Simpson for his comments on the manuscript and for alerting me to numerous errors. While I have been saved from many follies by these people, and others, it is perhaps too much for me to hope, in as wide-ranging a study as this, that I have expunged them all; and for the errors that remain I must claim full and exclusive responsibility.

This book has been written at a time when there has been a flourishing interest in the history of law and society, and in particular the intellectual history of law. It will be apparent to the reader how much I have benefited from much of the scholarship that has grown out of much of this recent work. In particular, I have gained a great deal from the scholarship and ideas of David

Lieberman and Gerald Postema, both of whom have mapped out new areas for exploration in the history of jurisprudence. It is my hope to add to this scholarship by concentrating more on the drier, pettifogging aspects of law; an approach which has its risks, but also, I hope, its rewards. Much of this work would not have been possible without the efforts of the Bentham Project at University College, London, and the scholars associated with them, who have, over a number of years, made Bentham seem a much more complex and sophisticated thinker than his early published works suggested and who have widened the access to this Bentham by making sense of his often cryptic manuscripts.

Material contained in Chapter 2 of this book appeared in an article on 'Blackstone and the Science of Law' in the *Historical Journal* in 1987 and I am grateful to the editors for permitting me to reproduce the material here.

I have been fortunate in being able to work on this project in the most congenial of environments, first as a graduate student at Corpus Christi College, Cambridge, and latterly at St John's College, Oxford. I am particularly grateful to the President and Fellows of St John's for electing me to a junior research fellowship which has enabled me to complete the work. I have benefited from the assistance of helpful and efficient librarians at the Cambridge University Library and the Squire Law Library, the Bodleian Library, the British Library, and the D. M. S. Watson Library of University College, London. Finally, I am delighted to record my gratitude for the constant support and intellectual stimulation, in other equally congenial environments, of my parents and the rest of my family. I would like to dedicate this book to them, and to the memory of my grandmother, who did not live to see its completion, but whose patient encouragement helped make it possible.

M.L.
March 1991

Contents

Abbreviations

Comm.	Blackstone, William, *Commentaries on the Laws of England*, 4 vols. (Oxford, 1965–9).
Comment/Fragment	Bentham, Jeremy, *A Comment on the Commentaries and A Fragment on Government*, ed. J. H. Burns and H. L. A. Hart (London, 1977).
IPML	Bentham, Jeremy, *An Introduction to the Principles of Morals and Legislation*, ed. J. H. Burns and H. L. A. Hart (London, 1977).
OLG	Bentham, Jeremy, *Of Laws in General*, ed. H. L. A. Hart (London, 1970).
Works	*The Works of Jeremy Bentham*, ed. J. Bowring, 11 vols. (Edinburgh, 1838–43).
UC	The Manuscripts of Jeremy Bentham held in University College, London.

Law Reports

A. & E.	Adolphus, John Leycester, and Thomas Flower Ellis, *Reports of Cases . . . in the Court of King's Bench*, 12 vols. (London, 1835–40).
Amb.	Ambler, Charles, *Reports of Cases . . . in the High Court of Chancery, with some few other courts*, 2nd edn. by J. E. Blount (London, 1828).
Atk.	Atkyns, John Tracy, *Reports of Cases . . . in the High Court of Chancery in the time of Lord Chancellor Hardwicke*, 3rd edn. by Francis William Saunders, 3 vols. (London, 1794).
B. & Ad.	Barnewall, Richard Vaughan, and John Leycester Adolphus, *Reports of Cases . . . in the Court of King's Bench*, 5 vols. (London, 1831–4).
B. & Ald.	Barnewall, Richard Vaughan, and Edward Hall Alderson, *Reports of Cases . . . in the Court of King's Bench*, 5 vols. (London, 1818–22).

B. & C.	Barnewall, Richard Vaughan, and Cresswell Cresswell, *Reports of Cases . . . in the Court of King's Bench*, 10 vols. (London, 1823–30).
B. & P.	Bosanquet, John Bernard, and Christopher Puller, *Reports of Cases . . . in the Courts of Common Pleas and Exchequer Chamber, and in the House of Lords, from . . . 1796, to . . . 1799*, 3rd edn., 3 vols. (London, 1826).
B. & S.	Best, William Mawdesley, and George James Philip Smith, *Reports of Cases . . . in the Court of Queen's Bench and the Court of Exchequer Chamber on appeal from the Court of Queen's Bench*, 10 vols. (London, 1862–71).
Bing.	Bingham, Peregrine, *Reports of Cases . . . in the Court of Common Pleas and Other Courts*, 10 vols. (London, 1824–34).
Bing. NC	Bingham, Peregrine, *New cases . . . in the Court of Common Pleas and Other Courts*, 6 vols. (London, 1835–40).
Bro. CC	Brown, William, *Reports of Cases argued and determined in the High Court of Chancery, during the time of Lord Chancellor Thurlow*, 5th edn. by Robert Belt, 4 vols. (London, 1820).
Brown PC	Brown, Josiah, *Reports of Cases upon Appeals and Writs of Error determined in the High Court of Parliament*, 8 vols. 2nd edn. (London, 1808).
Burr.	Burrow, James, *Reports of Cases . . . in the Court of King's Bench, during the time Lord Mansfield presided in that Court*, 5th edn., 5 vols. (London, 1812).
C. & J.	Crompton, Charles, and John Jervis, *Reports of Cases argued and determined in the Courts of Exchequer and Exchequer Chamber*, 2 vols. (London, 1832–3).
C. & P.	Carrington, F. A., and J. Payne, *Reports of Cases . . . at Nisi Prius, in the Courts of King's Bench and Common Pleas, and on the Circuit*, 9 vols. (London, 1825–41).
Camp.	Campbell, John, *Reports of Cases . . . at Nisi Prius, in the Courts of King's Bench and Common Pleas*

	and on the Home Circuit, 4 vols. (London, 1813–16).
CB	Manning, James, T. C. Granger, and John Scott, *Common Bench Reports. Cases . . . in the Court of Common Pleas*, 18 vols. (London, 1846–56).
CBNS	Scott, John, *Common Bench Reports. New Series. Cases . . . in the Court of Common Pleas, and in the Exchequer Chamber*, 20 vols. (London, 1857–66).
CCC	Cox, Edward William, *et al.* (ed.), *Reports of Cases in Criminal Law*, 31 vols. (London, 1846–1940).
Chitty	Chitty, Joseph, *Reports of Cases principally on Practice and Pleading determined in the Court of King's Bench*, 2 vols. (London, 1820–3).
Cl. & F.	Clark, C., and W. Finnelly, *Reports of Cases in the House of Lords, on Appeals and Writs of Error*, 12 vols. (London, 1832–46).
Co. Rep.	Thomas, J. H., and J. F. Fraser (ed.), *The Reports of Sir Edward Coke, Knt.*, 13 vols. (London, 1826).
Cowp.	Cowper, Henry, *Reports of Cases . . . in the Court of King's Bench from . . . 1774 to . . . 1778*, 2nd edn., 2 vols. (London, 1800).
Cox	Cox, Samual Compton, *Cases determined in the Courts of Equity from 1783 to 1796*, 2 vols. (London, 1816).
Cro. El.	Leach, Thomas (ed.), *Reports of Sir George Croke, Knight . . . of such select cases as were adjudged . . . during the reign of Queen Elizabeth . . . revised and published by Sir Harbottle Grimston*, 4th edn. (London, 1790).
Cro. Jac.	Leach, Thomas (ed.), *Reports of Sir George Croke, Knight . . . of such select cases as were adjudged . . . during the reign of James the First . . . revised and published by Sir Harbottle Grimston*, 4th edn. (London, 1791).
D. & R.	Dowling, James, and Arthur Ryland, *Reports of Cases . . . in the Court of King's Bench*, 9 vols. (London, 1822–31).
De G. M. & G.	De Gex, J. P., S. MacNaghten, and A. Gordon,

	Reports of Cases heard and determined by the Lord Chancellor and the Court of Appeal in Chancery, 8 vols. (London, 1853–7).
Dougl.	Douglas, Sylvester, *Reports of Cases . . . in the Court of King's Bench, in the nineteenth, twentieth, and twenty first years of the reign of George III*, 4th edn. by W. Frere and H. Roscoe, 4 vols. (London, 1813–31).
Dowl.	Dowling, Alfred Septimus, *Reports of Cases . . . in the Court of King's Bench*, 9 vols. (London, 1833–42).
E. & B.	Ellis, Thomas Flower, and Colin Blackburn, *Reports of Cases . . . in the Court of Queen's Bench and the Court of Exchequer Chamber on Error from the Court of Queen's Bench*, 8 vols. (London, 1853–8).
E. & E.	Ellis, Thomas Flower, and Francis Ellis, *Reports of Cases . . . in the Court of Queen's Bench and the Court of Exchequer Chamber on Error from the Court of Queen's Bench*, 3 vols. (London, 1863–7).
East	East, Edward Hyde, *Reports of Cases . . . in the Court of King's Bench*, 16 vols. (London, 1801–12).
Esp.	Espinasse, Isaac, *Reports of Cases . . . at Nisi Prius, in the Court of King's Bench and Common Pleas from . . . 1793 to . . . 1796*, 6 vols. (London, 1801–7).
Ex.	Welsby, W. N., E. T. Hurlstone, and J. Gordon, *The Exchequer Reports. Reports of cases . . . in the Courts of Exchequer and Exchequer Chamber*, 11 vols. (London, 1849–56).
F. &. F.	Foster, T. Campbell, and W. F. Finlason, *Reports of Cases . . . at Nisi Prius and at the Crown Side of Circuit; with select decisions at Chambers*, 4 vols. (London, 1860–7).
Freem. Ch.	Freeman, Richard, *Reports of Cases argued and determined in the High Court of Chancery principally between the years 1660 and 1706*. 2nd edn. by John Eykyn Hovenden (London, 1823).
Gilb. Rep.	*Cases in Law and Equity . . . printed from the ori-*

ginal manuscript of the late Lord Chief Baron Gilbert (London, 1760).

Godbolt Hughes, W. (ed.), *Reports of Certain Cases arising in the severall Courts of Record at Westminster in the Raignes of Q. Elizabeth, K. James and the late King Charles, collected . . . by the late learned Justice Godbolt* (London, 1652).

H. Bl. Blackstone, Henry, *Reports of Cases . . . in the Courts of Common Pleas and Exchequer Chamber*, 2 vols. (London, 1827).

H. & N. Hurlstone, E. T., and J. P. Norman, *The Exchequer Reports. Reports of Cases . . . in the Courts of Exchequer and Exchequer Chamber*, 7 vols. (London, 1857–62).

HLC Clark, C., and W. Finnelly, *Reports of Cases heard in the House of Lords*, 11 vols. (London, 1848–66).

Hob. *The Reports of the Reverend and learned Judge . . . Sir Henry Hobart*, 3rd edn. (London, 1671).

Keb. Keble, Joseph, *Reports in the Court of King's Bench at Westminster from the XII to the XXX year of the Reign of . . . King Charles II*, 3 vols. (London, 1685).

Ld. Raym. Raymond, Robert, Lord, *Reports of Cases . . . in the Courts of King's Bench and Common Pleas in the Reign of the late King William, Queen Anne, King George the First and King George the Second*, 4th edn. by J. Bailey, 3 vols. (London, 1792).

Leon. Leonard, William, *Reports and Cases of Law argued and adjudged in the Courts of Westminster, in the times of the late Queen Elizabeth and King James*, 4 vols. (London, 1687).

LJ *Law Journal Reports.*

LR *The Law Reports* (London, 1855–).

M. & S. Maule, George, and William Selwyn, *Reports of Cases . . . in the Court of King's Bench*, 6 vols. (London, 1813–17).

M. & W. Meeson, R., and W. N. Welsby, *Reports of Cases . . . in the Courts of Exchequer and Exchequer Chamber*, 16 vols. (London, 1837–47).

Macq. H. L. Sc.   Macqueen, John F., *Reports of Scotch Appeals and Writs of Error . . . in the House of Lords*, 4 vols. (Edinburgh, 1855–66).

Mod.   *Modern Reports: Or Select Cases adjudged in the Courts of King's Bench, Chancery, Common Pleas and Exchequer from the restoration of Charles the Second to the twenty eighth year of George the Second*, 12 vols., ed. T. Leach (London, 1793–6).

Moo. & Malk.   Moody, William, and Benjamin Heath Malkin, *Reports of Cases . . . at Nisi Prius, in the Courts of King's Bench and Common Pleas and on the Western and Oxford Circuits* (London, 1831).

Moo. & Sc.   Moore, John Bayly, and John Scott, *Reports of Cases . . . in the Courts of Common Pleas and Exchequer Chamber and in the House of Lords*, 4 vols. (London, 1833–4).

N. & M.   Nevile, Sandford, and William Montagu Manning, *Reports of Cases . . . in the Court of King's Bench*, 6 vols. (London, 1834–9).

P. Wms.   Williams, William Peere, *Reports of Cases . . . in the High Court of Chancery, and of some special Cases adjudged in the Court of King's Bench*, 4th edn. by Samuel Compton Cox, 3 vols. (London, 1787).

QB   Adolphus, John Leycester, and Thomas Flower Ellis, *Queens Bench Reports*, 18 vols. (London, 1843–52).

Railway Cas.   Nicholl, H. I., T, Hare, and J. M. Carrow, *Cases relating to Railways and Canals argued and adjudged in the Courts of Law and Equity*, 7 vols. (London, 1840–55).

Rol. Rep.   *Les Reports de Henry Rolle serjeant del' Ley, de divers Cases en le Court del' Banke le Roy*, 2 vols. (London, 1675).

Salk.   Salkeld, William, *Reports of Cases adjudged in the Court of King's Bench; with some special cases in the Courts of Chancery, Common Pleas and Exchequer*, 6th edn. by William David Evand, 3 vols. (1795).

Sayer	Sayer, Joseph, *Reports of Cases . . . in the Court of King's Bench* (London, 1790).
Sho.	Shower, Bartholomew, *Reports of cases adjudged in the Court of King's Bench during the Reigns of Charles the Second; James the Second; and William the Third*, 2nd edn. by Thomas Leach, 2 vols. (London, 1794).
Sid.	Siderfin, Thomas, *Les Reports des divers Special Cases Argue & Adjudge en le Court del bank le Roy, et auxy en le Co. Ba. & l'Exchequer*, 2nd edn., 2 vols. (London, 1714).
ST	*A Complete Collection of State Trials*, ed. T. B. Howell and T. J. Howell, 33 vols. (London, 1816–26).
Stark.	Starkie, Thomas, *Reports of Cases . . . at Nisi Prius, in the Courts of King's Bench and Common Pleas, and on the Circuit*, 3 vols. (London, 1817–20).
STNS	*Reports of State Trials. New Series*, ed. John Mac-Donell and John E. P. Wallis, 8 vols. (London, 1888–98).
Stra.	Strange, John, *Reports of Adjudged Cases in the Courts of Chancery, King's Bench, Common Pleas and Exchequer, from . . . the second year of George I to . . . the twenty first year of King George II*. 3rd. edn. by M. Nolan, 2 vols. (London, 1795).
T. & R.	Turner, George, and James Russell, *Reports of Cases . . . in the High Court of Chancery during the time of Lord Chancellor Eldon, 1822–24* (London, 1832).
T. Raym.	Raymond, Thomas, *Reports of Divers Special Cases . . . in the Courts of King's Bench, Common Pleas and Exchequer, in the Reign of Charles II*, 3rd. edn. (London, 1803).
Taunt.	Taunton, William Pyle, *Reports of Cases . . . in the Court of Common Pleas, and other Courts*, 8 vols. (London, 1810–19).
TR	Durnford, Charles, and Edward Hyde East, *Term Reports in the Court of King's Bench*, 8 vols. (London, 1817).

Vaugh.   Vaughan, Edward, *The Reports of that learned Judge Sir John Vaughan, Kt, late Chief Justice of His Majesties Court of Common Pleas . . . published by his son* (London, 1677).

Vent.   *The Reports of Sir Peyton Ventris . . . in two parts* (London, 1716).

Ves.   Vesey, Francis (jun.), *Reports of Cases . . . in the High Court of Chancery*, 2nd edn., 20 vols. (1827–33).

W. Bl.   Blackstone, William, *Reports of Cases . . . in the Several Courts of Westminster Hall from 1746 to 1779*, 3rd edn. by C. H. Elsley, 2 vols. (London, 1828).

Willes   Durnford, C. (ed.), *Reports of Adjudged Cases in the Court of Common Pleas during the time Lord Chief Justice Willes presided in that Court; together with some few cases of the same period determined in the House of Lords, Court of Exchequer and Exchequer Chamber* (London, 1800).

Wils.   Wilson, George, *Reports of Cases . . . in the King's Courts at Westminster*, 3 vols. (London, 1799).

Wils. KB   Wilson, George, *Reports of Cases argued and adjudged in the King's Courts at Westminster*, 3rd edn., 3 vols. (London, 1799).

Wms Saund.   *The Reports of the most learned Sir Edmund Saunders Knt late Lord Chief Justice in the Court of King's Bench, in the reign of his most excellent majesty, King Charles the second. Edited with notes and references to the Pleadings and Cases by John Williams*. 6th edn. by E. V. Williams, 2 vols. (London, 1845).

WR   *The Weekly Reporter*.

1

Introduction

THIS is a study of the debates about law and legal reasoning at the
end of the eighteenth and the beginning of the nineteenth centuries.
It seeks to address the question of what the common law was about,
and how theorists and practitioners conceived it, in such a way as to
make historians more sensitive to the legal framework. This is not
therefore a history of any particular doctrine or area of law, but a
discussion of the legal framework.

When historians discuss the common law, they tend to portray it
as a body of principles and rules that can be distinctly articulated and
defined. The standard view of the eighteenth-century common law is
perhaps that one taken by Morton Horwitz, which describes the pre-
industrial common law as being a fixed body of doctrine, based on
natural law and inflexible rules, which sought to provide fair
solutions.[1] Similarly, P. S. Atiyah has written that '[t]he law, to most
people of the eighteenth century, including the lawyers, had, in its
essentials, a sanctity and an unchangeability'.[2] The common law is
thus widely understood to have been seen as inflexible and
unchanging, the guarantor of fairness and justice, its perfect reason
guaranteed in its immemoriality. Flexibility, at least in theory, was to
be found in equity, which abated the rigours of the fixed common
law; yet by the 1770s, equity itself had largely hardened into a
precedent-based system, and precedent-minded common lawyers
were seeking to restrict equitable conceptions of the common law.[3] If
the law moved and grew, it was in a Burkean way, adding on to a
sturdy and solid ancient structure. At any rate, the common law was

---

[1] Morton J. Horwitz, *The Transformation of American Law* (London, 1977), ch. 1.

[2] *The Rise and Fall of Freedom of Contract* (Oxford, 1979), 97. He adds, 'Law could not
just be manipulated, and made out of nothing, as it were, to suit the passing fancies of
a political party, a King or even a Parliament; it was "there," it had an objective
existence of some sort; in its essentials it was unchanged and binding on everyone.'

[3] David Lieberman, *The Province of Legislation Determined: Legal Theory in Eighteenth
Century Britain* (Cambridge, 1989), 122–43.

not a tool of policy, nor a system to promote any short-term goal: for
it was based on natural law, with judges finding the single correct
solution to legal problems.

It is not surprising that historians have so characterized the law,
as a source-based system of positive rules, for by the eighteenth
century, most jurists discussing the nature of law discussed it in this
way. First of all, they described the common law as a set of rules and
guides to conduct. 'A Law', wrote Thomas Rutherforth, 'is a rule to
which men are obliged to make their moral actions conformable.'[4]
Law was seen increasingly as a distinct entity, but one issuing guides
to conduct. Ephraim Chambers's *Cyclopaedia* defined law as 'a
command, or precept, coming from some superior authority, which
an inferior is obliged to obey'.[5] This view stressed the legislative
nature of law above its adjudicative side. '[T]he power of all law is
from the *express*, and that of customs from the *supposed*, will of the
legislator,' wrote John Taylor in 1755.[6] This view had a pedigree, for
Hale had written of some customs which were now taken as being
immemorial, but which had originally been acts of parliament.[7] His
editor, Charles Runnington, could add, more positively, that
common law and statutes came originally from the legislature,
common law being 'nothing else but statutes, anciently written, but
which have been worn out by time'.[8] Similarly, Chief Justice
Vaughan had observed in 1672 that 'most of the *Common Law* cannot
be conceived to be Law otherwise than by *Acts of Parliament*, or
Power equivalent to them'.[9] Eighteenth-century writers who sought to
make definitions of the law could hence describe it in terms of rules
and in terms of bodies. Blackstone, describing what the common law
was, called it the law of custom,[10] which he divided into three types:
general customs, particular customs, and particular local laws.[11] For
Blackstone, there were certain positive tests to see whether the

---

[4] *Institutes of Natural Law*, 3rd edn. (London, 1754), 1.

[5] E. Chambers, *Cyclopaedia: Or, an Universal Dictionary of Arts and Sciences*, 7th edn.,
2 vols. (London, 1751; 1st edn. 1728), tit. Law.

[6] *Elements of the Civil Law*, 4th edn. (London, 1828), 245. Cf. *Collins v. Blantern*
(1767) 2 Wils. 347 at 348.

[7] Hale, *The History of the Common Law of England*, ed. C. M. Gray (Chicago, 1971), 45.

[8] M. Hale, *History of the Common Law*, 5th edn., ed. C. Runnington, 2 vols. (London,
1794), i. 5 n.

[9] *Sheppard v. Gosnold* (1672) Vaugh. 163. Quoted in Richard Tuck, *Natural Rights
Theories. Their Origin and Development* (Cambridge, 1979), 135.

[10] W. Blackstone, *Commentaries on the Laws of England*, 4 vols. (Oxford, 1765–9), i, 63
(henceforth as 1 *Comm.* 63).   [11] 1 *Comm.* 67.

custom was law: it had to be immemorial, continued, reasonable, certain, compulsory, and consistent.[12] This view of law as a tangible thing owed much to Coke's polemic against the crown, where he had argued for an ancient immemorial and unchanging common law. For if there was such a body, then it could be traced, so that even in the later eighteenth century, both Blackstone and Francis Sullivan were attempting to trace back the 'pure' feudal rules corrupted by the Norman conquest.[13]

The publication of Hale's *History of the Common Law* was a landmark in the establishment of a view of the law as a body based on a unified principle.[14] Hale's work sought to reconcile the political and historical polemics with a legal theory of the nature of the common law that was more sophisticated than Blackstone's static view. Given the recent historiography, which had shown how the law after the Conquest had differed from the pre-Norman law,[15] Hale reconciled the immemoriality of the common law with its flexibility by putting forward a Burkean view: the common law was a body, which grew and adapted itself to the people's needs, ever approaching perfection. Thus, 'by Use, Practice, Commerce, Study and Improvement of the English People, [the laws] arrived in Henry 2d's Time to a greater Improvement,'[16] he said, while under Edward I, the 'English Justinian', the law 'obtained a very great Perfection'.[17] According to Hale, the law was more or less settled by this time. For Hale, then, the law did change, but it was still a body, 'as Titius is the same Man he was 40 Years since, tho' Physicians tell us, That in a Tract of seven Years, the Body has scarce any of the same Material Substance it had before'.[18] The antiquity of the common law, which had always been a strand in English legal thought, now became a dominant one,[19] and the notion that one could not tell the origin of laws—and hence their reason—became a central idea in justifying

[12] 1 *Comm.* 77–8.

[13] 2 *Comm.* 52 and F. S. Sullivan, *Lectures on the Constitution and Laws of England*, 2nd edn. (London, 1776), 15.

[14] See Barbara J. Shapiro, 'Law and Science in Seventeenth Century England', *Stanford Law Review*, xxi (1968–9), 727–66. She shows that the seventeenth-century desire for certainty was manifested in Hale's attempt to see the whole law as a system.

[15] See J. G. A. Pocock, *The Ancient Constitution and the Feudal Law* (Cambridge, 1957).

[16] *History of the Common Law*, Gray ed., 84.

[17] Ibid. 101.   [18] Ibid. 40.

[19] Fortescue had praised the antiquity of the English law in ch. 17 of *De Laudibus Legum Angliae*. This was taken up vigorously by his nineteenth-century editor: see Andrew Amos's notes to chs. 17–20 of the work.

the common law. From Hale through Blackstone to Burke,[20] the idea
took root that the law was shaped by the collective reason of society,
and was not to be scrutinized in the light of its intrinsic reason.

Hale's view of law was one which stressed that there were right
answers to be found in the law. This can be seen in his response to
Hobbes's *Dialogue between a Philosopher and a Student of the Common
Laws of England*. Hobbes, discussing Coke's comment that nothing
was law which was not reason, dismissed this idea, saying that since
all men had reason, any man might disobey any law he felt
unreasonable, which was plainly absurd. From this, he argued that
'[i]t is not Wisdom, but Authority that makes a Law'.[21] Hobbes's
philosopher argued that reason could not be the arbiter of law, since
all disagreed on reason, so that law must be seen to come from the
sovereign.[22] Hale's response was to argue that the reason of law was
not the reason of every man, but, as in many other complex sciences,
needed learning and application.[23] Hale could thus rehabilitate an
idea of the artificial reason of the law, but he was still left with a rule-
based concept. For Hale argued that the natural reason Hobbes had
attacked led to an arbitrariness not found in the common law. '[T]hat
Law is best framed', he said, 'that at once hath Certainty, and yett
induceth as few particular mischiefs as may be.'[24] Since moral
actions were infinitely complex and varied, it was not natural reason
but the reason of time which produced solutions: 'Long Experience
makes more discoveries touching conveniences or Inconveniences of
Laws then is possible for the wisest Councill of Men att first to
foresee.'[25] This was a Burkean response to Hobbes's positivism,

---

[20] See J. G. A. Pocock, 'Burke and the Ancient Constitution', in his *Politics, Language and Time: Essays on Political Thought and History* (London, 1972), 202–32.

[21] *A Dialogue between a Philosopher and a Student of the Common Laws of England*, ed. J. Cropsey (Chicago and London, 1971), 55.

[22] Hence, Hobbes's positivist definition: 'A Law is the Command of him, or them that have the Soveraign Power, given to those that be his or their Subjects, declaring Publickly, and plainly what every of them may do, and what they must forbear to do.' Ibid. 71.

[23] '[T]ho' two, or more, men of ye Same perfection of the reasoning Facultie that have yett variously Exercised and applyed that Comon Facultie to their Severall objects, they are not Equally to Expect an equall aptitude and perfection in each othrs [sic] Science or art.' *Reflections by the Lrd. Cheife Justice Hale on Mr. Hobbes his Dialogue of the Lawe*, in W. S. Holdsworth, *History of English Law*, v. 500–13, at p. 502. For a discussion of the debate between Hale and Hobbes, see D. E. C. Yale, 'Hale and Hobbes on Law, Legislation and the Sovereign', *Cambridge Law Journal*, xxxi (1972), 121–56; R. Tuck, *Natural Rights Theories*, 135–9; and G. J. Postema, *Bentham and the Common Law Tradition* (Oxford, 1986), 46–66.

[24] Hale, *Reflections*, 503.   [25] Ibid. 504.

rejecting abstract reason, but none the less accepting the view that the law provided rules and tangible solutions within itself.

By the eighteenth century, Blackstone saw this artificial reason as being embodied in custom and the law of nature. However, this view of defined sources of law, and of positive rules that could be related to them, was relatively new. This is evident in earlier approaches to the law of nature. Lawyers like Fortescue did not consider that there was one universal system of natural law, but felt that the law grew from a number of sources. The common law was seen to conform to a natural law, but this natural law was no deductive or complete structure: rather, it was an innate rationality, to be seen and tested by the use of logic. Fortescue took his definition of law—'it is an holy sanction, commanding whatever is honest, and forbidding the contrary'[26]—from the civil law, but his method for discovering the reason of the laws was Aristotelian.[27] Fortescue saw no unitary system, but a multiplicity of good laws. 'If . . . under these three distinctions of the *Law of Nature, Customs* and *Statutes*, the fountains and originals of all laws, I shall prove the Law of *England* eminently to excel,' he wrote, 'then I shall have evinced it to be good and effectual for the government of that kingdom.'[28] He added,

The laws of *England*, as far as they agree with, and are deduced from the *Law of nature*, are neither better nor worse in their decisions than the laws of all other states or kingdoms in similar cases. For, as the *philosopher* says, in the fifth of his *Ethics*, 'The Law of Nature is the same, and has the same force all the world over.'[29]

This view could be interpreted, as it was by Selden, to see natural law as a base on which the body of the civil laws could grow.[30] It could equally be seen to use the law of nature as an external test of rationality, in a way which would give it a greater function in the practical reasoning of lawyers.

If the law of nature did not provide positive rules, and if common lawyers were suspicious of a Hobbesian sovereign, then their artificial reason implied a lawyerly craft which was inductive, drawing from what law existed, and analysing in an Aristotelian way. The result was that in the sixteenth and early seventeenth

---

[26] *De Laudibus Legum Angliae*, 8.
[27] Ibid. 20.   [28] Ibid. 47.   [29] Ibid. 48.
[30] See Tuck, *Natural Rights Theories*, 83–4. See also Lieberman, *The Province of Legislation Determined*, 44–5.

centuries, common-law theoreticians did not turn to the law of nature to provide a methodological framework, but, like John Dodderidge,[31] outlined the Aristotelian method as the necessary tool for anyone wishing to understand those sciences which were founded on reason. For Dodderidge, while all law might derive from the law of nature, the reason of the law had to be discovered by examining each rule through the rules of logic.[32]

This view of law as being derived from a form of reasoning was one shared by Coke, who had an essentially different conception of law from that held by those seeking to define all the law. For Coke had viewed the common law as being beyond definition, with an infinity of sources and guises. It was no coincidence that Coke never wrote a systematic treatise of the common law, but left his thoughts embedded in a chaotic commentary on Littleton and in his *Reports*; for to set down a complete defining treatise would have contradicted his idea of what the common law was about.[33] When Coke said what the common law was, he defined not one source, but twenty. More importantly, these sources were not sources of rules or guides, but were forms of reasoning. Coke's sources included the maxims and principles of the common law, books of authority, the original writs in the *Register*, correct entries of judgments and approved precedents, as well as such purely abstract ideas of the nature of reasoning as arguments from convenience, from the impossible, from greater to lesser conclusions and vice versa, from common presumptions, and from the opinions of learned men.[34] This definition of the common law was not a substantive one, seeing law

---

[31] *The Lawyer's Light: or a Due Direction for the Study of the Law* (London, 1629).

[32] Ibid. 10. See Richard J. Terrill, 'Humanism and Rhetoric in Legal Education: The Contribution of Sir John Dodderidge (1555–1628)', *Journal of Legal History*, ii (1981), 30–44.

[33] Coke's *Institutes* stand clearly in the common law tradition of unstructured descriptions of the law, for he made no attempt to reduce the law to a coherent, self-contained whole. Instead, the first book was a commentary on Littleton, being an unstructured presentation of a lifetime's learning, in which Littleton's structure was used to pass on a variety of facts and ideas in Coke's opinion central to the common law. For that reason, many of Coke's important comments bore little relation to the point being discussed in Littleton's text. Thus, his famous ideas on the embodiment of reason in the law were included in a commentary on Frankalmoigne. See *The First Part of the Institutes of the Laws of England; Or, a Commentary on Littleton*, 17th edn., ed. F. Hargrave and C. Butler, 2 vols. (London, 1817), 97b (henceforth as *Coke upon Littleton* 97b). The second book of the *Institutes* was a chronological description of statute, the third an alphabetical treatise on pleas of the crown, and the fourth an analysis of the courts.   [34] *Coke upon Littleton* 11a.

as a set of clear rules or as a system which contained in itself the answer to legal problems: it was rather a view of the law as a system of reasoning, where most of the 'sources' of law were modes of thinking. Coke's most famous definition of the law was that it was based on reason: '*Nihil quod est contra rationem est licitum*; for reason is the life of the law, nay the common law itselfe is nothing else but reason; which is to be understood of an artificiall perfection of reason, gotten by long study, observation, and experience, and not of every man's naturall reason.'[35] This definition cannot be taken as meaning that the common law was based on the reason of natural law, and that one judged the rules of the common law by a rational test: it meant that the common law was a system of reasoning, that the source of law lay in the way that judges thought about legal problems.

Common lawyers in Coke's era shared this view: for them, the law was not a set of rules from above, but a system of remedies responding to wrongs in society. Law was to be found not in rules, but in maxims, eruditions, and principles. As Plowden said,

Maxims are the Foundations of the Law and the Conclusions of Reason, and therefore they ought not to be impugned, but always to be admitted; yet these Maxims may by the Help of Reason, be compared together, and set one against another, (although they do not vary) where it may be distinguished by a Reason that a Thing is nearer to one Maxim than to another, or placed between two Maxims, nevertheless they ought never to be impeached or impugned, but always be observed and held as firm Principles and Authorities of themselves.[36]

Law was drawn from life. Not only did it have as many sources as life, but they interacted in a flexible way. John Dodderidge wrote,

[A]ll Grounds or Rules of the Law of *England* in respect of their matter which they doe concerne, are either such as are not restrained to any one proper or peculiar title of the Law, but as occasion serueth, are applicable into euery part, title or tractate of the law . . . All which, being either conclusions of Naturall reason, or drawne and deriued from the same, do not onely serue as directions and Principles of the Law, but are likewise as Positions and Axiomes to be obserued throughout all mans life and conuersation; hauing their originall from those Arts that are necessary and behoofull for maintenance of humane societie.[37]

---

[35] *Coke upon Littleton* 97b.
[36] *The Commentaries or Reports of Edmund Plowden* (London, 1779), 27.
[37] *The Lawyer's Light*, 7.

According to Dodderidge, the grounds of law included natural and moral philosophy, custom, civil and canon law. All these sources of law were multifarious and could not 'bee properly reduced . . . vnder any one peculiar title of the Law extant in any abridgement, table or dictionarie'.[38] To understand the law, the lawyer had to apply logic. This would reveal both the primary conclusions of reason, which were imprinted on the minds of all men, and the secondary principles 'which are not so well knowne by the light of nature, as by other meanes',[39] and which could be seen by speculation to be true, even though the manifest truth of them were unknown.

Dodderidge explained that legal rules came from two forms of reasoning, the one being manifestly true—the reason evident to all— and the other being a 'contingent veritie'. Contingent propositions, though framed on the observation of nature, were not equally manifest to all people, for reason was imperfect. 'Therefore,' he said, 'are those Grounds not vniuersally true, but subiect to many and manifould Exceptions: And yet never the lesse true in all such Cases as are not comprehended under these *Restraints* or *Exceptions*.'[40] There were instances where the rule could not cover all cases. Hence, the law was best left to each circumstance:

[I]t is more conuenient and profitable to the state of the common wealth to frame Law vpon deliberation and debate of reason, by men skilfull and learned in that facultie, when present occasion is offered to vse the same, by a case then falling out and requiring Iudiciall determination: for then it is likely, with much more care, industrie and diligence to be looked vnto; and much more time of deliberation is there taken for the mature decision thereof, then otherwise upon the establishing of any positiue Law, might be imported concerning the same.[41]

Justice and law hence came from reasoning on the case. New cases did not have anterior authority, but had to be decided by inference and application. The law was thus about deriving rules of reasoning, building the law from cases and circumstances, but not subsuming all under single rules. This conception of the common law as a system of reasoning was one that remained the practising lawyer's view. It will be seen that despite the rise of a jurisprudential view of the nature of the common law which stressed that it was built

---

[38] *The Lawyer's Light*, 15.   [39] Ibid. 45.
[40] Ibid. 58.   [41] Ibid. 90.

around single principles, a conception remained of it as a system of remedies that could be flexible and adaptive.[42]

At the beginning of the eighteenth century, most common lawyers did not seek to put their law into a rational form. Because they saw the law as a form of reasoning working within a set of remedies, most legal texts were written not in a systematic way, but as lists. The literature of the common law built from the bottom up, describing what law existed and assuming that it had an internal logic. The common law was seen to be based on the procedure of writs and actions as opposed to substantive laws or rights, so that the law was not seen as a self-contained whole, but developed in response to problems arising in society. Works outlining the various forms of writs were therefore a very important part of common law literature, the classic work still being Fitzherbert's *Natura Brevium*.[43] This form of literature remained popular in the eighteenth century, when William Bohun's *English Lawyer*, itself a summary of writs, explained that principle was to be discovered in the writs:

It is very justly observed by my Lord *Coke*[44] and others, That Original Writs are the Foundation on which the Common Law depends: And certainly a careful Perusal of, and attending to the various Forms of the Writs laid down in the *Register*, and in the *Natura Breviums*, will discover not only much of the Practice and Methods of Proceeding, but also in ma[n]y Cases, the very *rationale* and fundamental Principles upon which our Common Law is Built.[45]

Early eighteenth-century legal literature was dominated by the practitioners' books which displayed precedents of pleas. Such

---

[42] See S. F. C. Milsom, 'Reason in the Development of the Common Law', *Law Quarterly Review*, lxxxi (1965), 496–517.

[43] *The New Natura Brevium of the most reverend Judge Mr. Anthony Fitzherbert*, ed. William Rastall (London, 1652). The preface to this book illustrates how writs were seen to be the base of the common law: 'In every Art and Science, there are certain Rules and Foundations, to which a Man ought for to give credit, and which he cannot deny. In like manner there are divers Maxims and Fundamentals in the knowledge of the Common Laws of the Land, which a Man ought for to believe very necessary for those who will understand the same Law, especially at the beginning of their studies; for upon those Fundamentals the whole Law doth depend. For which purpose, in time past there was composed by a Learned Man, a very profitable book, cald, *The Register*, which doth contain sundry Principals, by which he would be well instructed who would study the Law. And also for that purpose was there composed by a Learned Man, a Book called *natura Brevium*, which Book doth declare and set forth the Diversities and natures of many Original Writs with their Process.' This book aimed to modernize the previous two.   [44] *Coke upon Littleton* 73b.

[45] William Bohun, *The English Lawyer* (London, 1732), 3–4.

books did not attempt to describe legal rules for the practitioner—for 'rules' followed cases, not vice versa—but neither did they attempt to analyse procedural rules. Instead, they merely showed the correct means with which to present a legal case, recording the pleas and the record of the averments in various cases without looking at all at the legal rules involved, the verdicts given, or the arguments of counsel. They were merely guides on how to draw up a good plea, for if the plea was correctly drawn, the case would be won. Among such works were Richard Aston's *Placita Latine Rediviva*, published in 1661, which was an alphabetical treatise listing various types of plea under each form of action. Thus, under the heading *Action sur le case* was listed 'Brief versus Tailer per deceit', 'Pre fauxment inditer de felony sans Clergy', and 'Versus Common carryer pur perder des Biens'. This type of book was extremely common.[46] For the practitioner, pleading was the entry to the reason of the law and legal texts focused on the forms of plea and presentation.[47] However, for the most part, there was no discussion of rationale in the textbooks.[48]

The other forms which the literature of the common law took equally reflected the idea that it grew from below, for the tendency was merely to describe the law as it was, with little systematic

---

[46] Others of the same ilk included Simon Theloall's *Le Digest des Briefs et des Choses concernant eux* (London, 1687); Henry Clift's *A New Book of Declarations, Pleadings, Verdicts, etc.* (London, 1719); and Robert Gardiner's *Instructor Clericalis* (London, 1693). See also Gardiner's *The Doctrine of Demurrers, setting the variety of precedents of Demurrers in all sorts of Actions and in all the several parts of Pleading* (London, 1706); *The English Pleader* (London, 1734); and the countless versions of the *Young Clerk's Tutor*.

[47] Thus Giles Jacob wrote in 1725 that the English laws were the most rational in the world, and that he had found 'the Fundamental Principles on which their great and Noble structure is built': yet the book he wrote was an alphabetical list of terms and procedures. *The Student's Companion* (London, 1725), iv. Jacob was the author of numerous texts on law, which reflected the common lawyers' method. One such was *A Law Grammar; or Rudiments of the Law*, which began by quoting Fortescue saying that 'as *etymology, orthography, prosody,* and *syntax,* are the springs and foundations of grammatical learning, so the *principles, causes* and *elements,* are the foundations of *learning in the law*'. This book was typical of its genre in its layout, being divided in six sections, covering definitions, the grounds and principles of law, maxims, moot points of practice, legal terms, and fictions. The fact that it reached a sixth edition in 1817 shows the tenacity of the thinking that lay behind it.

[48] For instance, William Bohun's *Institutio Legalis* (London, 1724) was divided into four parts: the first described terms and writs and the authority of the courts; the second covered crown informations, fines, the process of outlawry, and official writs; the third showed mixed and personal actions; and the fourth examined various pleas. Yet in all this, there was no discussion of the reason behind the system.

organization.[49] One such type of work was the abridgement of statutes, such as John Cay's, written in 1739, which stood in a long tradition of abridgements, whose major methodological tool was the alphabet.[50] Another type of work was the specific study of one aspect of the law, such as William Nelson's *Lex Maneriorum*, which collected all its information from case reports on copyholds, but arranged everything alphabetically.[51] A third form of legal literature which remained popular was the law dictionary and Nelson himself brought out an edition of Blount's dictionary.[52] Common law literature thus assumed that the law was not imposed, but grew out of society, and that therefore it could not be defined, but only described.

The problem with this view of the law was that it did little to explain the law's practical functioning. Law remained a mystery. '[The] knowledge of the law is like a deepe well,' Coke wrote, 'out of which each man draweth according to the strength of his understanding. He that reacheth deepest, he seeth the amiable and admirable secrets of the law, wherein, I assure you, the sages of the law in former times . . . have had the deepest, reach.'[53] The difficulty was that legal literature in the early eighteenth century did not inform the student how to achieve this, particularly since the demise of the early sixteenth-century works on method and logic.[54] Timothy Cunningham explained the problem of the modern approach: 'English law writers frequently begin their definitions with the words *is when*, which is erroneous,' he said, giving an example: '"Abatement," says Sir Edward Coke, *is when* a man died seised of an estate of inheritance, and between the heir and an estranger doth interpose himself and abate.'[55] The mere listing of large numbers of remedies

---

[49] For a survey of a typical selection of common law literature, see Louis A. Knafla, 'Law Studies of an Elizabethan Student', *Huntington Library Quarterly*, xxxii (1968–9), 221–40 and his 'The Matriculation Revolution and Education at the Inns of Court in Renaissance England', in A. J. Slavin (ed.), *Tudor Men and Institutions: Studies in English Law and Government* (Baton Rouge, 1972), 232–64. See also Wilfrid R. Prest, *The Inns of Court under Elizabeth I and the Early Stuarts, 1590–1640* (London, 1972), 132–49.

[50] John Cay, *An Abridgment of the Publick Statutes in Force*, 2 vols. (London, 1739).

[51] William Nelson, *Lex Maneriorum: or, the law and customs of England relating to manors and lords of manors*, 2nd edn. (London, 1733).

[52] Thomas Blount, *A Law Dictionary*, 3rd edn, ed. William Nelson (London, 1717).

[53] *Coke upon Littleton* 71a.

[54] See Abraham Fraunce's application of Ramist logic in *The Lawiers Logicke* (London, 1588), and William Fulbecke's *A Direction, or Preparation to the Study of the Law*, 2nd edn., ed. T. H. Stirling (London, 1829).

[55] T. Cunningham, *The History and Antiquities of the Four Inns of Court* (London, 1780), x.

left the common law unfathomable, and it was in this context that lawyers sought to make sense of it in bodies of rules.

This took several forms. At one level, the early eighteenth century, taking up this desire to define what the law was about, saw a growing interest in histories of doctrines and areas of the law, which sought to define the law. These treatises sought to analyse the law in terms of principle, showing the principle through history.[56] At another, it took the form of seeking to put the common law into a systematic framework, to show that it had rationality and comprehensiveness. This attempt, taken up by Blackstone, involved putting the law into a Roman structure, and showing that it could be related to a series of source-based rights, which could be derived from a natural law base. English lawyers had always seen the civil law as a source of principles and jurisprudence,[57] but they had not sought to reconcile their system with its forms. Blackstone sought to unite jurisprudence and common law practice into one framework, in order to show that the common law could be seen to fit a deductive system of reasoning from natural law principles, which were essential and epistemologically correct. This law saw the law as unfolding, as a matter of principle, in a deductive way from above, to produce a coherent and systematic structure which held within itself all the legal answers society might require. This was a new way of defining the common law, distinct from Hale's concept of a growing law.[58] This view, stressing the holistic nature and unity of law, was one shared by Bentham. Blackstone and Bentham are usually seen as

[56] Thomas Madox, in the preface to his *History and Antiquities of the Exchequer*, 2nd edn. (London, 1769), said it was useful to look at ancient law along with modern, so that 'by comparing them together, and by enquiring into the Causes of such Alteration as was afterwards superinduced, and the Manner in which it was brought about, he may comprehend the Subject-Matter in its full extent'. (vii) For a discussion of the histories, see Holdsworth, *History of English Law*, xii. 402–17.

[57] See Prest, *The Inns of Court* for the division of practical learning and theory in early seventeenth-century legal education. Donald R. Kelley in 'History, English Law and the Renaissance', *Past and Present*, lxv (1974), 24–51 argues that English legal education at the beginning of the sixteenth century was antitheoretical and ignorant of civilian works. This view is challenged, however, by Christopher Brooks and Kevin Sharpe in 'History, English Law and the Renaissance', *Past and Present*, lxxii (1976), 133–42, where they argue that English lawyers did not claim a perfection or immemoriality of the common law before Coke, but were aware of, and made use of, civilian jurisprudence.

[58] Hale had written, 'it is not possible for men to come to the Same Certainty, evidence and Demonstration touching [laws] as may be expected in Mathematicall Sciences'. *Reflections*, 502.

the great antagonists, the one representing an ancient common law tradition and a natural law theory, the other a modern legislative notion based on positivist ideas of law. However, it will be seen here that Bentham's Pannomion was a natural successor to Blackstone, and that the conceptions of law as a unity that both men held stood outside the common law view. For it was only when the work of Blackstone, attempting to show that it was an ideal holistic code, failed to make the content of the common law fit the structure and the theory, that Bentham saw that, in order to achieve the ideal rule-based code resting on coherent first principles deducing into a whole system of law, one had to abandon the common law framework, and define anew. It will be seen that the Blackstonian and Benthamic views of law—those essentially taken up by historians as the mainstream discussions of what the law was about—were in fact outside the mainstream of what lawyers thought the law was about. It will be seen also that in both men's attempts to redefine law, they were less unequivocal about the traditional method than has been supposed.

At the same time that Blackstone was seeking to create a rights-based structure of the common law, other lawyers were seeking a rationalization of law by organizing and ordering the notions of legal remedies they had. At the end of the eighteenth century, there was therefore a growth in interest in the science of pleading, as the heart of the law. This involved rationalizing and refining the intricacies of the rules of practice to create a framework where a theory of law based on logical forms of reasoning and a multiplicity of sources could be revived. The articulation of a theory of law as a system of remedies allowed the common lawyers to reject the Blackstonian and Benthamic visions, and is therefore a vital context for explaining the survival of a haphazard common law system into the nineteenth century, in the face of attempts to codify the law.

This is a study of the conception of law; but in order to understand developments in that conception, and the impact of legal ideas, it is necessary to understand how the law worked in practice. For the latter view of law we have discussed was a practitioner's view, which created a theory out of a view of how the law in fact worked. It is an aim of this study, then, to examine the interaction of legal theory and practice, to show how they influenced each other. It will be seen that we cannot look at law through the theoretical lenses of Blackstone and Bentham, and that historians cannot understand the

common law of the period unless they come to terms with its
intrinsic nature as a system of remedies, and see the importance of
the practitioners' view. It will be seen that this theory of law, of its
growth from below through the presentation of cases, had in the end
to be accommodated by jurisprudence, and that the jurisprudence of
men like Austin retreated importantly from the reformist view of law
put forward by Bentham. It will be seen that the essential theory of
the common law, and the one to survive into the nineteenth century,
was the one which stressed that the law was a system of remedies,
where the law did not contain within itself all the answers to legal
problems, but drew on a multiplicity of sources to arrive at its
solutions.

By examining the view of the common law as a series of remedies,
it can also be seen how the law reflected opinion, and turned to
politics, morals, and abstract notions of justice for solutions to cases.
The law, it will be seen, did not define right and wrong, but sought
to follow the needs and dictates of society, as interpreted by the
judges. Perhaps the most useful analysis of jurisprudence was
provided neither by Blackstone nor Bentham, but by Adam Smith's
idea of the impartial spectator. For Smith, rights did not derive from
imposition (whether by God, nature, or a sovereign) but from the
recognition an impartial spectator would give them. Thus, 'we may
conceive an injury was done when an impartial spectator would be
of opinion [that the sufferer] was injured, [and] would join with him
in his concern and go along with him when he defended the subject
in his possession against any violent attack'. The right was proved
by the sympathy of the impartial spectator. Thus, in the case of theft,
'[t]he cause of this sympathy or concurrence betwixt the spectator
and the possessor is, that he enters into his thoughts and concurs in
his opinion that he may form a reasonable expectation of using . . .
whatever it is in the manner he pleases'.[59] By this view, the law had
to find the appropriate remedy for the injured party from an
impartial point of view, thereby solving the case in a just way, but
bearing in mind moral questions which went beyond the case.

This was the substantive aim of the common law: not to apply
eternal rules, nor to regulate society from above, but to provide

---

[59] *Lectures on Jurisprudence*, ed. R. Meek, D. D. Raphael, and P. G. Stein (Oxford,
1978), 17. Smith elaborated this when discussing crimes: 'in all cases the measure of
the punishment to be inflicted on the delinquents is the concurrence of the impartial
spectator with the resentment of the injured.' Ibid. 104.

useful, just, and flexible solutions to individual cases. This was not done in a vacuum of arbitration, however, and there were strict rules on case presentation. Before the court could make substantive decisions based on justice or fairness, the parties had to fulfil the strict requirements of procedure and the technicalities of case presentation. Once a dispute was formally set, the court looked to a range of sources for a resolution of the case: but their range of solutions was itself limited and constricted by the forms in which they were presented. Legal solutions could thus be an odd mixture of notions of policy and justice, and technical arguments where substantive decisions were shaped by the form of action.

The discussion of legal reasoning in the courts will focus almost wholly on internal legal debates and considerations of legal doctrines without looking closely at social influences and political considerations outside the courts which influenced the development of law. This, it may be argued, is to make the study too narrow, and imply that the history of law can be written wholly from within, as if legal doctrine has its own logic blissfully impervious to the petty considerations of daily life.[60] However, there are reasons why, in this case, the approach is justified. First, while law is a social phenomenon, it works in an artificial forum with its own form of argument and its own language. As Ronald Dworkin has written, '[e]very actor in the practice understands that what it permits or requires depends on the truth of certain propositions that are given sense only by and within the practice; the practice consists in large part in deploying and arguing about these propositions'.[61] Law has a relative autonomy; and those who suggest that the law is wholly or mostly shaped by social considerations outside the legal forum would do well to remember that, in practice, legal constructs formulated and imposed in the artificial forum of the court often determine and shape those social identities and forces said to control the law.[62] Second, it will be seen that the law was not cut off from society, but that it was accepted that the law drew its rules from society and changed in response to social needs. As will be seen, this

---

[60] See especially the important introductory essay to G. R. Rubin and D. Sugarman, *Law, Economy and Society, 1750–1914: Essays in the History of English Law* (Abingdon, 1984), for an approach which relates law to society.

[61] *Law's Empire* (London, 1986), 13.

[62] This is why Critical Legal Scholars, seeking to delegitimize the law, focus almost wholly on doctrine. See Robert W. Gordon, 'Critical Legal Histories', *Stanford Law Review*, xxxvi (1984), 57–125.

was not at the first level, but at a secondary level. Law was more than an instrument of policy: but policy was part of law. Social and policy considerations remained central: but the peculiarity of the legal context in which, and how, these ideas were discussed means that we must first have a full understanding of that legal context before we can assess the importance of those external considerations.

The view of law shown here will therefore differ from most views of the common law of our period. It will be seen that the law was not based on any concept of the law of nature or any other single standard. Such standards imply that there is a single right answer to be found for legal problems and that there are clear standards of morals or justice which can be used to find those answers. This idea was bound to fail, for it proved impossible to find such solutions. In practice, courts could only find the *best* answer, answers which only had validity so long as they succeeded in their aims and were useful. Law had to reflect society and its needs: and just as there were no single answers in daily life, so there were none in law. It was this fact which most undermined the static constructs of Blackstone and Bentham. Law remained in essence procedural, not rule based. Within this series of forms, judges sought the best answers to problems, which could best benefit the community, which served the interests of justice—however they defined that—and which satisfied the litigants. Each case was set by the litigants, each dispute was new; and because judges were solving each case as presented to them by drawing on a multiplicity of sources, the legal answers they produced were a reflection of the haphazard morality of the society, shaped in the artificial forum.

2

The Common Law and the *Commentaries*

WHEN Blackstone sought to devise a course of lectures to give young gentlemen 'some acquaintance with the laws of the land',[1] he faced the problem not only of creating an adequate overall map of the hitherto unfathomable and chaotic nature of the law, but also of explaining the underlying principles of law that led to particular judgments in particular cases. For the Vinerian professor, the lawyer trained only in practice, uninstructed in the first principles on which the practice was based, would be bewildered if he encountered any case departing from precedent: '*ita lex scripta est* is the utmost his knowledge will arrive at,' Blackstone wrote; 'he must never aspire to form, and seldom expect to comprehend, any arguments drawn a priori, from the spirit of the laws and the natural foundations of justice'.[2]

Blackstone faced a double dilemma: not only was it difficult to extract principles, but there were very few written rules to draw on, for the common law was, as he put it, 'only handed down by tradition, use, and experience'.[3] In an era where statutes were perceived as secondary additions and modifications of the common law, which were piecemeal and fragmented rather than unified and general, and where law reporting was rudimentary, case adjudications rested on two often unfathomable institutions. On the one hand lay the twelve judges of the Courts of Westminster Hall, who could discuss legal matters among themselves and develop their legal ideas in an 'unwritten' manner. Much early eighteenth-century law was hence part of an oral culture, or the custom of judges in their practice.[4] On the other hand lay the jury, making decisions which

---

[1] 1 *Comm*. 6.   [2] 1 *Comm*. 32.   [3] 1 *Comm*. 17.
[4] See A. W. B. Simpson, 'The Common Law and Legal Theory', in Simpson (ed.), *Oxford Essays in Jurisprudence*, 2nd series (Oxford, 1973). This may be seen in the fact, for example, that in the 32 years when Lord Mansfield presided in the King's Bench,

failed to distinguish matters of law and fact, but mingled them in a single verdict.

In addressing these two tasks, Blackstone's *Commentaries* achieved both success and failure. His overall map of the law, its arrangement and categorizations, gave the common law a coherence and unity not seen before; he was widely praised for this, and as a result his work became the staple diet for the law student for over a century.[5] His methodology was similarly important, for in putting the law into an order and a method, and in seeking to analyse it as a system of rules, he allowed lawyers to treat specific areas of law as sciences capable of analysis, and not merely as terms of art to be followed.[6] He was less successful, however, in explaining the functioning of law at case level, as Bentham was quick to expose in his critique.[7] In fact, the *Commentaries* were not a treatise on legal reasoning, but a summary of the law; and when it came to a discussion of how the courts functioned, Blackstone relied more on a theory of customs and maxims than on positive rules. Hence, a gap remained between Blackstone's traditional view of judges, and his quest for principle. He attempted to fill this gap by using the law of nature, but his careless and casual use of the concept reveals his lack of success.[8] A view of the common law as based on natural law

there were only 20 cases where dissenting opinions were expressed, and only 6 cases were reversed on appeal. See C. H. S. Fifoot, *Lord Mansfield* (Oxford, 1936), 47 and Edmund Heward, *Lord Mansfield* (Chichester and London, 1979), 57–8.

[5] Lord Mansfield contrasted Blackstone's 'analytical reasoning' with the 'uncouth crabbed' nature of Coke's Commentary on Littleton. See John Holliday, *The Life of William late Earl of Mansfield* (London, 1797), 89. Jeremy Bentham praised him as the first accessible institutional writer: *A Comment on the Commentaries and a Fragment on Government*, ed. J. H. Burns and H. L. A. Hart (London, 1977). Sir William Jones said that 'his *Commentaries* are the most correct and beautiful outline that was ever exhibited of any human science'. *An Essay on the Law of Bailments*, 2nd edn. (London, 1798), 3.

[6] See S. F. C. Milsom, 'The Nature of Blackstone's Achievement', *Oxford Journal of Legal Studies*, i (1981), 1–12; and A. W. B. Simpson, 'The Rise and Fall of the Legal Treatise: Legal Principles and Forms of Legal Literature', *University of Chicago Law Review*, xlviii (1981), 632–79.   [7] See below, Ch. 6.

[8] See H. L. A. Hart, 'Blackstone's Use of the Law of Nature', *Butterworth's South African Law Review* (1956), 169–74 and J. M. Finnis, 'Blackstone's Theoretical Intentions', *Natural Law Forum*, xii (1967), 163–83 which both point to areas of logical consistency but reveal the irrelevance of much of Blackstone's theorizing to his substantive text; and H.-J. Rinck, 'Blackstone and the Law of Nature', *Ratio*, ii (1960), 162–80, which points to its logical flaws. Daniel J. Boorstin's *The Mysterious Science of the Law* (Cambridge, Mass., 1941) argues that Blackstone was both a rationalist and an anti-rationalist and that he identified all aspects of English law with the law of nature,

principles entailed a fundamentally different view of law from a theory of custom. What made them sit together in the *Commentaries* was Blackstone's use of an Institutional framework in which to locate a customary and remedies-based system of law.[9] The Institutional structure not only assisted his categorizations of the law, but also enabled Blackstone to use a theory of law based on rules with rational and determinate sources, in order to show that the common law was not a haphazard collection of customs and maxims, but a coherent whole. In borrowing the Institutional structure for the *Commentaries*, Blackstone had to borrow the natural law epistemology as an organizing concept to give it coherence; but since he did not seek to relate natural law to legal reasoning at case level, it could play no part in explaining the law. Blackstone's theorizing on natural law was cursory and derivative.[10] Instead of natural law being a positive source, it ended at best with reason being a curb on custom, so that unreasonable customs were prevented from being seen as law.[11] Yet this was not particularly informative, for an unreasonable custom was little more than a custom which was not recognized as a legally binding one. This required an explanation of how and when courts first recognized customs as legally binding; something Blackstone failed adequately to cover.

The Institutional Structure

Given the absence of a systematized English law and the decline of theoretical analyses of the common law, there was a growing interest

but also avoided all logical and empirical difficulties by casting a veil of mystery over the law. Ernest Barker's *Traditions of Civility* (Cambridge, 1948), 309–19 argued that natural law played no part in the common law and that it was paradoxical for Blackstone to include it. However, David Lieberman's *The Province of Legislation Determined*, 36–55 restates the importance of natural law for Blackstone by reconciling it with his history.

[9] On the Institutional influences on Blackstone, see J. W. Cairns, 'Blackstone, An English Institutist: Legal Literature and the Rise of the Nation State', *Oxford Journal of Legal Studies*, iv (1984), 318–60 and Alan Watson, 'The Structure of Blackstone's Commentaries', *Yale Law Journal*, xcvii (1988) 795–821. See also, K. Luig, 'The Institutes of National Law in the Seventeenth and Eighteenth Centuries', *Juridical Review*, xvii (1972), 193–226 and Alan Watson, *The Making of the Civil Law* (Cambridge, Mass., 1981).

[10] See Paul Lucas, '*Ex Parte* Sir William Blackstone, "Plagiarist:" A Note on Blackstone and Natural Law', *American Journal of Legal History*, vii (1963), 142–58.

[11] See, e.g., 1 *Comm.* 70, 2 *Comm.* 210, 3 *Comm.* 118.

in the Roman method, not as a practical system but as an intellectual one.[12] Thomas Wood said in 1727, 'Every one who pretends to be a Scholar, ought to read thus far in the Civil Law, and to know the best Books in that Profession', though he warned against any attempt to bring 'our Laws to the Standard of the Civil Law in *every point*'.[13] Roman jurisprudence was considered to be a science of principles, to be referred to when the common law was silent, and it was therefore praised by the English judges. Holt, for instance, said '[i]nasmuch as the laws of all nations are doubtless raised out of the ruins of the civil law, as all governments are sprung out of the Roman Empire, it must be assumed that the principles of our law are borrowed from the civil law, and therefore grounded upon the same reason in many things'.[14] Hale said that the reasons of the law were so well grounded in the civil law that the best way to learn law as a science was to read the Digest.[15] For principle, one looked to Roman jurisprudence. 'It is', wrote Samuel Hallifax,

admirably calculated to furnish the minds of youth with universal and leading notions . . . the student, who confines himself to the institutions of his own country, without joining to them any acquaintance with those of Imperial Rome, will never arrive at any considerable skill in the grounds and theory of his profession: though he may perhaps attain to a certain mechanical readiness in the forms and practical parts of the law, he will not be able to comprehend that enlarged and general idea of it, by which it is connected with the great system of Universal Jurisprudence.[16]

The Roman structure was a deductive one, moreover, and writers like Thomas Bever described the law in the context of a chain of principles in the universe, where all was interdependent, and where the destruction of one part would damage the whole.[17] This structure, he said, was best found in the *corpus juris*.

---

[12] Roman law was still derided as tyrannical and foreign, but since the decline of the Inns of Court by the 1700s, the only abstract analysis of law available was the civilian one. For the influence of civilian literature on early modern English legal thought, see Brian P. Levack, *The Civil Lawyers in England: A Political Study* (Oxford, 1973).

[13] Thomas Wood, *Some Thoughts concerning the Study of the Laws of England, particularly in the Two Universities*, 2nd edn. (London, 1727), 8–9. This work was first published in 1708.

[14] *Lane* v. *Sir Robert Cotton* (1701) 12 Mod. Rep. 482. See also *Windham* v. *Chetwynd* (1757) 1 Burr. 414.

[15] Gilbert Burnet, *The Life and Death of Sir Matthew Hale, Kt.* (London, 1682), 15.

[16] Samuel Hallifax, *An Analysis of the Roman Civil Law*, 2nd edn. (Cambridge, 1775), x, xxii.

[17] Thomas Bever, *A Discourse on the Study of Jurisprudence and the Civil Law* (Oxford,

The main form of civilian literature was the Institute, based on the structure of Justinian. The Institutes sought to relate the principles of law to the law of nature. Justinian's *Institutes* had been divided into four books, but only the first two titles of the first book were devoted to justice and natural law. Yet these raw materials of jurisprudence— the maxims *justitia est constans et perpetua voluntas jus suum cuique tribuendi* and *jurisprudentia est divinarum atque humanarum rerum notitia, justi atque injusti scientia*[18]—were the foundations of more developed deductions in later works. Eighteenth-century Institutists always prefaced their works with a chapter on laws in general, which stood as introductory pieces to guide the reader through the three subsequent books. This introduction stood as a theory of justice, as derived from God or the law of nature. This pattern was followed by the most scholarly and complete English Institute of the eighteenth century, John Ayliffe's *A New Pandect of Roman Civil Law*, published in 1734. Ayliffe began by asserting that justice existed before positive law, and that justice—the giving each man his due— was the basis of all laws. From here, the structure divided human and divine laws, and divided human law into universal and particular laws, and so on. But all worked up to one definition of law:

The Law is an Art directing us to the Knowledge of Justice, or (in other Terms) *Ars Boni et aequi*, that is to say, a collection of Precepts, teaching us, what is just and what is unjust, what is equitable and what savours of Iniquity. For the word *Ars* here signifies a system of certain propositions, *viz.* which are known to us by Practice and which lead Men to some profitable End of Life.[19]

Ayliffe's idea of legal education was the antithesis of the common law one: 'Persons ought not immediately in the beginning to commit themselves rashly to that vast Ocean, but to set out in their Searches

---

1766), 2–3: 'Nothing is more certain, than that a series of subordinate connexions established, by the great Lord and Father of All, between every part of the moral, as well of the material, world. The dependence is so necessary, that the interruption of any of the springs, whereby either is moved, will endanger the very being of the whole machine. In the one, the fabric of the universe would be dissolved: in the other, mankind would be totally disunited, and reduced to what is usually, though improperly, called a state of nature. The office therefore of jurisprudence is to frame such laws as are correspondent to the nature of man; to make THEM the perpetual standards of human actions; and by enforcing an uniform and consistent obedience, to prevent so fatal a dissipation.'

[18] *D. Justiniani Institutionum*, ed. George Harris, 2nd edn. (London, 1761), 5.
[19] John Ayliffe, *A New Pandect of the Roman Civil Law* (London, 1734), 2.

after this Knowledge from self-evident Principles, and from the Elements of the Law.'[20] These self-evident principles came from the law of nature, either the primary natural law, which was instinctive, or the secondary one, which came from reason.

The common lawyer looking at civilian jurisprudence was therefore faced with two things, a coherent science of principles serving as a source for legal arguments and jurisprudence, and also a structured body of law which could serve as an excellent model for the arrangement of substantive rules. As common lawyers sought to give an overall map of their system, it was obvious to follow a Romanist structure. However, the Roman structure was based on rules and principles which involved a distinct concept of law which often differed from the common lawyers' one. The price of the Institutional model was the jettisoning of a common law view of the sources of law. The alternative was merely using the Institutional model as an *aide-mémoire* which failed to explain the workings of the law. It was this dilemma that was fully taken on only in the *Commentaries*.

While there had been attempts before to put the common law into a Roman framework,[21] they had used the Institutes only as a structure, without adopting its view of the workings of law. Sir Henry Finch had sought to reduce the common law to a rational whole in *Nomotechnia*, published in 1613, and in *Law, or a Discourse thereof*, published in 1627, he had been influenced primarily, as Prest has shown, by Ramist methodology.[22] The influence of this work on Blackstone has long been recognized,[23] and indeed Blackstone praised Finch's *Law* as the most methodical text yet written, its main flaw being that it was out of date since the abolition of feudal tenures.[24] Finch argued that 'he that will take before him the whole Body of the Law, and proceed therein with Profoundness and

---

[20] Ayliffe, 3.

[21] See, e.g., John Cowell, *Institutiones iuris Anglicani ad Methodum et seriem Institutionum Imperialum compositae et digestae* (London, 1605).

[22] See W. Prest, 'The Dialectical Origins of Finch's *Law*', *Cambridge Law Journal*, xxxvi (1977), 326–52. The first book of *Nomotechnia*, translated in 1759 as *A Description of the Common Law of England*, was virtually identical to the first book of *Law*. The translator's preface (at v) called this work 'the first general Institute of the laws of England'.

[23] See W. S. Holdsworth, *History of English Law*, v. 399–401 and xii. 418.

[24] *An Analysis of the Laws of England*, 3rd edn. (Oxford, 1758), vi. Hallifax made a similar objection to Finch's work: *Analysis*, iii. Feudal tenures had been abolished in 1660.

Judgment, will not lay the Foundation of his Edifice upon Estates, Tenures, the Nature of Writs and such like, but upon the current and sound Principles, of which our books are full'.[25] Yet it was a very different work from the one Blackstone aimed to write. Finch drew not on a single source of law, but instead posited a theoretical schema with a multiplicity of sources of law and reason, so that he did not seek to deduce the law from first principles. 'Rules of reason', he wrote, 'are of two sorts; some taken from foreign learning, as well divine as human; the rest proper to the law itself.' His principles therefore included theology, grammar, logic, natural philosophy, physics, politics, economics, and ethics. Finch's method in his long third chapter in which he examined the rules of reason taken from outside the law was simply to list maxims which could be covered by these headings, and then to describe rules in English law which confirmed these maxims. The largest category was logic, and to prove the logic of the law, Finch used the following method: he first proposed a logical maxim—*Accessorum Sequitur Principale*—and then illustrated it with an English rule: 'A Servant procures a Stranger to kill his Master, this is not Petit Treason in the Servant, because it is only Felony in the Principal.'[26] Moving on to discuss law constructions, fictions, and positive laws, he wrote, '[t]he foregoing Rules were such as were derived but out of other sciences. These that follow are peculiar to ourselves, and are called Law-constructions.'[27] Finch therefore sought to explain the law by the application of method and logic, not by the application of clear rules.

Finch's work was seen as a pioneering attempt to methodize the law, and by the start of the eighteenth century, Thomas Wood was praising its Romanist structure, rather than its Ramist logic. Divided into parts on persons at common law, on rights and possessions, on offences, and on courts of judicature, 'it almost follows the Method of *Justinian's Institutes*,' Wood declared,[28] adding that if Finch were modernized, the problems of common law education would be solved. Wood criticized the obsession of the universities with the civil law, and urged greater practicality on them, accusing them of scholastic nitpicking and fruitless discussion of useless practice.[29] He said that it was a misconception to assume that there was a single

[25] Finch, *Common Law*, 5.
[26] Ibid. 17.   [27] Ibid. 41.
[28] *Some Thoughts concerning the Study of the Laws of England*, 43.
[29] Ibid. 16–17.

system of civil law: instead, it had changed and adapted in all countries practising it. He contended that the English had borrowed what they wanted from the civil law, and that the common law was 'infinitely of more use' than the abstract civil law.[30] The common lawyers, he said, were 'willing to be tried by those [Roman] Texts, and to enter into a Comparison'.[31]

Wood did this, for he wrote both *A New Institute of the Imperial or Civil Laws* and *An Institute of the Laws of England*. The body of the former was divided into three books, covering Persons, Things, and Actions, and a fourth book covering proceedings in courts. The latter also had four books, covering Persons, Estates, Pleas of the Crown, and Courts of Justice. Wood's English Institute was a reformist work, favouring the consolidation of the statute laws which were 'monstrously overgrown', and a simplification of the complex rules of pleading. He similarly felt that in the construction of conveyances, more regard should be had to the intention of the parties making the conveyance than the strictness of the expressions used.[32] Nevertheless, Wood still thought of the common law in the old terms, and in his advice to students, he recommended that the student should first read Littleton and Coke, as well as law dictionaries, abridgements, and collections of writs, and that he should always 'keep *Finch's* method in his Mind'.[33] The common law for Wood had six foundations: the law of nature, the revealed law of God, general customs, principles and maxims, particular customs, and statutes. Wood listed a number of rules, taken from Coke, which illustrated the common law, including the idea that nothing which was against reason was law and that law respected the order of nature. This was not a set of sources for positive rules. The notion of common law was in effect defined by the first four foundations mentioned. Therefore, 'when we say It is so by *Common Law*, it is as much as to say, By *Common* Right, or of *Common* Justice,' Wood wrote, adding, '[i]ndeed it is many times very difficult to know what Cases are grounded upon the Law of *Reason*, and what upon the *Custom* of the Kingdom; yet we must endeavour to understand this, to know the perfect Reason of the Law'.[34] Statutes had a relatively minor stature, to be construed according to that common law. Hence any statute that was against reason was void. For Wood, maxims were 'of the same

---

[30] Wood, 14.   [31] Ibid. 57.
[32] *An Institute of the Laws of England*, 2 vols. (London, 1720), iii–v.
[33] Ibid. 45.   [34] Ibid. 6.

strength as Acts of Parliament when once the judges have determined what is a Maxim'. As a result, Blackstone saw Wood's work as a failure, dismissing it as 'being little more than FINCH's discourse enlarged and so thoroughly modernised, as to leave us frequently in the Dark, with regard to the Reason and Original of many still subsisting laws, which are founded in remote antiquity'.[35]

Wood's view of the foundations of the common law was wholly different from his civilian jurisprudence. He prefixed to his civilian work a translation of Domat's *Treatise of Laws* to stand for the theoretical, introductory section. This had formed the preliminary book of Domat's *The Civil Law in its Natural Order,*[36] which attempted to put modern French law into the Institutional structure. The introductory section related the body of the laws to a set of rational first principles and rules through an epistemological analysis which sought to resolve and explain the ends of laws. No man, he argued, could be ignorant of natural law without being ignorant of himself, for the first principles of the law had an epistemological foundation in the will and the understanding. Man's first law, which derived from these points, was to love God, since that was his end in life. His second law, derived from the first, was to love his fellow man.[37] These two essential laws governed all the rest, which derived from them. This analysis allowed Domat to explain the division of immutable and indifferent laws, for the validity of any law was tested by the two fundamental laws, and not by their intrinsic merit. Indifferent laws had no essential justice, but were only useful in certain places and at certain times as need dictated, and were known by promulgation rather than by intrinsic reason.[38] Even immutable laws were governed by the two fundamental laws:

> Laws have their Justice and Authority, only because of the relation which they bear to the Order of Society, and to the Spirit of the two Fundamental Laws; So that if it happen, that the Order of Society and the Spirit of those Fundamental Laws, require that some of the Immutable Laws be restrained either by Exceptions or by Dispensations, they admit of those Mitigations.[39]

In Institutional works, natural law was not one source of many in the process of reasoning, but the central source of law. When Blackstone

---

[35] *Analysis*, vi.
[36] J. Domat, *The Civil Law in its Natural Order: Together with the Publick Law*, trans. William Strahan, 2 vols. (London, 1722).   [37] Ibid. i, pp. i–v.
[38] Ibid. i, pp. xxvii–xliv.   [39] Ibid. i, pp. xxxiii–xxxiv.

wrote the *Commentaries*, he was attempting to unite both the Romanist structure and its jurisprudence. Those who had hitherto sought to use the Institutional structure had only used it as a method of organization, not as a method of analysis, for they still saw the law as having a multiplicity of sources. No writer before Blackstone had therefore sought to use the Roman law on its own terms. He therefore wanted

to mark out a Plan of the laws of ENGLAND, so comprehensive, as that every Title might be reduced under some one of its general Heads, which the student might afterwards pursue to any Degree of Minuteness; and at the same time so contracted, that the Gentleman might with tolerable Application contemplate and understand the Whole.[40]

Writers on Blackstone have suggested that he wanted to systematize English law in order to prove that it worked, in the face of critics who attacked the common law from a rationalist standpoint.[41] However, given the genesis of the *Commentaries* in the 1750s, it seems unlikely that his intentions were quite so conservative.[42] The problem of the chaos of English legal analysis was an old one, which had induced others to make similar systematizations. The fact that he was attempting to systematize English law in Roman terms did not make Blackstone innovatory: what was unusual was the sophistication and the rigour of the attempt, and the fact that he used the Institutional structure as more than a set of labels with which to describe existing law. But, as shall be evident, he found the task impossible.

---

[40] *Analysis*, iv.

[41] See Duncan Kennedy, 'The Structure of Blackstone's Commentaries', *Buffalo Law Review*, xxviii (1979), 205–382 and Boorstin, *The Mysterious Science*. See also R. Willman, 'Blackstone and the Theoretical Perfection of English Law in the Reign of Charles II.' *Historical Journal*, xxvi (1983), 39–70 and P. Lucas, 'Blackstone and the Reform of the Legal Profession', *English Historical Review*, lxxvii (1962), 456–89.

[42] See I. G. Doolittle, 'Sir William Blackstone and his *Commentaries on the Laws of England* (1765–9): A Biographical Approach', *Oxford Journal of Legal Studies*, iii (1983), 99–112. To see Blackstone as a conservative fending off liberal attacks is perhaps to translate later attacks on the common law back to the era of Blackstone. A major critique of the common law at Blackstone's time was that it was unfathomable: the very act of defining it in terms of rules was hence a reformist measure. In addition, on matters of doctrine, Blackstone was not averse to challenging accepted orthodoxies, as his view of criminal law and his ideas on the course of descents at 2 *Comm*. 238 show.

Blackstone's Theoretical Foundations

To write a successful Institute of the type that Blackstone aimed to do, it was essential to sort out the theoretical structure, and to relate it to the first principles. Blackstone had great difficulty in making the common law fit into the structure for two reasons. First, his key sources of law were in effect marginalized, and played little part in explaining the substantive law. Second, his structure, which sought to relate all law to rights, failed to make sense of law in terms of rights. Blackstone was clearly impressed with the civilian method, which he described as 'a collection of written reason'.[43] He recognized the rivalry between English and Roman methods, and himself urged that it was more useful to know English law.[44] However, he urged the study of English law in an 'academical' way, noting that the English law could be 'a science, which distinguishes the criterions of right and wrong': it was not necessarily anti-theoretical.[45] The thrust of the chapter in the *Commentaries* on the study of laws was that it had to be done academically. If the student

can reason with precision, and separate argument from fallacy, by the clear simple rules of pure unsophisticated logic; if he can fix his attention, and steadily pursue truth through any the most intricate deduction, by the use of mathematical demonstrations; if he has enlarged his conceptions of nature and art, by a view of the several branches of genuine, experimental, philosophy; if he has impressed on his mind the sound maxims of the law of nature, the best and most authentic foundation of human laws; if, lastly, he has contemplated those maxims reduced to a practical system in the laws of imperial Rome . . . a student thus qualified may enter upon the study of law with incredible advantage and reputation.[46]

It is significant that Blackstone was attempting this reconciliation of the analytical method and the common law content, for he was thereby asserting that it was not enough to see the English law as reasonable, to have a collection of rules which could be rationalized in the light of some external test: instead, he was trying to show that reason was embodied in the English law. For that reason, the Roman structure was essential.

The fact that Blackstone was following an Institutional structure

---

[43] 1 *Comm.* 5.   [44] 1 *Comm.* 5–6.
[45] 1 *Comm.* 27.   [46] 1 *Comm.* 33.

explains his introductory section on law in general and his use of the law of nature, something that has created comment since Bentham's famous attack. If it is borne in mind that he was using this format, the position of natural law becomes clearer, for it was the custom to begin such works with a discourse on natural law, and to relate the structure to it. Blackstone was following convention in putting it forward as the key to the law: his problems came in making the structure fit the theory. Unlike Domat, Blackstone had not resolved the ends of law, nor did he define what he meant by the law of nature. Instead, he borrowed ideas from other writers he hoped could resolve the problem: in the section on the nature of laws, he relied heavily on Burlamaqui, who had used Pufendorf's view of natural law.[47] This created a problem for Blackstone in that it threw up a view of law which he sought to marginalize.

For Pufendorf, all law was the command of a superior, with the result that where there was no Divine or Human law, there could be no wrong act—all would be indifferent.[48] Human society and sovereignty was based on consent, not force, according to Pufendorf, but in conferring power to the sovereign, the subjects obliged themselves to non-resistance and to obedience.[49] Furthermore,

in as much as the Law of Nature cannot, amongst a great multitude, be conveniently exercis'd without the Assistance of Civil Government, 'tis manifest that God, who imposed the said Law on the Human Race, did command likewise the establishing of Civil Societies, so far as they serve for Instruments and Means of improving and enforcing the Law of Nature.[50]

As a consequence of the sovereign being a means to the furthering of natural law in civil society, it was supreme and above human laws. The sovereign's laws concerned matters to be observed by the subjects for the public good of the state: to bring Divine Laws into the question against these was 'no less absurd than impious'.[51] In this way, Pufendorf could reconcile a strong positive law with

---

[47] See P. Lucas, '*Ex parte* Sir William Blackstone'. Opinions on Blackstone's intellectual debts focus on his debts to European natural lawyers. Sir Henry Maine said that Blackstone had followed Burlamaqui (*Ancient Law* (London, 1861), 114); Holdsworth felt Blackstone had followed Grotius via Burlamaqui (*History of English Law*, xii, 733); while Joseph W. McKnight said that Blackstone borrowed, but did not plagiarize Burlamaqui. 'Blackstone, Quasi-Jurisprudent', *Southwestern Law Journal*, xiii (1959), 399–411.

[48] S. Pufendorf, *Of the Law of Nature and Nations*, ed. J. Barbeyrac, trans. Basil Kennet, 3rd edn. (London, 1717), I.ii.6, p. 17.   [49] Ibid. VII.iii.1, p. 484.

[50] Ibid. VII.iii.2, p. 485.   [51] Ibid. VII.vi.3, p. 518.

natural law, avoiding the problem of the one judging and overruling the other. For Pufendorf, while the laws of nature were of universal obligation, 'it is the *Civil Power* that gives them the force of Laws in the *Civil Court'*.[52]

Blackstone's theorizing echoed this view in his view of society in a confused way. In a state of nature, Blackstone wrote, there would be only natural law, 'for a law always supposes some superior who is to make it' which in the natural state could only be God.[53] However, men were incapable of living in this fragmented way, and hence they needed societies and states. This helps explain Blackstone's view of municipal law: it either declared (and was subordinate to) the law of nature or legislated for indifferent matters.[54] Municipal law was defined as 'a rule of civil conduct prescribed by the supreme power in a state, commanding what is right and prohibiting what is wrong'.[55] Blackstone's editor, Edward Christian, pointed to the flaws in this definition: either it meant that all that the law commanded was *ipso facto* right—in which case 'commanding right' was tautologous—or it meant that right and wrong could be referred to the law of nature. Christian felt that the latter idea was absurd, since the law often forbade what was morally justifiable,[56] and he there-fore inferred that municipal law was whatever was commanded, and that morals did not enter into the question.

For Blackstone, sovereignty and the legislature were convertible terms, but they were not to be equated with the people as a whole. His view of the sovereign had Hobbesian premises. Arguing that man's weakness drove him into society, he contended that government merited total obedience, if men were to avoid a return to the state of nature.[57] Whatever was ordered by the sovereign legislature had to be obeyed, or else the constitution would be at an end—which was for Blackstone the worst eventuality. The boundaries of right and wrong were therefore set by law:[58] even when it came to declaring natural law, this was down to 'the will and wisdom of the legislature' rather than to an autonomous law of nature itself. Immutable laws had no validity unless they were confirmed by the sovereign. Therefore, absolute rights derived from what was allowed by law: 'The absolute rights of every Englishman

---

[52] Ibid. VIII.i.1, p. 1.
[54] 1 *Comm.* 42.
[56] 1 *Comm.* (1803 edn.) 44n.
[57] 1 *Comm.* 48.

[53] 1 *Comm.* 43.
[55] 1 *Comm.* 44.

[58] 1 *Comm.* 53.

... as they are founded on nature and reason, so they are coeval with our form of government, though subject at times to fluctuate and change: their establishment (excellent as it is) being still human.'[59]

Blackstone's sovereign was therefore supreme. There was no fixed form of government, and the legislature could put the execution of the laws into new hands: 'obedience to superiors is the doctrine of revealed as well as of natural religion: but who those superiors shall be, and in what circumstances . . . is the province of human laws to determine'.[60] Whatever constitution was established, he said, 'there is and must be in all of them a supreme, irresistible, absolute, uncontrolled authority, in which the *jura summi imperii,* or the rights of sovereignty, reside'.[61] In England, this gave parliament absolute despotic powers, with uncontrollable authority to alter every facet of law and the constitution. For Blackstone, parliament 'can, in short, do every thing that is not naturally impossible . . . what they do, no authority upon earth can undo'.[62] Even if parliament decreed something against the law of nature, it would still have to be obeyed.[63]

This positivist concept of law contrasted with his initial arguments that the source of human laws was a more direct law of nature, to be derived from reason, the pursuit of happiness, and revelation.[64] His initial definition was potentially compatible with a customary view of society, but Blackstone preferred a contractarian vision of the relationship of individuals to the sovereign. However, he remained very uncomfortable with the notion of the contract, and therefore minimized the natural right to rebel. Although he acknowledged the right in theory, he denied it in practice and in law, for he argued that just as the sovereign was legally without limit, so the law could not acknowledge the possibility of its own end, as would occur in a revolution. While the constitution subsisted, the power of parliament was without limit.[65] Blackstone was clearly embarrassed about 1688. Having taken great pains to establish that there had been a pure, uncorrupted succession up to that point, he could only suggest

---

[59] 1 *Comm.* 123.   [60] 1 *Comm.* 55.
[61] 1 *Comm.* 49.   [62] 1 *Comm.* 156.

[63] 'If the parliament will positively enact a thing to be done which is unreasonable, I know of no power that can control it.' 1 *Comm.* 91.

[64] See 1 *Comm.* 39–42.

[65] 1 *Comm.* 157. See Gerald Stourzh, *Alexander Hamilton and the Idea of Republican Government* (Stanford, 1970), 9–30 for a discussion.

that James II had abdicated. He could neither justify nor explain the Glorious Revolution:

I . . . rather chuse to consider this great political measure, upon the solid footing of authority, than to reason in it's favour from it's justice, moderation, and expedience: because that might imply a right of dissenting or revolting from it, in case we should think it unjust, oppressive, or inexpedient. Whereas, our ancestors having most indisputably a competent jurisdiction to decide this great and important question, and having in fact decided it, it is now become our duty at this distance of time to acquiesce in their determination; being born under that establishment which was built upon this foundation, and being obliged by every tie, religious as well as civil, to maintain it.[66]

Looking back, he argued that since the terms of the original contract were disputed and only acknowledged as a matter of theory and therefore 'only deducible by reason and the rules of natural law, in which deduction different understandings might very considerably differ',[67] the 'contract' had to be declared expressly after the revolution, by positive enactment. Blackstone rejected the concept of an original contract as contradictory to the known origins of society, and found the concept of the state of nature 'too wild to be seriously admitted'.[68] In so doing, he removed the law of nature from having a function in guarding or guiding the sovereign, without positing an alternative customary vision of society.

The result of this theorizing, was that it marginalized natural law to such a degree that it was irrelevant. Blackstone tried various ways to explain natural law. The first was allied to his first definition of law, describing the physical law which all creatures obeyed. Blackstone wrote,

[A]s God, when he created matter, and endued it with a principle of mobility, established certain rules for the perpetual direction of that motion; so, when he created man, and endued him with freewill to conduct himself in all parts of life, he laid down certain immutable laws of nature, whereby that freewill is to some degree regulated and restrained, and gave him also the faculty of reason to discover the purport of those laws.[69]

---

[66] 1 *Comm.* 205. For further explorations of this dilemma in eighteenth-century political thought, see J. P. Kenyon, *Revolution Principles: the Politics of Party, 1689–1720* (Cambridge, 1977), and H. T. Dickinson, *Liberty and Property. Political Ideology in Eighteenth Century Britain* (London, 1977), 121–62.   [67] 1 *Comm.* 226.
[68] 1 *Comm.* 47.   [69] 1 *Comm.* 39–40.

Here it appeared that the law of nature was invariable and was always followed, and although he followed this passage with one claiming that natural law encompassed Justinian's moral rules, he went on with the theme of inevitability: since natural law had the same end as individual happiness, all men pursued what was right in any case when they pursued self-interest. By this, natural law would become merely empirical fact, not a criterion against which to test positive law.

Blackstone also used natural law in a second sense, as a rule of conscience. This is made clear in the notes on his lectures in the Hardwicke MS: 'Every municipal Law is a Rule of Civil Conduct; whereas the Law of nature is of moral conduct; and, as it is hereby distinguished from the Law of Nature, so it differs from Councel in that it is obligatory.'[70] Here the law of nature was only a rule of private morality and the implication was that law proper was binding regardless of morals. Blackstone stressed that private vices were beyond the reach of law and noted that human laws need not bind consciences, since they were indifferent.[71] In making this claim, he asserted that most laws were amoral, and could not be deduced from an epistemological base, such as the law of nature.[72] 'Let a man therefore be ever so abandoned in his principles, or vitious in his practice, provided he keeps his wickedness to himself, and does not offend against the rules of public decency, he is out of the reach of human laws.'[73] Beyond this, he noted that law proper had nothing to do with moral precepts, but only with social utility:

[H]uman laws can have no concern with any but social and relative duties; being intended only to regulate the conduct of man, considered under various relations, as a member of civil society. All crimes ought therefore to be estimated merely according to the mischiefs which they produce in civil society: and, of consequence private vices, or the breaches of *mere absolute duties*, which man is bound to perform considered only as an individual, are not, cannot be, the object of any municipal law.[74]

---

[70] Hardwicke MS, BL Add. MS 36093, fo. 9.   [71] 1 *Comm.* 57.

[72] See Hart's argument in 'Blackstone's Use of the Law of Nature'.

[73] 1 *Comm.* 120. James Sedgwick criticized Blackstone on this in *Remarks Critical and Miscellaneous on the Commentaries of Sir William Blackstone* (London, 1800), 56, saying that since it was difficult to discover crimes and to convict of them, if men were not motivated by conscience, the legislature would always have to impose ever more severe laws to secure compliance. For him, compliance with civil laws was a matter of conscience in itself. See also, Richard Wooddeson, *Elements of Jurisprudence* (London, 1783), 23–4, 33.   [74] 4 *Comm.* 41. My italics.

Blackstone's chapter on laws in general left him with a dilemma, for
it contradicted his view of English law presented in his next chapter
and in the rest of the *Commentaries*. For Blackstone's view of legal
reasoning henceforth was based on customs and maxims, and what
the judges did. In practice, he was suspicious of statute law, which
he saw as inferior and confused by comparison with the common
law.[75] Blackstone seemed to treat customs as rules, arguing that
'precedents and rules must be followed, unless flatly absurd or
unjust'.[76] At the same time, however, he seemed to equivocate, for
he denied any fundamental distinction between customs and
maxims. The authority of maxims, he said, rested on their general
reception and usage, so that the only way to show a maxim was a
rule of the common law was to show that it had always been the
custom to observe it.[77] Custom by this account was no rule, but
merely what judges did. Rather than the common law being found in
the will of the sovereign or in a rule-based law of nature, it was
determined by the judges, the 'living oracles, who must decide in all
cases of doubt'. The common law was made up of the decisions of
judges, so long as they were grounded in reason and were not
absurd, and records of them were to be found in the law reports.
Blackstone's discussion of the role of judges and judicial precedents
was confusing and allusive, largely because he placed this discussion
in the context of a treatise seeking to define law as a system of rules,
and because he therefore spent very little time discussing the process
of legal reasoning by judges. Yet the six and a half pages devoted to
the general customs of England suggested a wholly different view of
legal reasoning from that elaborated in his discussion of law in
general, and opened up the problem for the rest of the *Commentaries*
that would undermine his rule-based structure. If law was based on
custom, then the law could only be explained in effect through
history tracing those customs, and by looking at the mechanisms of
court procedure through which the judges articulated them. This
would be the method of the rest of the *Commentaries*. He could not
fill the gap between the practice of the courts and the map of the law.

[75] See Lieberman, *The Province of Legislation Determined*, 56–67.
[76] 1 *Comm.* 70.
[77] 1 *Comm.* 68.

The Content of the Commentaries

When it came to reconciling the content of the common law to the Roman structure, Blackstone faced further difficulties. For the common law did not fit the alien structure and theory, and he was compelled to resort to historical and customary explanations which would clarify the law, but which contradicted the structure.

It is clear that Blackstone believed in a systematic, deductive approach from the *Analysis* which preceded the *Commentaries*, for his structure, following Hale,[78] echoed the civilian system. The first two books, on the Rights of Persons and the Rights of Things, corresponded to the Roman division of Persons and Things, and the second two, on private and public wrongs, corresponded to Actions. The Rights of Persons divided into absolute rights, to personal security, liberty, and private property, and relative rights, in effect the relations of people in society, or their status. In the *Commentaries*, this was explained to mean that a person's absolute rights 'would belong to their persons merely in a state of nature',[79] while relative rights were those that arose in society. However, Blackstone soon revealed that these absolute rights based on natural law in fact were themselves rights deriving from the state. The right to life, for Blackstone, meant the right to survive: 'there is no man so indigent or wretched, but he may demand a supply sufficient for all the necessities of life, from the more opulent part of the community'.[80] However, this was not absolute, for Blackstone did not recognize the right to steal if one was starving, nor a return to the community of property in time of crisis. The absolute right did not trump civil rights: rather, it was a right deriving itself from the Poor Law statutes. Yet when he later discussed those laws, Blackstone commented,

[N]otwithstanding the pains that has [*sic*] been taken about them, they still remain very imperfect, and inadequate to the purposes they are designed for: a fate, that has generally attended most of our statute laws, where they have not the foundation of the common law to build on.[81]

---

[78] *The Analysis of the Law: Being a Scheme, or Abstract, of the Titles and Partitions of the Law of England, digested into a Method* (London, 1713).

[79] 1 *Comm.* 119.

[80] 1 *Comm.* 127.

[81] 1 *Comm.* 353.

The right to life similarly meant that a man's natural life could not be destroyed. For all that, Blackstone still saw capital punishments as divinely sanctioned. Although he claimed that statutes seldom and the common law never inflicted bodily harm except in cases of the highest necessity, he contradicted this in the fourth book.[82] The second absolute right was the right to liberty and free locomotion. However, the laws invoked in support of this right were statutory and not confirmed until the reign of Charles II.[83] All the guarantees of liberty offered by Blackstone were defined by statute, and could therefore be removed: the right to free locomotion, for instance, could be removed by the settlement regulations of the Poor Laws.

The third right he had initially defined as absolute, the right to property, was later treated, in Book II, as a positive right, not a natural one.[84] Blackstone once more made a distinction between the situation of a state of nature, and that of civil society. Following Pufendorf, he argued that in the natural state, 'he who first began to use [a thing], acquired therein a kind of transient property, that lasted so long as he was using it, and no longer',[85] but once he quitted it, anyone else might take it. The concept of property beyond a use right developed with the rise of a more refined society and when the population of the world grew to such proportions that there was not enough spare land for people to occupy without encroaching on the land of others. While Blackstone stressed the notion of first occupancy as a theoretical grounding for the notion of private property, he did not seek to develop this idea.[86] Instead, it was the rise of settled agricultural and commercial society that grounded property rights. 'Necessity begat property,' Blackstone wrote, 'and in order to insure that property, recourse was had to civil society, which brought along with it a train of inseparable concomitants; states, government, laws, punishments, and the public exercise of religious duties.'[87] Were it not for this, man would for ever remain in

---

[82] 4 *Comm*. 4–9, where he also justified (via Hale) the use of capital punishments for offences not *mala in se*.   [83] 1 *Comm*. 131; 3 *Comm*. 128–9; 4 *Comm*. 431.

[84] See Robert P. Burns, 'Blackstone's Theory of the "Absolute" Rights of Property', *University of Cincinnati Law Review*, liv (1985), 67–86.

[85] 2 *Comm*. 3.

[86] He therefore dismissed the disagreements between natural law thinkers over the grounding of the right of occupancy as savouring 'too much of nice and scholastic refinement!' 2 *Comm*. 8.

[87] 2 *Comm*. 8. The following pages discussed the need for rules of property in securing commercial transactions of property.

a state of nature, the world a forest, and men mere beasts of prey. This necessity also required that property should not cease with death, but be open to inheritance. Discussing the right of inheritance, as beginning before the right of devising to others by testament, Blackstone wrote,

We are apt to conceive at first view that it has nature on it's side; yet we often mistake for nature what we find established by long and inveterate custom. It is certainly a wise and effectual, but clearly a political establishment; since the permanent right of property, vested in the ancestor himself, was no *natural*, but merely a *civil*, right.[88]

Property rights were therefore rights established by society, through custom. Blackstone made it clear that natural rights here were inadequate and incomplete. Discussing the justice of the case where a man disinherited his son for a third man, he dismissed the idea that this went against a natural law that should favour the son. For, by the law of nature, the man's property would again become common land, and be open to the next occupant, 'unless otherwise ordered for the sake of civil peace by the positive law of society'.[89] Offences against property rights were therefore offences against positive, not natural, law.[90]

This discussion gives us an insight into the place of natural law in Blackstone's theory and how much it owed to his incomplete reworking of the Pufendorfian version. Natural law did not give any firm guide or rules to civil society, but it was incomplete and undeveloped. Natural law at most gave basic principles, of which the key was civil peace. Human society and progress required detailed rules to secure this, but these detailed rules came from positive law, whose contents came from custom and imposition. From this, we can see that the structure of the *Commentaries* was primarily addressed to civil rights, not natural ones. As the *Commentaries* progressed, it became clearer that these civil rules derived more from custom than imposition, but since Blackstone sought to show law as a coherent whole based on natural principles, he sought to rationalize customary rules. This involved him in looking at history, but also in 'purifying' history. 'It is impossible to understand, with any degree of accuracy, either the civil constitution of this kingdom, or the laws which regulate it's landed property,' he wrote, 'without

[88] 2 *Comm.* 11.   [89] 2 *Comm.* 13.   [90] 4 *Comm.* 9.

some general acquaintance with the nature and doctrine of feuds, or the feudal law.'[91] Blackstone attempted to argue that the feudal system was originally a 'plan of simplicity and liberty', one which had been corrupted but then purified and perfected over time.[92] By this device, he could argue that the modern law was a rational system, and also preserve the notion of a pure ancient constitution that could produce eternal principles. However, at every stage, he needed to resort to historical arguments to explain the reason of the modern device, for the examination of history showed 'the groundwork of many parts of our public polity'.[93] If the law of real property came neither from natural law nor from sovereign imposition, but from custom,[94] explained by the history of the feudal law, it nevertheless had a coherent rationality that was reducible to rules. The core of the second book was thus devoted to explaining the area of the common law which was the most well defined in terms of rules and had a substantial literature discussing its forms.

The customary law of real property was in effect the key organizing concept of the *Commentaries,* for the majority of the actions described in Book III, on private wrongs, and the crimes in Book IV, were designed in Blackstone's schema to correct infringements of rights defined in the second book.[95] The notable feature of the *Commentaries* is Blackstone's inability to find a place for a theory of obligations and actions that stood distinct from the defined rights of property set out in Book II. Book III, rather than being devoted to such a clear discussion of obligations, covering torts and contracts, was divided into chapters covering courts and their procedures, one chapter dealing with wrongs to the rights of persons, another dealing with wrongs to personal property, and seven concerning wrongs to real property. The division of the law into rights and wrongs made sense when related to the feudal core of English law, for the body of substantive rules of tenure could easily be set out in

---

[91] 2 *Comm.* 44.   [92] 2 *Comm.* 58.   [93] 2 *Comm.* 52.

[94] Discussing the impact of the Conquest, Blackstone argued that while feudal tenures were introduced in England after the Normans arrived, it was by consent and not by virtue of conquest. 2 *Comm.* 48–50. However, he also argued that the only remaining modern tenures, socage tenures, 'were the relicks of Saxon liberty' which had survived the Conquest. 2 *Comm.* 81. For a discussion of the seventeenth-century debates on this, see J. G. A. Pocock, *The Ancient Constitution and the Feudal Law.*

[95] As Kennedy argued, Blackstone divided rights into three sections, defining them, then addressing civil and criminal wrongs against them. See, 'The Structure of Blackstone's Commentaries', 231.

Book II, and then Book III could discuss the types of injuries that could be done to real property and their remedies, and to that end, he described six real injuries: ouster, trespass, nuisance, waste, subtraction, and disturbance.[96] These were all substantive categories of wrongs that could be related to the notion of property. Less clear, however, was both his definition of personal property, and of wrongs against it. The law of personal property was given relatively little space in Book II, being divided into goods in possession and *choses in action*. The latter concerned property not in a person's possession, but that he had the right to demand a court to give him; it therefore largely covered contracts. Blackstone gave a general definition of the nature of contracts here; but in this area of law he remained vague. '[U]pon all contracts or promises, either express or implied, and the infinite variety of cases into which they are and may be spun out,' he wrote, 'the law gives an action of some sort or other to the party injured.'[97] These were discussed in Book III, where he covered the different forms of action relating to contracts, covering actions of debt, covenant and assumpsits and actions on the case. The problem with this was that since personal property did not have the body of defined feudal rules for a base, it relied for its substance on rules from decisions in cases that were derived from actions. The rights of personal property were defined by wrongs against them, which in turn were defined through remedies.

In Book III, Blackstone found himself facing a tension between his rule-based concept and the remedial common law system. He had been able to discuss the common law in terms of rules where acknowledged rules existed, but had failed to reduce the system of remedies to a set of rules. Apologizing for the large variety of remedies he had outlined, he justified himself by saying that all sciences needed terms of art, saying that 'the more subdivided any branch of science is, the more terms must be used to express the nature of these several subdivisions, and mark out with sufficient precision the ideas they are meant to convey'. However, at the same time, he had to acknowledge that in fact many rights were not defined, so that the forms of action were more than subdivisions of a greater whole. The 'excellence of our English laws' was that they 'adapt their redress exactly to the circumstances of the injury, and do not furnish one and the same action for different wrongs, which are

---

[96] 3 *Comm.* 167.   [97] 2 *Comm.* 397.

impossible to be brought within one and the same description'. This, he concluded, came from the fact that there was hardly a possible injury for which the party could not find a remedial writ 'conceived in such terms as are properly adapted to his own particular grievance', which in turn limited the discretion of the judge in administering the remedy.[98] By this point, Blackstone was eulogizing the function of a system of remedies above that of legislation, for the system managed to extend and accommodate personal actions to new situations as they arose in society, in a way that could not be foreseen by legislation.[99]

This meant that, ultimately, Blackstone's structure was a series of forms into which to put the content of the common law, without explaining a concept of legal reasoning which would instruct the student how the common law worked. Blackstone had to admit that his methodology was a compromise, even in the area of the greatest number of rules:

To say the truth, the vast alterations which the doctrine of real property has undergone from the conquest to the present time; the infinite determinations upon points that continually arise, and which have been heaped one upon another for a course of seven centuries, without any order or method; and the multiplicity of acts of parliament which have amended, or sometimes only altered, the common law; these cases have made the study of this branch of our national jurisprudence a little perplexed and intricate. It hath been my endeavour principally to select such parts of it, as were of the most general use, where the principles were the most simple, the reasons of them the most obvious, and the practice least embarrassed. Yet I cannot presume that I have always been thoroughly intelligible to such of my readers, as were before strangers even to the very terms of art, which I have been obliged to make use of.[100]

To justify this, Blackstone quoted Coke's argument that although the student would not be able fully to understand the meanings of all things laid down in the *Institutes*, he should proceed, because all would become clear when the student had more learning and experience. This was to surrender the Institutional method: in place of covering all by comprehensible rules, Blackstone was forced to extract a few general principles when describing things which were essentially particularistic and infinitely variable.[101] Blackstone, like

[98] 3 *Comm.* 266.   [99] 3 *Comm.* 268.   [100] 2 *Comm.* 382–3.
[101] 2 *Comm.* 172: 'I trust [the student] will in some measure see the general reasons, upon which this nicety [contingent remainders] is founded. It were endless to attempt

Coke, had to assume a hidden and often inscrutable reason in the law. 'The causes ... of the multiplicity of the English laws', he argued, 'are the extent of the country which they govern ... Hence, a multitude of decisions, or cases adjudged, will arise; for seldom will it happen that any one rule will exactly suit with many cases.'[102] In this way, he ended by arguing that because it was rooted in experience, English law was more rational than Roman law, which he derided as a system that had to be manipulated by contradictory commentators to be truly applicable.[103] He could claim a reason in law even where it was hidden,[104] and argue that the law was inherently so reasonable that to disorder any part of it would unbalance the whole.

Blackstone's structure, particularly in its division of the Rights of Things and Private and Public Wrongs, made sense, for a division of the rules of real property, the criminal law, and an analysis of remedies reflected the main areas of the common law. His problem lay in his attempt to relate all the body of laws to a set of rights, and to attach that to a theory of law which did not fit the English system. Having begun with a natural lawyer's concepts, he could not adequately fit in the forms of action and the common law notion of remedies to wrongs. Blackstone's dilemma was to try to fit the common law into a theory of law he essentially did not believe and did not use. Since in his view the law rested on custom and maxims, he needed to explain more clearly how those customs and maxims were treated by the courts, and how they evolved in the legal procedure, for the entire basis of the remedies of the third book required it. The rights defined in the second book, particularly of personal property, were too inspecific to be a guide to the remedies in the third book. These remedies depended on the custom and the

to enter upon the particular subtleties and refinements, into which this doctrine, by the variety of cases which have occurred in the course of many centuries, has been spun out and subdivided.'

[102] 3 *Comm.* 327.

[103] 3 *Comm.* 328: 'When therefore a body of laws, of so high antiquity as the English, is in general so clear and perspicuous, it argues deep wisdom and foresight in such as laid the foundations, and with great care and circumspection, in such as have built the superstructure.'

[104] 2 *Comm.* 376: '[E]xperience soon shewed how difficult and hazardous a thing it is, even in matters of public utility, to depart from the rules of the common law; which are so nicely constructed and so artificially connected together, that the least breach in any one of them disorders for a time the texture of the whole.'

maxims and the reasoning of the courts, but Blackstone did not elaborate further how these worked.

The Dilemma Presented by Blackstone

Because Blackstone had sought to fit the common law into an institutional structure which stressed the importance of rules and natural law as an organizing concept, and had sought to portray the common law as static and unchanging in its principles, he failed adequately to explore the customary base of law or its remedial nature in a systematic way. Writers after Blackstone therefore faced three problems. The first was how to handle the role of history in law, and how to examine change in law. The second was how to treat sovereignty and the role of the state. The third was how to deal with the peculiar detail of English forms of action, and how to put them into a rational structure. Because Blackstone's attempt to bring these three together was unsuccessful, his successors had to look to different solutions. One solution was to stress the role of the sovereign; another was to focus on custom and the lawyer's craft.

The solution which Sir Robert Chambers, Blackstone's successor,[105] sought to give to the problem of balancing sovereignty, natural law, and history was one which led him away from explaining the complexities of law into disquisitions on the political constitution and the structure of the state. This entailed him abandoning the Blackstonian view of history and natural law. Chambers firstly warned against romanticizing and rationalizing the past. He pointed out that the historical laws of a country were rooted in such obscurity that they were often undiscoverable, and he warned of the dangers of assuming that legislation in the past was motivated by rationality and not by chance or capriciousness.[106] Similarly, he was sceptical about the use of natural law. He argued that 'the feeble spirit of mortals' was unable adequately to pry into the eternal law of God. Rather, knowledge of right and wrong was obtained by investigating the causes of why certain acts were good and others bad, and by looking to the consequences of actions. The

---

[105] He was elected to the Vinerian chair in 1766, but stopped delivering his lectures in 1773.

[106] Chambers, *A Course of Lectures on the English Law delivered at the University of Oxford 1767–73*, ed. T. M. Curley, 2 vols. (Oxford, 1986), i. 84, 133.

key to the Divine Law was hence to examine the utility of actions, something discovered and measured over time.[107] This not only cast doubt on the Blackstonian vision of history and the role of reason, but denied all the reservations Blackstone had about parliamentary competence. The second Vinerian professor elaborated the doctrine of parliamentary sovereignty to Austinian proportions:

As parliament unites, either in person or by representation, all the powers that can possibly subsist in a community, it necessarily possesses supreme jurisdiction, and consequently an unlimited and irresistible authority. Of the supreme power in every state however constituted the authority is unlimited, not merely by human compact but by physical necessity; for power can only be limited by a greater power, and that power which is subject to a greater is evidently not supreme.[108]

Chambers' lectures were divided in three parts, building on this positivist conception: public law, criminal law, and private law. The first covered the constitution, showing it as a hierarchical and feudal structure from the king. The second summarized the mass of criminal law, but began with a refutation that the criminal law had arisen from successive experiments and the raising of order gradually by degrees out of confusion. Rather, the law had positive origins.[109]

The third section, on private law, was devoted wholly to property, with the exception of four chapters on equity. The most obvious omission in this structure was an examination of the law of actions. In fact, the third book was very thin. Apart from six chapters that were a close commentary on Littleton's *Tenures*, and a further six chapters on real property, Chambers devoted only four chapters to personal property, which included its nature, its acquisition, and injuries to it. Virtually the whole of the law relating to torts and contracts was relegated to one short lecture on injuries to personal property.[110]

---

[107] *Lectures.* i. 84–5.   [108] *Lectures.* i. 140.

[109] 'The laws of God revealed to Adam and to Noah were undoubtedly propagated through their descendants. Accordingly, civil life may be traced back to the East, the laws of the Egyptians were borrowed by the Cretans, by them transmitted into Greece and from Greece adopted by the Romans.' He added, 'Had mankind received no original instructions from a superior being, they would probably have continued through all ages *mutum et turpe pecus*, fattening in the summer and starving in the winter, worrying the kid and flying from the tiger.' *Lectures*, i. 307–8.

[110] In addition, Chambers had discussed contract as a way to obtain property in the previous chapter.

Chambers' work was unusual in omitting discussion of so much of the law. His organizing concepts of the sovereign state, developed over time on a feudal model, allowed him to set forth a large division of property, and to deal with real property under his schema, but did not allow him to develop the extensive portion of law that was covered in the third book of the *Commentaries*. Chambers' Vinerian lectures thereby represented a further step away from the common lawyers: as a collaborative effort with Dr Johnson,[111] the lectures could be an elegant view of the origins and nature of civil government in England, and explain the constitutional structure for the gentleman. They could not, however, explain the workings of law. Like Blackstone's natural law, Chambers' sovereign legislature soared high above the detail of the law at ground level, without explaining. His direction was therefore one which would bear less fruit than the *Commentaries* in explaining the law.

Chambers' successor to the Vinerian chair, Richard Wooddeson, returned to the Roman tripartite division of persons, things, and actions, and laid greater stress on the importance of special pleading than his predecessors had done, comparing it with 'anatomical skill in the medical profession'.[112] Wooddeson, like Blackstone, began with a discussion of the law of nature, but for him, the functional role of the law of nature was smaller than it appeared to be in Blackstone's structure. Wooddeson began his lectures with a discussion of natural law, but based his arguments concerning the rights of sovereigns to rule, and on the consent given to laws, largely on custom.[113] Where Blackstone had found a potential tension between the decrees of the sovereign and the dictates of natural law, Wooddeson argued that all subjects must obey the laws, since any diminution of respect for the laws would 'be bringing a greater evil upon the whole community'.[114] As for the conscience of the individual, Wooddeson followed 'Locke's philosophical advice' that a private person should abstain from any action he regarded as

---

[111] See E. L. McAdam, *Dr. Johnson and the English Law* (Syracuse, 1951); J. E. Reibman, 'Dr. Johnson and the Law', unpublished Edinburgh University Ph.D., 1979; and T. L. Curley's editorial introduction to the *Lectures*. For a discussion of Chambers' structure, see J. W. Cairns, 'Eighteenth Century Professorial Classification of English Common Law', *McGill Law Journal*, xxxiii (1987), 225–44. See also, H. G. Hanbury, *The Vinerian Chair and Legal Education* (Oxford, 1958).

[112] *A Systematical View of the Laws of England*, 3 vols. (London, 1792–3), i. 107.

[113] *Systematical View*, i. 21–4, 28–9.

[114] Ibid. 48–9.

unlawful, but undergo any punishment due as a result of his action. For Wooddeson, the abstract law of nature thus had a lesser theoretical role than it seemed to have for Blackstone. Rather, he emphasized custom and history from the start: 'the separate interest of any individual is to be postponed to the common welfare of the state,' he said, 'since history and reason alike teach us, that the finished fabric of a well-ordered constitution is to be the work of succeeding generations and gradually to be improved by progressive experience.'[115]

The notion of custom and the nature of change and development in law through the courts was taken up by James Sedgwick, writing in 1800 under the influence of the Burkean reaction to natural rights arguments. He dismissed the notion of abstract rights, arguing that since the purpose of laws was to regulate the moral conduct of man, they 'could not precede in existence the agent whose actions they were expressly intended to control'.[116] The concept of right grew from the suffering of wrongs. Sedgwick criticized Blackstone's static view of the law, in particular attacking his views on the need to follow precedents strictly. The progress from feudal to commercial society, he said, required 'an occasional deviation from principle'[117] and he argued that the decrees of a magistrate should guide but not bind. 'The *common law*, it has been said, works itself pure, *by rules drawn from the fountain of justice*,' he said, 'but never could it thus purge and defecate itself, if its unsound and exceptionable principles are to be perpetuated and brought into system.' Indeed, for Sedgwick, the very idea of bringing a case to court implied that the question was itself unsettled and in need of determination: 'every resort to legal jurisdiction presumes, either that the matter in dispute is still *sub judice*, or that a judgment awarded in a case is such as the court might, on a considerate review, be induced to reverse'.[118]

It was this notion of the law as changing piecemeal through case disputes that would be most stressed by lawyers after Blackstone. The *Commentaries* were succeeded by a rush of minor treatises which sought to describe particular aspects of the law, by writers who saw from Blackstone's work the utility and practicality of looking at areas of law in principled terms.[119] However, these works sought more to

[115] Wooddeson, 42–3.
[116] *Remarks Critical and Miscellaneous on the Commentaries of Sir William Blackstone,* p. 3.   [117] *Remarks,* 66.   [118] *Remarks,* 69.
[119] See Milsom, 'The Nature of Blackstone's Achievement'.

tease principles out of masses of cases than to erect natural law structures. They were hence largely empirical and descriptive. One such was Sir William Jones's work on *Bailments*, which sought to describe this area of law analytically, tracing each rule to its reason, to check the law historically, and from these methods produce a rounded synthesis.[120] Jones was suspicious of natural law arguments, criticizing them for being too abstract. Instead, he felt that the courts should be bound by authority 'as firmly as the pagan deities were supposed to be bound by the decrees of fate'.[121] The treatises, while often claiming to be discovering the true natural principles behind law,[122] were summaries of the law as distilled from a mass of cases, something Blackstone had largely eschewed. It was an empirical view, which held that principle was to be found, not by abstract theorizing, but by a minute examination of the cases.[123] These treatises looked at law in an inductive way by examining judicial developments at ground level. As Robert Maugham wrote in 1825, there were two ways to arrange the subject of a treatise—either one could make a digest of the law and its doctrines, or one could report every statute and case. His view was that the writer should collect the law in a compendious form, and arrange it with cases sufficiently but not excessively described, in a convenient order.[124] The lesson to be learned from the *Commentaries* was that the law had to be examined in a detailed way, both through its history and through a detailed analysis of its workings.[125] The analysis provided

---

[120] Jones, *Bailments*, 3–4.   [121] Ibid. 59–60.

[122] See J. J. Powell, *Essay upon the Law of Contracts and Agreements*, 2 vols. (London, 1790), iv–v: 'All reasoning must be founded on first principles. The science of the Law derived its principles either from that artificial system which was incidental to the introduction of feuds, or from the science of morals. And without a knowledge of these principles, we can no more establish a conclusion in law, than we can see with our eyes shut.'

[123] 'To collect Cases under any head of the Law, without regard to principles or arrangement, is a matter of no difficulty,' wrote the law reporter Isaac Espinasse, 'but Cases deciding no principles are useless . . . With this view I was induced to attempt to extract principles from Cases where they were not obvious.' *A Digest of the Law of Actions and Trials at Nisi Prius*, 2nd edn. (London, 1792), xiv.

[124] Robert Maugham, *A Treatise on the Law of Attornies, Solicitors and Agents* (London, 1825).

[125] See, e.g., M. Dawes, *Epitome of the Law of Landed Property* (London, 1818): 'The first principles of the science are obscured in their bulk; a proficient is wanted to analyse them; and when the initiated have some knowledge of the old law, they discover that it is out of use; yet it is impossible to know the new with precision, without studying the old, which enables us to see the reasons of the one as grafted on the other.' (vii-viii).

in this way revealed that the law was not the perfect static system of pure principle often suggested by Blackstone, but a dynamic system. As Thomas Jarman, editor of Powell's *Essay on Devises*, said in the 1827 edition, '[t]he laws of every nation must continually be receiving large accessions from judicial expositions; but in proportion to the increase of adjudged cases, the number of unascertained questions—the *terra incognite* of legal investigation—will be diminished'.[126] It is in this context that we must turn to the response to Blackstone, and examine the practitioners' theorizing of the law.

---

[126] J. J. Powell, *An Essay on Devises*, ed. Thomas Jarman, 2 vols. (1827), vii–viii.

3

The Logic of the Law

THE *Commentaries* were widely praised as the first systematic view of English law. However, when lawyers praised the work, they admired it more as an introduction to the law for students and gentlemen than as a complete and accurate statement of the law. The *Commentaries* were indeed widely perceived as being 'one of the best books for the student to take for his foundation',[1] and for that reason, Blackstone's method was lauded: but professionals were less convinced by the work's status as a guide for lawyers.[2] In a sense, what made the *Commentaries* attractive to the gentlemanly reader made them unattractive to the profession. For what was important in law to the generation of lawyers after Blackstone looking at his work were those very particularistic parts of the common law which Blackstone had found to undermine his natural law deductivism. Practitioners ignored or rejected the notion that the law was a set of rational rules which could be set out in a systematic way from the law of nature.[3] In an important way, they felt that Blackstone had misconstrued the law: it was not, they believed, a system of principles and rules which only needed the occasional use of history to explain the odd idiosyncrasy, but it was rather a complex and detailed system of forms which could only be simplified and distorted by reducing it to the rules that Blackstone had. For many

---

[1] See *A Treatise on the Study of Law* (London, 1797), 63 n. Edward Wynne said, in his *Eunomus: or Dialogues concerning the Law and Constitution of England*, 3rd edn., 2 vols. (London, 1809) at i. 49, 'I do not know a more emphatical application of the Grecian sage's wish "to teach young persons in the early part of life, what they may use when they are men," than is given by the *Commentaries on the Laws of England.*'

[2] See Sir William Jones, *Bailments*, 3. Jones praised the *Commentaries* as the most 'beautiful outline that ever was exhibited of any human science', but added that 'they alone will no more form a lawyer, than a general map of the world, how accurately and elegantly soever it may be delineated, will make a geographer'.

[3] J. F. Schiefer, for instance, writing in 1792, was critical of Blackstone's over-theoretical view of law. He wrote, '[i]t is not what law is in theory, nor what people imagine it to be, *but what it is in practice and in fact*, that is the subject worthy of the philosopher's enquiry'. *An Explanation of the Practice of Law* (London, 1792), xi.

practitioners, therefore, the law had to be approached through analysing those aspects of the law that Blackstone had used only casually: it had to be studied through a close examination of its history, and of its practical forms.[4]

Criticism of particular legal doctrines elaborated in the work was inevitable, given Blackstone's task of elaborating all the areas of the law, and he was duly attacked, in particular for his politically contentious elaboration of the Toleration and Test Acts[5] and for his legally contentious arguments on the rules of descent.[6] A more serious and damaging criticism, however, was that the very nature of the work entailed superficiality which engendered error. This was a view taken of the *Commentaries* by lawyers, and it was a view elaborated by Samuel Warren when examining a paragraph on Bargain and Sale taken from Blackstone.[7] Warren stated that

Almost every sentence in the above paragraph contains the enumeration of a principle so important and difficult in its application, as to have called forth dozens of reported decisions; and if only one of each of them were proposed to the ablest and most laborious reader, fresh from his perusal of Blackstone . . . he would find, that the forgoing sentences would be about as serviceable in conducting him to a correct conclusion, as a chorus out of Sophocles.[8]

The *Treatise on the Study of Laws*, published in 1797, echoed these views, arguing that the success of the *Commentaries* was not deserved: they certainly presented the country with a readable system of law when it was needed, but they did no more: lawyers

---

[4] For a modern discussion of the gap between jurisprudence and legal practice, see Charles Fried, 'The Artificial Reason of the Law or: What Lawyers Know', *Texas Law Review*, lx (1981–2), 35–58.

[5] See P. Furneaux, *Letters to the Honourable Mr. Justice Blackstone* (London, 1770).

[6] See W. H. Rowe, *Observations on the Rules of Descent* (London, 1803).

[7] 2 *Comm*. 447–9.

[8] S. Warren, *A Popular and Practical Introduction to Law Studies* (London, 1835), 325. Similar criticism was made by Frederick Ritso in 1815. Ritso pointed out that the *Commentaries* were written for the enlightenment of an educated public, and he went so far as to say that they were therefore wholly unsuitable for the professional education of law students. For, he argued, Blackstone had taken care only to illustrate those detached parts of the law which were 'most capable of historical or critical ornament'. *An Introduction to the Science of Law* (London, 1815), 31. In his attempts to appeal to the general reader, Ritso said, Blackstone had opted for ornamental illustration in place of solid argument, something which was misleading and misinforming. Thus, he argued that even the most widely praised part of the *Commentaries*—the Second Book on property—was so superficial that it was impossible for any student to form any clear idea about key distinctions in legal rules from this alone. Ibid. 45.

would receive no benefit from them.[9] The criticism put forward here went further, in arguing that Blackstone was lazy and inept as a researcher, and that he did not go deeply enough into the history of the ancient laws to explain the modern law. Not only did Blackstone fail adequately to explain what the law was, but he further failed to explain why it was what it was: '[h]e found it a much easier task to deduce his subject from the conquest, and to transcribe, with a few improvements of language, the matter which is heaped together in Lord Coke or in Maddox, than to walk in a path where there was no such genius to direct him: a vast labyrinth presented itself to him; he was conscious of his weakness and recoiled'.[10] Despite the frequent republication of the *Commentaries*, the view remained that Blackstone had covered difficult and variegated ground with only style to save him. Thomas Starkie told his pupils at the Inner Temple in the 1830s that Blackstone's work was all very well as a systematic arrangement of principle; but for the practitioner, he said, only practice and minute study would do for an education.[11] Rather than being systematic and logical, the law for Starkie was complex. In the *Commentaries*, 'where the principle is already extracted for him, [the student] learns his principle, with less trouble, it is true,' Starkie said, 'but this is a dispensation with labour, which is one of the most useful exercises to the mind of a lawyer, and which leaves the mere idea of an abstract rule, without any knowledge of its practical application, or of the legal limits which the principle serves to define'.[12]

Thus, while Blackstone had managed to extract principles from the law, he had left untouched the prime problems facing the eighteenth-century lawyers in its application. First, he had left intact the notion of the common law being an oral tradition among the judges. Second, he had venerated the jury trial as 'the glory of the English law'.[13] Together, these made it very difficult for an outsider to a case either to predict what the rule might be that would determine the case, or even to know what the rule or reason was that swayed the jury to come to a decision. Blackstone had summarized the law: but his natural law structure left unexplained how the law worked at ground level. It was in the context of his failure to discuss

---

[9] *Treatise on the Study of Laws*, 62 n.
[10] Ibid.   [11] *Legal Examiner*, ii (1834), 450.
[12] Ibid. 451.   [13] 3 *Comm.* 379.

the workings of law at case level that the first full history of the
English law was written.

John Reeves: the Historian's View of Law

John Reeves's *History of English Law*, published in 1787, was both an
expansion of and a reaction to the *Commentaries*.[14] It was written,
Reeves said, to flesh out Blackstone's last chapter on 'The Rise,
Progress and Gradual Improvement of English Law', for Reeves felt
that his predecessors, Hale and Blackstone, had given very imperfect
sketches of the history of law. Blackstone had only reverted to
history when his deductive reason let him down, so that his use of
history was superficial and occasional. Such a historical method was
abhorrent to Reeves. It was, he said, distorting to look at ancient law
in modern terms, as Blackstone had done, for only when one looked
at the ancient law on its own terms could it be understood. However,
Reeves was not just writing a history, for he intended that the book
should explain the whole system of English law to the lawyer: it was
designed to perform a similar function to that of the *Commentaries*.
Reeves's historical method was in fact a wholesale rejection of
Blackstone's institutional framework, for he sought in his history to
'place many parts of [the law] in a new and more advantageous light,
than could be derived from any institutional system; in proportion as
an arrangement conformable with the nature of the subject,
surpasses one that is merely artificial'.[15]

The *History* was therefore not a mere antiquarian work, no simple
scholarly attempt to finish off Blackstone's last chapter. It was
instead intended as a legal treatise of its own, which sought to
analyse and examine the common law and its rules wholly through
history: '[t]he History which I now presume to offer to the
profession of the law', he wrote, 'is an attempt to investigate and
discover the first principles of that complicated system which we are
daily discussing'.[16] The book was indeed scarcely a work of history
for the general reader, for it made almost no reference to social and
political changes outside the courts, and it was, as Holdsworth put it,

---

[14] *History of English Law, from the Time of the Saxons to the End of the Reign of Philip and
Mary*, 4 vols. (London, 1787).
[15] Reeves, *History*, i. p. vi.   [16] Ibid. iii.

'indescribably dull':[17] a legal source, full of technicalities and detailed minutiae. The *History* ran to four long volumes,[18] each covering a mass of detailed rules and procedures culled from a painstakingly close analysis of the classic texts of Glanvil, Bracton, and Littleton, as well as the charters, ancient statutes, and year books.[19]

This history was altogether different from Hale's and Blackstone's, and reflected the practitioner's approach to law. Where Reeves was most notably different from his predecessors was in his close and detailed examination of legal actions and court processes, for whereas Blackstone and Hale had both written histories of law as bodies of rules, treating laws as defined things, Reeves examined the law at the level of writs and judicial decisions, showing that it was only through a close examination of the history of certain decisions, writs and forms of action, that one could understand the nature of modern legal actions and the rules of modern law. Reeves's *History* was hence the first attempt to analyse the law and its history as a whole by looking at the forms of action. By examining the law through the forms of action, he was able to show that it was not only a changing thing but a system which worked haphazardly and responsively, developing new rules in an *ad hoc* way in the courts. By stressing that procedures were central, Reeves could show that the rules derived by the common law were much more flexible and indeterminate than was suggested by Hale or Blackstone. For Reeves, the law was thus not a self-contained science, but a forum reflecting changing social needs, and this was a conception of law which contrasted with the Blackstonian view of it as a rule of action.

In the *History*, Reeves showed the haphazard and irregular growth of writs, noting that '[i]t was by degrees that writs increased to the

[17] W. S. Holdsworth, *History of English Law*, xii. 413. This criticism is not entirely fair. Not only was Reeves not aiming to write a contextualized history, but as Plucknett has pointed out, at the time when Reeves wrote, when the science of pleading was reaching its apogee, any history of law was likely to have been technical. T. F. T. Plucknett, 'John Reeves: Printer', *Columbia Law Review* lxi (1961), 1201–9.

[18] A fifth volume was added in 1829 extending the *History* to the end of Elizabeth's reign.

[19] By the time that Reeves wrote, it was common to write legal treatises on particular aspects of the law around their history, using the history to explain the law. The most important such work was Sir Martin Wright's *An Introduction to the Law of Tenures* (London, 1730), but there were also other lesser ones, such as Timothy Cunningham's *History of Taxes* (London, 1783). Blackstone, by writing a treatise on law as a whole which underplayed the detailed history, was thus moving away from these texts; Reeves was returning to see law as a whole in their terms.

multitude and variety which is exhibited in this volume'.[20] Focusing
on the forms of remedy, he gave a detailed discussion of the rise of
the actions of trespass and case, the commonest forms of action in
use in the late eighteenth century.[21] His view stressed the flexible
growth of law in the courts. The writ of trespass, for instance, was 'a
late invention not wholly approved by Bracton',[22] but 'though simple
in its first origin . . . [trespass] was by construction and legal
intendment rendered applicable to an infinitude of cases where an
injury was done either to the person or property'.[23] The focus of
attention was placed on the courts as the area of legal change, and on
the remedy used to effect change. Reeves's history of the action on
the case, for instance, showed how this remedy grew in the courts—
'when it [first] appeared in court,' he argued, 'it underwent a
discussion and debate that indicated great doubt about the propriety
and nature of the invention'.[24] He then traced the action through its
rise in various cases.[25] Reeves showed that the growth of this form of
action was haphazard and opportunistic: there were, he said,
'difficulties in this new remedy, which were left to be settled by the
refined notions that obtained in after-times upon this subject'.[26] This
view thus stressed the adaptability of law as new remedies were
established in the daily procedure of the courts.

The view Reeves gave was one which stressed the importance of
using the right writ and the correct form.[27] Thus, he spent much time
discussing the distinction between trespass and case, showing how
success in litigation depended on the plaintiff choosing the correct

---

[20] Reeves, *History*, iv. 429.

[21] For a history of the development of the various forms of action, see S. F. C.
Milsom, *Historical Foundations of the Common Law*, 2nd edn. (Cambridge, 1981).

[22] Reeves, *History*, i. 338.

[23] Ibid. iii. 84.   [24] Ibid. iii. 89.

[25] Reeves argued that the first case involving the new remedy of case was that of the
Humber Ferryman in 1338 (22 Lib. Ass. f. 94, pl. 41), where the plaintiff's horse had died
as a consequence of the ferry having been overloaded. Reeves showed that the
defendant argued that since there had been no force or violence used (as was
necessary for an action of trespass), the plaintiff could only use an action of covenant.
The judges found for the plaintiff, however, and Reeves argued that this was to take
the idea of trespass in its widest sense. He showed that henceforth other claims of
wrong were allied to trespass, thereby creating a new form of action. He then
discussed a range of cases where the new remedy evolved. See Reeves, *History*, iii.
244.   [26] Ibid. 93.

[27] Ibid. iii. 393: 'If a road was straitened or embanked, an action upon the case lay; if
it was entirely stopped, an assize of nuisance, says Moile; to which Prisot assented,
provided it was stopped by the tenant of the soil; for if it was by a stranger, he held it
should be an action on the case.'

form and laying his case in the correct terms. He showed, moreover, that while it was essential to choose the correct remedy, it was often unclear and debatable which remedy should be used. These were problems familiar enough to common law practitioners,[28] and also to writers of plea guides: yet they were the vital questions of law largely ignored in jurisprudence. Writers like Blackstone had made all seem simple and logical, but, as the critics pointed out, distilling principles was the easy part. Reeves stepped in to reveal the complexities of detail.

The idea that law was flexible and that it grew with social needs was nothing new: not only had Hale made it the central plank of his *History of the Common Law*, but many eighteenth-century legal historians had similarly stressed the idea of change in law.[29] What made Reeves important was hence not the fact that he argued that the law changed, but that he showed lawyers how it changed. The change he described was not one built around major hallmarks in the law, but around slow and gradual legal decisions. For Reeves, judges did not 'find' law from eternal rules fictitiously existing: they made decisions in cases to settle disputes, out of which were derived the bodies of rules.

This notion can be seen, for instance, in Reeves's description of the rise of the device of uses. He showed that this device had grown in an opportunistic way in response to the needs of society, by ingenuity in the courts: '[t]his disposition of property, though a novelty in the law,' he wrote, 'was not incompatible with any known rule . . . [so that], [c]onformably with such general principles of equity, these gifts, though not capable of being enforced by any common-law process, seemed, equally with many other questions, to deserve the cognisance of the supreme tribunal of the kingdom'.[30] The law grew in a negative way: if there was a wrong, which was not covered or contradicted by any other rule, it could be recognized. Reeves showed that the growth of legal forms was not cut-and-dried: thus, this form of legal conveyance, he argued, was declared void as late as 1428, when a judge ruled against it; but by 1454, a court had favoured it, and thenceforth it came into regular use.[31] The

---

[28] For a discussion, see M. J. Prichard, *Scott v Shepherd* (1773) *and the Emergence of the Tort of Negligence* (London, 1976).

[29] See especially, J. Dalrymple, *An Essay towards a General History of Feudal Property in Great Britain* (London, 1757).

[30] Reeves, *History*, iii. 177–8.   [31] Ibid. iii. 367.

law was therefore no core set of principles, but developed in a haphazard way as lawyers attempted to solve daily problems for their clients. It was fashioned by the ingenuity of lawyers often trying to evade problematic rules.[32] The law could change simply because it was not a fixed set of rules, but a reasoning process, working with a system of remedies.

Reeves's view was confirmed by his examination of statute. It was a common eighteenth-century view that the common law was derived from immemorial statutes or even from the ancient Saxon codes. Hale had seen the law in terms of these rules and had placed the origin of the modern common law in the era of Edward I, the 'English Justinian', who had ordered and settled the law.[33] Additionally, all lawyers agreed that while the common law was the major area of the law, with statutes being only minor additions, when a statute was passed, it took precedence over the common law in its sphere. Reeves, drawing on much eighteenth-century scholarship,[34] however, argued instead that statutes were responsive to the common law, either confirming evasive devices developed in the courts, or regulating those evasions.[35] Thus, he argued, although more statutes were passed in the reign of Edward I than ever before, 'the slow hand of time and experience had been long moulding our laws and judicature into a form capable of receiving the finishing touches which were made by Edward; and, in that respect, perhaps, the turbulent and unprosperous reign of his father Henry was more productive than his'.[36] Reeves saw the statutes as further foundations for the common law, providing the broad rules around which it could develop.[37]

The notion that the law was based around remedies and wrongs,

---

[32] For instance, in discussing the Statute of Uses, Reeves wrote, 'one would have thought that the learning of landed property was, by this statute, once more settled on the pure and simple principles of the common law' but showed that this was not the case by discussing the evasions and refinements of the statute. Reeves, *History*, iv. 246.

[33] *History of the Common Law*, Gray ed. 101–6. See the discussion in Ch. 1.

[34] In particular, Daines Barrington's *Observations on the Statutes*, 2nd edn. (London, 1766), and David Wilkins's *Leges Anglo-Saxonicae* (London, 1721).

[35] Noteworthy examples of this were the Statute of Fines and the Statute *Quia Emptores*, but Reeves cited others in addition. Thus, it took the Statute of Marlbridge to close off a device which enabled tenants to defraud their lords of wardships, to which they were entitled by the feudal law (*History*, ii. 60–4); while wardships needed further regulation by the first Statute of Westminster (*History*, ii. 110–11).

[36] Reeves, *History*, ii. 245–6.   [37] Ibid. ii. 245.

rather than rights, was most clearly shown in his view of the criminal law. This was, of course, the area in the law of the most clearly defined rules. However, Reeves spent little time actually defining wrongs, instead examining the modes of trial, the presentation of the wrong, and the punishment attached.[38] For Reeves, it was the allegation of the wrong, redressed by a court, which made the law, after the fact. For example, the '*crimen raptus* . . . was, when a woman declared herself to have suffered violence from a man in the king's peace; by which latter circumstance nothing more was meant, than that the offence was cognisable in the king's court only'.[39] Many crimes were not capable of definition at all, being merely the quality or circumstance of an otherwise legal act which made it wrong: such was the case, for instance, of 'laese-majesty' or sedition.[40] For Reeves, crimes became defined in two ways. The first was when the remedy became more strictly specified. For instance, he argued, in Henry III's time the offence of homicide became better established, when the courts became stricter over proofs, and insisted on correct forms of allegation.[41] The problem lay not in defining the offence, but in showing that a wrong had occurred, which required the production of correct and convincing evidence.[42] Thus, the law lay in the correct allegation of a wrong and in the remedy produced by the court. The second was when the punishment became more closely defined, something often done by statute. At common law, he showed, punishments were not at first strictly specified, for since the system was based on procedures for an infinity of circumstances, it was felt that just as what constituted a crime could vary, so could the punishment.[43] Reeves showed that in each era, punishments varied, depending upon circumstances,[44] and he suggested that crimes only

---

[38] Ibid. i. 195.   [39] Ibid. i. 200.

[40] Ibid. ii. 8: 'We see that laese-majesty was not the description of any specific offence, which was attended with punishment peculiar to itself.'

[41] This was at the time when the older modes of trial by compurgation and ordeal were being replaced by more reliable methods of ascertaining evidence of guilt.

[42] Reeves, *History*, ii. 25. By the reign of Henry III, he said, 'In all appeals of felony it was required, that the year, day, hour, and place, should be stated precisely; and it was charged *de visu et auditu* upon the testimony of the party's own senses.' Such finding of the evidence was seen as more important than defining the wrong, which was seen as obvious, if the evidence was correct.   [43] Ibid. ii. 33 ff.

[44] Ibid. i. 201, and ii. 37, where Reeves writes that in the reign of Henry III. 'The punishment of robbery depended upon the nature of the crime; it was sometimes punished with loss of life, sometimes with loss of limb. The felonies of this time were punished variously, according to the circumstances of the case, by death or mutilation.'

became more strictly defined when statutes attached punishments to them.[45]

Reeves's *History* thus presented a view of the common law which was the antithesis of the rule-bound theory. His institute for the practitioner, seeing the law as a system of forms and remedies changing over time in response to the newly perceived wrongs emerging in society as they were presented in court, reflects the practitioners' view that the law was a system of logical reasoning with which to redress any type of wrong. This was a view concentrating on the law as a series of forms of action, and contrasted with Blackstone's more jurisprudential view which had seen law as a body with eternal cohesion that could be seen in terms of rules. However, there was a reformist lesson to be culled from Reeves. The book was unreadable, its method of explaining the forms and actions of the common law so intricate that it was clear that much had to be simplified to make sense of the workings of the law.

The Challenge to Deductivism

In the late eighteenth century, many lawyers were empiricists, drawing their inspiration more from Montesquieu than the Institutists, and looking more to the nature of law through history and practice than through theory.[46] The lesson from Montesquieu was that law was not to be seen through abstract simple terms, but through detailed empirical investigation. This was not to say that there were no theoretical truths to be found: rather, that this had to be done through the empirical method. When James Mackintosh wrote his *Discourse on the Study of the Law of Nature and Nations* in 1799, therefore, he argued that deductions from abstract theory were

---

[45] Reeves therefore called statutes 'laws made for the punishing of offenders'. Ibid. ii. 455. Hence, rape was only fully defined by a statute of Edward I which made it punishable by mutilation; while sodomy, which before had been 'variously punished', was only settled by a statute of Henry VIII making it felony. Ibid. ii. 125, iv. 317–18.

[46] In the preface to his *Essay towards a General History of Property in Great Britain*, John Dalrymple spoke of the influence of both Montesquieu and Lord Kames: 'The Spirit of Laws first suggested in France, and the considerations upon forfeiture first suggested in England, that it was possible to unite philosophy and history with jurisprudence, and to write even upon the subject of law like a scholar and a gentleman.'

specious, being inapplicable to human affairs.[47] Mackintosh was highly critical of the idea that a single theory could produce a legal system:

[N]o human foresight is sufficient to establish such a system at once, and . . . if it were so established, the occurrence of unforeseen cases would shortly altogether change it . . . there is but one way of forming a civil code, either consonant with common sense, or that has ever been practised in any country, namely, that of gradually building up the law in proportion as the facts arise which it is to regulate.[48]

This suspicion of the deductive method was reflected in the practitioners' response to Blackstone's methodology. Blackstone was most attacked for spending too much time discussing abstract speculations, and too little time expounding the detailed differences of law. Law, it was urged, was not a speculative science, as the *Commentaries* seemed to imply, but a practical one.[49] Frederick Ritso criticized Blackstone's 'mathematical' approach as being inapplicable to law. To use the deductive method in law, he said, was inappropriate, for there was

this difference to be observed between the two sciences *of law* and *of mathematics*, that in the latter, in which the reasoning is always upon lines and angles, which are self-evident, we reason from the cause to the effect; while the proportions themselves are of a nature to succeed each other, so that the preceding are regularly the key or the clue to those which follow. In the law, on the contrary, the order of our reasoning is usually the reverse of this.[50]

This did not mean that Ritso was hostile to reason in law.[51] However, this reason was wholly different from the deductive, mathematical reason which he felt that Blackstone was seeing in it. Ritso's notion of legal reasoning was that of Coke, and he therefore urged the student to study the artificial reason of the law, by means of long

---

[47] He attacked the 'attempt to give an air of system, of simplicity, and of rigorous demonstration, to subjects which do not admit it'. This, he said, could only be done 'by referring to a few simple causes, what, in truth, arose from immense and intricate combinations, and successions of causes'. Mackintosh, *Discourse on the Study of the Law of Nature and Nations* (London, 1799), 54. [48] Ibid. 58.

[49] See F. Ritso, *An Introduction to the Science of Law*, 17.

[50] Ibid. 32.

[51] His preface boldly stated that the 'law is not a mere series of unconnected decrees and ordinances, but, in the strictest sense of the word, a science founded on principle, and claiming an exalted rank in the empire of reason'.

study and deep investigation.[52] It is significant that what Ritso found worst in Blackstone was his introductory section discussing the epistemological nature of right and wrong, as if it were the mathematical cause. Ritso did not, as Bentham did, feel that Blackstone's epistemology was superficial or incorrect: he rather felt that the entire epistemological approach to legal reasoning was deeply flawed. 'The philosophy of right and wrong is a plain doctrine,' Ritso asserted, 'and it stands in no need of being vindicated by the subtilising refinements of casuistical distinction.'[53] Speculating on the abstract and philosophical nature of right and wrong would not settle or aid the mind of the student: it would only 'lead him into endless perplexities and contradictions'.[54] This was an old-fashioned common law view: right and wrong were obvious and needed no prior definition in that they would become clear at the end of the process of artificial reasoning. Right and wrong were not abstract entities or rules to which the law would conform: rather, they emerged naturally out of legal reasoning and the legal solution of practical problems. As Ritso saw it, Blackstone's introductory methodology infected and corrupted the whole body of the *Commentaries*, for the premises extended beyond the Introduction; and, he wrote, 'if the substance itself is infected with the same discolourings, if the manner of instruction is superficial and the materials defective, if conclusions of science are often misconceived, and points of practice mistaken or misrepresented, these are strong arguments . . . that this is no substitute for educating and forming lawyers'.[55]

The argument of Ritso's book was that one approached the science of law not through Blackstone's institutional method, but via the method of *Coke upon Littleton*. To that end, he advised the student in detail on how to approach and use the master's great work.[56]

---

[52] Law, he said (quoting Coke), 'implies that perfection of reason whereunto a man attains by long study, often conference, long experience, and continued observation . . . we must, therefore, diligently apply ourselves . . . to a timely and orderly course of reading that by searching into the arguments and reasons of the law, we may bring them home to our natural reason, that we may perfectly understand them as our own.' Ibid. 17–18.   [53] Ibid. 34.

[54] Ibid.   [55] Ibid. 38–9.

[56] Part II of Ritso's work was thus entirely devoted to this task. Ritso's advice to common law students on how to approach their studies was exactly the same as Sir Thomas Reeve's advice to his nephew: *Lord Chief Justice Reeve's Instructions to his Nephew concerning the Study of Law* (London, 1791). First, he should obtain a precise idea of the terms and general meaning of the law; second, learn the general reason on

Practical knowledge was of the essence for Ritso, while systematic arrangement was only a shorthand to aid the memory. He therefore rejected the notion that there could be a single point of deduction, or that there could be a single source of law.[57] Instead, he reverted to the Cokean idea that there were multifarious sources of law; and, like Coke, he chose to list 20 sources which showed that the law was based not on rules, but on methods of legal reasoning.[58] This argument reverted to the common lawyers' notion of law as a reasoning process, whose sources were arguments and modes of thought. It was a practitioner's view, for in most cases there was no rule, but only a reasoning process to work from.

The Cokean approach to legal reasoning was thus far from extinct in the late eighteenth century, and was well able to withstand Blackstone's institutional alternative.[59] Lawyers turning their minds to legal education at that time were concerned more that the student should look at logic and history than that he should look at natural law theory. Lord Ashburton, for instance, argued that the lawyer should study grammar, rhetoric, and logic along with history, and he urged the student to read Coke, Littleton, Plowden, Bacon, and the old reports as well as Blackstone.[60] Lord Thurlow similarly argued

which the law was founded; third, 'form some authentic system, to collect the great leading points of law in their natural order, as the first heads or divisions of our future inquiry'; and fourth, collect and arrange particular points of law. Ritso, *Introduction*, 150–1.

[57] Ibid. 180.

[58] Ritso listed as sources the Year Books, Original Writs, Pleas, Precedents and Entries of Judgment, as well as methods of pure reasoning: arguments from convenience, as well as *ab impossibilii* and *ab inconvenienti*.

[59] That is, despite the approach suggested by the *Commentaries*, legal education at the end of the eighteenth century and on into the nineteenth remained based on Coke's conception. Blackstone's work fitted into this pattern of legal education because his was an excellent overview, but its theory and methodology could not displace the dominant one. Therefore, the late eighteenth century saw new editions of numerous legal texts written in the seventeenth and early eighteenth centuries. Charles Barton published an edition of William Noy's *The Grounds and Maxims and also an Analysis of the English Laws* in 1794, which followed Finch on the multiple sources of law. Similarly, John Mallory's *Modern Entries in English*, first published in 1734, reached a fourth edition in 1791. Most interesting, perhaps, was J. H. Thomas's *A Systematic Arrangement of Lord Coke's First Institute* (3 vols., London, 1818), which arranged Coke's ideas under Blackstone's categories, a concrete example of lawyers liking Blackstone's arrangement, but preferring Coke's theory. For a view of what books were recommended to young lawyers in the nineteenth century, see R. W. Bridgman, *A Short View of Legal Bibliography* (London, 1807), and W. Wright, *Advice on the Study and Practice of the Law*, 3rd edn. (London, 1824).

[60] *Treatise on the Study of Law*, 56 ff.

that the lawyer needed first to have a '[g]ood scholastic education, founded upon grammar',[61] while the editor who drew these views together in a *Treatise on the Study of Law* also urged the study of logic and rhetoric. For him, logic gave the thinker precision and accurate reasoning, while rhetoric 'teaches the effect of proper arrangement of principles and propositions, constituting a gradation of truths, each arising out of that which preceded it, and all mutually supporting and confirming one another'.[62]

Behind this view lay the assumption that law derived its principles from other sciences. This notion was clearly elaborated in Edward Wynne's *Eunomus: Or Dialogues concerning the Law and Constitution of England*, written in 1767 and reaching a third edition in 1807.[63] In the first dialogue, Eunomus advised the student Policrites on the study of law, and told him that he should study not only his own science but others as well. The lawyer had to be able to argue from general principles, since 'the idea of obedience to laws would often be very imperfect without recurring at times to a pure source of obligations and stronger motives than any that laws themselves can furnish'.[64] This was not a view that there was a natural law which was the measure and key to other laws. Rather, it was a view which held that 'all arts and sciences have some kind of connection with one another: and that law, as one of these, is not . . . like one left on a desert island, and shut out from all society'.[65] There was, rather, 'a mutual intercourse constantly kept up between the law and other sciences'. In his argument, Eunomus referred to Finch's celebrated comment that the sparks of all sciences in the world were raked up in the ashes of the law.[66] It was a significant citation, for it was to suggest that law drew on all other areas of knowledge as it required, without being able to define all in terms of strict rules. The lawyer therefore needed a smattering of all sciences, as well as a knowledge of history, natural law, and civil law. Instead of being a self-contained science looking to its own principles for the solution of its problems, law was at the heart of all society and all thought, and was influenced by ideas contained in and derived from others. The law was 'a science not only connected with others, but in some measure containing

---

[61] *Treatise on the Study of Law*, 67.   [62] Ibid. 97–8.

[63] Wynne was a lawyer who had written some *Observations on Fitzherbert's Natura Brevium* in 1760 (published in *Miscellany concerning several Law Tracts*, 1765), which saw writs as the ancient basis of the common law.

[64] *Eunomus*, i. 57.   [65] Ibid. i. 59.

[66] H. Finch, *Common Law*, 5.

them all'.[67] The vital thing for the lawyer was to use these to learn how to think.

Thus, at the same time that Blackstone was seeking to analyse the law as a whole, there was a growing interest in looking at the law as a system of remedies and forms, with which to process other sciences and discover right and wrong in each case. Practising lawyers had, of course, always seen the law as such: but in the late eighteenth century they took this view and presented it as the key way to look at law, from a theoretical point of view, against the deductive view put forward by men like Blackstone. This view can be seen in the growing focus of attention at the end of the eighteenth century on the science of pleading, the logic of the law.

The Defence of Pleading

As far as practitioners were concerned, pleading was the most important part of law. Coke wrote that '[g]ood Pleading is the touchstone of the true sense of the law'.[68] The bases of pleading were the principles of logic and rhetoric;[69] its theory was the antithesis of a rule-bound deductivist one. An articulation of the science of pleading could be informative about the workings of law in a way the institutional structure could not. It explained the fluid workings of the law which Reeves had described, and allowed the law to embrace the other sciences. It also focused a case to produce a precise point for a rule. Finally, in its reformist aspect, it evaded the vagueness of the jury verdict. For the more pleas were focused on points of law for the judges to rule on, the more a science of special pleas was developed, the less would be left to the undefined capriciousness of juries.

Broadly, it was held that the law would provide a remedy for any

---

[67] *Eunomus*, i. 113.

[68] *A Booke of Entries* (London, 1614), preface. See also *Coke upon Littleton* 303a.

[69] See J. H. Baker, *The Reports of Sir John Spelman*, Selden Society, vol. 94 (London, 1978), 143; R. J. Schoek, 'Rhetoric and Law in Sixteenth Century England', *Studies in Philology*, l (1953), 110–27; D. S. Bland, 'Rhetoric and the Law Student in Sixteenth Century England', *Studies in Philology*, liv (1957), 498; R. J. Terrill, 'Humanism and Rhetoric in Legal Education: The Contribution of Sir John Dodderidge (1555–1628)', *Journal of Legal History*, ii (1981), 30–44; C. P. Rodgers, 'Humanism, History and the Common Law', *Journal of Legal History*, vi (1985), 129–56; A. Giuliani, 'The Influence of Rhetoric on the Law of Evidence and Pleading', *Juridical Review* (1962), 216–51.

wrong correctly presented, following strict rules. A legal action was defined to be the lawful demand of one's right;[70] yet this right was undefined in terms of rules. Right was only defined in the broadest sense: 'In Life, Liberty and Estate, every one (who has not forfeited them), has a Property and a Right; and if they are violated, the Law gives an action to redress the Wrong, and punish the Wrong-Doer.'[71] By this theory, any wrong correctly presented, which could be shown to be fit to be recognized by the courts, could be redressed.[72] It was through the rules of pleading that wrongs were presented to the court. By these rules, there was no need to define the right a priori: instead, only the procedure was strictly outlined. The rules of pleading were a form of rhetoric to pinpoint the question of dispute, a formally structured argument and counter-argument inviting the judge to come to a conclusion. When the issue had been defined, however, the judge could rule from any of the sources he chose, provided they tallied with the dispute as set forth to the court. In a sense, the judge acted as umpire between the contestants, and while he was taken to follow precedents and customs, he was able to rule *ab inconvenienti* or take his decision from another science if need be.[73]

In the second half of the eighteenth century, at the time that Blackstone was writing, lawyers began to discuss pleading as a logical science.[74] In place of listing the forms and precedents, writers began to treat pleading as a whole system. A key work in the development of this interest was Gilbert's *History and Practice of Civil Actions*,[75] published in 1737 and reaching a fourth edition in 1792. By

[70] *Coke upon Littleton* 285a.

[71] J. Comyns, *A Digest of the Laws of England*, 5 vols, (London, 1762), i. tit. 'Action', 113, citing *Thomas* v. *Sorrell* (1674) Vaugh. 330 at 337.

[72] *Tot erunt formulae brevium quot sunt genera actionum*, as Bracton put it. Quoted by F. W. Maitland in *Equity. Also the Forms of Action at Common Law. Two Courses of Lectures*, ed. A. H. Chaytor and W. J. Whittaker (Cambridge, 1909), 300.

[73] Baker quotes Fitzherbert's view thus: 'the law is nothing other than by right to show and declare the truth of every matter in good sentence; and if the parties cannot agree, if they vary upon matter in fact, then to make issue thereof and put it to the country, and then the judges, upon the truth of the matter in such sentence shown and tried, according to right, will adjudge it *secundum allegata et probata*; but if they agree upon the matter, then they shall show this is good sentence so that the truth of the matter appears, and submit it to the discretion of the order of the law, and the judges will adjudge it upon the truth of the matter.' *Reports of Sir John Spelman*, 152.

[74] See W. S. Holdsworth, *History of English Law*, ix, 311, and 'The New Rules of Pleading of the Hilary Term 1834', *Cambridge Law Journal*, i (1921–3), 261–78.

[75] The full title was: *The History and Practice of Civil Actions, particularly in the Court of Common Pleas, being an Historical Account of the Parts and Order of Judicial Proceedings, viz. Writs, Appearance, Bail, Declarations, Pleadings, Issues, Trials, Verdicts, Judgments, Errors*

tracing the history of a doctrine, it was felt that the historian could unlock its reason. Gilbert's work was a treatise on pleading and procedure, explaining each stage of the process from the declaration and pleas to the jury process and outlawry, explaining the stages in the legal process in a sequential way, and explaining the rules by reference to history. The first systematic outline of pleading, however, was provided by Comyns's *Digest*, published in 1762, which devoted 340 pages to the subject, explaining each stage of the pleadings with reference to all the relevant rules and precedents.[76] Comyns's work elaborated the various principles behind pleading, which served to articulate the principles of the science, describing a system where the contending parties stated their precise point of dispute for the court to deliberate on, by following strict rules.[77] The science of pleading was further elaborated in 1766 with the publication of Richard Boote's highly influential *Historical Treatise of an Action or Suit at Law*. Together, these two books represent an attempt to clarify and systematize what before had been seen as haphazard procedure, and their aspiration was to demystify the law and reveal its reason. Boote's work was a critical treatise, beginning with the premiss that there had been so many complex and unnecessary additions to the rules of pleading, particularly since the seventeenth century, that by the time he wrote, 'the proceedings in a suit [are] not only contradictory, but altogether dark and mysterious' to half the profession.[78] Boote's work was explicitly reformist: 'by omitting or lopping off many merely formal and fictititous matters now used in a suit, and thereby reducing our Writs and Pleadings to more concise, plain and significant forms,' he argued, 'it will be no difficult matter to set aside in a great measure, if not altogether, the objections that are made to the ordinary proceedings in Suits at Law, and to render the whole more intelligible and less expensive'.[79] Boote in fact favoured an entire reform of pleading to simplify matters: but, that lacking, his treatise aimed to explain the grounds and reasons of pleading, so that students and practitioners would no longer satisfy

---

and Costs; with the several changes introduced into these Proceedings and Practice by the several Statutes of Amendments, Jeofails and Costs: And containing a general Account of the Principles of Special-Pleading in all Civil Suits, 3rd edn. (London, 1779).

[76] Comyns, *Digest*, vol. v.

[77] For a concise summary of the principles of pleading, see Baker, *Reports of Sir John Spelman*, 142–63.

[78] R. Boote, *An Historical Treatise of an Action or Suit at Law* (London, 1766), viii.

[79] Ibid. xi–xii.

themselves with that 'superficial knowledge only, just as they find them directed to be used in the books of practice', as had traditionally been the case.[80]

In the late eighteenth century, we can perceive a strong defence of the theory of pleading, as if that were the heart of law. Pleading was perceived not merely as the tool of the practitioner but as the only way a legal system could function, which sought to solve disputes. Thus, at the same time that Blackstone was systematizing the law and Bentham attacking its technicality, practitioners reverted to the old texts and rehabilitated them, as well as writing new books of the same type. There continued a regular outcrop of practitioners' books, stretching from new editions of old collections of pleas, such as *The English Pleader*, a modernized edition of a work first published in 1738,[81] to new collections, such as the *Pleader's Assistant* and John Wentworth's *A Complete System of Pleading*, published at the end of the century, which ran to ten volumes of precedents, systematically arranged under the substantive heads of Contract, Tort, Trespass, and so on.[82] Writers justified their works and the need for such works vigorously. 'Pleading is confessed, by the most learned and experienced in the profession,' wrote John Impey in 1794, 'to be the best guide to the knowledge of the common law.'[83] Impey thus sought in his book to explain its rules. Similarly, the editor of a revised version of Samson Euer's *System of Pleading* approvingly quoted Coke to support his view of pleas: 'one of the best arguments or proofs in law is drawn from the right entries or course of pleading, as if that were *ipsius legis viva vox*'.[84] Practitioners' books were thus

---

[80] R. Boote, *An Historical Treatise of an Action or Suit at Law*, viii.

[81] *The English Pleader*, by a Gentleman of Lincoln's Inn (Dublin, 1783).

[82] *The Pleader's Assistant* (London, 1786); J. Wentworth, *A Complete System of Pleading: Comprehending the most approved precedents and forms of practice; consisting of such as have never before been published*, 10 vols. (London, 1797–9). See also *The Crown Circuit Companion*, 7th edn., ed. Thomas Dogherty (London, 1799).

[83] *The Modern Pleader* (London, 1794), v.

[84] *A System of Pleading. Including a Translation of the Doctrina Placitandi; Or the Art and Science of Pleading* (Dublin, 1791; 1st edn. London, 1677). The editor told his readers of the importance of pleading: 'There is a kind of systematic method to be used in pleading, which form and order we must be perfectly well acquainted with, to enable us advantageously to avail ourselves of matters that may chance to fall out in the progress of a suit, from the first commencement to its final close. Consequently an acquisition of this knowledge must be obtained by the study of such singular forms, and precise correct order. For, as it is said, *Forma legis, forma essentialis*, 10 Co 100. And by the same Author in another place *Forma non observata infertur adnullatio actus* 12 Co 7.' (xix).

continually popular and necessary; but increasingly their authors sought to ground the rules in reason and to justify them.

Legal theorists similarly defended the science, and even raised it on a pedestal. They stressed the old notion that the law was built on the foundation of logic and that that logic in law was to be found through the science of pleading. Sir William Jones thus wrote,

Our science of special pleading is an excellent Logick; it is admirably calculated for the purpose of analysing a cause, of extracting, like the roots of an equation, the true points in dispute, and referring them, with all imaginable distinctness, to the court or jury: it is reducible to the strictest rules of pure dialectick, and . . . [tends] to fix the attention, give a habit of reasoning closely, quicken the apprehension, and invigorate the under-standing.[85]

Lord Mansfield was thus by no means alone when he described the rules of pleading as being founded in 'soundest and closest logic'.[86] Wynne's *Eunomus* showed a similar attachment to the science of pleading. Writers who praised pleading saw it as more than a system of case presentation: for instance, in the argument of *Eunomus*, pleading was the technical and strict intermediary which let lawyers make sense of the rationality of morality and law. For Wynne, neither law nor morals were deductive sciences:

Demonstrations in morality are not in every instance so absolute as in geometry; because this depends on external figures, unalterable in their nature and independent of the mind; whereas the other depending on a mind, must depend on the clearness and precision of our ideas; which must be communicated by words, but will as often be entangled by them. Nor, when I speak of morality or law, as a science, can I be understood to mean, that all the truths they contain are so chained and connected together, as to be deduced from a single proposition.[87]

Morality and law were sciences, Wynne elaborated, in so far as their principles were either self-evident or derived from such truths. The problem was that the sciences of morals and law were hampered by the inadequacies of words; so that the key to logic, and to the discovery of those truths, lay in technical precision. Wynne therefore defended the system of pleading strongly, arguing that '[t]he structure of a record . . . is not less solid than the demonstration of a

---

[85] *Prefatory Discourse to the Speeches of Isaeus*, in *The Works of Sir William Jones*, 6 vols. (London, 1799), iv. 34.

[86] *Robinson* v. *Raley* (1757) 1 Burr. 319.   [87] *Eunomus*, i. 149–50.

proposition in Euclid: and pleading, formed on these maxims, is not only matter of science, but, perhaps, affords some of the best specimens of strict genuine logic'.[88] This was a view of science well away from the Institutional method: it perceived a rationality and order in law (and in morals), but a rationality which could not be defined in holistic or a priori terms, nor one which could be wholly grasped by an onlooker. The rationality in law was to be discovered by the application of logic, by the use of formal rules of pleading. The corollary of this was that Wynne lacked the rule-based conception of law that Blackstone had put forward. His conception was of two parties bringing a dispute before a legal umpire:

if in point of prudence as well as justice, [the plaintiff] ought to demand no more than he can prove; in point of general convenience he ought to demand it, with that certainty and precision . . . that the defendant may know how to answer the demand; and a third person, an entire stranger to both, sitting in a court of justice, may know how to judge between them.[89]

What the plaintiff demanded was guided by reason or common sense, and could not be strictly defined by rules. In the demand, he sought arbitration: but he needed precise rules of procedure to guide him in the presentation of his claim, so that the court knew exactly what to give judgment on.

This logical view was one shared by other lawyers at the end of the eighteenth century. John Frederic Schiefer wrote in 1792 that, in order to understand law, it was essential to grasp practice, and most notably the art of special pleading. He thus wrote,

A judgment given in a court of justice is nothing more than the just conclusion resulting from the premises. And those premises are, first, the record; and secondly, the evidence to be applied to that record: by comparing, therefore, the testimony of the witnesses, with written altercations of the plaintiff and the defendant themselves, we become able, and by no other means can we become so, of judging who is right, and knowing who is wrong.[90]

---

[88] *Eunomus*, i. 163.   [89] Ibid. i. 155.

[90] Schiefer, *Explanation*, iii-iv. Predictably, Frederick Ritso was also a great devotee of special pleading, as that science supported his Cokean view of legal rationality. Like Wynne, he felt that the law needed a technical language, and he felt that those who opposed pleading only did so because they failed to understand its technicalities. Pleading was a logical science: 'The science of pleading is not more difficult to be explained by a teacher, than the science of rhetoric itself. Having succeeded in distinctly and fairly understanding the *terms of art*, we are enabled to perceive, in a

The terms of art used in pleading were the logical terms from which precedents were derived: for only where there was a logical point of dispute clearly elaborated could there be a decision which could act as a precedent. The formulation of precise disputes would help the evolution of a body of law that was more than the oral custom of judges. Precise points could be articulated, ruled upon, and then reported,[91] to allow practising lawyers to see clearly how a ruling had evolved in a case, and what it meant. From these examples, it is clear that many lawyers turning their minds to a theory of the common law did not follow the rule-based thinking of Blackstone or Bentham, and that their view of the common law was not one of a system based on an eternal ancient constitution or on natural law or abstract justice, as historians so often assume. An articulation of the science of pleading did not give a map of the law like Blackstone's: but it did more fully explain how the law worked. The common law behaved in a very different way from that which is often assumed; and to understand the novelty of Blackstone and the context of Bentham, we must briefly examine the workings of the system.

Defining the Issue in Common Law Adjudication

The common law was in essence a system of adjudication, which drew its substantive notions from below through cases presented to courts.[92] By looking at the theory of pleading, and the way it was used, it can be seen that the common law aimed to work as a system to remedy any wrong correctly presented, and that the courts, in making their rulings, drew on a multiplicity of sources. In this way, it

short time, and with very little labour, that the various doctrines and rules of pleading are of a nature to be demonstrated upon the principles, upon which they were originally suggested, of plain reason and common intendment; and that they have usually no further authority in practice, than in proportion as they are calculated to promote the ends of substantial justice.' Ritso, *Introduction*, 184.

[91] It is, perhaps, no coincidence that law reporting should have grown so rapidly from the mid-eighteenth century, at the time of the revival in interest in pleading; nor that it should have commenced with Burrow's reports of Mansfield's King's Bench, since it was Mansfield who worked so hard to obtain special verdicts and special points of law for determination by the court.

[92] For a comparison of the contrasting English and French legal procedures, see P. Stein, 'The Procedural Models of the Sixteenth Century', *Juridical Review* (1982), 186–97.

can be seen that the law was no autonomous set of rules, but was interwoven into the fabric of society, drawing its rules thence.

In common law theory, the lawful claim of a right depended on the correct following of procedures from the outset, and in theory, the first step in the process was the obtaining of an original writ, to secure the defendant's appearance in court. A historical examination of the original writ showed that the courts in theory only sought to do justice between two contestants, without defining rules a priori. George Crompton described the process in this way:

Original writs were in their nature twofold, and were mandatory letters from the King, sealed with the seal in the Chancellor's custody, directed to the Sheriff, and either required him to command the defendant to do justice to the complainant, or appear in the Common Pleas at Westminster on the return, to shew why he did not comply; or else required the Sheriff immediately, without making any previous command to give up what was demanded, or take a security from his appearance in court . . . When the Original writs was returned to the Court of Common Pleas, the court thereby became possessed of the cause and all further process relating thereto issued from thence.[93]

In essence, then, the writ was a demand to 'do justice', a justice undefined. Indeed, Crompton defined the King's Bench as 'the *Custos morum* of the people, as, upon hearing of any offence militating against the first principles of justice or morality, it was impowered to inflict a proper punishment for it, and for that purpose might issue process returnable before itself'.[94] By the eighteenth century, the original writ was in practice insignificant and usually fictitious, for in effect the commonest ways to secure a defendant's appearance in court was via a bill of Middlesex or a capias.[95] However, it remained the theoretical grounding of any case.[96]

[93] G. Crompton, *Practice Common-Placed: Or the Rules and Cases of Practice in the Courts of King's Bench and Common Pleas Methodically Arranged*, 2 vols. (London, 1780), i, pp. xlvi-xlviii.   [94] Ibid. xxxiii.

[95] The Bill of Middlesex, used for the King's Bench, was itself based on a fiction that the defendant was in the custody of the King's Bench prison, or was an officer of the court.

[96] The first report of the commissioners on the Common Law Courts wrote in 1829, 'Great technical importance . . . has from time immemorial been attached to these instruments; and they have been considered not as mere process for compelling the defendant's appearance, but as necessary to found the jurisdiction of the court of Common Law between subject and subject, for unless where proceeding is in bill (which is in the nature of an exception from the regular course), the maxim is, that no suit can be commenced but by original writ.' *First Report of His Majesty's Commissioners*

More importantly, the plaintiff had to choose the correct form of action and make the claim conformable to the writ.[97] In theory, the common law had a remedy for every conceivable wrong, and it was a maxim that there was no right without a remedy.[98] In practice, however, remedies were constrained by the forms of action available. By the eighteenth century, the commonest forms of action were trespass and case,[99] the former alleging direct injuries, the latter consequential harms. The action on the case was a particularly flexible form of action, with the writ being adapted according to the facts of the case. In theory, it could remedy any wrong; but in fact there were distinct limitations, for not only did case not lie for acts covered by other remedies—notably trespasses, felonies, and misdemeanours—but one could equally not use the remedy unless there was particular damage suffered by the plaintiff alone,[100] nor where the act committed was not prohibited by law.[101] The law did not allow one action on several distinct causes of action, and a

appointed to Inquire into the Practice and Proceedings of the Superior Courts of Common Law, Parliamentary Papers, 1829 (46) IX. p. 79. Boote was highly critical of the continuing need to insert these technical formalities in a case, since they had no proper function any more. Historical Treatise, 23–33.

[97] The various forms of action were laid out and systematized in F. Buller (ed.), An Introduction to the Law relative to trials at Nisi Prius, 2nd edn. (London, 1775).

[98] The leading case for this doctrine was Ashby v. White (1703) 2 Ld. Raym. 938, where Holt ruled that every injury imported a damage, even where there was no pecuniary loss: 'And it is no objection to say, that it will occasion multiplicity of actions; for if men will multiply injuries, actions must be multiplied too; for every man that is injured ought to have his recompense.' See also Winsmore v. Greenbank (1745) Willes 578, Chapman v. Pickersgill (1762) 1 Wils. 146, and Pasley v. Freeman (1789) 3 TR 51.

[99] See S. F. C. Milsom, Historical Foundations of the Common Law, 283–313 on the development of these actions.

[100] See Iveson v. Moore (1699) 1 Ld. Raym. 486, which ruled that there could be no action for a public nuisance unless there was special damage alleged. Here, Rokeby J opposed allowing an action (as opposed to an indictment) on the grounds that 'if one man may have an action, for the same reason a hundred thousand may'. He went on, 'if the stopping be a particular damage to a particular person, he may have an action: but then the particular and special damage must be particularly and certainly alleged, which is wanting in this action'. See also The Governor and Company of the British Cast Plate Manufacturers v. Meredith (1792) 4 TR 794: Chichester v. Lethbridge (1738) Willes 71; R v. Lloyd (1802) 4 Esp. 200; and Rose v. Miles (1815) 4 M. & S. 101. See also R v. Wheatly (1761) 2 Burr. 1125 which ruled that the defendant, who was indicted for selling goods underweight, could not be charged criminally, but needed an action on the case, since here the damage was particular and not general.

[101] '[I]t does not lie for an Act not prohibited by Law, tho' it be to the Damage of the Party.' Comyns, Digest, i. 141, citing The Countess of Salop v. Crompton (1600) Cro. El. 777, 784, and Cudlip v. Rundall (1691) 4 Mod. 9.

plaintiff could not therefore join causes of a different nature in the same declaration.[102] This was a particular problem given the difficulty of establishing the precise boundary between actions, particularly between trespass and case, when it was unclear whether a set of facts constituted direct or consequential damage.[103] The nature of the remedy therefore limited the facts that could be presented before the court. Not every wrong therefore had a remedy: there were *damna sine injuria* for which the law gave no redress if the plaintiff could not find the legal remedy which ascribed particular guilt and responsibility to the chosen defendant.

The essence of common law pleading was to show the court that one had suffered a wrong for which the defendant was to blame. The system of pleading was thus a set of alternate allegations and denials which sought to establish that there had been a right which had been breached by the defendant, and which should be redressed by the court. The most important part was the declaration, the 'instrument framed to set forth the complaint or demand of the plaintiff or demandant, against the defendant or tenant, and which ought to contain the whole matter or substance thereof'.[104] There were several key rules behind the declaration. The first point was that it had to be conformable to the writ, since the declaration was an exposition of the writ, so that the claimant could not put all manner of multifarious claims in the declaration.[105] What was more important

---

[102] Comyns, *Digest*, i. 120.

[103] The most celebrated case of this was *Scott* v. *Shepherd* (1773) 2 W. Bl. 892, where the court had to decide whether the damage caused by a man throwing a lighted squib into a fairground, which was then thrown from one stall to another by others seeking to protect themselves, and which injured the last man, was immediate or consequential damage, and therefore whether the form of action to be used should be trespass or case. For an examination, see M. J. Prichard, *Scott* v. *Shepherd (1773) and the Emergence of the Tort of Negligence*. The literature on the distinction between trespass and case, and the significance of this distinction for the development of substantive law, is extensive. See Prichard, 'Trespass, Case and the Rule in *Williams* v. *Holland'*, *Cambridge Law Journal* (1964), 234–53; P. H. Winfield and A. L. Goodhart, 'Trespass and Negligence', *Law Quarterly Review*, xlix (1933), 359–78; C. H. S. Fifoot, *The History and Sources of the Common Law: Tort and Contract* (London, 1949); and P. H. Winfield, 'The History of Negligence and the Law of Torts', *Law Quarterly Review*, xlii (1926), 184–201.   [104] Boote, *Historical Treatise*, 75–6.

[105] Gilbert, *History*, 4; Comyns, *Digest*, v. 16; *Coke upon Littleton* 17a, 303b. Although the plaintiff had initially to choose the correct form of action, it was the facts pleaded which determined whether he had so chosen. In *Haward* v. *Bankes* (1760) 2 Burr. 1113, there was a dispute whether the plaintiff should have chosen case or trespass, and the court ruled, '[t]he plaintiff describes, in his Declaration, a Fact which, *as it comes out* at the Trial, *may* or *may not*, be a proper strict Trespass: It might, at the Trial, be proved

was that the writ had to be clear, unequivocal, and certain. The declaration therefore had to get the names of the parties correct and the names of the places right.

The plaintiff had to allege a wrong recognized by the court, but more than that, he had to show that his claim was precise.[106] 'So, a Declaration ought to have Certainty of the Things demanded: And therefore in Trespass for taking his Fish, the Declaration is bad if it does not shew the number and Kinds of Fish in certain.'[107] As explained by Chief Justice Holt, 'where a man brings trespass for taking his goods, he must declare of the quantity, because he, by having the possession, may know what he had, and therefore must know what he lost'.[108] Therefore, Lord Mansfield said an allegation that the defendant took 'divers goods' was insufficient, for 'the defendant cannot justify, unless the particulars are specified'.[109] The reason for this was clear: if the plaintiff had not correctly alleged the wrong, there was nothing for the court to adjudicate on, and no clear case for the defendant to answer.[110]

Precision was thus of the essence in making the claim, for the court could only consider what was alleged on the record.[111] This

to be *either* Trespass or Case; either one or the other of them, *according to the Evidence'.* In this case, the judge said, it was indifferent whether it was the one or the other, before the case began: but the evidence proved was of consequential damage, and hence the plaintiff had been right to proceed in case.

[106] See *Chamberlain* v. *Williamson* (1814) 2 M. & S. 408, where an administrator attempted to bring an action for a breach of promise of marriage to the testator. Here Lord Ellenborough ruled that the question was wholly novel, but he added 'that would not be a decisive ground of objection, if in reason and principle it could strictly be maintained'. But he said, the general rule was *actio personalis moritur cum persona*, so that 'the special damage ought to be stated on the record; otherwise the court cannot intend it'.

[107] Comyns, *Digest*, v. 26, citing *Playter's Case* (1582) 5 Co. Rep. 34b.

[108] *Keeble* v. *Hickerington* (1705) 11 East 574 n. See also *Chamberlain* v. *Greenfield* (1772) 2 W. Bl. 810, which ruled that the court could find damages only for so much as was laid in the declaration.

[109] *Bertie* v. *Pickering* (1769) 4 Burr. 2455. See also *Martin* v *Hendrickson* (1703) 2 Ld. Raym. 1007; *Crowther* v. *Ramsbottom* (1798) 7 TR 654; *Richardson* v. *the Mayor of Oxford* (1793) 2 H. Bl. 182; *Pinkney* v. *the Inhabitants of East Hundred* (1671) 2 Wms. Saund. 379; *Martin* v. *Kesterton* (1776) 2 W. Bl. 1089.

[110] For Mansfield's attitude to pleading, see below, Ch. 4.

[111] See *Turner* v. *Eyles* (1803) 3 B. & P. 456, where it was ruled that in an action of escape out of execution, the plaintiff had to prove that the party who escaped had been committed by a judge of the King's Bench. It was held that evidence of the commitment which was not filed on the record could not support the action. Further, it was held that the allegation—even if unnecessary to the cause—had to be proved as laid. See also, *Wigley* v. *Jones* (1804) 5 East 440; *Cooper* v. *Jones* (1813) 2 M. & S. 202; *Draper v Garratt* (1823) 2 B. & C. 2; and *Barnes* v. *Eyles* (1818) 8 Taunt. 512.

was particularly evident in libel cases.[112] In 1777, John Horne was prosecuted for a seditious libel for publishing an advertisement for a public meeting to raise funds for the families of Americans killed at Lexington and Concord.[113] Horne in his defence claimed the technical ground that the indictment did not sufficiently aver whether it was a libel on the king and government—and therefore seditious—or if it only referred to individual soldiers. Horne lost his appeal, but the point of pleading he argued was well established. The judgment of Lord Chief Justice De Grey summed up the theory of the law on this point:

> The charge must contain such a description of the crime, that the defendant may know what crime it is which he is called upon to answer; that the jury may appear to be warranted in their conclusion of 'guilty' or 'not guilty' upon the premises delivered to them and that the court may see such a definite crime, that they may apply the punishment which the law prescribes.[114]

In some cases, such as murder or burglary, the judge said, a direct and positive averment was needed, in specific terms, 'as, where the law has affixed and appropriated technical terms to describe a crime', while in cases such as libels, where the facts were descriptive and constitutive of the crime, those facts needed positive averment. Libels were mere words which were not unlawful save in their context and given their meaning: thus, those contexts and their meanings needed allegation. The wrong needed a precise statement: only if the case was properly laid could the case proceed.[115]

---

[112] See my 'From Seditious Libel to Unlawful Assembly: Peterloo and the Changing Face of Political Crime in England, c. 1770–1820', *Oxford Journal of Legal Studies*, x (1990), 307–52.

[113] *R* v. *John Horne* (1777) 20 *State Trials* 651 and 2 Cowp. 672.

[114] 2 Cowp. 682.

[115] These rules applied equally to non-criminal libels. In 1807, Lord Ellenborough reiterated the rule that wherever words were unclear or ambiguous, they 'require explanation by reference to some extrinsic matter to make them actionable', so that 'it must not only be predicated that such matter existed, but also that the words were spoken of and concerning that matter'. *Hawkes* v. *Hawkey* 8 East 427 at 431. See also *R* v. *Alderton* (1756) 2 Sayer 280, where the plaintiff lost his action for the want of a simple averment. In a similar case in 1815, *The King* v. *Marsden*, 4 M. & S. 164, Lord Ellenborough had ruled that in an indictment charging the defendant with intending to vilify one W.S., the libel had to allege specifically that the libel was 'of and concerning W.S.'. It was argued that there was nothing to connect W.S. with the insult, and it was impossible, looking at the record, to infer that the libel referred explicitly to that person. Similarly, in *Cartwright* v. *Wright* (1822) 1 D. & R. 230, the plaintiff lost his case for not stating in the declaration that the words used by the defendant about the

Even before the reforms in pleading, the courts were therefore strict in forcing the plaintiff to allege his wrong with all due precision; and sometimes this was taken to seemingly absurd degrees. Thus, in *Kearney* v. *King*,[116] the court ruled that if a declaration on a bill of exchange stated that the bill was drawn in Dublin, without averring that Dublin was in Ireland, and that the currency was therefore Irish, it had to be assumed that the currency in question was English, so that proof showing that the bill was drawn in Irish money would be a variation fatal to the case. 'Is there any thing in this declaration from which the judge would be informed that the parties did not mean money of England, but the money of some other part of the United Kingdom?' asked Chief Justice Abbott. 'No such information is any where to be found upon the record.'[117]

The most extreme cases involved statutes, of course, since here there were precise words to go on. Thus, in *R* v. *Morgan* in 1788,[118] the conviction against the defendant under the game laws was quashed: the indictment had charged that he had 'killed a hare', whereas in the words of the counsel moving to overturn the conviction, 'the words of the 5 *Ann*, c. 14, are prohibitory against *keeping or using a gun*, &c to kill, and not against *killing*'. For all that the court knew, the defendant might have killed the hare by mistake. Thus, Morgan escaped due to a bad declaration by the prosecution.

The declaration had similarly to show that the plaintiff had a right to that which was claimed.[119] The plaintiff therefore had to show the right by which he held the land claimed, or claim a right to the use of that which had been violated. For example, 'it is necessary that the Plaintiff should shew the Common or Way, &c. to be his own, otherwise it may be the Common, &c. of the Defendant'.[120] This needed great precision, and the plaintiff had to aver every fact necessary to maintain his action and prove his right: 'therefore in all cases where the estate or Interest commences on a condition

---

plaintiff were quotations from another source, as became apparent in the evidence. Since the case laid was different from that proved, the plaintiff lost his action. See *Goldstein* v. *Foss* (1827) 6 B. & C. 154, and *Clement* v. *Fisher* (1827) 7 B. & C. 459.

[116] (1819) in J. Chitty, *Reports of Cases Principally on Practice and Pleading determined in the Court of King's Bench*, 2 vols. (1820–3), i. 28.

[117] Ibid. 31–2.   [118] Ibid. ii. 563.

[119] *The King* v. *the Bishop of Worcester* (1669) Vaugh. 53.

[120] Comyns, *Digest*, v. 34. See also, *Strode* v. *Birt* (1696) 4 Mod. 418.

precedent, be the Condition or act in the Affirmative or Negative, and to be performed by the Plaintiff, the Defendant or any other, the Plaintiff ought in his count to aver Performance'.[121] Similarly, in an action founded upon a statute, the plaintiff had to aver every fact necessary to show the court that his case was within the statute. Finally, the plaintiff could only claim his due and no more—'[a]s, in Debt on a Bond for 40 Pounds, if the Declaration concludes his Demand for 40 Marks, it is bad, if he does not shew how the Residue is discharged'.[122]

Thus, in *Morton* v. *Lamb*,[123] it was ruled that in an action for non-delivery of corn, where the parties had agreed to sell and buy the corn, it was held to be incumbent on the plaintiff to aver a tendering of the price, since the delivery and payment were concurrent acts, and each side had to prove that the other had done his part before he could have an action against the other. Lord Kenyon explained why in this case the plaintiff had lost. 'It is not imputed to the defendant that he did not carry the corn to Shardlow, but that he did not deliver it to the plaintiff,' he said, 'and to this declaration the defendant objects, and says, "I did not deliver the corn to you (the plaintiff) because you do not say that you were ready to pay for it; and if you were not ready, I am not bound to deliver the corn."'[124] Since both acts were to be done at the same time, the plaintiff had to aver he was ready to pay.[125] A similar ruling was made in *The Duke of St Albans* v. *Shore* in 1789.[126] 'It is clear in this case,' said Lord Loughborough, 'that unless the plaintiff has done all that was incumbent on him to do, in order to create a performance by the defendant', then he could not maintain the action: '[i]f he has not set forth a sufficient title, judgment must be against him whatever the plea is, and if the plea be a good bar, the same consequences must follow.'[127]

Similarly, it was essential to prove that it was the defendant who was responsible for the wrong alleged. The fact that the common law saw disputes in terms of two individual antagonists, one of whom was wronged by the direct fault of the other, created problems for

[121] Comyns, *Digest*, v. 39.   [122] Ibid. v. 53.
[123] (1797) 7 TR 125.   [124] 7 TR 129.
[125] See *Merrit* v. *Rane* (1720) 1 Stra. 458 and *Waterhouse* v. *Skinner* (1801) 2 B. & P. 447.   [126] 1 H. Bl. 270.
[127] 1 H. Bl. 278. This rule was only applicable, however, where the condition precedent was necessary to support the title. See *Campbell* v. *Jones* (1796) 6 TR 570; *Glazebrook* v. *Woodrow* (1799) 8 TR 366; and *Ferry* v. *Williams* (1817) 8 Taunt. 61.

wrongs committed by middlemen or employees.[128] In 1795, for instance, in *Stone* v. *Cartwright*,[129] the plaintiff sued the defendant for so negligently supporting his mine, which ran under the plaintiff's house, that the ground subsided and the house was damaged. The defendant was not the owner of the mine, but the manager, with full powers in its conduct. The owner took no part in the running of the mine, and was not present when the accident occurred. In this case, the plaintiff lost, for the court held that since the manager had no interest in the mine, he could not be held liable for the negligence.[130] Yet the owner could not have been sued either, for he was not personally negligent, nor at fault for the accident. In this case, then, there was a clear wrong, with damage, but the plaintiff could find no specific individual who was responsible for the wrong, so that in effect he had no remedy. The individualism of the common law could thus frustrate cases with obvious wrongs.[131] The plaintiff thus had to ascribe a legal duty or responsibility to the defendant, something which was often impossible. When in 1815, one Harris and his wife sued the trustees of a public road, whose public duty it was to place street lamps along the road, for compensation for an injury sustained by falling over a heap of scrapings left on the pavement in the dark by workers employed by these trustees, the court held that to say 'that every trustee of a road is liable in damages for such an accident as this . . . would be going farther than any case warrants'.[132] The trustees could not be held liable here; but neither could anyone else. The wrong was without remedy simply because there was no one on whom to attach blame.[133] Similarly, the

---

[128] This was to hamper the evolution of the law of employer liability for industrial accidents in the nineteenth century after *Priestley* v. *Fowler* (1837) 3 M. & W. 1.

[129] 6 TR 411.

[130] Justice Grose ruled, 'It frequently happens that a person's gardener employs labourers under him, yet it could never be contended that on that account he would be answerable for damage done by them in the course of their employment.' 6 TR 413.

[131] In *Bush* v. *Steinman* (1799) 1 B. & P. 404, it was ruled that he who had work done for his benefit was civilly liable for acts done by workmen for his benefit. However, it remained difficult in many cases to ascribe responsibility to distant owners. For a contrasting case where a manager was held responsible, see *Witte* v *Hague* (1823) 2 D. & R. 33.   [132] *Harris* v. *Baker* (1815) 4 M. & S. 27.

[133] Thus, in 1766 in *Postlethwaite* v. *Parkes* 3 Burr. 1878, the plaintiff sued in an action of trespass *vi et armis* for an assault on his daughter, for getting her with child, *per quod servitium amisit*. The father claimed that since she was pregnant, she lost her employment, and had had to return home under his care. The court here held that no action lay: since she was over 21, the father had no duty to maintain her, and since she was someone else's servant, the father lost nothing. Here was a wrong which had

courts were strict on the forms of legal justification allowed. This can be seen in cases of nuisance. In *Cooper* v. *Marshall*,[134] the defendant, in an action of trespass for spoiling the plaintiff's coney burrows, claimed that a right of common had been interfered with, and therefore justified his acts by saying that he had merely been abating a nuisance. The court rejected the plea, saying first that the defendant had the right to remove only so much of the coney burrows as constituted a nuisance; and second, that merely calling something a nuisance would not make it a nuisance at law justifying acts as his.[135]

Once the declaration had been made, the defendant replied by his plea, which could be either general or special.[136] The rules of special pleading were strict, supporting the notion that it was the parties themselves who produced the issue. The plea had therefore to be conformable to the count and had to answer every part of it. Similarly, it could not allege several matters at once,[137] it could not be argumentative but had to be a direct and positive denial of the charge, and it had to be certain. The special plea gave precise matter of justification,[138] and joined issue on a precise point. However, one could equally give a general plea, which was 'a concise and direct Answer of the Defendant to the plaintiff's Declaration, framed and contrived of old in such sords as were proper to deny the whole part of the Declaration: As if the defendant was charged with a Trespass,

---

harmed the father, yet he had no remedy. The father attempted unsuccessfully to argue here that the daughter had to be considered a servant, and that he had lost her services, for it was a well-established principle that no action lay for such a case, except where there had been a loss of service. See also *Hunt* v. *Wotton* (1679) T. Raym. 259. For a discussion of the doctrine, see G. H. Jones, 'Per Quod Servitium Amisit', *Law Quarterly Review*, lxxiv (1958), 39–58.

[134] (1757) 1 Burr. 259.

[135] This question was further considered in 1795 in *Sadgrove* v *Kirby*, 6 TR 483, where the court ruled that a commoner could not justify the cutting down of trees planted by the lord on waste ground even though this removed much of the common land: instead, he had to seek his remedy by an action on the case. Here, the court was clearly influenced by policy considerations, for both Lord Kenyon and Justice Abbott said that the lord's trees were of potential benefit to the community, so that it needed a formal consideration by the court to decide whether he should be allowed to keep the trees. For a discussion of policy, see below, Ch. 4.

[136] There were two types of pleas: pleas in abatement, which only delayed the proceedings, and pleas in bar, which challenged the declaration and produced the issue. Only the latter are outlined here.

[137] However, by the statute 4 Anne c. 16, the defendant could give several pleas to the counts. The plaintiff could lay as many counts as he chose.

[138] *Coke upon Littleton*, 282b.

the general plea was, that he was not guilty thereof, which is now commonly called the general Issue'.[139] The general issue denied the whole charge and thereby threw the onus of proving all conceivable matters on the plaintiff, and because of this it had great advantages. The general issue gave great power to the jury, in so far as it mixed together denials of law and fact.

After the plea, the plaintiff replied to the defendant, via the replication, in which the plaintiff had to answer the whole plea. Once more, the matter alleged had to conform to the count and be relevant to the plea. For instance, 'in Trespass for a wrongful taking and Detaining in Prison, the Defendant justifies by Process &c., and the Plaintiff replies that a Supersedeas afterwards issued, after which he detained him, it will be bad; for by his Replication he does not maintain the wrongful Taking but only the Detention'.[140] The replication could not include subsequent matter, which was not directly relevant to what was alleged in the declaration: it could only specify more clearly what was in the declaration, in reply to the defendant's plea. The replication was followed by the defendant's rejoinder, and, if need be, any number of further allegations, before the precise issue was reached. The issue was when both parties put their cause on a point of fact disputed to be tried by a jury[141] 'proceeding out of the several allegations on the way'.[142] The issue was produced when there was a fact which was disputed or where there was a point of law referred to the court. As Comyns described it, any material fact had either to be confessed and avoided, admitted or traversed. If traversed, then there was produced an issue of fact.[143] However, the parties could equally admit all the facts and demur to the court, by referring the question to the judge, to decide if there was a legal case to be answered on the facts presented. The demurrer came when one party felt that there was no legal case to answer; but to demur, one had to admit all the facts.[144]

The system thus depended upon precise claims and counter-claims by the parties. Any error in the proceedings at common law was fatal.[145] Comyns noted, '[i]f pleading be bad, Judgment shall be

---

[139] Gilbert, *History and Practice of Civil Actions*, 106.
[140] Comyns, *Digest*, v. 88.
[141] Ibid. v. 129.   [142] *Coke upon Littleton*, 126a.
[143] Comyns, *Digest*, v. 98 ff.   [144] Comyns, *Digest*, v. 124.
[145] However, various statutes of jeofails had given parties powers to amend their pleas where the fault was merely formal and did not affect the substance of the case. See Gilbert, *History*, 107–31.

against him who made the first default: as, if a Count or Declaration be bad, there shall be Judgment against the Plaintiff; though the Bar is insufficient'.[146] Simply, if the pleas were bad, there was no case to answer, for all rested on the presentation of the issue, not on an abstract right. Similarly, the verdict had to conform to the declaration and the pleading. As Gilbert put it, '[w]hat is Substance and what not, must be determined in every Action, according to its Nature: That seems properly to be the Essence of the Action, without which the Court would have no sufficient Grounds to give Jugment [sic]'.[147] There had to be a clear foundation for a verdict; and it was a cardinal rule that a jury could not find anything contrary to the record, nor could it find anything not set out upon the record.[148] In its finding, the jury was not guided by an abstract rule, but by the case as presented to it.

These particular rules were those used by practitioners in their daily practice, and the common law, seen from this ground level, was therefore a very different beast from that conceived by high theory. For this view of law, stressing the science of pleading, contained its own rhetorical theory, that theory seeing law as a reasoning process. It stressed that law grew out of practice, in the correct presentation of wrongs and in the logical structuring of a record. This 'practitioner's theory' had always been latent in the common law; but it is very important that at this time writers should have sought to systematize the rules of pleading through their treatises, and that there should have evolved a notion of a 'science' of pleading. For these haphazard rules of practice were becoming more clearly articulated as a theory that the common law was not a body of clear rules and initial rights, but a set of remedies with which to redress any number of wrongs. According to the theory, rules came later, inferred from cases and principles, and rules and decisions could be influenced by all manner of 'sources of law', provided that the law obeyed its own forms. The pleas did not decide the law, but only defined the fact at dispute, leaving the court to rule whether the wrong was illegal, from all manner of sources. This view of the common law explains how the courts could function by taking as their sources of law such questions as policy or expedience, as well as precedent and past rules. In a sense, the courts could make utilitarian adjudications in cases, acting flexibly with a view to

---

[146] Comyns, *Digest*, v. 113.
[147] Gilbert, *History*, 121.   [148] Comyns, *Digest*, v. 136 ff.

particular justice, since the question to be decided had already been well defined. This view of the law showed that the common law was not a self-contained science, but derived its rules and solutions from below, in a constant feeding from society. The law was no abstract set of defined guides and rules: it was a flexible system of adjudication responding to society's problems.[149] The science of pleading had two functions: first, it defined the point to be adjudicated; and second, it produced a legal point that could act as a precedent. As we shall see, the first was more important than the second, for the second was not a *rule* but evidence of what judges had done in the past, and hence one reason why judges should adjudicate in like manner again.[150]

---

[149] The respective positions held by Blackstone and Bentham on the one hand, and by the devotees of pleading on the other, reflect a division in contemporary jurisprudence between those positivists who seek to find and apply source-based positive rules of law and those who see law as a form of institutionalized adjudication. See George P. Fletcher, 'Two Modes of Legal Thought', *Yale Law Journal*, xc (1980–1), 970–1003; Stephen R. Perry, 'Judicial Obligation, Precedent and the Common Law', *Oxford Journal of Legal Studies*, vii (1987), 215–57; and Lon L. Fuller, 'The Forms and Limits of Adjudication', in *The Principles of Social Order: Selected Essays of Lon L. Fuller*, ed. K. I. Winston (Durham, NC, 1981), 86–124.

[150] This is to follow Simpson's view that the common law was the custom of judges making similar adjudications. A clearly focused precedent would articulate the custom better than the oral culture of judges; but it was not binding. See A. W. B. Simpson, 'The Common Law and Legal Theory', in A. W. B. Simpson (ed.), *Oxford Essays in Jurisprudence*, 2nd series (Oxford, 1973), 77–99.

4

The Sources of Legal Judgment

GIVEN that the common law was based on a system of pleas and
forms of action and that common lawyers sought for its sources
outside that law, it can be seen that it was no static set of eternal
rules, nor was it divorced from society and social considerations. As
Lord Kenyon put it, judges were not 'men writing from their closets
without any knowledge of the affairs of life, but persons mixing with
the mass of society, and capable of receiving practical experience of
the soundness of the maxims they inculcate'.[1] The common law was
not a self-contained science: it was rather based on a system of forms
which allowed lawyers to look outside the law for solutions to legal
problems, once the terms of the legal dispute had been set.[2] This did
not mean that every case was a wholly new adjudication, where the
judges were free to rule as they pleased, based on their ideological or
political prejudices, however:[3] for the common law was an artificial
forum, where the judges were constrained by the forms of law, its
analogies and precedents. Judges remained faithful to a consensus
on legal rules, where that consensus existed;[4] and in most cases,
there was little dispute as to what the law was, since the force of
precedent and analogy could give uncontentious answers to legal
problems. In these cases, judges did not need to look to social
considerations very far, but could answer legal problems from the
idealist position that doctrine held all the answers. However, there
were a number of occasions where the case at issue was wholly

---

[1] *R v. Waddington* (1800) 1 East 143 at 157. Quoted in F. E. Dowrick, *Justice According
to the English Common Lawyers* (London, 1961).

[2] As Roscoe Pound argued, there is a hard balance to be struck in any legal system
between technical and discretionary rules, and legal systems must balance the two to
allow the law to grow. See Pound, 'Justice According to Law', in *Essays on Jurisprudence from the Columbia Law Review* (New York, 1963).

[3] The law was more than what the judge had for breakfast, as the Realists would
claim, and more than a flexible ideological tool. See C. H. S. Fifoot, *English Law and its
Background* (London, 1932).

[4] See A. W. B. Simpson, 'The Common Law and Legal Theory'.

novel or contentious, where the judges disagreed over what the law was, or agreed that there was no law. Here, analogy was insufficient to solve the problem, for the materials of legal science did not contain all the answers. In such cases, judges often had theoretical disagreements over what the principles of law dictated, and could only solve those disagreements by reference to extra-legal considerations shaped by politics, morals, or philosophy. These novel cases in turn influenced the development of doctrine since they were, in a sense, the cutting edge of the law. In this way, doctrinal developments were flexible in such a way as to reflect social concerns. In a sense, the common law is best described as a conventionalism of forms, where lawyers agreed on the forms and processes which made up the legal framework, but were free to disagree within that framework, allowing the law to reflect the needs and moral choices of the community, without undermining the status of the law and its perceived legitimacy.

When it came to these contentious cases, each judge often had a different conception of what the common law was about. Probably the best-known example of this in the eighteenth century occurred in *Millar* v. *Taylor*[5] where the judges in turn argued that the law was based on justice, natural law, custom, and convenience. John Miller, looking back on the case in 1825, mused that the vagueness and inconsistency of the notions which here appeared to have been floating in the minds of some of 'the ablest doctors who ever sat in Westminster Hall, upon so fundamental an article of judicial faith' would necessarily create much 'doubt and perplexity respecting the foundation upon which a large portion of the Common Law of England really rests'.[6] For Miller, this case proved that law was not the simple uncontentious application of doctrine, the articulation of answers from within the law. It showed, rather, that 'the most considerable portion of the whole is composed of determinations and resolutions of the judges, proceeding upon analogy, public policy, and natural justice'.[7]

There were two types of legal arguments used by the courts, often concurrently, in solving these cases. One was the form of argument internal to the law, where judges argued from precedents, analogies,

---

[5] (1769) 4 Burr. 2303. See the discussion of this case in David Lieberman, *The Province of Legislation Determined*, 95–8.

[6] John Miller, *An Inquiry into the Present State of the Civil Law of England* (London, 1825), 236.   [7] Ibid. 237.

and forms, in their desire to articulate the true 'law', and where they urged the need for stability and certainty in law. The second type was external to the law, for the courts held that, where a case had been sufficiently alleged, the courts could rule from the grounds of fitness and justice alone. It was not unusual for judges to make comments like '[c]ommon sense is sufficient to decide this case, without having recourse to any legal decisions on the subject'.[8] For ultimately, the common law was a system of remedies, to correct any wrong, to adjudicate in the best manner for society and the litigants. The first two sections of this chapter will examine these types of reasoning, which are to be found in clear cases and in novel cases. However, it is also important to examine how these types of reasoning could sit together in cases which were not wholly novel, but which still developed the law. In many cases, there was a complex and subtle relationship between the dictates of technicality, the arguments from analogy and precedent, and the influence of extra-legal factors. While technicalities restricted the scope of social influences in the courts, these influences were nevertheless important, so that it can be seen that in many cases technical and extra-legal reasonings worked together, the one influencing the other, to allow a flexible and creative growth in law.[9] This process will be examined in the final section, looking at Lord Mansfield's judgments.

Reasoning from Within the Law

Perhaps the clearest articulation of the view that lawyers reasoned in a compromise of analogy, precedent, and policy was made by Justice Parke in 1833. 'Our common-law system', he said,

consists in the applying to new combinations of circumstances those rules of law which we derive from legal principles and judicial precedents; and for the sake of attaining uniformity, consistency and certainty, we must apply

---

[8] *Porter* v. *Shephard* (1796) 6 TR 665 at 669.

[9] The judge, as Fifoot pointed out, acted like an artist: 'He is necessarily conditioned by the material fortuitously given to him, by the anxiety not to impair judicial consistency and by the predominant feeling of the profession. Working within these limits, he transmutes experience into law, and, by generalising, performs a genuine act of creation.' C. H. S. Fifoot, *Judge and Jurist in the Reign of Queen Victoria* (London, 1959), 37.

those rules, where they are not plainly unreasonable and inconvenient to all cases which arise; and we are not at liberty to reject them, and abandon all analogy to them, to those to which they have not yet been judicially applied, because we think that the rules are not as convenient and reasonable as we ourselves could have devised. It appears to me to be of great importance to keep this principle of decision steadily in view, not merely for the determination of the particular case, but for the interests of law as a science.[10]

This was an account of the common law as a set of clear rules which could be applied to new situations. To a large degree, the law appeared to be the simple application of rules derived from precedents to the facts of new cases.[11] English jurisprudence, according to Burke, had no other sure foundation than decided cases, 'nor, consequently, have the lives and properties of the subject any sure hold, but in the maxims, rules and principles, and juridically traditionary line of decisions' to be found in law reports and authorities.[12] In making judgments, judges often seemed only to apply clear precedential rules. Thus, Lord Tenterden said in *Selby* v. *Bardons* that '[t]he decisions of our predecessors, the judges of former times, ought to be followed and adopted, unless we can see very clearly that they are erroneous, for otherwise there will be no certainty in the administration of the law'.[13]

However, precedents were not absolute, nor did they create precise rules. Rather, they acted as a source of legal analogy. Since there was, as yet, no concept of *stare decisis* established in England, there was no absolute need to follow precedent.[14] However, judges usually followed the guides of precedent even where their own

[10] *Mirehouse* v. *Rennell* (1833) 1 Cl. and F. 527 at 546. In this case, it was ruled that where an advowson attached to a prebend fell vacant, and before filling it the prebendary died, the presentation would belong to the administratrix, and not to the successor.

[11] See C. K. Allen, *Law in the Making*, 6th edn. (London, 1958), and R. A. Cross, *Precedent in English Law*, 3rd edn. (Oxford, 1977).

[12] *The Works of the Right Honourable Edmund Burke*, ed. W. King and F. Laurence, 16 vols. (London, 1826–7), xiv. 332. Best put it similarly when arguing that 'the judgments of Westminster Hall are the only authority that we have for by far the greatest part of the law of England'. *Fletcher* v. *Lord Sondes* (1826) 3 Bing. 501 at 588. See also *Coke upon Littleton*, 285a.

[13] *Selby* v. *Bardons* (1832) 3 B. & Ad. 1 at 17.

[14] J. P. Dawson writes, 'Even as late as Lord Mansfield, the notion that the law was to be found in particular cases would have seemed strange indeed.' *The Oracles of the Law* (Ann Arbor), 1968, 78. As he points out, there could be no firm notion of binding precedents until there were comprehensive and reliable law reports, which did not occur in England before the early nineteenth century.

judgment went against it, not out of any reverence for the past but because it was more convenient to do so, the long-term utility of having apparently consistent cases outweighing particular injustices. This was because the law, as a system of remedies, sought the best legal answer to the problem presented, and as such, had to take into account the prior expectations of the litigants, expectations which would be shaped by a continuing trend of decisions. There was hence great flexibility even where precedents existed. Because the law was a reasoning process to redress wrongs, judges could look to the most useful and just solution to the problem. As Wynne argued, in the beginning of law, judges ruled simply *ex aequo et bono*, and where precedents were lacking they did the same in modern times.[15] Yet judges also remained faithful to precedent in many cases, and did not treat each case as if it were a unique adjudication. This seems a dilemma at first, until it is noted that following precedent, and maintaining certainty in the law, was often the most useful and fair thing to do. For instance, in *The King* v. *The Inhabitants of Brighthelmston*,[16] the court had to consider a delicate question on the settlement regulations of the Poor Laws, and in their judgments, each judge was very anxious not to introduce any doubt into the law. Both Justices Buller and Grose made it clear that the court should follow authority and precedent in this case, rather than considering first principles, for it was now too late to resort to that type of reasoning. Lord Kenyon said that the ruling he would give was not the same as his personal view of the case, since 'the modern cases are certainly against such a decision' as he would naturally choose. Since these cases were uniform, he would follow them: '[w]ith those decisions I acquiesce,' he said, 'because these subjects should not remain in doubt'.[17] Clearly, the Poor Law was too intricate and important a question to be undermined: it had importance beyond the case at hand.

Lord Kenyon ruled similarly in *Goodtitle* v. *Otway* in 1797,[18] a case concerning a deed of settlement and involving the doctrine of the revocation of wills. Counsel in this case had argued that the doctrine of revocations was not grounded in reason and said that it would be absurd to apply it here. However, Lord Kenyon said that this was an argument which could be used against all manner of doctrines which had no abstract rationality, and that it was now too late to challenge

[15] Wynne, *Eunomus*, ii. 115–16.
[17] 5 TR 192.
[16] (1793) 5 TR 188.
[18] 7 TR 399.

common recoveries, since so much property was based on this form. While he might decide one way if the case were new, he could not do so now that the law was settled:

Those who are confident in their superior abilities, may perhaps fancy that they could erect a new system of laws less objectionable than that under which they live: I have not that confidence in mine, and am satisfied by the decisions, and series of decisions, of great and learned men on the rules under which the landed property of this country is now held; and it is my duty, as well as my inclination, to follow and give effect to those rules.[19]

Behind this lay the need for stability and certainty. As Justice Ashhurst said, the law needed predictability, particularly where property was concerned. 'The decisions of the law are great landmarks for the safety and regulation of real property,' he said, '[a]nd perhaps it is of less importance how the law is determined, than that it should be determined and certain; and that such determinations should be adhered to, for every man may know how the law is.'[20] The clearest elaboration of the scope for judicial creativity when set against the binding force of precedent had been made by Chief Justice Vaughan in 1670. 'Where the law is known and clear, though it be inequitable and inconvenient,' he said, 'the judges must determine as the law is, without the inequitableness or inconveniency.' There, the fault needed remedy by legislation. However, 'where the law is doubtful, and not clear, the judges ought to interpret the law to be as is most consonant to equity, and least inconvenient'.[21] Judges made a choice on whether to follow precedent or not: that choice was influenced by the effect their decision would have.

Precedent was therefore no clear-cut thing.[22] In practice, it was

---

[19] 7 TR 415.

[20] 7 TR 419. See also *Butler* v. *Duncomb* (1718) 1 P. Wms. 448 at 452, and *Doe dem. Clarke* v. *Ludlam* (1831) 7 Bing. 280.

[21] *Dixon* v. *Harrison* Vaugh. 37–8.

[22] See A. W. B. Simpson, 'The *Ratio Decidendi* of a Case and the Doctrine of Binding Precedent', in A. E. Guest (ed.), (*Oxford Essays in Jurisprudence* (Oxford, 1961), 148–75. At 151, he summarizes a sceptical view of precedent: 'it is mistaken to think of the doctrine of precedent as a body of legal rules which impose legal obligations on courts; the doctrine must consist only in a set of propositions (which may be true or false) about what the judges in various courts as a matter of fact do. Thus cases on the doctrine of precedent can only sensibly be cited as evidence of certain facts of judicial behaviour.' Simpson associates this view with Glanville Williams's, as stated in his edition of J. Salmond's *Jurisprudence* (11th edn. 187–8).

extremely difficult to extract the *ratio decidendi* from the case,[23] for in many contentious cases, the judges might give different reasons for the same conclusion, or might conclude differently from the same premises. The theory was that the court should look to the reason of the precedent, the principle behind its rule:[24] but in many cases it was difficult to discover exactly what that reason was. In hard cases, it was very difficult to extract any clear rule at all; something which was exacerbated by the fact that the case was bound up with the circumstances of the particular facts at issue. Since precedent was unclear, and worked only by rough analogies from decided cases, the law could be favourable to flexibility and certainty at the same time. Because the law was a system of reasoning and not a set of clear rules, it was not inconsistent for judges to hold both the view that the law could adapt itself to the dictates of public policy and that it should strive for stability and certainty. Even Lord Mansfield, that doyen of judicial creativity, remained aware of the limits on innovation: 'where we are not tied down by any erroneous opinions, which have prevailed so far in practice, that property would be shook by an alteration of them,' he said, 'arguments of convenience and inconvenience are always to be taken into consideration'.[25] It was a competition of conveniences, between modifying the law and undermining it. Convenience and policy was to be taken into account not to control the established law but to decide in new cases.[26] In contentious cases, it was not difficult to evade precedent, if that was felt necessary. Precedent was indeterminate, for by the rules of pleading, what made a case were all the particular circumstances of the dispute, focused into the issue; and to that extent, every case was distinct. Blackstone, in what appeared to be one of his most cryptic statements, had said that precedents were evidence of the law, without being law in themselves.[27] Put thus, in

---

[23] A. L. Goodhart, 'Determining the Ratio Decidendi of a Case', in his *Essays in Jurisprudence and the Common Law* (Cambridge, 1931), 1–26.

[24] See *Jones* v. *Randall* (1774) 1 Cowp. 37; *Lewis* v. *Lewellyn* (1823) 1 T. & R. 104; *Nye* v. *Moseley* (1826) 6 B. & C. 138; *Glazebrook* v. *Woodrow* (1799) 8 TR 366. In *Bole* v. *Horton* (1673) 3 Vaugh. 382, it was said, 'if a Court give judgement juridically, another Court is not bound to give like judgement, unless it think that judgement first given was according to law'.

[25] *Burgess* v. *Wheate* (1759) 1 W. Bl. 123 at 165–6. Mansfield sometimes showed a strong devotion to precedent, where he felt that overriding them would be unsettling. See *R* v. *Dawes and Marten* (1767) 4 Burr. 2120.

[26] See Lord Kenyon's comments in *The King* v. *the Master and Fellows of St. Catherine's Hall, Cambridge* (1791) 4 TR 233 at 243.   [27] 1 *Comm.* 70.

the context of a theory of rules, it made little sense; but in a context of seeing law as a reasoning process it was much clearer. As Wynne argued, no single determination could bind any other case, simply because no two cases were identical.[28] There could be no monolithic rules, derived either from legislation or from precedent, to cover all cases: rather, there were only guidelines for future determination. For Wynne, law arising out of precedent evolved from new determinations of facts and issues presenting themselves via pleading before the court, as decided by judges.[29] Similarly, there was some danger in analogy from case to case, since each case was distinct.[30]

This notion that every case was distinct was articulated by Best CJ in 1826, in *Fletcher* v. *Lord Sondes*, where the court had to consider the validity of a bond for resigning an ecclesiastical living in favour of another. Best, who wanted to allow the bond, on the grounds of public policy and his notion of justice which 'encourages us to provide for our children, relations and friends, and allows us to bestow in them offices for which they are duly qualified',[31] realized that his argument was undermined by the precedent of *The Bishop of London* v. *Ffytche*,[32] which had declared such bonds to be simoniacal. However, the judge used the pleader's logic to get around this precedent. 'A slight variation in circumstances vitiates the validity of a precedent,' he argued, 'and the ground on which it vitiates it is, that we cannot tell whether this variation of circumstances, had it been contemplated by the court which first established the precedent, might not have operated so as to produce a different judgment.'[33] This is an important comment: it reveals that every legal case was in effect a new deliberation of circumstances, to be guided but not bound by past analogies.

The notion that each case determined the law explains why judges were so often reluctant to give much weight to *obiter dicta*. As Best CJ put it in *Richardson* v. *Mellish* in 1824,[34] '[t]he expressions of every Judge must be taken with reference to the case on which he decides,

---

[28] Edward Wynne, *Eunomus*, ii, 114.   [29] Ibid. 143.

[30] Best CJ once observed, '[i]n all sciences analogical reasoning must be pursued with great caution. Minute differences in the circumstances of two cases will prevent any argument from being pursued from the one to the other'. *Rennell* v. *the Bishop of Lincoln* (1825) 3 Bing. 223 at 264.   [31] 3 Bing. 526 at 589.

[32] *The Bishop of London* v. *Ffytche* (1782), cited in T. Cunningham, *The Law of Simony* (London, 1784), 56.

[33] 3 Bing. 570.   [34] 2 Bing. 248.

otherwise the law will get into extreme confusion'. This was an idea reiterated by Lord Tenterden seven years later. '[G]eneral words, whether uttered by a Judge in Court, or spoken elsewhere, or published in a treatise,' he said, 'must, on sound principles of logic and criticism, be limited to the subject matter on which they are employed: the attempt to carry them further only leads to error.'[35] Mere *dicta* therefore often had very little weight.[36]

Arguments from within the law, such as precedents, were therefore one aspect of legal reasoning that would not necessarily determine the outcome of a case. Each legal case being a new problem for a court, and the process of adjudication being a process of legal debate, all manner of sources were used to attain a conclusion. Nevertheless, in wholly novel cases, judges often used arguments from within the legal framework to achieve answers to problems. For example, it was not uncommon, in the absence of precedent, for judges to use deductions from the nature of acceptable pleas and writs to see if a new plea was valid. 'Pleading,' said Holt CJ, 'though it does not make the law, yet is good evidence of the law, because it is made conformable to it.'[37] Holt could thus make a concrete division based on reasoning on the nature of the plea, and on analogies from relevant pleas. Similarly, Ashhurst J turned to the books of entries and returns of writs to guide him in deciding a new case, since these technical forms were 'the best authorities in the absence of decided cases'.[38] Lord Kenyon, in deciding the extent of the liability of an executor, drew heavily on reasoning based on the nature of the writ. For Kenyon, 'the very form of proceeding' dictated the solution to the case.[39] Clearly, then, the legal reasoning

---

[35] *The King* v. *the Master and Wardens of the Merchant Tailors Company* (1831) 2 B. and Ad. 115 at 124. It was, however, up to the judge in each case to decide what had been *obiter* and what had been an essential ground of the ruling. See *Brisbane* v. *Dacres* (1813) 5 Taunt. 143 at 159.

[36] See *R* v. *Maurice Jarvis* (1757) 1 Burr. 153 and *Sanderson* v. *Rowles* (1767) 4 Burr. 2968.   [37] *Cage* v. *Acton* (1698) 1 Ld. Raym. 515 at 522.

[38] *Boothman* v. *the Earl of Surry* (1787) 2 TR 5 at 10.

[39] *Farr* v. *Newman* (1792) 4 TR 621 at 648. In this case, it was ruled that the goods of a testator in the hands of his executor could not be seized in execution of a judgment against the executor in his own right. To arrive at the decision, Kenyon argued thus from legal forms: 'in an action against an executor the judgment is, that the debt shall be levied *de bonis testatoris*, if there be sufficient goods of the testator in the hands of the executor to be administered, and the damages and costs in certain events to be levied *de bonis propriis*. In executing such a writ the sheriff must abide by the terms of the writ, and make a distinction between the two sorts of goods; and if, in the execution of such a writ he cannot find goods sufficient to answer the debt of the

process could use as a base for argument the very forms of law presented.[40]

The judges equally used legal maxims and accepted notions as grounds for legal decision. It should be noted that the courts did not solely base their decisions on maxims, but rather used maxims to support arguments based on the justice or expediency of the case. This can be seen for instance in the case of *Brisbane v. Dacres*,[41] where the court had to decide whether a man who, under a mistake of law, had given a sum of money he was not compellable to pay to the captain of a ship, could recover it back when he discovered his legal error, given that it would not be against conscience for the captain to keep it. The court decided that in essence it would be unreasonable for the captain to have to repay the sum (after this length of time),[42] and justified its decision on two legal maxims. The first was *ignorantia legis non excusat*, which was used to show that the plaintiff's error was just his bad luck; while the second was *volenti non fit injuria*, which was used to argue that as he had handed the sum over freely, he could not have been wronged by the defendant. By a clever use of legal maxims, the court found as it wanted.

In other cases, the legal notion was more vague. In *Milbourn v. Ewart* in 1793,[43] the plaintiffs argued that a bond made to a woman to induce her to marry a man, which promised her money after his death, was rendered invalid by their marriage. They used for their contention an analogy from the law which ruled that when a debtor married his creditor, that debt was dissolved. However, the court rejected these 'flimsy and technical reasonings' and held, in the absence of any precedent, that they would find for the widow on the strength of the legal principle that the law would not work a wrong.[44]

---

testator's creditor, he cannot have recourse to the other fund; but the creditor must institute a new action, alleging a *devastavit*, before he can have resort to that other fund, and have execution against the executor's goods. This shews the distinction between the two funds beyond all doubt, and is of greater authority than even adjudged cases, because the writs and records form the law of the land.'

[40] See also *R v. Woolf* (1819) 2 B. and Ald. 609.

[41] (1813) 5 Taunt. 143.

[42] Sir James Mansfield CJ ruled that it would be 'most contrary to *aequum et bonum*, if he were obliged to repay it back. For see how it is! If the sum be large, it probably alters the habits of his life, he increases his expences, he has spent it over and over again; perhaps he cannot repay it all, or not without great distress: is he then, five years and eleven months after, to be called on to repay it?'

[43] 5 TR 381.   [44] 5 TR 385.

Reasoning from Outside the Law

When it came to considering novel cases, where reasoning from analogy was unclear, the courts' process was one of solving legal problems which arose out of society by using a range of arguments which could be applied to the case at hand. In making their decisions, the judges drew on a vast range of 'sources', invoking natural law, justice, political philosophy, political economy, and convenience. This was natural, for once the bounds of the debate had been set by the pleas, the judges had merely to adjudicate on the rightness of the issue, by whatever reasonings and debates they saw fit. It will be seen in this section how legal cases were often abstract debates, with judges disagreeing on their beliefs and the grounds of their judgments, and often leaving the law wholly unsettled.

Essentially, what was uppermost in judges' minds was to provide the legal answer which best served the needs of society, so that the common law was based less on concepts of 'justice' or 'natural law' and more on expedience and public policy. Lord Chief Justice Lee thus rescinded a bargain between two parties to procure a public office in 1750, on the ground that it sought to introduce unworthy objects into public offices. He said,

Political arguments, in the fullest sense of the word, as they concern the government of a nation, must, and always have been of great weight, in the consideration of this court, and tho' there may be no *dolus malus*, by contracts as to other persons, yet if the rest of mankind are concerned as well as the parties, it may properly be said, that it regards the public utility.[45]

In the cases which follow, it can be seen that there was no defined *law* but that the legal decision arrived at was produced in the courts by judges drawing for their interpretations on considerations of policy, justice, religion, and fairness, as well as philosophy, logic, and analogy. The legal process here was one of legal *debate*, with judges disagreeing on how to obtain the best legal conclusion from the premises on the record. In these cases, the judges disagreed fundamentally on what they felt the legal solutions should be, and for their justifications they went well beyond law. This sort of reasoning can be seen in *Steel* v. *Houghton* in 1788, which revolved around the question whether there was a common law right to glean

[45] *Earl of Chesterfield* v. *Sir Abraham Janssen* (1750) 1 Atk. 305 at 352.

after the harvest.[46] This was a novel case, and one of particular significance, involving as it did the right of the poor to glean from enclosed lands and to interfere with commercial agriculture. In this case, the plaintiff sued the defendant for trespass, declaring that the defendant had broken his close at Timworth in Suffolk, and had trodden down much grass and corn and carried it away. Against this, the defence claimed a general custom in favour of gleaning, and claimed authority in Hale's *Trials per Pais* and Blackstone's *Commentaries*.[47] This case provides a good insight into legal reasoning, for, in a divided court, the majority of the judges found for the plaintiff. In this case, all the judges had clear conceptions of what the law should be, but each justified his argument by abstract and extra-legal arguments.

Justice Gould found for the defendants, confirming that the right to glean did exist at common law. For him, this was as clear a case in favour of a general custom of gleaning as there could be. He understood the custom to prevail in all areas he knew of, and he ascribed the absence of discussions of gleaning in legal authorities to the fact that the custom was 'too notorious to be disputed'.[48] Gould's arguments extended beyond this, however, into a range of philosophical and biblical sources, saying, '[f]rom what better fountain could it be drawn than the Holy Scriptures?'[49] In addition, he cited authorities from Selden[50] to Plato,[51] and ended his judgment by citing cases and a local statute which seemed to presume that a general right to glean existed.[52] Thus, no clear case or legal authority

---

[46] 1 H. Bl. 51. This case has attracted much attention. See Peter King, 'Gleaners, Farmers and the Failure of Legal Sanctions in England 1750–1850', *Past and Present*, cxxv (1990), 116–50 and his 'The Origins of the Gleaning Judgement of 1788: A Case Study of Legal Change, Customary Right and Social Conflict in Late Eighteenth Century England' (forthcoming).

[47] The defence cited *Trials per Pais*, 54 and 3 *Comm*. 212–13, as well as Gilbert's *Law of Evidence*.   [48] 1 H. Bl. 53–4.

[49] 1 H. Bl. 55. In particular, he cited *Leviticus* 19: 9–10 and 23: 22.

[50] He cited Selden's *De Jure Naturali et Gentium*, saying (at 55), '[f]rom Selden, it appears that the actual property was vested in the poor . . . it did not accrue to the poor as a donation but a legal right'.

[51] His citation of Plato came in another curious line of reasoning. The custom of gleaning, he said, had to be established, since the etymology of the names by which the custom was known in England proved that it was a custom known in Europe as well: '[i]t is clear to me, the word leasing was brought from the Germans, and gleaning from the Normans'. Following this argument that the custom had a shared etymology, he quoted Plato: 'Qui intelligit nomina, res etiam intelligit.' 1 H. Bl. 57.

[52] Gould's use of the statute is important: he used the local statute, whose provisions he argued presumed a right to glean at common law within that locality, as a

could be used, but other sources could be invoked to show that the right had to exist.

This was a minority view, however, and Lord Loughborough put forward a view more congenial to the other judges. The right claimed, he said, was against the fundamental nature of property, which favoured exclusive enjoyment, and it was therefore destructive of the good order of society. Beyond this, it would encourage vagrancy, and was a right which would be totally impossible to enjoy, 'since nothing which is not inexhaustible, like a perennial stream, can be capable of universal promiscuous enjoyment'.[53] At base, his ruling was founded on his ideas of the economic well-being of society: 'The consequences which would arise from this custom being established as a right, would be injurious to the poor themselves,' he urged:

Their sustenance can only arise from the surplus of productive industry; and whatever is a charge on industry, is a very improvident diminution of the fund for that sustenance; for the profits of the farmer being lessened, he would be the less able to contribute his share to the rate of the parish; and thus the poor, from the exercise of this supposed right in the autumn, would be liable to starve in the spring.[54]

This view was echoed by Justice Heath. Against Justice Gould, he argued that '[t]he law of Moses is not obligatory on us',[55] and went on to say '[t]he inconvenience arising from this custom being considered as a right by the poor, would be infinite; and in doubtful

legal source to show that the law did recognize that right. He said, 'By an Act of Parliament passed in the year 1786, for inclosing the common fields of Basingstoke, the gleaning or leasing is to begin after the crop is carried. Times are mentioned, one for wheat, and another for other species of grain, for the exercise of this right; and the owners of the land are restrained under penalties (a strong circumstance to shew their sense of the right of the poor) from putting in cattle or hogs, within those respective times.' (1 H. Bl. 57) It is a case showing the eighteenth-century judges' use of statutes, not as absolute guides of right and wrong, but as additional sources of legal opinion. Statute was part of the common law. For modern discussions of the problem, see T. R. S. Allen, 'Legislative Supremacy and the Rule of Law', *Cambridge Law Journal*, xliv (1985), 111–43 and P. S. Atiyah, 'Common Law and Statute Law', *Modern Law Review*, xlviii (1985), 1–28.

[53] 1 H. Bl. 53.   [54] Ibid.

[55] 1 H. Bl. 61. He added, 'It is indeed agreeable to Christian charity and common humanity, that the rich should provide for the impotent poor; but the mode of such provision must be of positive institution. We have pledged all the landed property of the kingdom for the maintenance of the poor, who have in some instances exhausted the source.'

cases, arguments from inconvenience are of great weight'. In support of this, he argued that to allow the right would encourage fraud and lead to disputes, since the labourer would sow in a way as to get the best gleanings, thereby defrauding the farmer. Besides this, at harvest time, gleaning was a great drain on the manpower available to the farmers and should therefore not be encouraged. But what of the opinion that the labourers should join in and benefit from the harvest as well? Once more, economics took over: '[t]o that it may be answered,' he said, 'that they recover from the advanced price of labour, a recompense in proportion to their industry'.[56] In this way, the court rejected the claimed common law right, on a mixture of public policy, political economy, and convenience.

This shows that legal cases were not clear-cut applications of rules and precedents, but were rather reasoned debates to settle disputed points in line with what the policy of the law required. Besides policy and convenience, judges were often guided by their notions of humanity, justice, and natural morality. In *Gifford* v. *Lord Yarborough*,[57] the court had to decide for the first time who owned the land formed by the alluvion of the sea. In his judgment, which decided that the owner of the adjoining land rather than the king owned this new land, Best quoted from Locke on the nature of property settlements, drawing the conclusion that divine authority and human reason commanded men to subdue the earth and improve it by cultivation. From this base, he urged that it was reasonable, just, and convenient that the landowner should acquire the soil. It would be beneficial to the public, he argued, since land which would otherwise be barren would be cultivated. The grounds for his decision were thus wholly extra-legal, being a mixture of political philosophy, political economy, and a sense of fairness: '[t]he original deposit constitutes not a tenth part of its value, the other nine tenths are created by the labour of the person who occupied it; and in the words of Locke the fruits of his labour cannot, without injury, be taken from him'.[58]

Considerations of policy needs and convenience were used on occasions in place of more obvious legal analogies,[59] as can be seen in

---

[56] 1 H. Bl. 61–2.
[57] (1828) 5 Bing. 163.   [58] 5 Bing. 166.
[59] Cf. *Russell* v. *the Men of Devon* (1788) 2 TR 667 at 673, where Justice Ashhurst made the comment, 'it has been said that there is a principle of law on which this action might be maintained, namely, that where an individual sustains an injury by

Nicholson v. *Chapman*.[60] In many cases, judges had a choice whether to follow legal analogy or their abstract ideas of what was required; and not infrequently they chose the latter where their decision had important ramifications for commerce. In this case, a quantity of timber had been rescued after floating accidentally down the Thames, and the court ruled that the man who had rescued the timber had no lien on it for the trouble or expense he had put himself to in the carriage of it. Rather, he was liable to an action of trover if he did not return it to the owner. At first sight, it appeared that the rescuer was entitled to something for his trouble, and counsel argued that the case was analogous to that of salvage, where it was an established legal principle that the the party salvaging was entitled to a reward.[61] There seemed a prima facie case that the rule of salvage should be extended by analogy to this case, but this was rejected by the court on the grounds of policy and a conjecture of the consequences. Lord Chief Justice Eyre ruled that '[p]rinciples of public policy and commercial necessity support the lien in the case of salvage. Not only public policy and commercial necessity do not require that it should be established in this case, but very great inconvenience may be apprehended from it, if it were to be established'.[62] This, he explained, was because the owners of craft and goods would be forced thereby to guard against 'the wilful attempts of ill-designing people to turn their floats and vessels adrift, in order that they might be paid for finding them'.[63] This was a case of the court deciding on the possible consequences of their decision and its effect on trade: the answer demanded by both abstract justice and legal analogy—a reward to the rescuer—was not the expedient one. The court in effect created the rule to suit the needs of society, as it was perceived.[64]

the neglect or default of another, the law gives him a remedy. But there is another general principle which is more applicable to this case, that it is better that an individual should sustain an injury than that the public should suffer an inconvenience.'

[60] (1793) 2 H. Bl. 254.
[61] *Hartford* v. *Jones* (1699) 1 Ld. Raym. 393, Salk. 654.
[62] 2 H. Bl. 258–9.   [63] 2 H. Bl. 259.
[64] See especially *R* v. *Russell* (1827) 6 B. & C. 566. In this case, the court ruled that it was no nuisance to erect staiths in a public navigable river, which might interfere with the common right of passage, on the grounds that the staiths facilitated trade by allowing the faster unloading of goods, and were therefore a public benefit. Justice Bayley's arguments here were pure economic theory. It was true, he said, that people traded for selfish and private benefit, but, echoing *The Wealth of Nations*, he said that

Convenience was a clear ground of judgment, and was often cited in cases to support a verdict.[65] However, this was not always public convenience, for often private inconvenience overruled public need. When judges considered the consequences of their decision and the policy of the law, they did not look unfailingly at what solution was best for society in the abstract, for the economy, or even for their class. We must bear in mind the artificiality of the legal forum and the point that the judges were debating a defined issue before them. That being the case, judges could as easily be swayed by private convenience and wrong as by public priorities. This was apparent in *Ball v. Herbert*,[66] which ruled that the public had no common law right to tow along the banks of navigable rivers. The defendant, charged with trespass, argued that he had such a right, and that if his (public) right clashed with the (private) right of the plaintiff, then the latter had to give way. Lord Kenyon was unmoved, pointing to the complete absence of authority. He said, 'on account of the extreme inconvenience, to which individuals having lands adjoining the public rivers would be subject, I cannot bring my mind to say that the defendant's justifications can be supported', adding,

this benefited the public. 'If then,' he said, 'the exportation of the produce of a neighbourhood will increase the trade and commerce of a port, and that trade and commerce will benefit every place to which that produce is sent, how is that exportation to be advanced? By giving facilities to exportation, by reducing the expense to the owner of that produce, by enabling him to export upon terms which will ensure him a profit and a market.' He went on to say, 'Exclude the question of public benefit to the London market from the staiths in question, and must it not be excluded from each and every one of those staiths, and what will be the state of the London market when the purchaser can meet with nothing but keel coal?'

[65] See for example *Raynard v. Chase* (1756) 1 Burr. 2. Here it was ruled that a person not qualified to exercise a trade, who entered into a partnership with a qualified person without actually participating in the trade itself, could not be prosecuted under the Elizabethan statute of Artificers for trading without having served an apprenticeship. In this case, Lord Mansfield ruled that in many undertakings it was essential that partners should take a risk, and that 'the general usage and practice of mankind ought to have weight in determinations of this sort, affecting trade, commerce, and the manner of carrying them on'. While it would throw great confusion in the way trade was conducted if the court found against the defendant, on 'the other hand, I see no inconvenience; it is exactly the same thing as to the trade, in every iota, whether the partner has or has not served an apprenticeship'. (1 Burr. 7) For other cases determined on the grounds of convenience, see *R* v. *Vaughan* (1769) 4 Burr. 2494; *Chase* v. *Westmore* (1816) 5 M. & S. 180; *Deane* v. *Clayton* (1817) 7 Taunt. 489; *R* v. *Beeston* (1789) 3 TR 592; *Deeks* v. *Strutt* (1794) 5 TR 690; *May* v. *Brown* (1824) 3 B. & C. 113; *R* v. *the Mayor and Aldermen of the Borough of Portsmouth* (1824) 3 B. & C. 152; *Richardson* v. *Mellish* (1824) 2 Bing. 229; and *R* v. *the Inhabitants of St. Gregory, Canterbury* (1834) 2 N. & M. 440.   [66] (1789) 3 TR 253.

'[p]erhaps small evidence of usage before a jury would establish a right by custom on the ground of public convenience; but the right here claimed extends to every bank of every navigable river throughout the kingdom'.[67]

In some cases, the convenience and policy was not clear, and judges were divided on which side to follow. This was evident in the case of *Blundell* v. *Caterall*,[68] a case discussing whether the public had a common law right to bathe in the sea, and whether they therefore had the right to cross the sea-shore owned by a private proprietor in order to reach it. Justice Best ruled that there was such a right, and in the absence of authority, he based his ruling on the question of policy. 'The reason on which my judgment is grounded is public advantage,' he said, adding that '[t]he right of bathing in the sea, which is essential to the health of so many persons, is as beneficial to the public as that of fishing, and must have been as well secured to the subjects of this country by the common law'.[69] This right, he felt, was too important to be left to the landowners, and here the rights of the various parties had to be balanced for the maximum good. However, Best was here in a minority, for the other three judges took a different view of policy. Justice Holroyd for instance said that the right claimed was 'inconsistent with the nature of permanent private property', concluding that it was supported by neither necessity nor authority.[70] Chief Justice Abbott put a different perspective on the case. Here, he said, the defendant had set up a profitable business carrying bathers over the plaintiff's land in bathing machines. Since bathing machines were a new invention, there could be no ancient rights with respect to them. As a consequence, the defendant had no right to complain if the owner of the land should wish to participate in the profits, and maintain his private right.[71] The convenience here was that of private property and the freedom from opportunistic traders.

Clearly, in determining what was actionable or wrong, the courts were at liberty to use their vague notions of justice and fitness. This was reiterated in *Forbes* v. *Cochrane*,[72] which held that where slaves had escaped on to a British ship, those slaves could not be recovered by their owner. It was ruled that the Law of England was based on the law of nature and of God, and that since the right claimed was

---

[67] 3 TR 262.   [68] (1821) 5 B. & Ald. 282.
[69] 5 B. & Ald. 287.   [70] 5 B. & Ald. 300–1.
[71] 5 B. & Ald. 316.   [72] (1824) 2 B. & C. 449.

inconsistent with these, it could not be recognized. Indeed Best CJ even went so far as to suggest—in 1824–that if there were a statute allowing for the recovery of slaves, the court would have to consider overruling it.[73] Elsewhere, he had argued that while the law did not compel every kind of conduct required by humanity, 'there is no act which Christianity forbids, that the law will not reach: if otherwise, Christianity would not be, as it has always been held to be, part of the law of *England*'.[74]

Occasionally, the reasons for a decision derived from considerations internal to the law clashed with those notions of justice or convenience external to it. In these cases, it depended on the weight of arguments in the court to see who would be victorious, and on occasion, it resulted in a legal stalemate. The influence of justice and the need for correct pleading can be seen in the contrasting cases of *Horwood* v. *Heffer*[75] and *Houliston v Smyth*.[76] In the first case, it was ruled that no ill treatment by the husband of a wife short of personal violence would enable a stranger to maintain an action of assumpsit against the husband for furnishing her with necessaries, whereas the second ruled that if a wife left her husband under a reasonable fear of violence, he would be liable for necessaries. In the first case, the plaintiff lost because he stressed not the wife's fear of violence, but the fact that the husband had allowed his mistress to take her place in the household. Thus, Lawrence J ruled that while this might be abhorrent and humiliating, it did not show that she could not have had all the necessaries she required by staying in the house. Besides this, there were other remedies: she could have sued for alimony. The decision in *Horwood* v. *Heffer* thus stated there had been no legal wrong alleged—and indeed it was held that to allow this action would undermine other remedies at common law for this situation.[77] This view was overruled in *Houliston* v. *Smyth*, where Best CJ argued that it was indecent for a woman to have to share her house with a prostitute. 'The law can never require any woman to act contrary to

---

[73] The idea that a statute against reason could be overruled was elaborated by Coke in *Bonham's Case* (1610) 8 Co. Rep. 114, and reiterated by Blackstone at 1 *Comm.* 42. However, by the nineteenth century, this idea had no practical application, and few jurists would have defended it. For a discussion, see C. K. Allen, *Law in the Making*, 432–6.

[74] *Bird* v. *Holbrook* (1828) 4 Bing. 628. See also *Ilott* v. *Wilkes* (1820) 3 B. & Ald. 304.
[75] (1811) 3 Taunt. 421.   [76] (1825) 3 Bing. 127.
[77] Mansfield CJ ruled that to allow this action would wholly supersede the necessity for a suit of alimony or a divorce *a mensa et thoro*. 3 Taunt. 422.

decency,' he said, in an opinion echoed by his brother Park, who condemned the previous decision as being 'abhorrent from every feeling of a man and a Christian'. 'That cannot be the law of England,' Park concluded, 'because it is not the law of morality and religion.'[78] These cases are important, for they show the compromise between correct form and a sense of justice, and they reveal the leeway the courts had in determining what was legal and what not. For while in the first case, the court felt that the question put before the court did not show sufficient grounds for an action, in the second, the court was so convinced of the immorality of the case, that it determined it to be an actionable wrong.

The law thus was a flexible system of reasoning, with even its legal maxims and rules liable to reinterpretation and change in the light of new contexts.[79] The cases we have examined in this section were unusual ones, for they were cases which had little law to settle them, where the gap to be filled from outside the law was large indeed. To understand how the law functioned in a flexible and dynamic way, it is necessary to look at cases which were dominated neither by straightforward determinations from within the law, nor by philosophizing outside it, but where these two combined, with the substantive adjudication being mediated by the technicalities of the pleas. To elaborate this, it is useful to examine some of the decisions of Lord Mansfield.

Lord Mansfield: Reasoning and the Art of Pleading

Lord Mansfield is usually seen as a great rationalizer and innovator in the law, who based his judgments on broad principles of jurisprudence and justice rather than pettifogging on particulars.[80] Indeed, for Bentham, Mansfield was 'at the head of the gods of my idolatry . . . Days and weeks together have I made my morning pilgrimage to the chief seat of the living idol.'[81] As such, Mansfield is

---

[78] 3 Bing. 131.

[79] For a case which demonstrates well how much the common law was a system based on legal debates and uncertainties, rather than a system of clear answers, see *Reg* v. *Millis* (1843–4) 10 Cl. & F. 534. Here, the court was divided, with some judges arguing from legal analogies, some from the position of justice or fairness. Thus, in the end, the case was settled, but the law remained unclear.

[80] See D. Lieberman, *The Province of Legislation Determined*, 99–121; C. H. S. Fifoot, *Lord Mansfield*; E. Heward, *Lord Mansfield*; *Jones* v. *Randall* (1774) 1 Cowp. 37.

[81] *Works*, i. 247, quoted in Holdsworth, *History of English law*, xii. 554–5.

easily seen as a judge whose attitudes to the common law were unusual and innovative. Three features of his legal reasoning stand out. First, he is known for judgments based on principle and justice, looking to settle disputes on the substantive merits of the case rather than on technicalities. Second, he is noted for his desire to lay down clear rules and principles to guide future conduct, which explains his keenness for special verdicts allowing the judge to elaborate complex points of law, and for special juries of experts whose decisions would ensure the principles elaborated were ones which reflected public needs. In particular, this was best seen in his developing of commercial law, where Mansfield applied general principles to what had hitherto been a mass of unintelligible cases.[82] Thirdly, Mansfield is noted for his hostility to over-technicality, where cases were lost through formal slips or errors of pleading. His reputation is that of a creative and speculative judge, a widely read and philosophical Scot with little patience for the ancient complications of law.

An analysis of Mansfield's judicial reasoning can reveal that this latter characterization is somewhat misleading. For it can be seen that Mansfield's reasoning was not wholly untypical of the usual common law method: indeed, were that not the case, it would be hard to explain why so few of his rulings were overturned, and why his brother judges on the Bench usually agreed with him. An examination of Mansfield's reasoning is useful for two purposes. First, as an illustration of the nature of common law reasoning, we can see how his judicial attitudes fitted an adjudicative theory based on correct pleading. Second, by examining Mansfield's most controversial judgments, and his attempts to develop clear rules in law, we can see the limitations of common law reasoning and flexibility in modern society.

Initially, it is evident that Mansfield was not hostile to the technical precision required by the rules of pleading, defending it in several cases. In *Bristow* v. *Wright* he said that 'the rules of pleading are founded in good sense. Their objects are precision and brevity.'[83] Mansfield's dictum was not an aberration: nor merely (as it has sometimes been taken) the chiding of a plaintiff who had been caught in his own snare by setting forth too full and complex a

---

[82] See the comments of Buller J in *Lickbarrow* v. *Mason* (1787) 2 TR 63.

[83] (1781) 2 Dougl. 665 at 666–7. Mansfield was keen that pleas be brief and simple, to get to the issue as soon as possible. See *Dundas* v. *Lord Weymouth* (1777) 2 Cowp. 665; *Price* v. *Fletcher* (1778) 2 Cowp. 727; *Alder* v. *Chip* (1759) 2 Burr. 755.

declaration. For on other occasions Mansfield ruled that defects in pleas settled the case, before the substantive issues could be brought to trial.[84] In *Combe* v. *Pitt*,[85] Mansfield made the comment that it was unnecessary to look at subsequent pleadings if the first plea was bad. Here, in an action of debt, the defendant had pleaded in abatement that another action had been brought against him in the same term, 'whereas he ought to have shown that the Right of Action was attached in some other Person, before the present Plaintiff's Action was commenced'.[86]

Mansfield sought to ensure that there was a ground of action and that it was correctly laid under the right form. Thus, in *Purdy* v. *Stacey*,[87] a case for defamatory words, he ruled on the declaration 'that the charge was so loose, that it did not of itself import a crime'. If it was not totally clear by the declaration that the words were necessarily defamatory, the court could not cure them. Similarly, in *Ross* v. *Johnson* in 1772, where the plaintiff had used an incorrect form of action against a wharfinger for detaining his goods, Mansfield ruled that although he disliked nonsuiting plaintiffs on objections unconnected with the merits of the case, the distinction between the action of trover and action on the case was one founded in principle.[88] Mansfield's strictness over forms of action can be seen in *Hambly* v. *Trott*,[89] where the ruling was that the action of trover could not lie against an executor for conversion by a testator. The court pointed out that the maxim *actio personalis moritur cum persona* was not universally true, but there was a clear distinction to be made. Where the declaration was of a sort as to call for a plea of not guilty—where the cause of action lay *ex delicto*—there the wrong was buried with the offender. However, in so far as there was a benefit or property acquired, there an action for its value lay against the executor. In this case, therefore, the plaintiff lost for using the wrong form and eliciting the wrong plea: for here the cause of action was founded in a duty, not a wrong, and 'upon principles of civil obligation, another form of action may be brought, as an action for money had and received'.[90]

---

[84] See *R* v. *Lookup* (1766) 3 Burr. 1901.   [85] (1763) 3 Burr. 1423.
[86] 3 Burr. 1432–3. The defendant was given leave to answer over.
[87] (1771) 5 Burr. 2698.
[88] 5 Burr. 2825.   [89] (1776) 1 Cowp. 371.
[90] 1 Cowp. 377. For Mansfield's attitude towards allowing the flexibility of actions on the case, in contrast to other actions in tort, see *Bird* v. *Randall* (1762) 3 Burr. 1345; and also (for indebitatus assumpsit) *Moses* v. *Macferlan* (1760) 2 Burr. 1005. Occasion-

Mansfield's hostility to the technicality of pleading was seen mainly when counsel tried to capitalize on formal slips; and there are many cases where he dismissed mere objections of form, such as clerical errors.[91] Yet this was not untypical of English judges. The arcane science of pleading was not technical merely for its own sake, and where a formal slip could be corrected by facts presumed from the verdict or by correcting the error of a clerk, it had frequently been done.[92] For this reason, Mansfield took care when granting a rule for a new trial: 'a new trial ought to be granted to attain real justice; but not to gratify litigious passions upon every point of summum jus'.[93] Similarly, he said that it did not always follow that there should be a new trial whenever the verdict was contrary to evidence, for 'it is possible that the Verdict may still be on the side of the real justice and equity of the case'.[94] Realizing the dangers of excessive technicality, Mansfield was keen to overcome technical slips.[95] Thus, while he acknowledged that 'a verdict will not mend the matter, where the gist of the action is not laid in the declaration', he added that 'it will cure ambiguity'.[96] The function of pleading, for Mansfield, then, was to bring the point of dispute to the court in the most simple way, to attain justice.[97] Therefore, when in *Anderson* v. *George*[98] the plaintiff, instead of trying the substantive issue between them (seeing problems in his own evidence), attempted to use a trick of pleading to win, Mansfield ruled that he had taken an unfair

ally, Mansfield found himself lagging behind his brother judges over new forms of declaration. See *Stuart* v. *Wilkins* (1778) 1 Dougl. 18.

[91] See *Hart* v. *Weston* (1770) 5 Burr. 2586; *Trueman* v. *Fenton* (1777) 2 Cowp. 544. In *Sulston* v. *Norton* (1761) 3 Burr. 1235, he ruled that 'if, by mistake, [the verdict] has been entered upon a count not proved, instead of the count which was proved, that is no reason for a new trial'.

[92] See *Cowper* v. *Spencer* (1725) 8 Mod. 376.

[93] *Farewell* v. *Chaffey* (1756) 1 Burr. 54. In *Macrow* v. *Hull* (1764) 1 Burr. 11, the plaintiff was denied a new trial he was strictly entitled to on the grounds that prospective damages were so small it 'would even be a cruelty' to him to grant one.

[94] *Dr Burton* v. *Thompson* (1758) 2 Burr. 664. This was a libel case, where instead of finding for the plaintiff in a case where he would be entitled to only very small damages, the jury had found for the defendant.

[95] However, if justice demanded it, he was willing to uphold technical slips. In *Bennet* v. *Smith* (1757) 1 Burr. 401, the court decided that a common informer who sued for punishment only, and had been guilty of a mere slip which entitled the defendant to a non pros., was not to be given the chance to set it aside.

[96] *Avery* v. *Hoole* (1778) 2 Cowp. 825.

[97] See *Gardiner* v. *Croasdale* (1760) 2 Burr. 904 and *Mayor of Yarmouth* v. *Eaton* (1763) 3 Burr. 1402.   [98] (1757) 1 Burr. 352.

advantage, 'contrary to justice and good conscience'. The rules of practice, he said, must be general, but 'he who abused them in a particular case could not shelter a trick by regularity'. By keeping a tight rein on the rules of pleading, when and how they were to be used, they would clear the path to, and not obstruct, substantial justice.[99] Nevertheless, Mansfield was always aware of the dangers of paying too close a heed to the justice of a case at the expense of established legal precedents: 'Favourable cases make bad precedents.'[100]

The fact that Mansfield subscribed to the underlying adjudicative theory of pleading can be seen most clearly in *Rushton v. Aspinall*.[101] This was an action of assumpsit on a bill of exchange, drawn on one Meyer indorsed to Rushton and then to Aspinall. The declaration stated that the bill had been presented to Meyer, who refused to pay, and that Rushton was therefore liable. The plaintiff in error claimed that the declaration was bad for failing correctly to allege a demand on the acceptor, and for failing to state notice to the defendant of the acceptor's refusal to pay; to which the defendant in error replied that these defects were cured by the verdict. Mansfield declared the rule to be

that, where the plaintiff has stated his title, or ground of action inaccurately—because to entitle him to recover, all circumstances necessary, in form or substance, to complete the title so imperfectly stated, must be proved at the trial—it is a fair presumption, after a verdict, that they were proved; but that, where the plaintiff totally omits to state his title or cause of action, it need not be proved at the trial, and, therefore, there is no room for presumption.

The conclusion was a clear principle of pleading: 'The promise alleged to have been made by the defendant is an inference of law, and the declaration does not contain premises from which such an inference can be drawn.'[102] The plaintiff had failed to supply the necessary premises; and hence the law had no dispute to adjudicate upon.

Even in cases when Mansfield had a clear idea of what was substantial justice, the first hurdle was to have correct pleas. In 1783,

---

[99] See *Rice v. Shute* (1770) 5 Burr. 2611. For a case where Mansfield made a ruling by going through the intricacies of the pleas to see if the substantive merits had been tried and concluded that it was a simple slip that prevented a trial of justice, see *R v. Roger Philips* (1757) 1 Burr. 292.   [100] *Sadler v. Evans* (1766) 4 Burr. 1984.
[101] (1781) 2 Dougl. 679.   [102] 2 Dougl. 683.

an insurance company tried to sue the hundredors of London to recover money they had paid to a client as a consequence of damages during the Gordon Riots, after the client had recovered money from the hundredors under the Riot Act for the damage done, who had deducted the amount he had been paid by the insurance. Mansfield clearly thought it was a hardship that the insurers could not recover the money, for it seemed unfair that they should pay what should have come from elsewhere. However, he found that to allow both owner and insurer to sue the hundredors contradicted the rules and principles of pleading: 'I take it to be a maxim, that as against the person sued the action cannot be transferred. As between the parties themselves,' he explained, 'the law has long supported it for the benefit of commerce, but the assignee must sue in the name of the assignor; by which the defence is not varied.' The injustice produced would be this: if the insurer could sue, no realease by the insured would bar the action, so that two (or more) would have the right of action for the same wrong.[103] It was a great hardship here, Mansfield concluded, but one for which there was no remedy.

Occasionally, Mansfield's decisions followed a strict reading of the allegations, against what seemed just. In *Rich* v. *Coe*,[104] the master of a vessel had covenanted with its owners to have the sole management of the ship for a certain term, and to repair and maintain it at his own cost; but the plaintiff, who had supplied necessaries, sued the owners for the money. The court held that the owners were liable, even though they did not have knowledge of what was being supplied, for Mansfield held that their agreement with the master was wholly private, and that the plaintiffs were total strangers to it.[105] 'To be sure, if it appeared that a tradesman had notice of such a contract, and, in consequence of it, gave credit to the captain individually as the responsible person, particular circumstances of that sort might afford a ground to say, he meant to absolve the owners, and to look singly to the personal security of the master,' Mansfield said, '[b]ut here it is stated, that the plaintiff had no notice whatever of the contract.' The owners therefore ran the risk. Here, the judgment showed the defendants had failed clearly to lay blame

---

[103] *The London Assurance Company* v. *Sainsbury* (1783) 3 Dougl. 245.

[104] (1777) 2 Cowp. 636.

[105] This point, he said, was 'an answer to the observation, that the plaintiff must have known the real situation of the master in this case, from the general usage and custom of the country in that respect'. 2 Cowp. 639.

elsewhere in a case which was of great importance to the owners of ships who leased them.[106]

Mansfield's attitude to pleading helps explain his often contentious attitude to juries, for in many areas—most notably libel—he was seen as wanting to emasculate the jury. In his commercial cases, not only did Mansfield use special juries of expert merchants, but he also encouraged the finding of special verdicts to enable the court to elaborate on the law later, in studied judgments. In some cases, therefore, the key issue of what was the custom of merchants was left to the expert jury which outlined the rule by their finding.[107] In others, however, the jury was encouraged to give two alternative verdicts, subject to the opinion of the court on the matter of law.[108] This enabled the court to focus on a clear and deliberate point of dispute, and to make an adjudication on it, while avoiding the indeterminacy of a general jury verdict. In *Tyrie* v. *Fletcher*[109] he therefore said it was proper to save the question for determination by the court 'because in all mercantile transactions, certainty is of much more consequence, than which way the point is decided'.[110] Mansfield was seeking to make clear rules for merchants: but it was done by determined reasoning on a precise point of dispute refined both through pleas and special verdict, for higher deliberation by the court.

Once the correct system of pleas had been gone through, however, the judge was able to decide on the justice of the case. Hence, Mansfield was not untypical in using arguments from policy or logic. Thus, in *Tyrie* v. *Fletcher*, he said '[t]here is no case or practice in point; and, therefore, we must argue from the general principles applicable to all policies of insurance'. He then determined from what he saw as the nature and principles of insurance. In *Heylyn* v. *Adamson*, the question for the court was whether, in an action brought on an inland bill of exchange, by the indorsee against the indorser, the objection that it did not appear that the drawer of

---

[106] See also *Wilkins* v. *Carmichael* (1779) 1 Dougl. 101.

[107] e.g. *Lewis* v. *Rucker* (1761) 2 Burr. 1167.

[108] e.g. *Hamilton* v. *Mendes* (1761) 2 Burr. 1198. Sometimes in insurance cases, the matter being a written instrument to be construed, it was wholly a matter for the court's interpretation of words and meanings. Thus in *Simond* v. *Boydell* (1779) 1 Dougl. 268, Mansfield was critical of merchants who made unclear contracts of insurance.   [109] (1777) 2 Cowp. 666.

[110] He made the same point in *Pelly* v. *Royal Exchange Assurance Company* (1757) 1 Burr. 341, and *Vallejo* v. *Wheeler* (1774) 1 Cowp. 143.

the bill had any notice of non-payment or that any demand had been made of him was the grounds of a nonsuit: a clear question on the pleas. This, according to Mansfield, had to be 'determined upon the nature of the transaction, general convenience, and the authority of deliberate resolutions in court'.[111] He therefore discussed the nature of bills of exchange and argued from general convenience: 'everybody knows that the more indorsements a bill has, the greater credit it bears: whereas if those demands are all necessary to be made, it must naturally diminish the value, by how much more difficult it renders the calling in the money'.[112] Mansfield then explained the analogy with promissory notes and the significant differences, concluding that in bills of exchange, there was no need to make a demand on the first drawer, because the indorsor was the drawer, each new indorsement acting as a new bill. 'The indorsee does not trust to the credit of the original drawer: he does not know whether such a person exists.'[113] By examining the nature of bills of exchange and convenience, Mansfield was able to decide whether the wrong alleged in the pleas was one correctly set out.[114]

Mansfield drew on similarly broad sources, mixing reasoning internal to and external to the law, in *Hamilton* v. *Mendes*,[115] where the court had to decide whether the insured party could recover the whole value of a ship, or only the actual loss, when the ship had been captured by a foreign enemy but later recaptured. Here, the jury found two different sets of damages, leaving the court to decide which to award. Mansfield ruled that the plaintiff could not recover on the whole loss, and in so doing he used three types of arguments. First, he used logic. 'It is a contradiction in terms, to bring an action for indemnity, when, upon the whole event, no damage has been

---

[111] (1758) 2 Burr. 669 at 674.

[112] 2 Burr. 675.   [113] 2 Burr. 675.

[114] See also *Grant* v. *Vaughan* (1764) 3 Burr. 1516, where it was held that the bearer of a bill of exchange could maintain an action against a drawer. In this case, it was impossible to bring the action in the name of the person to whom the note was originally made payable, since it was made out to a ship 'or bearer'; but even if there had been a person named that would not have changed matters. '[T]he person so originally named may become bankrupt; or may be indebted to the drawer of the note, so as to give the drawer a right to set off such debt against the demand of the money due upon the note. So that if the courts of law should not allow the bearer to bring the action in his own name, there might be no relief at all. And it can never be supposed reasonable or legal, that the banker should have it left in his discretion or choice, to pay the money to one or the other as his fancy or inclination should lead him.' 3 Burr. 1523. This was clear reasoning on the need for the pleas to give a remedy.

[115] (1761) 2 Burr. 1198.

sustained. This reasoning is so much founded in sense, that the common law of England adopts it.' To back this up, he drew an analogy from the law of landlord and tenant, regarding waste.[116] Analogy was used further in drawing an inference from a precedent case which under different circumstances had come to an opposite conclusion. The third ground of judgment, and the most elaborated, was convenience and consequence. The only reason why anyone would want to abandon ship in these circumstances, Mansfield said, was because the ship had been overvalued or the market had collapsed: and it was unfair that the insurer should suffer for falls in the market, most clearly because over-valuations were against the principles of maritime law.

Such arguments of convenience are to be found throughout Mansfield's commercial cases. In *Lewis* v. *Rucker*,[117] the plaintiffs had insured their consignment of sugar on a voyage from St Thomas Island to Hamburg, but on the way the sugar was damaged and had to be sold at once at a low price. The sugar was insured at £30 per hogshead, the price on arrival at Hamburg was £23, and the sugars were sold at £20. The question was, at what rate should damages be estimated? The defendants claimed they should pay the difference between the price they obtained and the current market price, the plaintiffs claimed the difference to the higher price, on the grounds that if the whole consigment had been lost, then the insurers would have had to pay the full value, and on the grounds that they had to sell the sugar at once, and not hold it pending a price rise. Mansfield's ruling confirmed the special jury's finding for the defendant. Central in this finding was the question of convenience: if the plaintiff's contention succeeded, it would involve the underwriter in the rise or fall of the market, subjecting him sometimes to pay much more than the loss and at other times depriving the insured of any payment. 'If speculative destinations of the merchant, and the success of such speculations were to be regarded,' Mansfield said, 'it would introduce the greatest injustice and inconvenience. The underwriter knows nothing of them.'[118]

Mansfield drew on convenience elsewhere. In *Wigglesworth* v. *Dallison*,[119] the defendant was sued in trespass for taking away the plaintiff's corn. The defendant had been a tenant on the land, who

---

[116] If the tenant repaired the waste before any action was brought, no action could be brought.   [117] (1761) 2 Burr. 1167.
[118] 2 Burr. 1173.   [119] (1779) 1 Dougl. 201.

had taken away his crop after the expiry of his term, and, in the case, he pleaded a local custom which justified him. The plaintiff challenged this, claiming the custom was uncertain, unreasonable, and against the deed. The court therefore had to decide on the custom, and part of the grounds for the decision was convenience. 'It is just,' the Chief Justice ruled, 'for he who sows ought to reap, and it is for the benefit and encouragement of agriculture.' Though this went against the general law which held that tenants, who sowed when they knew their term was going to expire had to be responsible for their own mistake, here the custom of the place could 'rectify what otherwise would be imprudence or folly'. The custom was reasonable and certain, and only added to the deed, therefore.

On occasion, particularly with mercantile law, Mansfield drew on wider sources beyond the law. In *Luke* v. *Lyde*,[120] where the question was one of determining how much freight had to be paid in case of loss at sea, where there had been salvage, he quoted from the ancient Rhodian laws, as well as from Roccius and an ordinance of Louis XIV. In *Vallejo* v. *Wheeler*, where the court had to define barratry, he drew on dictionary definitions, particularly from the Italians, 'who were the first great traders of the modern world'.[121] In this case, as in *Glover* v. *Black*,[122] Mansfield first consulted with traders before making his decision, since '[i]t might be greatly inconvenient, to introduce a practice contrary to general usage [a]nd there may be some opening to fraud if it be not specified'.[123] It was not only experts he conversed with. In one case, he noted, 'I have mooted the point with many who are not lawyers, upon the morality and rectitude of the transaction.'[124] In this case, the grounds of the decision, against the plaintiff in an action against an auctioneer for selling a horse at the highest price contrary to express instructions from the owner not to go below a certain level, were that he had acted in bad faith and in a dishonest and fraudulent manner, by expecting the auctioneer to bid secretly on his behalf in his own sale.

The type of reasoning that Mansfield used then was not untypical of the common law reasoning we have encountered already. Indeed, given that many of Mansfield's most innovative cases were in

---

[120] (1759) 2 Burr. 882.
[121] (1774) 1 Cowp. 143. [122] (1763) 3 Burr. 1394.
[123] Mansfield was prepared to change his mind, when the commercial community disapproved of his decisions. See *Lilly* v. *Ewer* (1779) 1 Dougl. 72.
[124] *Bexwell* v. *Christie* (1776) 1 Cowp. 395.

contract and the commercial law of insurance, where there existed a definite mercantile practice and definite contracts and policies to interpret, there was often less room for the wide-ranging philosophical speculation that can be seen in other areas. Mansfield was not a maverick in looking to justice, convenience, or authority. However, he did encounter problems in attempting to make general rules for future cases, particularly when this was done by breaking or modifying the rules of pleading.

This can be seen in some of his most contentious and challenged cases in contract law, where Mansfield attempted to modify the notion of consideration. As Blackstone had put it, in any contract, there had to be a consideration laid, so 'that a *nudum pactum* or agreement to do or pay anything on one side, without any compensation on the other, is totally void in law'.[125] In cases of assumpsit, a consideration therefore had to be clearly set forward, since that was the basis of the obligation.[126] Mansfield was seen to undermine this in two areas. One of these was in *Pillans* v. *Van Mierop*[127] which held that in written contracts there was no need to show any consideration. This was a commercial case concerning the liability for a bill of exchange. White, an Irish merchant, had drawn a bill of exchange from the plaintiffs, offering to give them credit on the defendants' house in London. The defendants agreed, but after White's bankruptcy, they refused to pay. The question for the court was who should suffer because of White's bankruptcy, and whether the pleas sufficiently connected the plaintiff and defendant, to make the defendants liable. The defendants argued that there was no consideration to make them liable: the only consideration was past.

In fact there were two points of issue here. The first was whether the defendants had made a valid acceptance of the bill; the second was the question of consideration. This being a commercial case, the second issue could have been accommodated, for while in assumpsit it was usually necessary to show consideration, this was not so in the case of bills of exchange, governed by the law and custom of merchants.[128] Because a bill of exchange was assignable and

---

[125] 2 *Comm.* 445.
[126] See below, Ch. 9 for a fuller discussion.
[127] (1765) 3 Burr. 1663.
[128] Chitty put it thus: 'It is not . . . owing to the *form* of a Bill of Exchange, nor to the circumstance of its being in *writing*, that the law gives it this effect, but in order to strengthen and facilitate that commercial intercourse which is carried on through the

negotiable, it imported a consideration unless the contrary was shown.[129] It was thus well established that bonds and notes could be seen as prima facie evidence of good consideration without it being proved.[130] Thus, in 1747, Lee CJ ruled in a case where the plaintiffs had made a bill of exchange over to the defendants, who were to pay money to a company in Spain, which they failed to do, leaving the plaintiff to pay the company with additional interest, that

The count says, that the defendants accepted the bill, and became liable by the custom, and being so liable, neglected payment, and thereby the plaintiff was obliged to pay it, and did pay it; by reason of which premises and the custom the defendant became liable, and so promised to pay the plaintiff. This seems to me, as at present advised, to be a good consideration to raise the promise.[131]

Thus, on the question of consideration as applied to this case, Mansfield was being uncontroversial in saying that '[t]he law of merchants and the law of the land is the same', and '[a] nudum pactum does not exist in the usage and law of merchants'.[132]

The first issue was more problematic, potentially, for it had to be clear that there was an accepted link between the parties. Here, Mansfield allowed the mere verbal agreement to suffice, the words 'I will give the bill due honour' being in effect an acceptance. This aspect of Mansfield's decision was much more contentious, and was narrowed by Mansfield himself in a subsequent case,[133] and in later cases there tended to be much more focused and precise argument as to whether facts laid in declarations amounted in effect

medium of this species of security.' *A Practical Treatise on Bills of Exchange*, 5th edn. (London, 1818), 13–14.

[129] '[T]he want of consideration, as between the maker and payee of a note or bill, cannot be set up in an action against either of them at the suit of an indorsee, unless it be proved that he was acquainted with this circumstance at the time of taking the note or bill. And the reason why third persons ought not to be affected by this rule is, that bills and notes being negotiable instruments, by mere indorsement and delivery, it would be enabling the original parties to assist in a fraud, if they were to be allowed to set up the want of consideration as between themselves, in bar to an action.' S. Comyn, *The Law of Contracts and Promises upon various subjects*, 2nd edn. (London, 1824), 10.

[130] See *Guichard* v. *Roberts* (1763) 1 W. Bl. 445; *Crawley* v. *Crowther* (1702) 2 Freem. Ch. 257; *Meredith* v. *Chute* (1702) 2 Ld. Raym. 759.

[131] *Simmonds* v. *Parminter* 1 Wils. KB 185 at 189.

[132] 3 Burr. 1669. This was overstating the case: but the onus probandi lay with the plaintiff. See *Collins* v. *Martin* (1797) 1 B. & P. 648.

[133] *Pierson* v. *Dunlop* (1777) 2 Cowp. 571.

to acceptances.[134] However, his final argument that if this *was* an acceptance, then it 'would be very destructive to trade, and to trust in commercial dealing, if they could' afterwards retract it, was perfectly reasonable.

The problem in *Pillans* v. *Van Mierop* occurred when the judges attempted to generalize. Mansfield did this in holding 'that the ancient notion about the want of consideration was one for the sake of evidence only', so that what should have been a mere determination in a commercial case was extended into a rule about the nature of consideration in general. Wilmot went much further, drawing on Grotius, Pufendorf, and Bracton to show that the reason for holding parol contracts void without consideration was because they might be rashly entered into: since this did not apply to written contracts, they needed no consideration to be shown.[135] These were dangerous speculations: not being arguments based on the question at hand but seeking to introduce substantive arguments at the level of the pleadings, to alter and disrupt a settled mode of pleading. This contrasts with the attitude of Yates, whose judgment concurred, but whose arguments were more tied to matching his conclusions to the pleas:

The acceptance of a bill of exchange is an obligation to pay it: the end of their institution, their currency, requires that it should be so. On this principle, bills of exchange are considered, and are declared upon as special contracts; though, legally, they are only simple contracts: the declaration sets forth the bill and acceptance specifically: and that thereby the defendants, by the custom of merchants, became liable to pay it.[136]

By making a sweeping rule that written contracts needed to show no consideration, Mansfield and Wilmot flew in the face of a standard rule and sought to bring arguments from convenience and justice in at a level where they could not usually be introduced.[137] Yates's contention, that the custom of merchants implied a consideration,

---

[134] See *Johnson* v. *Collings* (1800) 1 East 98; *Clarke* v. *Cock* (1803) 4 East 57. The judges in these cases were much more careful than Mansfield had been in *Pillans* v. *Van Mierop*, but shied away from overruling his holding.

[135] Wilmot, however, also said the reason why the acceptance of a bill of exchange should bind was for the convenience of commerce, and in these arguments he was repeating orthodoxy.

[136] 3 Burr. 1674.

[137] It should be noted that it was Wilmot's views, not Mansfield's, that were the more extensive, and therefore the ones most subject to criticism afterwards.

seemed more modest, and seemed better to follow the need to comply with the formalities of proceeding.

The notion that there could be no *nudum pactum* in writing was overruled in *Rann* v. *Hughes*,[138] an altogether very different case: here, to allow the general rule to be applied to the facts at hand would produce substantive injustice. The case was one against an executrix, who was being sued in her personal capacity to pay a legacy she had undertaken to pay. The key problem was whether and why an executrix should be personally liable.[139] According to Skynner LCB, 'The being indebted is of itself a sufficient consideration to ground a promise, but the promise must be co-extensive with the consideration unless some particular consideration of fact can be found here to warrant the extension of it against the defendant in her personal capacity.'[140] Here, the executrix gained no benefit. Moreover, the declaration failed to show there were sufficient assets in the legacy to pay; but assumed that once she promised to pay, she became personally liable. There was no reason why she should be, beyond merely having written a promise to the plaintiff that she would pay.[141] 'If a person indebted in one right in consideration of forbearance for a particular time promise to pay in another right, this convenience will be a sufficient consideration to warrant an action against him or her in the latter right,' Skynner went on, 'but here no sufficient consideration occurs to support this demand . . . for she derives no advantage or convenience from the promise here made.'[142] The contrast of the two cases may thus be explained in good part as a result of the difference in their nature, and in the different pleadings thereon. While it made sense to hold banks to their written engagements, because of the justice and practice of the case, it did not do so for the executrix who might be forced to pay more than she ought. The problem posed by Mansfield lay then in his seeking to make clear rules out of the details of precise cases.[143]

[138] (1778) 7 TR 350 n., 4 Brown PC 27.

[139] No action could be brought in a court of law against a legacy, since testaments were under the jurisdiction of the ecclesiastical courts or equity. However, to enable beneficiaries to recover legacies due in a quicker way, actions of assumpsit were brought against executors for promises.   [140] 7 TR 350 n.

[141] Contrast *Atkins* v. *Hill* (1775) 1 Cowp. 284, where Mansfield had held that where there were sufficient assets left in a legacy, that was sufficient consideration to force the executor to pay a promised legacy.   [142] 7 TR 350 n.

[143] This led him to contradictions in his own judgments. *Tyrie* v. *Fletcher* therefore appeared to contradict the decision he had made in *Stevenson* v. *Snow* (1761) 3 Burr. 1237, the decisions differing at base in the interpretation made of similar contracts.

Mansfield had similar problems where he attempted to introduce the notion that a moral consideration was sufficient to bind a contract, elaborated in *Trueman* v. *Fenton*.[144] In that case, it was held that a creditor who had given a debtor a new bill worth half of the old, which he would not claim under a commission of bankruptcy, but would recover later, was entitled to payment. The objection to this was that it was reviving an old debt under a new promise and was hence a *nudum pactum*, but against that Mansfield noted that 'all the debts of a bankrupt are due in conscience . . . and there is no honest man who does not discharge them, if he afterwards has it in his power to do so'.[145] The doctrine was applied in *Hawkes* v. *Saunders*.[146] The facts of this case were very similar to *Rann* v. *Hughes*, but here there were enough assets left in the legacy to pay the claim. Mansfield and his fellow judges held that this fact was a sufficient consideration to force an executrix to pay in her personal capacity, although the nature of the pleadings ruled out the judgment being given *de bonis testatoris*. The reasoning seemed clear enough: the executrix should be held to her bare promise to pay, because as executrix she had enough money to pay, and the plaintiff had suffered owing to her omission. It seemed like substantive justice: she had promised, and she had the money. But this was to conflate two legal personalities: she was forced to pay in her personal capacity for a claim on the legacy because her moral obligation to pay as executrix implied sufficient consideration for her to uphold her promise as an individual.[147] The problem was this. If common law pleadings involved the allegation of a wrong for which the other party was responsible, the court had to connect those two parties to each other by the case they set out on the pleas. When that was done, the court decided whether what was done was a wrong. Here, however, the court made the *connection* between the parties who on the face of the pleas were not connected save by a bare promise, by invoking substantive arguments of a moral nature. This was upsetting the applecart: common law required formality in pleadings at the first level and allowed substantive arguments at a second-higher level of judgment: it did not easily countenance the upsetting of the formality of pleading by substantive arguments there.

---

[144] (1777) 2 Cowp. 544.

[145] 2 Cowp. 548.   [146] (1782) 1 Cowp. 289.

[147] This was the key difference from *Atkins* v. *Hill*: in that case, the defendant was sued *qua* executor.

The moral consideration doctrine was highly problematic, for the moral question was a vague one to introduce. Subsequent cases cast doubt on the doctrine and sought to revive the strictness of pleadings that Mansfield had undermined.[148] The law reporters Bosanquet and Puller, in a famous note to *Wennall v. Adney*,[149] sought to restrict the import of Mansfield's idea,[150] for they argued that the term moral consideration, instead of being vague, only applied to 'those imperative duties which would be enforceable by law, were it not for some positive rule, which, with a view to general benefit, exempts the party in that particular instance from legal liability'.[151] The reporters cited *Mitchinson v. Hewson*[152]—which held a husband was not liable to be sued alone for the debt of his wife contracted before marriage—to draw the principle that an obligation to pay in one right would not support an assumpsit to pay in another right, 'even though it be a legal obligation, and coupled with an express promise'.

In *Littlefield v. Shee*,[153] Lord Tenterden noted that the moral consideration doctrine 'is one which should be received with some limitation', and the judgment went against the plaintiff on the pleas. Elizabeth Shee had had goods supplied to her while living apart from her husband, which she promised to pay for after his death. Here, it was held that as the price of the goods was originally a debt of her husband's, the ground of the supposed moral obligation had not been set forth clearly in the declaration, and the plaintiff could not recover.[154] The doctrine was finally overruled in *Eastwood v.*

---

[148] In *Deeks v. Strutt* (1794) 5 TR 690, Lord Kenyon ruled against *Atkins v. Hill* and *Hawkes v. Saunders* by maintaining that no action at law could be maintained for a legacy. Kenyon noted that the arguments in favour of this action were founded on 'the supposed justice of the case and the convenience of the parties', but showed that it was in fact highly inconvenient to introduce this action, in so far as it encroached on equity territory and undermined the guarantees supplied at equity. In this case, however, there had been no express promise to pay.

[149] (1802) 3 B. & P. 247.

[150] '[H]owever general the expressions used by Lord Mansfield may at first appear, yet the instances adduced by him as illustrative of the rule of law, do not carry that rule beyond what the older authorities seem to recognize as its proper limits; for in each instance the party bound by the promise had received a benefit previous to the promise.'

[151] They concluded that an express promise 'can give no original right of action if the obligation on which it is founded never could have been enforced at law, though not barred by any legal maxim or statute provision'.

[152] (1797) 7 TR 348.   [153] (1831) 2 B. & Ad. 809.

[154] This was, he said, in contrast to *Lee v. Muggeridge* (1813) 5 Taunt. 36, where the moral consideration was clearly laid.

Kenyon[155] in 1840, where the executor of the plaintiff's wife's father was suing for the recovery of money he had spent himself on her maintenance as a minor. Lord Denman argued that here there was only a declaration of a benefit voluntarily conferred and an express promise by the defendant to pay. The declaration was bad because there was no consideration beyond past benefits, and all the allegations were insufficient:

If the subsequent assent of the defendant could have amounted to a ratihabitio, the declaration should have stated the money to have been expended at his request, and the ratification should have been relied on as matter of evidence; but this was obviously impossible because the defendant was in no way connected with the property or with the plaintiff, when the money was expended. If the ratification of the wife while sole were relied on, then a debt from her would have been shewn, and the defendant could not have been charged in his own right without some further consideration, as of forbearance after marriage, or something of that sort; and then another point would have arisen upon the Statute of Frauds which did not arise as it was, but which might in that case have been available under the plea of non assumpsit.

This was to require a strictness of allegation that could not be achieved by the vague moral doctrine, and to restore the strictness of forms Mansfield had sought to undermine.

This view of Mansfield's reasoning and the fate of two of his more contentious innovations thus tells us much both about Mansfield and the common law. It can be seen that, in many ways, he was no simple iconoclast wishing to usurp the functions of a legislator, but continued to work within the common law tradition of using wide sources for substantive decisions. On the other hand, his attempts to lay down clear broad rules that went beyond the instant case ran into problems. Mansfield was unable to work as a grand legislator, if only because the common law system could not make the jump from being a collection of atomized adjudications on the case at hand to being a clear system of rules. Grand substantive rules that sought to usurp the place of the technical and formal rules at the level of pleading encountered hostility from many judges, who, in the contentious areas, sought to restrict Mansfield's wider ambitions. There remained limits to the common law horizon: it would not be judges, but legislators and textbook writers who would make sense of the grand sweeps of law.

[155] 11 A. & E. 438.

The cases and the system of reasoning we have examined provide the vital context in which to put Bentham. It is important to realize that at the same time that Blackstone was writing, there was a sharp contrast to his natural law based, rule-bound way of looking at the common law, which was to be found in the reasoning and behaviour of judges and lawyers. Bentham thus had two things to react to: not only Blackstone's characterization of the common law, but the flexible adjudicative system we have been examining. It is to Bentham's responses that we must now turn.

5

Bentham and the Complete Code of Laws

THE story of how Jeremy Bentham grew disenchanted with the common law, seeing it as unable to provide either the clear rules needed for a modernizing society or the certainty that a legal system required, is now a very familiar one.[1] Bentham's critique of the common law—that it was 'dog law', whereby men were punished for their actions *ex post facto*, as you would beat a dog, that it existed nowhere but in the vague minds of the judges, and that it was in danger of being inflexible[2]—led him, by the early 1780s, to seek to abandon it, or even a statutory digest of it, and put in its place a Pannomion, a complete and perfect code of laws. In so doing, Bentham had found his life's work: the creation and completion of such a code.[3] This was to be the reverse of the common law method:

[1] See D. Lieberman, *The Province of Legislation Determined*, 219–76 and G. J. Postema, *Bentham and the Common Law Tradition* (Oxford, 1986). Lieberman in particular explores Bentham's progress from a critique of the common law to the creation of the Pannomion. See also J. H. Burns, 'Bentham and Blackstone: A Lifetime's Dialectic', *Utilitas*, i (1989), 22–40. There have, in addition, been a number of important recent studies of Bentham examining his critique of the common law, his ideas on definition, and his substantive proposals. See R. Harrison, *Bentham* (London, 1983); L. J. Hume, *Bentham and Bureaucracy* (Cambridge, 1981); D. G. Long, *Bentham on Liberty: Jeremy Bentham's Idea of Liberty in relation to his Utilitarianism* (Toronto, 1977); D. Lyons, *In the Interest of the Governed* (Oxford, 1973); F. Rosen, *Jeremy Bentham and Representative Democracy* (Oxford, 1983); and J. Steintrager, *Bentham* (Ithaca, NY, 1977). For older studies, see D. Baumgardt, *Bentham and the Ethics of Today* (Princeton, 1952); M. Mack, *Jeremy Bentham: An Odyssey of Ideas 1748–92* (London, 1962); and E. Halévy, *The Growth of Philosophic Radicalism* (London, 1928).

[2] See *Of Laws in General*, ed. H. L. A. Hart (London, 1970; henceforth *OLG*), 185; *Truth v. Ashhurst*, in *The Works of Jeremy Bentham*, ed. J. Bowring, 11 vols. (Edinburgh, 1838–43; henceforth as *Works*), v. 231–7 at 235; *A Comment on the Commentaries and a Fragment on Government*, ed. J. H. Burns and H. L. A. Hart (London, 1977; henceforth *Comment/Fragment*), 197–9. For a discussion of the paradox of the law being at the same time arbitrary and inflexible, see Postema, *Bentham and the Common Law Tradition*, 280. See also S. R. Letwin, *The Pursuit of Certainty: David Hume, Jeremy Bentham, John Stuart Mill, Beatrice Webb* (Cambridge, 1964), 164.

[3] See Bentham to Revd John Forster, *The Correspondence of Jeremy Bentham*, vol. ii, ed. T. L. S. Sprigge (London, 1968), 100.

in place of the dog-law, there would be a body of clearly defined rules for judges to apply; in place of the technical rigidity of common law procedure would come flexibility in adjudication, with an absence of strictly defined procedural rules.[4]

Historians are divided over what type of code Bentham envisaged. On the one hand historians like L. J. Hume and S. R. Letwin have argued that it should be wholly comprehensive, so that judges would adjudicate in a fairly mechanical manner following the substantive rules of the code. This interpretation rests on Bentham's persuasion that social reality had a structure that could be uncovered by classification, so that it was possible to outline all possible modes of action.[5] On the other side, Gerald Postema has argued that Bentham's theory of adjudication was much more flexible than has hitherto been realized. For Postema, Bentham's theory of law was built on a commitment to a direct-utilitarian theory of practical reasoning: by this, the code guaranteed a co-ordination of social interaction and secured expectations, but guaranteed that, at case level, the practical reasoning of the judges would remain a direct-utilitarian one that could dispense with the code. The Benthamic code was thus only a broad set of principles which could be fleshed out by reference to utility, and the judges could ignore the code when utility dictated.[6]

Bentham is an ambiguous character, and there is room for both interpretations. It may even be argued that both are true, for there is a tension between Bentham the legislator and Bentham the adjudicator. We should not be surprised to find major tensions in Bentham's work. First, as David Lieberman has shown, he changed his view of what he was doing in the 1770s, moving from a Digest to a Pannomion. At the same time that he was writing a critique of

---

[4] For an examination of Bentham's view that the common law failed as a system of rules, see G. J. Postema, 'The Expositor, the Censor and the Common Law', *Canadian Journal of Philosophy*, ix (1979), 643–70.

[5] L. J. Hume, *Bentham and Bureaucracy*, 170–4, 60–75; S. R. Letwin, *The Pursuit of Certainty* 128. See also Long, *Bentham on Liberty*, 100, 151; E. Halévy, *The Growth of Philosophic Radicalism*, 27–8.

[6] G. J. Postema, *Bentham and the Common Law Tradition*, 147, 403–39. My interpretation of the function of the code will agree with Postema's at 428–34. However, it will be suggested that the code had a slightly stronger function than Postema suggests (405, 454) and that judges would not be free to make utilitarian adjudications case by case, possibly by-passing and without feeding into the code. For an alternative interpretation, see the important argument of P. J. Kelly, in *Utilitarianism and Distributive Justice: Jeremy Bentham and the Civil Law* (Oxford, 1990).

Blackstone and the common law concept of law, he was outlining his key visions of positive law for the rest of his life. Second, Bentham was to an important degree starting from scratch. Not only did English law lack clear substantive rules, it equally lacked an analytical vocabulary. The common law in the eighteenth century was still based on an oral tradition, not a dogmatic one. Lacking a Roman base, England could not produce a Pothier or Thibaut or Savigny, since the English analyst had no clear foundation of concepts to build on. Devising a code and devising an analytical system thus went hand in hand. Bentham's analytical disquisitions are traditionally seen as being the theoretical precursors for his complete code; yet it may equally be argued that much of Bentham's codifying of the law served as a vehicle towards the building of a dogmatic system.

In fact, we can see two Benthams at the same time: one aiming to construct an ideal all-comprehensive real code of laws to be put into practice (a code of rules), another the critic of the common law, developing a metaphysics of law with which to reform the mass of common law materials (a code of concepts). These two Benthams reflect the two problems he was addressing. Blackstone's failure to show the common law as a united body of rules induced Bentham to seek to throw away the common law and start again; but the problem Blackstone ignored of knowing how judges came to decisions in concrete cases was also one Bentham addressed that took him in a different direction. Bentham was known best in his life as a reformer, and hence it is the first view that has traditionally prevailed. Indeed, it is clear that he envisaged drawing up large and extensive substantive codes of laws for any government that would let him, offering his services to President Madison of the United States, as well as several Latin American and Southern European states in the 1820s.[7] Throughout his life, Bentham drew up codes of Penal, Civil, and Procedural Law, culminating in the 1820s with his *Constitutional Code*. Moreover, he remained resolute in his commit-

---

[7] *Codification Proposal*, in *Works*, iv. 535–94. See M. Williford, *Jeremy Bentham on Spanish America* (Baton Rouge, 1980). For discussion of Bentham on codification, see Dean Alfange Jr., 'Bentham and the Codification of Law', *Cornell Law Review*, lv (1969), 58–77; T. DiFilippo, 'Jeremy Bentham's Codification Proposals and some remarks on their place in history', *Buffalo Law Review*, xxii (1972–3), 239–51; and L. Radzinowicz, *A History of English Criminal Law and its Administration from 1750*, 4 vols. (London, 1948–68), iii. 431–47. See also, M. Berger, 'Codification', in E. Attwool, *Perspectives in Jurisprudence* (Glasgow, 1977), 142–59.

ment to a complete code, seeing it in 1828, at the time of the wave of law reform, as being 'altogether indispensable', while consolidation was 'unendurable' and the mere reinforcement of the corrupt system.[8] Yet the most salient feature of Bentham's substantive proposals—whether in the form of writing a code or even in the more modest project of building and running his Panopticon—was their failure. Not only did he fail to get any government to adopt his code, but he never managed to complete a satisfactory one. Yet his ideas and his approach to law were highly influential. We must therefore distinguish between codification as an idea and as a substantive proposal.

The interpretation one takes of Bentham's jurisprudence depends on one's interpretation of his intentions for his code.[9] His positivism seems to lend itself most naturally to a rule-utilitarian interpretation. If we view Bentham as the positivist antagonist of the common law and its way of working, and ally this to his epistemological speculations on the possibility of uncovering all the springs of human action, and to his role as the man who wanted to throw away the common law, then we must see his code as a deductive antithesis to the common law system.[10] It will be seen, however, that

[8] Bentham was therefore very dismissive of Peel's efforts, tartly remarking that 'Judge and Co.' could now be renamed 'Peel and Co.'. He dismissed consolidation because 'it saves trouble to Co. in statute hunting; while, to Lay gents, by having the all-pervading fiction of Judge-made law unexpelled, it leaves the rule of action as unknowable as ever'. University College, London, Bentham MSS, Box lxxxv, fos. 87–90 (henceforth as UC lxxxv. 87–90).

[9] This may also be related to Bentham's radical politics. Bentham's most complete substantive codes, particularly the *Constitutional Code*, formed part of his radical political project. Much of his analytical work, particularly in the 1770s, was aimed at improving legal reasoning as it existed. It may thus be argued that while Bentham in the 1820s may have wanted the kind of rigid substantive system as outlined in the *Constitutional Code*, he also wanted at the same time to influence practising lawyers not convinced by the need to reform root and branch through his analytical jurisprudence. At any event, it may be suggested that the desire for a complete and rigid code was a *political* one rather than a *legal* one. This may explain the different types of projects he engaged in during the 1820s, discussed below. For Bentham and radicalism, see J. R. Dinwiddy, 'Bentham's Transition to Political Radicalism, 1809–10', *Journal of the History of Ideas*, xxxvi (1975), 683–700 and Douglas Long, 'Censorial Jurisprudence and Political Radicalism: A Reconsideration of the Early Bentham', *Bentham Newsletter*, no. XII (1988), 4–23.

[10] The difficulty with seeing him as a direct-utilitarian is that it appears to undermine his theory of law: if there were complete flexibility in adjudication, and the rules of the code were only loose guides to expectation, the system could be as capricious at case level, and as unpredictable, as the common law one. In so far as it sought to avoid precedents, it would make the system one of adjudication, but would

Bentham's rigid deductive code was practically unworkable as a system of law. On the other hand, if we examine Bentham's code as an analytical code of concepts, we can make better sense of the possibility he allowed of flexibility in adjudication.

Bentham was best known in the first guise, not least because his analytical work on the nature of law remained unpublished until the twentieth century. Much of this analytical work is concerned with looking at the law which existed, and trying to make sense of it. It will be argued in this and the following chapter that Bentham's rejection of Blackstone led him to a desire to make a complete body of rules, but that the more he developed his theory of law, the less feasible this became. The complete Pannomion was an unworkable aspiration, though it could serve as an ideal-type against which to measure real law. Ultimately, the thrust of Bentham's jurisprudence was less the building of a code of complete rules than the constructing of one of concepts; yet, as we shall see, Bentham, drawn increasingly into substantive code making, never succeded in devising an analytical code.

This has important ramifications. If we view him as favouring flexible adjudication and differences in law at case level, it may be seen that his system was not dissimilar to the common law one; and that his prime intention was therefore not to rewrite the substantive law in its entirety, but to alter the way men *thought* about it. Yet this means that, at the point of adjudication, we can see him as neither a rule-utilitarian nor a direct-utilitarian: we can see rather that his flexible adjudicative system would in some degree reflect a simplified, pruned version of the common law one.

Bentham's Pannomion

(i) *The Deductive Code*

Bentham's desire to codify was inspired by his critique of the common law which was shaped by his positivist conception of the law as a set of rules to guide conduct. Law was a positive institution: it existed to focus expectations, to provide security, and to co-

---

hardly allow the growth of *law* in Bentham's sense. Postema points out that the theory of adjudication he argued for Bentham had some problems of coherence: *Bentham and the Common Law Tradition*, 440–64.

ordinate social interaction.[11] The most important thing was for law to be known and understood: and hence the notion of command was central to the notion of law.[12] It had to be expressed through rules for 'it is only by means of a rule that any moving force can be applied to the active faculty, or any guide [be given] to the intellectual . . . [or] any instruction given'.[13] The problem with the common law was that it failed the rules test. 'Right', Bentham said, 'is the conformity to a rule, wrong the deviation from it: but here there is no rule established, no measure to discern by, no standard to appeal to: all is uncertainty, darkness and confusion.'[14] At best, the common law was a set of rules by fiction, arrived at by treating it as if it were statute.[15] However, in fact the only authoritative part of common law was the decision in the case at hand, the individual command of the judge. As for the body of common law, it consisted of 'a system of *inductions* from those elements, which inductions are unauthoritative, made by every man for himself'.[16] Bentham's critique of the common law was that it offered no general commands to guide conduct, but only particular commands and punishments. The common law was made up 'either 1st of Particular Commands or 2dly of General assertive propositions assumed as the ground of those Commands'.[17] Indeed, the common law could hardly be said to be *law* at all, in so far as a judicial order could not be a law because it did not extend to persons in succession, but only to a case at hand.[18] The command of the common law expired with the case: it was only by inference from the perceived grounds of judgment of the case that any rules, or guide for future action could be found. The rules of common law were therefore inferred by every man 'at hazard'. However, '[t]o serve as ingredients in a system of Law, we must have not ideas of individual articles of conduct, but ideas of sorts of articles of conduct'.[19] In common law, each man drew his own conclusions from the individual case: but there was no guarantee of agreement.

---

[11] See Postema, *Bentham and the Common Law Tradition*, 147–90. See also his 'Bentham on the Public Character of Law', *Utilitas*, i (1989), 41–61.
[12] See UC lxix. 104.
[13] *Pannomial Fragments* in *Works*, iii. 211–30 at 215.
[14] *OLG* 184.   [15] *OLG* 194.
[16] UC lxix. 115. See *Comment/Fragment*, 211, 251 note g.
[17] UC lxix. 119.   [18] UC lxix. 98.
[19] UC lxix. 108, 115, 151.

Hence, it was impossible to focus on any rule of the common law:

To the whole mass together we give the name of common law: but take any article of it (separately) from the rest, we know not what name to give it . . . we know in general, at least we recognize I suppose when we are told as much, that the office of law is to command: that that is called common law must therefore exert itself somehow or other in commands. But to pick out any such proposition or any greater parcel, and to understand how it concurs to the imposing of a command, this is what appears not to have been ever so much as thought of.[20]

All that could be done was to look at the mass of common law cases and to tease a rule out of them: but even this method failed, for every case was made up of an infinity of circumstances, the majority of which were not reported.[21]

Bentham's rule-based concept of law informed his attacks on judicial legislation and his arguments that the function of the judge and the legislator should be kept distinct.[22] For Bentham, arbitrariness was the worst feature law could have: he therefore preferred a system of *stare decisis*, where judges were bound by the rule in the first case, to a system allowing flexibility.[23] For the same reason, Bentham in the mid-1770s favoured the setting up of an authoritative system of law reporting. Even if the reports were bad, the subject would be better off, having something he could trust. Only authenticated reports could be quoted—these portable in small-print volumes going back only to the Revolution—and each year new cases would be added, the most recent first.[24] The reports would be extensively indexed, so that 'a Catalogue might be formed of all the topics that would come under consideration'.[25] Only through consistency in cases could people know what to expect in law, and thence know how to guide their actions. Bentham's attacks on the method of the common law thus reflected his statist views, of the sovereign through law directing the actions of its subordinates,[26]

---

[20] UC lxix. 111.

[21] One had to look to the judicial record of the case, but '[t]his record being copied from precedents of the darkest antiquity instead of being a complete history of the case which it purports to be the record, is in fact a partial and imperfect history . . . applied to [the new] case in question it is in consequence . . . imperfect'. OLG 185.

[22] *Comment/Fragment*, 223–4.

[23] *Comment/Fragment*, 196–7. See Postema, *Bentham and the Common Law Tradition*, 193 ff for a discussion.

[24] UC lxx(a). 118, 128.   [25] UC lxx(a). 137.

[26] See G. Himmelfarb, 'The Haunted House of Jeremy Bentham', in her *Victorian Minds* (London, 1968), 32–81. For a discussion of Bentham as a theorist for the modern

a concept quite different from the common lawyers'. Indeed, Bentham's concept of legislation and sovereignty was bound to lead him to reject the common law, for even the most rigid common law system, following precedent in a mechanical way, would be imperfect as a method of creating rules.

The practical implications of Bentham's legislative view were profound.[27] Bentham held that judges both should not and could not legislate: *ex post facto* decisions made a rule for the punished party, but made no future direct rule, since the judge's command was limited to the case. Hence, law required positive rules to be imposed by the legislator; but if the role of judges was to be limited to applying pre-determined rules, then the code of legislation needed to be complete. Bentham argued in *Of Laws in General* that in the code there could be no law which was not complete, because this was the only place where the legislative will was laid out: while one could look at different parts of the code, one could not look beyond it.[28] Bentham had high ambitions: if there were any ambiguous passages, which required the assistance of a dictionary or interpretation to elicit the meaning, then the code would not be complete, for to use a dictionary was to make its author the superior legislator, 'to interpret a law is to alter it'.[29] To be complete, 'all exemptive clauses expressive of all the grounds of exemption . . . should be set down'.[30]

However, if he was to jettison the common law, Bentham needed a theory to prove that it was possible for legislation to provide every rule to make judicial legislation redundant. He had to show that it was logically and epistemologically possible to create a system of law that was rational, coherent, and valid. He needed a deductive system: what Blackstone attempted to do within the bounds of the common law, Bentham tried to do from scratch. Bentham thus wrote of his project, 'This is not an assemblage of unconnected observations: it is a systematical [work] in which the minutest positions are regularly deduced as consequences from the most general and important principles.'[31] He declared his aim to be to 'compose a work

economic age, see J. Annette, 'Bentham's Fear of Hobgoblins: Law, Political Economy and Social Discipline', in B. Fine *et al.*, *Capitalism and the Rule of Law: From Deviancy Theory to Marxism* (London, 1979), 65–75. See also N. Rosenblum, *Bentham's Theory of the Modern State* (Cambridge, Mass., 1978).

[27] For a discussion of the development of theories of legislation, see J. H. Burns, *The Fabric of Felicity: The Legislator and the Human Condition* (London, 1967).
[28] *OLG* 158.   [29] *OLG* 159, 163.
[30] *OLG* 168.   [31] UC xxvii. 110.

in which admitting the principle of utility (as a postulate) the politician might find a solution of every question tha[t] can arise upon the subject of punishment'.[32]

Bentham's ambition was hence analogous to Blackstone's. Like the commentator, he aimed to unite substantive law and jurisprudence in one structure, where substantive law would follow from theoretical rigour. It was only in proportion as one understood terms and concepts that one could come to grips with law in practice.[33] Thus, as Bentham saw it in 1780, the work would have three parts: an Institutional part to show the relation of the several provisions that followed, to show the method that was used in the work, and to show that it was exhaustive; the operative part, divided into the main text and a glossary; and the justificative part to explain the reasons for the provisions in the operative part.[34] The main text of the operative part would be accessible to the public,[35] the justificative part being kept in the form of notes. Similarly, in the *Constitutional Code*, Bentham wrote that all existing law would have to be abolished, the new system replacing it having the rationale behind every regulation defined before law was enacted.[36] Bentham's aim was hence to make law into a science where rationality and connection would take the place of disorder, where the form and matter of law would be reconciled, with the form revealing the rationale of the law and guaranteeing cognoscibility.[37]

For Bentham, the foundations of the ideal code lay in a correct epistemology, in discovering a 'natural' arrangement of law, 'which takes such properties to characterize [laws] by, as men in general are, by the common constitution of man's *nature*, disposed to attend to'.[38] It seemed possible to him to legislate for all actions, thereby removing the need for judicial legislation, because it was possible to classify and take into account all men's needs, and all aspects of their

---

[32] UC xxvii. 111. Later, he spoke of clarifying the law of evidence, in a way to 'put men's reason in a train; and . . . furnish fundamental principles from whence by an easy deduction, they might proceed to conclusion which should point directly at that mark'. UC xxvii. 125.

[33] *A General View of a Complete Code of Laws*, in *Works*, iii (henceforth *General View*), 155–210 at 158.   [34] UC xxvii. 118.

[35] It 'ought to be read over once or often in the course of the year by being distributed into portions as the Bible is according to the order appointed in the English Liturgy.' UC xxvii. 118.

[36] *Constitutional Code*, in *Works*, ix. 1–3. (henceforth *Constitutional Code*).

[37] *Codification Proposal*, in *Works*, iv. 539–44.

[38] *Comment/Fragment*, 415.

nature. Through Bentham's method of classification and organization, the complete code would be set, a system which would be
concise, clear, compact, and complete:[39]

> In a system thus constructed upon this plan, a man need but open the book
> in order to inform himself what the aspect borne by the law bears to every
> imaginable act that can come within the possible sphere of human agency:
> what acts it is his duty to perform for the sake of himself, his neighbour or
> the public: what acts he has a right to do, what other acts he has a right to
> have others perform for his advantage, whatever he has either to fear or to
> hope from the law.[40]

This system would leave 'no *terrae incognitae*, no blank spaces'.[41]
Although in *Of Laws in General* he talked of the vast expanse of
jurisprudence being 'collected and condensed into a compact sphere
which the eye at a moment's warning can traverse in all imaginable
directions', this did not mean that the code would be a simple overall
map of the law. Bentham held that the law did not have to be wholly
covered in a single code, for he argued that provided every
individual could easily get access to that aspect of the law that he
was concerned with, it was irrelevant how bulky the Pannomion
itself was.[42] His plan was this: 'let the whole mass of legislative
matter be broken down into parts, carried out in such sort, that in
hand, and thence in mind, each man may receive that portion in
which he has a personal and peculiar concern, apart from all matter
in which he has no concern'.[43] One could have any number of codes,
provided one knew where to look when one wanted, something
guaranteed by a system of cross-references.[44] Bentham argued that

---

[39] *Papers Relative to Codification and Public Instruction*, in *Works*, iv. 451–533 at 480.
[40] *OLG* 246.
[41] Bentham said that his code would have to include many provisions which might
seem of little use to the general multitude, but that these were necessary since the
legislator had to anticipate all evils. When the code was complete, 'villainy can not plot
nor can imagination conceive that injury/mischief against which the law has not made
provision of a remedy'. UC xxvii. 122, 144.
[42] *Nomography; Or the Art of Inditing Laws*, in *Works*, iii (henceforth *Nomography*),
231–83 at 239. The code would be divided '[s]o as each individual have but the
advantage and comfort of beholding effectually within his reach—within the reach of
his purse, as well as of the mastery of his mind, whatsoever parts he is in any way
concerned in point of interest to be acquainted with, the bulk of the whole, how vast
soever, is with reference to him a matter of indifference: overbulkiness is not with
relation to him among the properties that belong to it.'
[43] *Nomography*, 255.
[44] This system of cross-references was elaborated in the *General View*. The divisions
he proposed were the central one of substantive and adjective law, and others such as

every man should be able to be his own lawyer, for not only could many not afford to hire expensive barristers, but no one knew a man's interest better than he did himself.[45] This was no idle hope: it was a practical proposal that there should not only be guidelines for general conduct, but also the supporting legislated detail to allow any man to check minutiae.

Hence, the key division was that between penal law and civil law. The penal law had logical primacy, for one could only conceive of law through the notion of an offence. However, no law was purely penal or purely civil, but rather any law comprised both. Therefore, the division between the two was not a logical but a typographical one. The bare act that was commanded was simple and could be covered within a short span: it was the circumstances belonging to it that were 'capable of being infinitely diversified'. Thus, the penal part was the commanding part of law, the civil was the expository part: or, the penal law was the skeleton, the civil law the flesh.[46]

Indeed, this system of division was for Bentham not merely practically desirable but a conceptual necessity. For Bentham, a complete law consisted of everything connected with a single command or rule: a law was only complete when everything concerning it had been taken into consideration. If a legislated command had no qualifications or expository matter (such as 'thou shalt not ,kill'), it was complete; but 'if it has expositions, it is not complete without those expositions: if qualifications, without those qualifications'.[47] Thus, a genus of offences was not completely defined until 'all the circumstances are described by which the act in question may be attended'. In reality, any enumeration of all the circumstances in which an act was prohibited 'would be to give a description of all the phaenomena that are observable in the world': for that reason, the shorter way was to enumerate the circumstances in which the act was not prohibited.[48]

The key to the Benthamic code was therefore to be the rational deductive method. Bentham argued that while it was impossible to

direct/indirect, general/particular, and permanent/transitory. Similarly, he discussed the need for separate codes for different areas of law, such as codes for penal, civil, constitutional, international, maritime, military, ecclesiastical, financial, and procedural law. *General View*, 157, 200 ff., and *Papers Relative to Codification*, 451–60. See also Lieberman, *The Province of Legislation Determined*, 269.

[45] *Papers Relative to Codification*, 482–3.   [46] *OLG* 198, UC xxx. 41–2.
[47] *OLG* 157.   [48] UC lxix. 35.

foresee every possible circumstance, the legislator could nevertheless foresee every species of offence likely to emerge. '[B]e the
occasion what it may, if *in specie* the language cannot always be all-
comprehensive . . . yet *in genere* it may always be: and, as every
individual is contained within its species, so is every species within
its *genus*.'[49] Thus, while the code would not be absolutely precise on
all details, the details could be deduced from the specific provisions
that did exist within the code. Indeed, when Bentham noted in the
passage just quoted that one could not cover every detail, but only
species, it was only after he had stressed, with great force, that the
legislator should seek all-comprehensiveness. For Bentham, the code
would be complete and vast—'[w]hatever is not in the code of laws,
ought not to be law'.[50] The details left out by the code would be
minute indeed.

(ii) Natural Procedure

The corollary of the defined code would be an undefined procedure.[51] For Bentham, the law of procedure was an adjective law to
the substantive law of the code, and the only point in having a
procedural law was to accomplish the will manifested in the
substantive law.[52] Bentham hated the technicalities of common law
procedure, feeling that all was designed to frustrate the litigants, and
to earn lawyers and judges as much money as possible.[53] In its place,
he proposed a 'natural' procedure, which involved giving as much
freedom to the judge as possible. However, flexible procedure
depended upon the existence of a well-defined substantive code, for
the law of procedure had no validity except when tested against the
substantive law:

As in fact every act by which a course of procedure is commenced has for its
end or object, the bringing about the execution of some law of the
substantive class, so, in point of utility, it may be said that the course of

---

[49] *Codification Proposal*, 538.   [50] *General View*, 205.

[51] For examinations of Bentham on procedure, see W. Twining, *Theories of Evidence:
Bentham and Wigmore* (London, 1985); M. I. Zagday, 'Bentham on Civil Procedure', in
G. W. Keeton and G. Schwarzenberger, *Jeremy Bentham and the Law* (London, 1948),
68–78, and G. W. Keeton and O. R. Marshall, 'Bentham's Influence on the Law of
Evidence', in ibid. 79–100. See also, G. J. Postema, 'The Principle of Utility and the
Law of Procedure: Bentham's Theory of Adjudication', *Georgia Law Review*, XI (1977),
1393–1424.

[52] See *Principles of Judicial Procedure*, in *Works*, ii. 1–188.

[53] See ibid. 46–8.

procedure ought to have in every instance, for its main and primary end at least, the accomplishment of the will manifested in the body of the substantive laws.[54]

This was an important idea, for it confirms the fact that judges would make adjudications by reference to a clear body of deductive rules for all situations. '[T]he substantive code should, as mathematicians say, be given, or the adjective can have no meaning,' he said, 'the substantive being throughout a necessary object of reference.'[55] Given that there would be a clear substantive code, with a defined will for every circumstance, there could be a simple procedure. Thus, the reverse side of his abhorring the absence of rules in the common law was Bentham's abhorrence of its procedures.

Bentham argued that the procedures in English courts served directly to frustrate justice, for they encouraged mendacity and vexatious suits, and served to cause clients huge expenses and delays before any settlement was reached. The whole system seemed to be founded with the aim of gathering fees. Just as all men sought to maximize their interests via their actions, so judges, who were the authors of procedural rules, used this opportunity to maximize their profits, in diametrical opposition to the interests of those who sought justice.[56] The end of the technical system was thus to collect fees and to remunerate the judges, by multiplying the steps necessary before the case was heard; the means used to this end was to extend a tissue of lies, 'the instruments, by which on every occasion the dirty part of [the judges'] work was done'.[57] The crowning part of this system of mendacity was to be found in the system of special pleas, whose very art was that of forgery and libel to obtain better fees.[58] Bentham found it absurd that a man could win a case upon technicalities, that he could be acquitted on a charge merely because a written plea had been improperly drafted. Because of this, he argued, the law was in effect taken out of the hands of the parties and judges and put into the hands of those who drew up the

---

[54] *Principles of Judicial Procedure*, 6.   [55] Ibid. 15.

[56] Ibid. 12–16. In *Scotch Reform*, in *Works*, v. 1–53 at 6–7, he similarly said that the aim of the technical system was to exact fees: 'System of procedure generated by the influence of this sinister interest, the *technical* or *fee-gathering* system: technical from its nature; fee-gathering from its object and its cause.'

[57] See *Principles of Judicial Procedure*, 12; *Rationale of Judicial Evidence*, in *Works*, vi. 269 and vii. 199 ff.

[58] *Rationale of Judicial Evidence*, in *Works*, vi. 307. Bentham added, 'forgery carries men to the gallows, special pleading to the bench'.

pleas. Thus, Bentham complained that the 'power of granting effectual pardon to all criminals—murderers in particular, not excepted—belongs incontestably to every person by whom the function of penning the instrument of accusation is performed'.[59] English procedure was not merely nonsensical, but also dangerous: 'if rogues did but know all the pains that the law has taken for their benefit, honest men would have nothing left they could call their own'.[60] What is noteworthy in his analysis of English procedure is the absence of any recognition of the practitioner's view of pleading outlined above. From first to last, Bentham saw the common law of procedure as being the gravy-train of Judge & Co. alone.[61]

In place of this, Bentham sought to establish a natural system, with almost no rules at all, based on common sense and common experience. It was a system that was universal, and that would need none of the procedural divisions and differences to be found in the English division of courts.[62] Bentham's theory was designed to avoid a number of evils associated with the technical system: frustration of well-grounded claims and allowance of ill-grounded claims, expense, vexation, delay, precipitation, and complication. To that end, he made numerous proposals in the *Principles of Judicial Procedure* and in the *Constitutional Code*. There would be only one judge per judicatory, who would be omnicompetent, able to hear every type of cause. The system was to be an elaborate form of summary jurisdiction, with local courts in every district, easily accessible.[63] Justice was to be cheap and readily available—indeed, Bentham even went so far as to suggest that the judge should always be on call, sleeping in court to be available for night duty.[64]

---

[59] *Principles of Judicial Procedure*, 14.

[60] *Rationale of Judicial Evidence*, in *Works*, vi. 205.

[61] Bentham's ostensible view of common law procedure thus seemed informed more by invective than by an understanding of the theory of pleading, and has led some to argue that he was less successful than Blackstone in accounting for the practice of law in settling cases and determining precedents. See Sir Rupert Cross, 'Blackstone v. Bentham', *Law Quarterly Review*, xcii (1976), 516–27. However, Bentham's rhetoric was deceptive of his understanding: see below.

[62] *Principles of Judicial Procedure*, 7.

[63] *Constitutional Code*, 473: 'Conceive the seat of the principal justice chamber, to be in a town, occupying the middle of the square: in such sort, that from the spot the most remote from the justice chamber, a grown person, in a state of ordinary health and strength, will be able to travel on foot, from his or her place of residence to and from the justice chamber in the course of any day of 24 hours, without sleeping elsewhere than at home: an interval of—say six hours—being left for the performance of the judicial service.'   [64] *Constitutional Code*, 541.

The aim was to allow the judge and the parties direct access to one another, and to allow the judge the scope to determine the precise point at issue. It is apparent how strong Bentham's notion of domestic justice was, and how deeply he loathed the system of pleading, where the matter of dispute was decided before the parties came to court. Thus, he wrote,

Father of a family! when you have a dispute to settle between two of your children, do you ever begin by driving them from your presence?—do you send them to attorney, special pleader, serjeant or barrister? Think you that by any such assistance, any better chance would be afforded you for coming at the truth, than by hearing what the parties had to say for themselves?[65]

Bentham would thus do away with pleas entirely, and would allow the judge to hear everything that might be relevant, directly from the mouths of the parties. He put his simplified proposals forward in *Scotch Reform*, where he contrasted the natural system with the technical one. In the natural system, the parties would confront each other face to face, giving *viva voce* testimony in simple day-to-day language before a single judge who would hear the whole cause in a single sitting. Truth was the watchword of the court, and the judge had to give his reasons for the decision he came to.[66] For all the looseness of procedure, however, the case had to revolve around the dictates of 209 substantive law.

This, then, would be the reverse of the common law method: a strong code of rules, a flexible code of procedure. It required a Herculean legislator, but this was not something that daunted Bentham:

Lawyer.—And so you look upon it as possible, do you, sir, to compose a complete body of statute law, extending over all causes, as well as over all persons?
Non-lawyer.—Indeed I do, sir; and, for these fifty years or more, the more I have thought of the task, the greater does the facility of it appear to me. Not

---

[65] *Justice and Codification Petitions*, in *Works*, v. 437–548, at 450. For other examples of Bentham's ideal of domestic justice, see *Rationale of Judicial Evidence*, in *Works*, vi. 505 and *Justice and Codification Proposals*, 446.

[66] *Principles of Judicial Procedure*, 29: 'On each individual occasion, as a security for the maximization of the aggregate of good, and the minimization of the aggregate of evil, he will settle in his own mind, and make public declaration of, the reasons by the consideration of which his conduct has been determined; which reasons will consist in the allegation of so many items in the account of evil, on both sides: magnitude, propinquity, certainty, or say probability and extent,—being in relation to each head of good and evil, taken into the account.'

a cause is ever decided, or, so much as begun, but all this, though never done, is supposed to be done. Which, according to you, is productive of most labour and most difficulties?—to form an article of real law once and for all; or by an endless series of suppositions never realized, to make it over and over again in the imagination?[67]

The Benthamic code therefore would allow flexibility in the handling of procedure and the receiving of evidence, but the judge was not to be allowed the same flexibility in substantive matters.[68] Bentham's legislator was to have 'one eye that of an eagle: the other that of a mole'.[69]

The Incomplete Code

This glance suggests that Bentham indeed felt that the legislator could start from scratch and encompass within his code all manner of foreseeable circumstances, so that all old law could be thrown away and be replaced by a new static system.[70] However, it can be seen that Bentham's ambition to form a complete deductive code a priori was logically impossible, in two ways. First, his theory of man could never descend into sufficient details for such a complete epistemology as was required by his code to be formed. This was also complicated because of the relationship between men's expectations and the law. Second, Bentham's theory of how rules worked in action, and how they were devised, was more subtle than the 'one-way' process that was implied by the legislative theory given above.

---

[67] *Rationale of Judicial Evidence*, in *Works*, vii. 271. See also UC xxvii. 144: 'When the code has that degree of amplitude and discrimination which it ought to have and which it has been here understood to give it, villainy cannot plot nor can imagination conceive that injury/mischief against which the law has not made provision of a remedy.'

[68] Thus, Bentham wrote of his system of ready written pleas, 'On the part of the plaintiff, a description of the demand in this permanent form is in general necessary for the use of the judge; to the end that, in the event of its being acceded to by him, the decision, the judgment, pronounced by him, and the execution of that judgment, may be sure to be correspondent to it.' *Rationale of Judicial Evidence*, in *Works*, vii. 271.

[69] UC xxvii. 152.

[70] Bentham wrote, 'What is to be done with the body of statutes now subsisting? What is to be done with the Roman Law? Burn them.' UC xxvii. 123. In putting forward his codification ideas, Bentham further stressed that decisions concerning the construction of words should not be preserved, since the construction of words applied to particular circumstances was a question of fact. UC lxix. 31. His essentially static view of his code can be seen in his proposal of 1780: 'Once in a hundred years let the Laws be revised, for the sake of changing such terms and expressions as by that time may have become obsolete.' UC c. 91.

This can be seen especially in his view of how the civil law grew from below. Similarly, it can be seen that Bentham's purported natural procedure was in fact much more technical than it seemed, being in a sense a purified form of common law adjudication.

(i) Expectations and Sensibilities

It will be argued in this section that because Bentham's concept of law was based on the sociological notion of a habit of obedience, and hence on the idea that law had to reflect popular needs and fulfil popular expectations, he was compelled, in the attempt to construct a perfect code, to discover in full detail the motives and sensibilities which conditioned people's expectations. This, it will be seen, was impossible, which in turn meant that the attempt to create a perfect deductive code was flawed.[71]

For Bentham, 'the ultimate efficient cause . . . of the power of the sovereign is neither more nor less than the disposition to obedience on the part of the people'.[72] This idea, and its importance for Bentham's concept of sovereignty, has had much discussion in recent years.[73] As H. L. A. Hart has pointed out, for Bentham, the sovereign's legislative powers were not conferred by law nor by any 'duty-generating transaction or social relationship',[74] but instead they came from 'a social situation for the description of which no normative terms were required'. This social situation was the habit of people to obey. Much of the debate about Bentham's concept of the habit of obedience has focused on the question of the validity of

---

[71] Karl Olivecrona has argued that Bentham attempted an empirical investigation of the facts to which law applied, but failed to succeed in his empirical task because he began with a preconceived idea of law as the expression of the sovereign will alone. It will be shown here that the empirical investigation undermined Bentham's concept as a prescriptive formula. See 'The Will of the Sovereign: Some Reflections on Bentham's Concept of "a Law"', *American Journal of Jurisprudence*, xx (1975), 95–110. In his important recent study of Bentham's civil law writing, P. J. Kelly suggests that Bentham's theory was based on a psychological hedonism that was concerned with the pursuit of pleasure as a final efficient cause of action, not on an egoism that was empirically true in every case, with every action directly being concerned with seeking pleasure. Hence, he argues that Bentham did not seek mathematical precision in defining the springs of action. *Utilitarianism and Distributive Justice*, 25–68.

[72] *OLG* 18n.

[73] See H. L. A. Hart, 'Sovereignty and Legally Limited Government', in his *Essays on Bentham: Studies in Jurisprudence and Political Theory* (Oxford, 1982), 220–42; and J. H. Burns, 'Bentham on Sovereignty: an Exploration', *Northern Ireland Legal Quarterly*, xxiv (1973), 399–416. See also Postema, *Bentham and the Common Law Tradition*, 220 ff.

[74] Hart, *Essays on Bentham*, 221.

laws. That is, many writers feel that Bentham did not use the habit of obedience as a test for any specific legislated rule, but only as a test for the right of the sovereign to legislate; so that people would obey rules they saw as valid, even if they opposed the content.[75]

However, we may go further, to argue that it was not merely the validity of a law, but its utility, that was under the people's scrutiny.[76] For Bentham, the subjects did not only watch for the validity of laws, but also their usefulness. While he agreed that defined limits to the sovereign might be useful signs to tell men when rebellion was in order, in the end all was a question of feeling: '[i]t is the principle of *utility*, accurately apprehended and steadily applied, that affords the only clue to guide a man through these straits'.[77] Bentham elaborated, saying that men would rebel if they felt that the overall good resulting from it would exceed the harm from the uprising. The defined limitation on the sovereign would help here, but it was not the end word: ultimately, the habit of obedience was a sociological concept, not a philosophical one, depending upon what people did in practice in each situation. The habit was 'an affair of calculation: and this calculation each one must make for himself according to circumstances'.[78]

As Bentham put it, where there was no contract between the sovereign and subjects, 'the force and efficacy of the law may depend in a considerable degree on the existence, real or supposed, of some customs to which it is or pretends to be conformable. When therefore a law *in principem* is established having custom for its foundation, the appealing to that custom is a sort of step taken towards the ensuring observance of it'.[79] Furthermore, Bentham made it clear that the motives to obeying any law were not solely

---

[75] Hart argues that '[t]he validity or invalidity of legislation is not to be identified with its effectiveness or ineffectiveness in securing obedience' (*Essays on Bentham*, 234). In Hart's view, single acts of disobedience would not invalidate a law, but there had to be different tests of the law's validity. Cf. Postema, *Bentham and the Common Law Tradition*, 245–55.

[76] The view stressing the validity of a law may be argued to be one which makes Bentham seem more of a contractarian than he was, stressing too heavily the need for a signal before one could rebel. For this might parallel the natural law view that one could rebel if the contract between sovereign and subject were broken. It might similarly be seen to parallel the idea in natural law treatises that one could not challenge an indifferent law on the grounds that it was useless or immoral, provided that it had been promulgated by the sovereign. However, Bentham was distinguished from the natural lawyers in seeing that all laws had to be subject to the test of utility at each stage.   [77] *Comment/Fragment*, 483. See also 491.

[78] *Pannomial Fragments*, 219.   [79] *OLG* 109.

political but also moral and religious:[80] no law could survive which did not have moral and religious support as well as political support.[81] This point was of especial importance when it came to constitutional law, for there were no political sanctions against the sovereign, since the sovereign was the highest political body, and no one could judge the sovereign while it subsisted. Therefore, in constitutional law, the only sanction against the sovereign was the moral one;[82] but this moral one naturally included the disposition to rebel on utilitarian grounds.

This interpretation of the habit of obedience is essential, given Bentham's anxiety to avoid Blackstone's natural law positivism and given his desire for a theory where the rules could be tested at each level. Bentham's notion of law thus extended beyond his conception of it as commanded rules: rules were not to be imposed regardless, but were to be digests of what was acceptable. This is evident in his discussion of expectation. For Bentham, one of the fundamental tasks of law was to secure men's expectations by setting out a framework on which they could be focused.[83] An equally important strand in his theory was the notion that the law was itself as much shaped by people's expectations as it focused them. Law was built up from what people needed and expected, so that it had to conform to popular needs in order to be perceived as useful, and hence as valid. For the law 'is not the master of the dispositions of the human heart: [it] is only their interpreter and their servant'. Hence, '[t]he goodness of the laws depends upon their conformity to the general *expectation*'.[84] In many areas, the law did not define expectation, but followed a strong prior natural expectation. Hence,

There are some laws naturally more easily understood than others; such are, laws conformable to expectations already formed; laws which repose upon *natural* expectations . . . Natural expectation directs itself towards the laws which are most important to society; and the foreigner who should be guilty of theft, fraud, or assassination, would not be permitted to plead his

---

[80] *OLG* 133.   [81] *OLG* 70.

[82] Discussing sanctions against the sovereign, Bentham writes, 'The force of the political sanction is inapplicable to this purpose: by the supposition within the dominion of the sovereign there is no one who while sovereignty subsists can judge so as to coerce the sovereign: to maintain the affirmative would be to maintain a contradiction. But the force of the religious sanction is as applicable to this purpose as to any other . . . [t]he same may be said of the force of the moral sanction.' *OLG* 68–70.

[83] See Postema, *Bentham and the Common Law Tradition*, 147–90.

[84] *Principles of the Civil Code*, in *Works*, i. 297–364, 322. Cf. Postema, 175.

ignorance of the laws of the country, because he could not but have known that acts, so manifestly hurtful, were every where considered as crimes.[85]

For this reason, legislation could not be an a priori science, but had to be founded on empirical investigation. 'Legislation,' wrote Bentham, 'which has hitherto been founded principally upon the quicksands of interest and prejudice, ought to be placed upon the immoveable base of feelings and experience: a moral thermometer is required, which should exhibit every degree of happiness and suffering.'[86] This would be the foundation of the deduction: only when the legislator had resolved and understood the people's aims, aspirations, and desires, could any deductive framework be set up. It was this search for an epistemology to decode people's expectations in every case that Bentham was engaged in in *An Introduction to the Principles of Morals and Legislation* and the *Table of the Springs of Action*. He therefore wrote,

The feelings of men are sufficiently regular to become the object of a science or an art; and till this is done, we can only grope our way by making irregular and ill-directed efforts. Medicine is founded upon the axioms of physical pathology: morals are the medicine of the soul: legislation is the practical branch; it ought, therefore, to be founded upon the axioms of mental pathology.[87]

Bentham wrote that mankind was governed by pleasure and pains, and that this point had to be the foundation of any system of law.[88] In proportion as this was borne in mind, the science would be exact.[89] This meant that the sources and nature of pleasures and pains had to be calculated and quantified, and the first twelve chapters of *An Introduction to the Principles of Morals and Legislation* thus examined in some detail how to measure pleasures and pains, their kinds, and how they affected people's sensibilities and

---

[85] *Principles of the Civil Code*, 323. Bentham said that the law should be anterior to the formation of expectations, so that it could shape them, but he added that there existed a multitude of expectations founded on custom and usage. This reflects the natural lawyers' division of fundamental and indifferent laws: the legislator could shape expectations on matters on which no opinion had hitherto been formed, but he could only follow expectation on fundamentals. Cf. UC lxix. 147: 'It is not difficult therefore to understand, how the same expectation should produce the same action or forbearance even without a law.'

[86] *Principles of the Civil Code*, 304.

[87] Ibid. 304–5. Cf. Harrison, *Bentham*, 141, Long, *Bentham on Liberty*, 100, 124.

[88] *An Introduction to the Principles of Morals and Legislation*, ed. J. H. Burns and H. L. A. Hart (London, 1977; henceforth as *IPML*), 11.   [89] *IPML* 40.

consciousness. One had to be clear on these points before one began to discuss offences and the law.

Pleasures and the avoidance of pain were 'the ends which the legislator has in view: it behoves him to understand their value'.[90] In other words, since pleasures and pains were the instruments the legislator had to work with, he needed a full understanding of their force. This is what Bentham sought to supply in outline. He therefore listed the circumstances which had to be taken into account, both as relating to the individual and to groups. One had to weigh up the intensity, duration, certainty or uncertainty, propinquity or remoteness, fecundity, purity, and extent of a pleasure or a pain, in estimating its value. Using these tools, one could calculate the tendency of any act in the community, by counting all the relative immediate and distant pleasures and pains caused by it on each side and weighing them against each other. It was only in proportion as these things were borne in mind that the science of legislation could be rigorous.

An examination of Bentham's analysis reveals that the sensibilities he enumerated could not be deduced in any logical way, but would vary from case to case. He was therefore enumerating, albeit in an exhaustive manner, things that had to be taken into account. Thus, his 14 simple pleasures—'pure' pleasures which could not be resolved into other entities—were subjective: they were pleasures of sense, wealth, skill, amity, a good name, power, piety, benevolence, malevolence, memory, imagination, expectation, relief, and pleasures dependent on association.[91] 'Of all these several sorts of pleasures and pains,' he wrote, 'there is scarce any one which is not liable, on more accounts than one, to come under the consideration of the law.'[92] The law had to take these things into account: but that did not mean the law could predict their details.

This was particularly true since the same causes of pleasure or pain could produce different effects on different individuals, since people's individual sensibilities affected this influence. The efficacy of any cause of happiness was precarious, for 'in the same mind such and such cause of pain or pleasure will produce more pain or pleasure than such or such other causes of pain or pleasure: and this proportion will in different minds be different'.[93] One man might be influenced most by pleasures of taste, another by pleasures of the

90 *IPML* 38.   91 *IPML* 42.
92 *IPML* 49.   93 *IPML* 51.

ear. This was apparent in the case of wealth distribution: a rich man would get less happiness from an increase in his fortune than a poor man would. Although in his *Principles of the Civil Code* Bentham tried to establish some sort of guideline for the circumstances in which wealth could be divided to produce the greatest happiness, he found it was impossible to make a fixed guide. At some undefinable stage, a rich man's unhappiness at losing money would be the same as the poor man's happiness at receiving it: however the boundaries were impossible to determine.[94]

There were hence always variations in sensibilities to be taken into account. Bentham listed 32 circumstances influencing sensibility. These included moral factors such as 'strength of intellectual powers', 'bent of inclination', 'moral sensibility', and 'sympathetic sensibility' as well as physical factors such as 'sex', 'age', 'insanity', and 'climate', along with what may be dubbed political consider-ations, 'government', 'lineage', and 'religious profession'.[95] The influence of these was not constant either. Thus, one circumstance affecting sensibility was 'antipathy', yet 'there is no primeval and constant source of antipathy in human nature . . . [t]here are no permanent sets of persons who are naturally and of course the objects of antipathy to a man'.[96] It is therefore clear that these were not capable of being integrated into a complete and entire code. Rather, they were factors that had to be taken into account both by the legislator and the judge, in matching the law to people's expect-ations, and making the correct utilitarian laws and judgments.[97] Hence he wrote of the process of summing up pleasures and pains,

It is not to be expected that this process should be strictly pursued previ-ously to every moral judgment, or to every legislative or judicial operation. It may, however, be always kept in view: and as near as the process actually pursued on these occasions approaches to it, so near will such process approach to the character of an exact one.[98]

These detailed pointers were hence more a question for the judge than the legislator. Bentham said that while some factors affected all people,

---

[94] *Principles of the Civil Code*, 305 ff.
[95] *IPML* 52 and ff.   [96] *IPML* 61.
[97] See Kelly, *Utilitarianism and Distributive Justice*, 34–5.
[98] *IPML* 40.

yet in their application to different individuals are susceptible of perhaps an indefinite variety of degrees. These cannot be fully provided for by the legis-lator; but, as the existence of them, in every sort of case, is capable of being ascertained, and the degree in which they take place is capable of being measured, provision may be made for them by the judge.[99]

The precision in exploring sensibilities that Bentham sought would therefore be a precision of *kinds* rather than contents. By his epis-temology, Bentham outlined all the factors he saw that had to be taken into account in the legal process, without being able to show the precise influence of each at ground level. As Mill pointed out, his method could make men clear thinkers, but it could not guarantee completeness. 'It is a security for accuracy,' Mill said, 'but not for comprehensiveness.'[100] The project was to reduce all manner of things until men knew what they were looking for.

Ultimately, therefore, legislation would only be an approximate science, in which exactness would come at case level:

[T]hough each of these propositions may be found false or inexact in each particular case, it will neither militate against their speculative correctness, nor their practical utility. It is sufficient,—1st, if they approach more nearly to the truth than any others which can be substituted for them; and, 2dly, If they may be employed by the legislator, as the foundation of his labours, with less inconvenience than any others.[101]

It would therefore be difficult to create a legislative science a priori from the top down, with the principle of utility as the thread through all.[102]

---

[99] *IPML* 69.

[100] Mill added, 'rather, it is a security for one sort of comprehensiveness, but not for another'. 'Bentham' republished in B. Parekh (ed.), *Jeremy Bentham: Ten Critical Essays* (London, 1974), 1–40 at 11–12.

[101] *Principles of the Civil Code*, 305. Cf. Harrison, *Bentham*, 155.

[102] Kelly has recently argued that the *Table of the Springs of Action* was not meant to provide an exhaustive catalogue of all possible motives, but rather that '[h]e wanted to provide a practical classification of certain basic types of motivation in order to facilitate the legislator's task of constructing a utilitarian science of legislation'. *Utilitarianism and Distributive Justice*, 22. However, we may distinguish the usefulness of the *Table* to the *legislator* and to the *judge*. If the former were to construct a complete code that would omit nothing, then the *Table* would have to be infinitely complete. If he were not, a catalogue of distinct motives to be taken into account in every case and decoded by the judge would be useful to make the process of adjudication more precise. We can hence see the *Table* as a tool as much for judges as legislators.

(ii) Rules and Commands

Bentham criticized the common law for being composed of only inferential rules. In fact, it will be seen here that even in Bentham's schema a rule did not descend to detail, but was only a general guide that described in outline what was done at case level.[103] The law only existed in reality at case level, where the will of the legislator was inextricably bound up with the judgment of the magistrate: it was not a simple matter of application. As shall be seen, in the civil aspect of law, what the parties and the judge did was far more important than what the legislator did: so that we shall see that Bentham's idea of law included its *adoption* as strongly as its enactment.

The fact that the legislator would not descend into every detail can be seen in the distinction Bentham makes between the power of imperation *de singulis*—the power of enacting particular laws or of judging the effect of general laws upon particular people—and the power of imperation *de classibus*, the making of general laws. The latter had a far greater extent than the former, but was 'liable to peculiar limitations by which its force may be diminished or even utterly destroyed'. These limitations, Bentham wrote, gave room for other powers that were complementary. The power of enacting general laws was the power of legislation. This might seem at first sight to be absolute, and to 'absorb as it were into its substance, every other power that could have existence in a state'.[104] However, it was not such an absolute power, since it was too general, being unable to define the precise classes which would compose the whole.

Bentham argued that the legislator's commands were shaped and limited by the language in which they were expressed. He noted,

By these general terms or names, things and persons, acts, and so forth are brought to view in parcels; which parcels are the larger and the more comprehensive in proportion as the extent or logical amplitude (if so it may be called) of such names is the more comprehensible. This being the case the legislator in the grouping of the persons things and acts which he takes for the subjects and objects of his laws is limited to such parcels as correspond to the generic names which are furnished by the language.[105]

---

[103] Its advantage over the common law rule was that it gave a better guide to judges and to the public's expectation.

[104] *OLG* 81.   [105] *OLG* 82.

The legislator was thus limited to broad and general terms, by the nature of the language; but each class was composed of individuals which were too specific and detailed to be covered by the general definition. Thus, while the legislator determined the class, others determined what composed it. Hence, the power of legislating *de classibus* could never be absolute and unlimited—'[i]t can never so much as amount to the entire power of imperation: it will fall short of being equal to that power by so much as is contained in whatever powers of aggregation or disaggregation are established in the state'.[106] In matters of property, ownership was not determined a priori by legislation *de classibus*, but by the power of conveyancing, a power *de singulis* determined in each particular case. The legislator had to adopt conveyances as legally binding; but he could not take notice of them all. All he could do was to describe in general terms the forms he saw proper to adopt—the content of those forms was infinitely variable.[107]

Bentham thus had to acknowledge that his code could not descend into detail. It was only by a general description of their effects rather than by direct specification that individual acts could come under a general class.[108] Thus, he sought to define the narrowest offences definable, the *genera infima*. These stood for vast areas of detail:

Were [no definitions] to be made use of but what would result from the enumeration of all the circumstances necessary to constitute the description of the *species infimae* there would be no such thing as carrying on any discourse upon the subject whatsoever . . . for even one of the generic names now employed it would be necessary to substitute a little volume.[109]

Moreover, the general rule was only one part of the legal process. In the criminal law,

To juries, in most cases belongs in conjunction with the regular judges as also with prosecutors, witnesses and individual officers of justice, and other persons whose share in this power however inconspicuous is not the less real, the power of aggregating persons in most cases to the disadvantageous class of delinquents.[110]

Law and its application required both an act of will and one of judgment. For Bentham, the common law failed to enunciate a real will; but these courts did exercise real and valid judgments. Indeed,

---

[106] *OLG* 91.   [107] *OLG* 180.
[108] *OLG* 23.   [109] *OLG* 175.   [110] *OLG* 88.

the judgment could be expressed in general terms 'and as such may stand as a proposition fit to be tacked on as appenditious matter, to a general command . . . concerning acts of that *sort* of which the particular command in question is'.[111] In statute law, the expression of will was clear, but it could not become real until applied to a case. Bentham argued that a law had two parts—a directive part expressing the will or command, and a predictive part, 'requiring some person to verify the prediction that accompanied the first'. This person was primarily the judge,[112] who not only fulfilled the prediction by applying the law, but made a judgment whether the prediction should be applied here.[113] The judge remained central to the legal process.[114]

In this process, the problem lay in matching the general (predictive) commands of the legislator to the particular commands of the judge in the case. The general command from above was mediated by the judgment of facts below:

The acts of judges are commands, and commands are volitions. But the volitions are governed by acts of the understanding/Judgments. The judgment formed the command follows of course. Tis in forming the judgment that all the trouble and difficulty consists.[115]

Thus the judgment depended upon the nature of the case before him, every judgment having reference to some obnoxious act, which either had been committed (in the case of penal law) or which was

---

[111] UC lxix. 115.

[112] *OLG* 137–40. It also applied to 'witnesses, registers, court-keepers, jail-keepers, bailiffs, executioners, and so forth'.

[113] It may be argued that Bentham still felt that all circumstances imaginable should be legislated for, since the directive part was the expression of will and the comminative was the act of the understanding of the legislator. For Bentham wrote, '[a]s the former then in order to be complete, must be a full and faithful picture of the legislator's mind, so the latter must be a full and faithful picture of the future state of things, of future exterior events'. *OLG* 167. However, Bentham's comminative parts were in fact *procedural* rules, seeking to ensure that law was not frustrated by capricious and accidental forms. They therefore did not predict circumstances and their application to the will of the law via the judgment.

[114] 'The Law says, who so hath stolen, let the Sheriff hang him: not this man or that man in particular, but any man that hath stolen: What is it that the Sheriff does in consequence? He does not of his own accord take and hang the individual John Thomas, who he thinks is of the *sort* of person who has stolen; but he waits and hears the *opinion* of the Judge, telling him that John Thomas is the person who has stolen, and the Command of the judge telling him that John Thomas is the person he is to hang.' UC lxix. 118.   [115] UC lxix. 111.

sought to be prohibited in future (in the case of civil suits).[116] A judge issued commands, but 'he can issue commands to such [individuals] only as are called before him by other individuals.[117]

Bentham recognized that law would always work through this partnership of judge and legislator. In his analysis of judgment, he saw that in order to facilitate the complex problem of judgment, the point of law should be as clearly demarcated as possible. In the common law, Bentham felt that the intrinsic difficulty was magnified, since there were only indeterminate ideas of what the law was, and since law and fact were habitually jumbled together in court.[118] He considered how one would find a simple question of fact, in the case of a man accused of theft. Only by describing facts without reference to legal words could one decide purely a question of fact—in a way as done in a special verdict.[119] Otherwise, the question of law—whether the act was illegal—might be taken for granted under the analysis of facts. To avoid this problem, Bentham wanted the terms of the charge to be always the same as the words in the statute. The form would be settled by the legislator, the allegations necessary could then be proposed as questions to the jury. In either case, what was essential to know was what a term such as 'theft' meant. Bentham's discussion of the function of special verdicts showed the need to distinguish the class covered (the *genera infima*) from the specific circumstances of the case, so that the one could be seen to fit the other without begging the question. The danger in any case was of the jury making use of an inspecific word in their verdict, which did not define the offence precisely. Thus, it was essential in law to have notions like theft well defined.[120] However, the notion

---

[116] *OLG* 220–1. Hence, the judge did in effect make laws: 'This right then which the judgment has reference to is either constituted by the judgment or is not: if it be created by the judgment it could not have been violated before the judgment, consequently there could not have been any offence created or committed on the score of that right previously to the judgment.'   [117] UC lxix. 159.

[118] In discussing the relationship between law and fact in English courts—particularly in the light of the controversy over political libels in the 1770s—Bentham noted that juries always considered questions of law (especially in any general verdict) while judges always found fact. Such was the business of drawing inferences from testimony. '[T]here is no business whatever that occurs upon a legal trial that is not business of Law.' UC lxix. 194.

[119] To decide whether the act done fell within the law, one would have to describe the acts and circumstances of the defendant 'taking care that none of the words used in the description of either act or circumstances, convey any intimation of the manner in which it is regarded by Law'. UC lxix. 176.

[120] UC lxix. 177. Hence, Bentham argued that many disputes were resolved into

defined was a general notion. The process of law was not complete until the rule was complemented by the judgment, which descended into particular details.

In the civil law, this question of definition was even more important, because the whole question rested not on decisions as to whether certain acts had been done, but whether certain conditions existed. Thus, in an action of ejectment, brought against someone claiming title to lands because he was the heir to the last proprietor, the question revolved solely around the events by which he became heir. If he lost, it was not because of any acts of his, but because of the 'non-existence of any of these circumstances constitutive of title one or other of which ought to have existed for him to have been a party not comprised in the general prohibition issued by the general law'.[121]

Whereas in the criminal law the directive and predictive parts were united, in the civil law, there was no expression of will prior to the case, so that the only offence was the 'consequential contingent' one, the one associated with the prediction.[122] There, the right claimed was determined in the court, and the question of penalty was entirely contingent, depending on the possibility of the determination being ignored.

In the civil law, moreover, the rules grew out of adjudication, not prior legislation. 'A judgment,' Bentham said, 'if it be a civil one, must if it does anything create an offence.' However, 'what offence there is in the case comes after it'.[123] In a civil suit, the plaintiff did not claim a *liquidated* right had been violated (since that would be a criminal offence), but he asked the judge to liquidate the right for him. He claimed the right to a right.[124] The judge gave the mandate that acted as law: in effect, every civil suit resulted in a new law from the judge, with '[t]he parties contributing the *directive* rules, the Legislation the *sanctionative*'.[125] Thus, it can be seen that Bentham did not have in mind the total enumeration of particular cases that could come before a court. As Bentham pointed out, in the law of property, 'we have a different law for every distinct proprietary subject: and matter is infinitely divisible'.[126]

---

verbal or metaphysical disputes. The entire dispute with the American colonies, he said, was of this nature.

[121] UC lxix. 196.
[122] *OLG* 227.
[123] *OLG* 226.
[124] *OLG* 227.
[125] *Constitutional Code. Volume I*, ed. F. Rosen and J. H. Burns (Oxford, 1983), IX.4.A39.
[126] *OLG* 177.

This has added significance when we observe that Bentham acknowledged the importance of the civil law. He wrote,

With relation to the civil code,—taking the mass of its arrangements for an intermediate end, the matter of the penal code is but a means. By the arrangements contained in the civil code, so many directive rules are furnished; what the penal code does, is but to furnish sanctions, by which provision is made for the observance of those directive rules.[127]

This has important ramifications for the meaning of Bentham's classic definition of law. He defined law as 'an assemblage of signs declarative of a volition conceived or adopted by the *sovereign* in a state, concerning the conduct to be observed in a certain *case* by a certain person or class of persons, who in the case in question are or are supposed to be subject to his power'.[128] For this definition includes the notion of a command *adopted* in a *case*—allowing room for judicial legislation. Indeed Bentham said that a mandate could belong to the sovereign by conception or adoption, if it issued from someone else.[129] Bentham held that in the case of adoption, there were two parties involved: the sovereign and the party from whom the law emanates. They might have divergent ends in view concerning the law: for the party, his own satisfaction, for the sovereign the pursuit of the greatest good of the community, according to the principle of utility; though usually they coincided.[130] Bentham was here talking of the mandates of the master, parent or husband, adopted by the legislator: but it clearly also applied to the mandates given by judges on the basis of claims put by plaintiffs.[131] By that token, law could have as its source the rights claimed in litigation, by men seeking self-interest: once given legal sanction by the judge, for reasons of general utility, they became part of law. In this way, it may be argued that Bentham's theoretical system allowed for the growth of law from below, at least in civil cases.[132]

---

[127] *Constitutional Code*, 12.

[128] *OLG* 1.   [129] *OLG* 21, 27–31.

[130] '[T]he proper end of the sovereign who adopts, and that of the subordinate who issues the mandate, coincide: being each of them not the particular good of the author of the mandate but the general good of the community at large.' *OLG* 32.

[131] Bentham says that it is by adoption that conveyances and covenants acquire their validity: 'adopted by the sovereign, they are converted into mandates'. *OLG* 23–5. See also UC lxix. 95.

[132] This seems clearly contradicted by statements such as 'The Power of Judge of our Superior Courts extends not in any instance that I know of to the making of a Substantive Law' (UC lxix. 89). However, Bentham was here contrasting the powers of judges

Bentham's Pannomion can therefore be seen as an exercise in separating the spheres of law and fact more clearly, rather than elaborating the detail of factual circumstances where law would apply. Defining offences did not tell the judge what to do in every case: but it at least allowed him to know what he was doing. The code would be deductive, but not simply so: rather, the judge, faced with the facts before him, would have to figure out what the relevant questions were relative to the law, and what the law was that was best applicable. It is significant that Bentham never wrote a minute elaboration of details: in a sense, it was not necessary:

> To describe and distinguish the several contrivances by which in different cases this concentration may be effected, would require a volume. All that can be done here is to give notice to the reader: inasmuch that being aware of the metamorphoses, he may be master of a thread which will conduct him at any time from the artificial and super-induced, to the native and primeval form of the several provisions of the law.[133]

For a mechanical code, allowing judges no choice at case level, would have to be perfect, not in covering every detail in the body of the code, but in having a system of deduction that would allow perfect movement from the principle of utility down to the instant case. It will be seen that this was impossible to achieve, and that Bentham's inductivist methodology disallowed it; but that this being so, Bentham's theoretical ideal type of law was unworkable. This interpretation reconciles the theoretical dilemma, but undermines the practicality of the code and the rejection of the common law. The Pannomion worked as an ideal-type system of theory, a tool for the critique and improvement of the common law. If we probe into the details of the Pannomion, we will find that, in substance, Bentham did not propose a system of law fundamentally different from the common law one: but that he was central for the attack on the irrationality and chaos of the old system, and consequentially that his achievement was to force men to think of law in substantive terms. Bentham remained a common law revisionist.

to make adjective rules of procedure for their courts, and their inability to make clear substantive rules in the same way. The implication is that judges cannot legislate *in banc*: the judge can act no otherwise 'than at the instigation of some party and that a party concerned in a precise and determinable matter' (UC lxix. 145, 203). It does not imply that in the process of adjudication they may not issue mandates that are adopted by the sovereign and become law.

[133] *OLG* 179.

Bentham's Structured Procedure

Bentham's proposed system of natural procedure was in fact more structured than might at first be realized. This is evident when we look at his key objections to common law pleading. In essence, Bentham's hostility to the common law system was based around the view that it was not so much that the theoretical principles of pleading were wrong, but that they had become so complex and irrational over time that they no longer served the function of justice.[134] The problem with the technical system was that because it was irrational, it was impossible to know, save for the abstruse lawyer-learning.[135] This was above all what made the law abundant with vexation, delays and expense: not only were there endless fees for documents to be drawn up, but because so little was explained by the system, the parties had to come prepared with all the evidence they might find necessary.

Most evident was the way that the technical system gave the key power to the clerks who drew up pleas. The judge could nullify a cause, where the merits were clear, simply because a lawyer had omitted to state a word 'which neither the legislator nor the judge had ever ordered to be employed'.[136] The law thus became subservient to quibbles: which in turn frustrated the substantive law, undermining statute, and also making the substantive common law even harder to divine.[137] The strict technicality of the common law also led the judges to be mechanical, exempting them from the responsibility of examining the merits. Whatever cruelty or injustice was committed by the court could be seen as the fruit of the rules, the fault not lying with the judge, but in 'the nature of things, the imperfection of human institutions, and so forth'.[138] At the same time, the law became capricious, because of the 'double-fountain' principle, giving the judge the discretion to favour the plaintiff or defendant at will. It can be seen that this principle was a result of *procedure*:

---

[134] *Rationale of Judicial Evidence*, in *Works*, vii. 211–14: 'In many of these instances . . . the mischief of it, stole on at an imperceptible rate: being, therefore, not the work of any one judge or judges to the exclusion of the rest, the effect produced by the sinister interest is rather the preservation of the practice, than the generation of it.'

[135] *Rationale of Judicial Evidence*, in *Works*, vii. 206–7.

[136] Ibid. 255, 246.   [137] Ibid. 256–7.   [138] Ibid. 248.

Decide against the merits, on the ground of the quirk, the fiction, the jargon, you receive the joint praise of profound science and inflexible steadiness—the praise of adhering to the rule *stare decisis*. Decide in favour of the merits, disallowing the quirk, discarding the fiction, the jargon, you receive the praise of liberality—of attachment to the laws of substantial justice.[139]

Bentham had no intrinsic distrust of allowing judges freedom in adjudication: his qualms concerned giving them the choice on what to adjudicate on—the merits or the pleas. Indeed, the system of pleading was a 'mendacity licence', falsehood being an integral part of it. Because the pleas were drawn first, and the evidence was only required much later, a plaintiff was at liberty to cause a defendant much expense and trouble merely by bringing a false and vexatious suit.[140] Bentham dismissed the whole system of pleas as corrupt and mendacious, sacrificing the truth for a precise allegation, and therefore requiring multiple and contradictory counts. All the precision of pleading could still avoid getting to the essential points: thus, in trover, Bentham said, the declaration focused on how the defendant got hold of the goods rather than explaining the plaintiff's right to them; while in actions for real property, all was masked by the fictions of John Doe and Richard Roe.[141]

Much of Bentham's time in the *Rationale of Judicial Evidence* was therefore taken in a critique of the workings of the common law and equity systems of pleading, showing how the irrationality of the pleas, the overlapping of jurisdictions, and the delayed stages in the cause frustrated litigants and prevented the courts from arriving at the issue in a clear manner. In other words, the common law system of pleading did not live up to its claims. Bentham's alternative therefore can be seen as a means of simplifying pleading and reducing it to its logic. He outlined the stages that the parties should go through as follows. As for the plaintiff, he should begin by stating the nature of his demand, or the service he expected at the hands of the judge. The second stage was '[t]o state on what *title* such demand is grounded, viz. in point of law: ex. gr. *delinquency, contract, succession,* &c. &c.: referring to the tenor of the *law*, where there exists such a law'. Then, he would state the facts he would rely on, for example,

they being such as, in virtue of such law, have given to him such his *title* to such *service*: events or other facts *investitive*, or say *collative*,—having the

---

[139] Ibid. 308.   [140] Ibid. 263–5.   [141] Ibid. 275–81.

effect of *investing* him with, or *conferring* upon him, such his title to such service.[142]

Bentham would require more detail on the evidence: the plaintiff would have to state the grounds of his persuasion of such collative or investitive facts, whether the evidence was direct or circumstantial, what witnesses he would call, and what written evidence he would use. The plaintiff would receive the counter-allegations of the defendant. As for the defendant, he would first admit or contest the claim, then (if he contested) would state whether it was on the ground of law or fact. He would then follow similar steps to the plaintiff's. Both parties together would discard what evidence it was not necessary to produce, that they could agree on.

This could be done in 'ready written pleadings'. Although he consistently favoured the oral presentation of cases before the judge, whereby the judge could correct errors on the spot and get to the issue between the parties at once,[143] Bentham nevertheless also proposed a system of pleading where all that the parties had to do was to specify the service demanded, and the relevant facts and laws that entitled them to the judge's service. This required a fully comprehensive system of substantive laws, for 'there can be no such thing as *good pleading*, without a complete body of laws in the form of statute law'.[144] Thus, Bentham favoured simplified forms of plea where the plaintiff only had to fill in his particular facts:

The general nature of the plaintiff's demand, and of the grounds on which it rests, in respect of title, in point of fact as well as law, [should be] consigned, as far as consignable, to *printed forms*; and so in regard to the defence: the allegations individualized by names, places, times, &c. inserted in the blanks: as in the forms provided by divers statutes, and those given in Burn's Justice.[145]

It can be seen that this was in effect a system of defining the case quite precisely by the parties coming before the court. It was a system of formal pleading.[146] The patriarchal court did not therefore

---

[142] *Rationale of Judicial Evidence*, 228, 270–1.
[143] See e.g. ibid. 247–8.   [144] Ibid. 271.
[145] *Scotch Reform*, 11. Bentham's reference is to Richard Burn's *The Justice of the Peace and Parish Officer*, which was the standard guide on the law for magistrates in the later eighteenth and early nineteenth centuries. See also UC lvii. 5.
[146] 'Should justice ever become an object, a system of pleading might be devised, which, creating no delay, and giving no mendacity-licence, should at the same time give real information to the parties, and bind in chains the despotism of the judge.' *Rationale of Judicial Evidence*, in *Works*, vii. 270.

seek to treat the litigants like naughty children: it required them to define the dispute between them. Bentham further recognized that the question of substantive law would not always be as straightforward as was desirable. Thus, his system provided for the defendant to dispute the question of law that was applicable to those facts within the development of the case. In addition he wrote,

Whenever the burthen of delay, vexation, and expense, attached to the collection of the evidence, constitutes an object worth regarding,—if any *point of law* is in question, the collection may on both sides be postponed till after the determination of the point of law: for, suppose the point of law given (for example) against the plaintiff, all evidence . . . will be altogether useless.[147]

If the parties might need adjudication from the judge on a matter of law, they might need the help of 'legal advisers' in drawing up the demand paper.[148] In addition, Bentham allowed for a system of appeals, the reasons for which included dissatisfaction with the judge's decrees, including questions of law and fact. Bentham significantly noted that this stage would involve 'incidental costs, fees for argumentation by law practitioners'.[149]

Bentham's attitude to pleading can be seen in his attitude to the exclusion of evidence. His general rule is well known: he would allow all evidence to be heard, '[e]xcept where the letting in of such light is attended with preponderant collateral inconvenience, in the shape of vexation, expense and delay'.[150] Bentham spent much time discussing what evidence was proper to be excluded as well as what was improperly excluded under the current system. Among the latter, he argued that much evidence was excluded by the rule that it must be confined to the point in issue. What is of note is that Bentham felt it was perfectly proper to exclude all evidence irrelevant to the points in dispute, but that the current system of pleading only determined that very imperfectly. He therefore proposed that the rule should be kept that evidence should be accepted only of 'either those [facts] on which the decision immediately turns, or

---

[147] *Rationale of Judicial Evidence,* in *Works,* vii. 231. Similarly, where there was very much evidence to be collected, the defendant could postpone the collection of his until the plaintiff had made out his case, to see if the defendant had one to answer.

[148] *Principles of Judicial Procedure,* 66.

[149] *Ibid.* 93.

[150] *Rationale of Judicial Evidence,* in *Works,* vii. 336. See M. Menlowe, 'Bentham, Self-Incrimination, and the Law of Evidence', *Law Quarterly Review,* civ. (1988), 286–307.

other facts which are evidentiary of them'.[151] Rather, he proposed a greater flexibility in the pleadings, to allow the court to ascertain what evidence was relevant.

It can be seen that Bentham was not hostile to formalities from his examination of preappointed evidence. This was evidence which was essential in civil law, most notably contract and property. The question of fact needed to be far more precisely defined at the outset in such cases, because in the civil law, 'it is only through the medium of facts to which . . . the law has imparted those prolific and distinctive powers, that the law has it in its power to give birth or termination to rights and obligations'.[152] Since contractual law was framed by the contracting parties, it was most certainly ascertained by having formalities to be observed, to serve as a simple type of preappointed evidence for the court, when disputes arose. Bentham preferred a high degree of formality: contracts should be written on fixed forms of contract paper, there being different species of these for each species of contract, the forms of which should be notorious. The contract should be witnessed by a notary, to attest to its fairness. The notary could also secure the propriety of the contract, ensuring that the party contracting was one of those regarded by the legislator as fit to do so; that he should know his resulting rights or obligations; and that the contract was not illegal. Clearly, contracts needed careful drawing up, and the ordinary man would need the assistance of a lawyer.[153] What led Bentham to desire such clear fixed forms was the lack of notoriety of contemporary contract law, which could be cured by having notorious forms. However, since the system to be fair depended on the parties knowing of the required formalities and it being in their power to observe them, Bentham felt it should still be possible for the court to allow contracts where the formalities had not been observed, if the parties could explain why they had not done so. Provided the contract was fair, it should not be frustrated by the absence of formalities.

What would be flexible and open therefore in the presentation of cases would be the allowing the judge to assist the parties in arriving at the point of dispute, and at amending errors in the procedure. The problem with common law pleading thus seemed not to be its desire for precise allegations of disputes, but its rigid formality, which

---

[151] *Rationale of Judicial Evidence*, in *Works*, vii. 560.
[152] Ibid. vi. 509.
[153] Ibid. vi. 521–8.

disallowed the correction of simple errors. Bentham wanted the parties to appear in person before the judge at the commencement of the suit in order that the judge and the other party could question them on their allegations. By this means, the judge could flesh out the declaration, and understand more clearly what was at issue than could be done by strict pleas.

The advantage of this would be that it would be flexible. Thus, the plaintiff could easily and quickly amend his declaration as he needed to in the progress of the case. To guard against this being vexatious, Bentham proposed that the plaintiff should pay for the amendment if he could have foreseen at the outset that the second ground would have been more fruitful than the first. Bentham favoured allowing amendments at any stage, since the precise description of an act could vary between the telling it extrajudicially and judicially or as new evidence emerged.[154] The judge, under this system, would have to enunciate the reasons for all of his decisions. This may be taken as allowing the judge to adjudicate in a direct-utilitarian way, following free natural adjudication. However, it should be noted that the judge was explaining his actions in light of his reaction to the demands of a party. 'No such intercourse will be commenced,' he wrote, 'unless from the applicant's statement, made under responsibility, the judge is satisfied that, taking it for correct, he will be justified in the exaction of the *service* demanded.'[155] At every stage, the judge had to be convinced that there was still a correct case made out to answer; and it may be suggested that the reasons that the judge gave of his actions related at all times to the case that was being presented by the parties.

Judicial Creativity

In spite of Bentham's hostility to judicial lawmaking, he none the less found himself acknowledging the need for judicial legislation even within the code. In 1776, when first contemplating codification, he wrote that judges should have the power not only to make ordinances regulating questions of procedure, but also to 'propound Substantive Regulations in matters of Contract and Conveyancing'. Bentham's proposals show how ready he was to admit that law grew

---

[154] *Principles of Judicial Procedure*, in *Works*, ii. 66–72.
[155] Ibid. 80.

best from the details of cases from below that had to be incorporated into any code; for he wrote,

If any particular cause suggested the inconvenience which it is the intent of the ordinance to remedy that it be an instruction to the judges to state the name of the cause and give a short history of it in as far as relates to the point in question. The reason being grounded in matter of actual experience will strike more forcibly than if grounded on supposition or probability. That will tend to the improvement of the law: and not less to the certainty of it, by taking away all pretence for irregular decisions.[156]

By the 1820s, when Bentham was engaged in writing the *Constitutional Code*, seeking a defined system of concrete law, he still allowed judges either to dispense with the law, or alter it. In his elaboration of the 'Executive-Staying' or 'Sistitive' function of the judge, Bentham argued that the judge here did not derive his notion of justice from the code, but from somewhere else. For the judge could dispense with the code whenever he saw 'something in the law, which, having appeared to him to be an imperfection, such as, in case of execution and effect thereto given, will be productive of injustice, and thence of contravention to the intention of the legislature'.[157] The judge would have to choose between two evils—the evil of the injustice to the party affected if the unjust law was executed against the evil of failing to exercise what was clear law; but he opted for what he perceived to be the lesser evil. The end of government— justice and utility—had primacy over the mere words of law, and ultimately, the judge should decide on utilitarian considerations. The judges were to be given a power to undermine the substantive law:

When, by exercise given to the Judges' sistitive function, execution, to a portion of law as it stands, has been, as above, refused, the effect of such refusal will be liable to be *retroactive*: disfulfilling thus an engagement, which (though, as supposed, through oversight) has been entered into by the law.[158]

Equally, the judges could contribute to the code as a result of their decisions, through the 'Contested Interpretation Reporting Function' described in the *Constitutional Code*.[159] By this, the judge could propose changes in the wording of the law that could be adopted into the Pannomion. Although Bentham elaborated on a detailed system of checks on this power—the interpretation of the law made

---

[156] UC lxix. 200.   [157] *Constitutional Code*, 508.
[158] Ibid. 509.   [159] Ibid. 502 ff.

by the judge had to be submitted to a higher judicatory, the Justice and Legislation Ministers and a Contested Interpretation Committee of the legislature before it became law—if these bodies did nothing, merely accepting the judge's word, then the interpretation would become law without any positive legislation by the sovereign. Thus Article 16 of the relevant section of the *Constitutional Code*:

At the end of [. . .] days after the receipt of a Justice Minister's Contested Interpretation Report by the said committee, (if within that time no motion has therein been made for the taking such Report into consideration), the interpretation, if any, which has been sanctioned or proposed by the Justice Minister, shall be considered as adopted by the Legislature, and corresponding amendment, directive or re-editive, as the case may appear to require, be, by the Legislation Minister, (subject to direction by the Legislative and the Contested Interpretation Committee,) applied to the part or parts in question of the Pannomion.[160]

Amendments would work their way up from the bottom, and would be adopted by a tacit form of legislation. In this way could be given 'to the Pannomion at all times, the benefit of such experience, information and correspondent skill, as cannot, in any other situations, in an equal degree, have place'.[161] Similarly, the judge could declare what the law was or what a provision in the code meant, for Bentham defined the 'Declaratory-Directive' function of the law to be 'declaring that the meaning of the law is so and so: with the inference as to the state of rights and obligations on both sides'.[162] This was to admit that the Pannomion could not deduce all law from above, and to admit that when it came to substantive content, it would be built up from the details of local circumstance.[163]

This can equally be seen in Bentham's discussion of judicial interpretation. Bentham argued that the need for interpretation came from a want of understanding in the legislator. This was either because

---

[160] Ibid. 504.   [161] Ibid. 431.   [162] Ibid. 481.

[163] We should note that these powers given to judges are distinct from the power of utilitarian case adjudication which Postema ascribes to the Benthamic judge. These powers were not allowing the judge to dispense with the code and make decisions on utilitarian lines with direct reference to the relative happinesses involved, but were powers to amend the code, requiring the agreement of the legislator. When a judge made a Sistitive Judgment, he gave three decrees: one giving execution to the law as it stood, one giving the decision the judge desired, and one suspending the execution of the others until the will of the legislature was clear. See *Constitutional Code*, 508, and the discussion of these issues in J. R. Dinwiddy, 'Adjudication under Bentham's Pannomion', *Utilitas*, i (1989), 283–9.

all the facts which went to constitute the mischief or which might control it were not present in his mind, or because his judgment concerning them may have been a wrong one. Bentham thus acknowledged the possibility that the legislator could act in an incomplete manner; and he recognized the need for a liberal interpretation of the legislator's will, that is attributing a will to the legislator which he did not express, but which one supposed he failed to express because of his inadvertency or haste in making the rule. Here, the judge supposed what the legislator would have done in the case at hand.[164] Bentham favoured that whenever the judge made a liberal interpretation, he should declare openly that he had done so, and that he should draw up a general provision expressing the alteration to be certified to the legislator, which would become a part of the law by tacit consent if not negatived by the legislator.[165] In effect, though, this was to create a kind of customary law from the judges.[166] Interpretation would clearly play a larger role in Bentham's system than he initially acknowledged: for if penal laws were to be interpreted strictly, in matters of civil law—which did not involve direct punishment—Bentham would still allow a liberal interpretation.[167]

Thus it is evident that Bentham's view of law neither allowed him to create a complete code of laws to cover every circumstance by legislation, nor to create a system where judges would not legislate and where there would be free procedure. Bentham's stated intentions were undermined by his developed ideas, so that many features that were to be found in the common law system would find their way into his. In the end, his Pannomion could not be a practicable scheme. 'My object', Bentham wrote in 1775, 'has been to exhibit a standard of perfection.' That being shown, 'it is to be considered what sacrifices are required by the necessities of the times'.[168] Bentham's system could be one to purify the common law of its absurdities. It is to this aspect that we must now turn.

---

[164] *OLG* 162. This was to be a part of the code: UC c. 90.
[165] *OLG* 241.   [166] Cf. *OLG* 163n.
[167] *OLG* 241: 'As to the individual case by which the propriety of the general alteration comes to be suggested, the authority of the judge in this line should be confined to operations of the remedial kind: it should not extend to positive punishment [but] should be confined to the case in which whatever burthen was thrown upon one party would be so much taken off the shoulders of the other: and that no man be left in possession of a clear profit reaped in fraud of the old law: for by punishment past mischiefs cannot be recalled and whatever is yet to come may as effectually be prevented by a new law which may be made on purpose.'
[168] UC xxvii. 126.

6

Bentham's Classifications
and Analyses

If we reject Bentham's substantive efforts at codification, we must
address the 'other' Bentham, the classifier and analyst. Bentham's
main objections to the common law did not lie in what the judges did
at case level, but in the inability of the common lawyers to create a
set of terms and concepts to explain and hence to know what they
were doing. His aim in writing *An Introduction to the Principles of
Morals and Legislation* was therefore to create a code *'in terminis'*, and
his delay in publishing the project resulted from him getting
'unexpectedly entangled in . . . the metaphysical maze', that led him
on to *Of Laws in General*.[1] These early words should give us a clue to
the nature of Bentham's project: it was not to list offences in a simple
penal code, but to create a structure of concepts and terms. *An
Introduction* was perceived by Bentham to be a 'metaphysical' work,
standing in relation to the substantive law as a treatise of pure
mathematics stood to natural philosophy.[2] His interest in 1780 may
therefore be said to have been as much in classification as in codification:

As Laws are inventions calculated to the producing the greatest possible
Happiness in Society, by restraining action in those instances where it is
disposed to detract from that maximum of Happiness the most natural and
satisfactory Classification will be that which exhibits in the plainest light
their influence on it.[3]

The use of such an arrangement was to guide those who were
'unacquainted with the articles comprized in it to the finding of any
article which they are desirous to become acquainted with'. A correct
classification and arrangement was essential in order to unravel the
details of a case, to get to the dispute at hand. Thus, Bentham argued

---

[1] *IPML* 1.   [2] *IPML* 5.   [3] UC lxiii. 73.

that one could classify offences by their physical appearance, or by their moral nature and political effect. 'By offences scarce distinguishable in their Physical Basis,' he wrote, 'will be produced mischiefs infinitely different as well in quality as in quantity.'[4] Hence, they needed to be distinguished by a different arrangement, that would be more revealing.

Bentham attacked the common law via Blackstone; but we can see that he had an ambiguous view of both. Bentham was not unwilling either to praise Blackstone's achievement or to acknowledge his own debt to the commentator.[5] Indeed, Blackstone's achievement lay in his arrangement—'[t]he rest was little more than compilation'.[6] Yet in his arrangement and classification of law—both in theory and in practice—lay Blackstone's errors, thanks to the fact that he chose to arrange his view of law in a technical, not a natural way. This, in turn, was shaped by the common law he was describing, which itself was bound by technical, nonsensical forms. Bentham was not, however, hostile to the substantive rules in the common law, such as were to be found. His works are peppered with references to actual law and cases when he discussed a point of arrangement, and his critique of Blackstone was often based on the argument that Blackstone had misunderstood the law, because of his misunderstanding of terms. Bentham's key critique of the common law was that it was nowhere to be found, and that everyone who wanted a standard of rule by which to guide his conduct had to construct it for himself. On the one hand, this meant that there were no clear rules emanating from a legislator in the form of statute; but equally, it was due to the fact that the forms of the common law were wholly irrational, and that there were no conceptual materials which men could put together to form their own rules.

Bentham's central task in his lifelong project was hence not detailed legislation but definition, classification, and arrangement. At the same time as he was setting out to create a code, he was also writing a treatise of universal jurisprudence.[7] Such a treatise would

---

[4] UC lxiii. 83.

[5] *Comment/Fragment*, 414–15; Bentham wrote, 'How to estimate in my own instance the obligations which the science is under to him I know not: by him I know what I know: without him I might very likely have known nothing.' UC xxvii. 99, 107.

[6] *Comment/Fragment*, 396.

[7] Bentham therefore proposed the following titles for his work: 'A Key to Universal Jurisprudence', 'Elements of Jurisprudence', 'Novum Organon Juris', and 'A Key to the Nomenclature of Universal Jurisprudence'. UC lxix. 214.

be equally comprehensible in any state, since the terms which lay behind the rights, powers, duties, and restraints would be the same, even though the substantive matter differed according to place. These terms would be 'a common standard of interpretation for the several technical terms as they are called in the several systems of jurisprudence'. Thus, whereas a treatise of English law written in technical terms, like the *Commentaries*, would be comprehensible only to a technical English lawyer, a French, Spanish, or Swedish lawyer would equally understand a treatise written in universal terms. Hence, the great want of definition was 'not for words of municipal jurisprudence; but for terms of universal jurisprudence'.[8] Bentham was therefore concerned above all in the seeking of definitions, rather than the providing of substantive rules. 'Every science then has its metaphysics,' Bentham asserted, '[n]ow the metaphysics of this our science law, consists in ascertaining the ideas belonging to the several terms of universal jurisprudence by means of which the . . . terms of the particular jurisprudence of any one country are endeavoured to be explained.'[9] This system of definitions would stand as a perpetual touchstone for trying the truth and significance of any speculations on law.[10]

Bentham in 1775 clearly had in mind a reordering of existing law in order to make sense of it. His main criticism of not just Blackstone, but also Beccaria, Montesquieu, and Adam Smith, was that while they began with general principles, they failed to work them out in practical detail. Bentham's work, on the other hand, 'commences with Metaphysics; it terminates with Old Bailey practise'.[11] Significantly, Bentham in 1828 was still engaged in the same task, when he began the work entitled *A Familiar View of Blackstone* or *Blackstone Familiarized*. He explained his intentions thus:

This paper has for its object or end in view, the giving to the people of England and its dependencies in as far sound as possible . . . a conception as clear as possible of the state of the law as it is in England. On considering how this can be done, it has been found that by no other means could any

---

[8] UC lxix. 126, 148; lxiii. 73. Bentham said that it would be of use for students therefore to arrange the materials of their national jurisprudence under the headings he had delineated for universal jurisprudence. UC xxvii. 121.

[9] UC lxix. 153.　　　　　　　　　　　　　　　　　[10] UC xxvii. 103.

[11] UC xxvii. 133. Bentham went on, 'It begins with the principle of utility, with pains and pleasures in the abstract, with intentions, consciousness, motives and dispositions. It ends with Indictments, Informations, Certiorari, . . . and Capiases. It was begun in the garret of a metaphysician; it was concluded at the desk of an attorney.'

conception be given of law as it is, so clear, if at all, as by means of law as it ought to be.[12]

This project was undertaken after the *Constitutional Code*, and at the same time that Bentham was lambasting Peel and Brougham for their reforming timidity. Yet it reveals much of the nature of his ambitions for the code.[13] Bentham's work would be censorial and expository at the same time. At one level, the 'model of Absolute perfection' which he sought to create in his definitional science would be a standard against which to measure practical legal systems;[14] on the other, arranging existing jurisprudence under the headings he had devised—an exercise in *expository* jurisprudence— would reveal the confusions in the law, and be censorial.[15] A correct arrangement would therefore not *create* the perfect deduction; but, like the methodology of natural sciences, it would allow the observer to see what was good and necessary to the system, and what not. This was seen by the position of bad laws:

Now, a bad Law is that which prohibits a mode of conduct that is *not* mischievous. Thus would it be found impracticable to place the mode of conduct prohibited by a bad law under any denomination of offence, without asserting such a matter of fact as is contradicted by experience. Thus cultivated, in short, the soil of Jurisprudence would be found to repel in a manner every evil institution.[16]

The law would censor itself once there were clear determinate ideas about its nature.

---

[12] UC xxxi. 75.

[13] Indeed, it may be asked how far Bentham thought the Pannomion to be achievable. In 1780 he had written, 'The reformation (of the Laws) is not a work for the people in this age. The man who shall exercise this great work, the man who shall unite the zeal of a Sully, the disinterestedness of a Vane, the probity of a Clarendon, with the favour of a Buckingham, the legal knowledge of a Comyns, the eloquence and popularity of a Pit[t] the philosophy of a Bacon is yet to come.' UC xxvii. 124. The fact that he began the *Familiar View of Blackstone* in his eightieth year may suggest he recognised the time had still not come.

[14] UC xxvii. 126, UC xxxi. 104.

[15] 'By a brief statement of such arrangements under these several heads as here presented themselves as in the highest degree conducive to the above general purposes, a standard of reference will be established, by reference to which such arrangements as actually have place under our law may be explained, and some judgment at the same time formed of the conduciveness to that same end.' UC xxxi. 170. See also *Comment/Fragment*, 404, 416.

[16] *Comment/Fragment*, 416–17.

Bentham and Arrangement

If Galileo and Newton had undermined the notion of final causes in science, cutting the sciences free of theology, eighteenth-century thinkers none the less still perceived a unity in the physical world, and hence sought a unification of all knowledge into a single system.[17] There were, however, alternative ways of perceiving this unity. For some, all disputes in philosophy could ultimately be reduced to verbal disputes: once the moral sciences were as precise in their terms as mathematics was, they could be as exact a science. Thus, Leibniz spoke of forming an alphabet of human thoughts and of the time 'when we should be able to form conclusions concerning God and the Mind, with not less certainty than we do at present concerning figures and numbers'.[18] Similarly, Condillac spoke of the art of reasoning as being no more than a language well arranged, so that a perfect language was a perfect system of analysis.[19] Bentham's Pannomion, coupled with his increasing fascination for coining new words and recasting the system of language, may be seen to have fitted clearly into this view of the world. Yet Bentham eschewed Condillac's confidence in the universal success of terms. His intellectual debts were not to Leibniz or German philosophy, but to the French enlightenment, and hence his method was less mathematical, and owed far more to that of D'Alembert, who was considerably more cautious about the possibility of decoding the universe, and whose concepts of logic, classification, and arrangement differed.[20]

Bentham was influenced by two important methodological ideas of D'Alembert's. First, he realized that there would always remain gaps in human knowledge, that the philosopher could only stitch

[17] See R. McRae, 'The Unity of the Sciences: Bacon, Descartes and Leibniz', *Journal of the History of Ideas*, 18 (1957), 27–48.

[18] Letters to Oldenburg, quoted in D. Stewart, *Elements of the Philosophy of the Human Mind*, vol. 2, (1814), p 139–40.

[19] *La Logique* (Paris, 1780).

[20] D'Alembert saw the universe as being made up of interdependent parts, whose interrelations derived from the unity of the whole: by classification and definition, the scientist could begin to explore the labyrinth. See *Essai sur les élémens de philosophie ou sur les principes des connoissances humaines*, in *Mélanges de littérature, d'histoire et de philosophie*, 4th edn., 5 vols. (Amsterdam, 1767). See also, *Encyclopédie, ou Dictionnaire raisonné des sciences, des arts et des métiers, par une société de gens de lettres*, 17 vols. (Paris 1751–65), art 'Cosmiques'.

together his ideas from the limited information at his disposal.[21] This information came from the facts that one could see.[22] D'Alembert's *Preliminary Discourse* to the *Encyclopédie* spoke of the encyclopaedical order as being a kind of map of the world of sciences and arts. And just as the map depended on the position of the cartographer, so the encyclopaedia depended on one's view of the world—as well as the limitations of one's knowledge.[23] Hence, he advocated that care should be taken to observe exactly the mutual dependence of the objects of the science, and to leave gaps where knowledge was lacking, rather than fill the gaps with false links.[24] Second, D'Alembert argued that the way to put together the map was by resolving these simple facts and creating clear definitions of their relations.[25] Hence, the overall view of the world was one created by a synthesis of simple ideas, but a synthesis that would always remain to some degree provisional.[26] D'Alembert's method was to 'analyse our experience introspectively in order to reconstitute it in a clearer and more exhaustive way'.[27] This involved distinguishing the simple ideas that made up each notion, particularly in the case of abstract (or fictitious) ideas.[28] For him, logic could be reduced to the simple principle of finding and developing intermediary objects and definitions to link diverse objects.

Bentham's work shares these twin concerns of forming a clear definition of concepts and terms to make sense of the data that is being dealt with and a clear methodological arrangement of the

---

[21] *Encyclopédie*, Art Cosmologie, *Élémens de philosophie*, iv. 16.

[22] The view one had of the world thus came not from axioms, but from '[d]es faits simples et reconnus, qui n'en supposent point d'autres, et qu'on ne puisse par conséquent ni expliquer ni contester'. *Élémens de philosophie*, iv. 27.

[23] '[L'ordre encyclopédique] consiste à rassembler [nos connaissances] dans le plus petit espace possible, et à placer, pour ainsi dire, le Philosophe au-dessus de ce vaste labyrinthe dans un point de vue fort élevé d'où il puisse appercevoir à la fois les Sciences et les Arts principaux; voir d'un coup d'oeil les objets de ses spéculations, et les opérations qu'il peut faire sur ces objets; distinguer les branches générales des connoissances humaines, les points qui les séparent ou qui les unissent; et entrevoir même quelquefois les routes secrètes qui les rapprochent. C'est une espèce de mappemonde.' *Encyclopédie*, i, p. xv.

[24] *Élémens de philosophie*, iv. 39.

[25] '[D]ans les Sciences où le raisonnement a la meilleure part, c'est sur des définitions nettes et exactes que la plupart de nos connoissances sont appuyées.' *Élémens de philosophie*, iv. 30.

[26] See R. Grimsley, *Jean D'Alembert* (Oxford, 1963), 245–6.

[27] Ibid. 229.

[28] *Élémens de philosophie*, iv. 31 ff.; *Éclaircissemens sur differens endroits des élémens de philosophie*, in *Mélanges*, v. 19–20.

whole science. Bentham acknowledged his intellectual debts in this field to Locke, to James Harris and to Linnaeus, in the fields of analysis and classification.[29] Yet he reserved a special place for D'Alembert. He wrote to the French philosopher in 1778, saying '[c]'est de vous que je tiens le fil du labyrinthe des connoissances humaines',[30] and planned to send him samples of his works on arrangement and logic.[31] Bentham described his methodology thus: 'Little by little I framed to myself a kind of method which may be stiled the method of analytical exhaustion. This consisted in taking the (logical) whole and dividing it and subdividing it, till I had broken it down into parcels to which the names in question were applicable.'[32] Yet having completed the analysis, Bentham saw the need for a synthesis 'as a key to it'.[33] An understanding of his concerns when dealing with logic, classification, and arrangement helps us understand his vision of the function of legal terms. It will be seen that Bentham's system was concerned not with elaborating substantive facts, but with providing a clear logical exposition of the relations of things, in order to understand the substance.

Bentham saw his project as one of metaphysics, 'to examine what ideas we have belonging to the terms we use'.[34] His attitude to metaphysics sheds important light on the nature of his enterprise. Bentham noted that judges were habitually suspicious of metaphysics[35] but argued that those (like Burke) who declared their hatred of it were like Cacus who declared he hated light. For Bentham, all questions in law were in effect questions concerning the import of words, questions whose solution therefore depended on skill in verbal definitions.[36] Metaphysics was not idle speculations: those who hated it therefore hated the principles by which controverted points in law could be settled. Hence jurisprudence needed an architect to build up a set of terms and definitions which unravelled the

---

[29] He wrote to D'Alembert of his work on complex ideas such as pleasure, pain, will, substance, space, that '[t]out cela forme un Travail dont l'idée m'est venue principalement de la part de Locke'. UC clxix. 52. For Harris, see UC xxvii. 164, and for Linnaeus, see, e.g., UC xxvii. 109. Bentham wrote, 'to Mr. Harris . . . [I owe] the idea of attempting to analyse a subject upon an exhaustive plan: to M. D'Alembert the distinction between real and verbal or fictitious entities which has been of such infinite use to me in the way of definition'. UC xxvii. 144.

[30] *Correspondence*, ii. 117. He was referring to both D'Alembert and Helvetius.

[31] UC clxix. 50–65.

[32] UC xxvii. 160.

[33] UC lxix. 105.

[34] UC lxix. 153, 155.

[35] He referred to *Millar v. Taylor* (1769) 4 Burr. 2303. UC lxix. 182.

[36] UC lxix. 182.

meanings currently muddled in the obscure nomenclature of the law.[37] The process of definition aimed to discover the simple ideas behind all legal terms.[38] When definition and classification were complete, the judge (or the scientist) would be better placed to make sense of what he did at ground level.[39]

Bentham however stressed that it was not possible to fix the import of words by unconnected definitions. There needed to be a well-ordered, unbroken chain of definitions, constructing 'the only sure ladder whereby a man can climb up to the heights of science'.[40] There were some things that simply could not be defined *per genus et differentiam*, for not every word could be traced directly up to a simple idea. As a result, the ideal form of definition went with classification. Definitions 'must all be struck upon a Common Center'.[41] In this discussion, the point was especially related to law, since legal terms needed to be defined in chains, as standing isolated they would make no sense. Thus, he wrote that 'it is requisite that it should be capable of being divided further as often as there may be occasion: and that, if possible, upon the same plan as it was begun upon'.[42]

The connections between ideas were as important as the ideas.[43] This view can be seen reflected in Bentham's view of logic, which was essentially an encyclopaedical one. It was logic that united the materials sorted out by analysis. For Bentham, any complete institute of logic could not leave unvisited any part of art and science nor any aspect of human thought or action. Hence an institute of logic and a complete methodological encyclopaedia would be one and the same thing: save that logic gave the bird's-eye view, while the encyclopaedia filled in the detail.[44] The function of logic was therefore to set up clear and definite ideas, and to arrange them in a clear and useful manner.[45] Bentham rejected scholastic logic, and indeed

---

[37] UC lxix. 176, 182.

[38] 'Simple ideas are the *ne plus ultra* of expository investigation.' UC lxix. 118.

[39] 'The words defined are all so many given quantities and possessing them, the jurist finds himself rich in means for the solution of any problem in his science.' UC lxix. 161.   [40] UC lxix. 159.

[41] UC lxix. 134.   [42] UC lxix. 229.

[43] Cf. D'Alembert, *Élémens de philosophie*, iv. 39: 'Pour comparer deux ou plusieurs objets éloignés les uns des autres, on se sert de plusieurs objets intermédiaires; il en est de même quand on veut comparer deux ou plusieurs idées. L'art du raisonnement n'est que le développement de ce principe, et des conséquences qui résultent.'

[44] *Essay on Logic*, in *Works*, viii. 213–93, at 219.

[45] Ibid. 221–2.

showed no interest in discussing the nature and function of the syllogism or logical reasoning.[46] Rather, the method of acquiring knowledge was through induction and observation—proceeding from particulars to generals—and then arranging it correctly.[47] Understanding Bentham's encyclopaedical view of logic thus helps us to understand the nature of the Pannomion.

Bentham talked of the need to 'draw a circle' around all the possible cases and circumstances that could occur. The method of exhaustion which drew this circle was hence analogous to the arithmetic of infinities in mathematics—'[b]y it everything, without it nothing can be done'.[48] The exhaustive method aimed for the first time to give the legislator a comprehensive and clear view of his subject. It was to create a system of comprehensive categories in which to put things. However, a system of classification and logical deduction could not in itself be a substitute for induction. Thus, in *Chrestomathia*, Bentham's most ambitious project of classification, he wrote that 'upon *observation* made of individual *perceptions*, and upon the correctness with which it has been made' depended the truth of all general propositions. Bentham rejected syllogistic reasoning in saying that '[b]y general words, a truth, in so far as ascertained by individual observation, may indeed be *expressed*: but it is not by stringing together general words . . . that truth can be *proved*'. The function of definitional all-comprehensiveness was therefore not to allow a simple deduction from the general first principles to the individual instance, but to 'point the attention of the reader to the individual matters of fact, on which the possession of this property depends'.[49] As a consequence, any general formulary was provisional, with observation and experiment being the only ultimate definitive tests to be made:[50]

Of *Logic* with its divisions, all that it is in the power to do is, to arrange and display in the most instructive manner whatsoever matters have been extracted from those sources. What it can do is, to *methodise*; and in that unimmediate way *promote creation*:—what it can *not* do is, *to create*.[51]

---

[46] See G. Bentham, *Outline of a New System of Logic, with a Critical Examination of Dr. Whately's Elements of Logic* (London, 1827), p. ix.

[47] *Comment/Fragment*, 96–7. Bentham said that until Locke, logic was only concerned with the art of disputation. UC lxix. 153.

[48] UC xxvii. 169.

[49] *Chrestomathia*, ed. M. J. Smith and W. H. Burston (Oxford, 1983), 237 note b.

[50] *Chrestomathia*, 239 n.   [51] *Chrestomathia*, 251.

It was Bentham's desire for completeness that led him to espouse the exhaustive mode of division, and the method of bifurcation.[52] There should be no 'dark spots'—rather, everything should find its place in the system. The system would be based on the contradictory formula: what was classed in one division would thus be contradictory to what was classed in the other. Bentham took the 'Ramean tree' as his ideal model of method.[53] This method, though '[p]lanted and firmly rooted, by the logical work of Saunderson', had scarcely been used by English logicians 'for any other purpose than the being slighted'.[54] Bentham chose for his targets Sanderson, Watts, and Reid and Kames.[55] The first two had merely failed to see the uses of a completely bifurcate model, but the latter had attacked Ramus. Reid had objected that by the contradictory formula one could divide England into Middlesex and what is not Middlesex: so that the 'complete' division would not in fact be complete. Bentham rejected this, saying that in the bifurcate division, two properties had to be given, one in which the two individuals agreed, two in which they did not: '[b]ut, of no one property,—whether as possessed, either by all *'England,'* or by itself, or by anything that *'is not'* itself,—does the word *'Middlesex'* give any intimation'.[56]

[52] *Chrestomathia*, 218.

[53] Bentham confused Ramus's method of bifurcation and the Porphyrian tree. *Chrestomathia*, 223 n., 241 n. Bentham was on occasion quite confused about Ramus: in the 1770s, he identified Ramus with Scotus and the very Parisian scholastic logicians he was opposing. *Comment/Fragment*, 341 & n. It seems that Bentham never in fact read Ramus's works directly, and thought that given the passage of time, Ramus's attacks on Aristotle would be of little use: *Chrestomathia*, 241–2 n. Nevertheless, he identified the method of exhaustiveness and bifurcation with Ramus, and his method of beginning with the largest and most familiar classes and then proceeding to the lower ones, as in UC lxix. 10, echoed Ramus. Bentham's interest in Ramist ideas is significant, given Ramus's great obscurity in eighteenth-century England. However, Ramist ideas are mentioned in Sanderson's *Logicae Artis Compendium* (11th edn. Oxford, 1741; 1st edn. 1618) as useful, and Bentham acknowledged his interest in them to have come from that source. See W. S. Howell, *Eighteenth Century British Logic and Rhetoric* (Princeton, 1971), 16–21; Walter J. Ong, *Ramus, Method and the Decay of Dialogue* (Cambridge, Mass., 1958).

[54] *Chrestomathia*, 242, 244.

[55] Sanderson and Watts, whose works were the standard logics at Oxford in Bentham's day, both expressed an interest in method and arrangement ignored by Aristotelians like Aldrich and later Whately. See Watts, *Logic: Or the Right Use of Reason in the Inquiry after Truth* (London 1792 edn.; 1st edn. 1725), 304 ff. Reid took up the challenge against the Aristotelians more strongly, attacking the syllogism as a means to attain truth, and stressing the need for induction, published in Kames's *Sketches of the History of Man*, 2 vols. (Edinburgh, 1774).

[56] *Chrestomathia*, 250.

The method of exhaustiveness and bifurcation could therefore give an overarching view of all knowledge. For Bentham, '[m]ethod is of use to let us know where to meet with things: and to let us see that nothing is forgotten [or] omitted',[57] His critique of earlier Encyclopaedical sketches was that they had failed to do this. Bentham focused in particular on D'Alembert and Bacon's distributions, as well as Chambers',[58] and found these sketches to be inadequate. D'Alembert had divided his scheme according to the three faculties of the mind, memory, reason, and imagination, corresponding to the arts of history, philosophy, and poetry. Bentham rejected this, since the source of the division was not the nature of the subject but the nature of human faculties. One objection to this was that it was incomplete, omitting perception. D'Alembert's error was to have begun not with a single subject to divide but rather with three. This meant that within the details of the scheme, there were many repetitions, with the same object treated under different headings.[59] In its place Bentham put an exhaustive method which showed how all the sciences related to each other and to the end-in-view. It may be argued that Bentham's quest for completeness stands in contrast to D'Alembert's recognition that blank spaces should be left where knowledge was incomplete. However, this paradox is resolved when we observe that the completeness Bentham was seeking was not factual but analytical.

Bentham borrowed D'Alembert's simile of the cartographer,[60] but sought to unite classification and definition much more closely. As he wrote in a draft to D'Alembert in 1778,

Or un arrangement, une classification, une arbre systematique qu'est ce c'est si non il n'est qu'un suite des mots qui sont generiques et specifics par

---

[57] UC xxvii. 127b.

[58] D'Alembert's sketch came from his *Preliminary Discourse* to the *Encyclopédie*, Bacon's from 'The Platforme of the Designe' in his *Of the Advancement and Proficience of Learning, or the Partitions of the Sciences* (Oxford, 1640), and Chambers' from his *Cyclopaedia*.

[59] For Bentham's criticisms, see *Chrestomathia*, 160–78. Bentham similarly criticized Linnaeus for not observing a strictly bifurcate division. UC lxix. 209.

[60] Just as the map maker first locates the overall position of the country, before moving on to details, so he saw his own task. UC xxvii. 14. Jurisprudence, he said, could not be perfectly treated without a general map of knowledge 'as, by the help of the commanding arrangements given by a Bacon and a D'Alembert any man of a plain understanding and a suitable degree of industry may easily stamp upon his own mind'. UC xxvii. 137.

rapport les uns aux autres: generiques par rapport a ceux qui recupent une position plus bass, specifiques par rapport a ceux qui recupent une position plus haute.[61]

The object of classification, as that of arithmetic, was to find a common divisor to other quantities.[62] Bentham's new Encyclopedical Table in *Chrestomathia* was therefore much more analytical than the one in the *Encyclopédie*, being rigidly divided into bifurcate contradictories, each of which had a new word coined by Bentham.[63]

Bentham's exhaustive method was important for his view of the legislator. This method did not depend on amassing knowledge, for a man became intelligent not by what he knew, but by the attention he bestowed on things.[64] Thus, the man who could give an exhaustive view of the entire range of the objects of government would have the whole field of legislation at his feet: 'nothing will be new . . . everything incident that can present itself will find a place ready prepared for it in his system'.[65] Bentham made a distinction therefore between legislation and administration: success in the former depending on an acquaintance with man and things in general, success in the latter on acquaintance with particular men and things.[66] The business of classification—and hence legislation—was to create an arrangement into which new facts and new cases could be fitted as they came along.

Definition and classification could not take the place of empirical observation, however, for definition was only a substitute for enumeration: 'it is only used either because the particulars to be enumerated are not all known, or if known, are too numerous to mention'. Where the particulars were all known and not too extensive, enumeration was always to be preferred.[67] Nevertheless, for practical purposes, enumeration was not always necessary and definition could suffice:

Description is a detailed exposition of those properties, the exhibition of which is not necessary in order to distinguish the object in question from all such which are not designated by the same name. It may, accordingly, be

---

[61] UC clxix. 58. Cf. UC lxix. 24.

[62] UC lxix. 169.   [63] *Chrestomathia*, Table V.

[64] UC xxvii. 154: 'The same number of plants were seen every day by Linnaeus and by the boy who weeded in his garden.'   [65] UC xxvii. 149a.

[66] Note the parallel of this with Bentham's views on legal commands and legal judgments. See above, Ch. 5.   [67] UC lxix. 154.

more and more ample to an infinite degree. A definition is a concise description, a description is an enlarged definition.[68]

There was a limit to the detail one needed to know in order to classify; and a limit to how far one could descend in detail. Although he aimed at perfection, Bentham knew his classifications would fall short. This did not matter, so long as they were useful. Thus, he wrote in *Chrestomathia*,

Yes, true it is that, no otherwise than through individual objects, can any clear ideas be imbibed, from the names of those ideal aggregates or bundles, of different sorts and sizes, into which, by the associating and dividing power of those appellations, they are collected and distributed. But, from a comparatively small number of individual objects, may be obtained very instructive and practically serviceable ideas, of very extensive aggregates . . . In this tract, approximation is, throughout, the utmost that can be hoped for. But, unless and until some other scheme of distribution shall have been found, such as shall be exempt from, or at least in a less degree exposed to, this imputation of indistinctness, than that which is here submitted, the imperfection, so long as the work has any use, will not afford any sufficient reason for leaving it unattempted'.[69]

Indeed, in that work, Bentham eschewed an excessive descent into details, pointing out that it was only in its primary and most extensive divisions that any acquaintance was needed.[70] Nevertheless, for practical purposes, particulars were always more reliable than generals, nowhere more than in law.[71]

Definition had another function, however. For Bentham sought to engage in both an analytical and a synthetic exercise. Much of his work—in *Of Laws in General* and the *Preparatory Principles*—was analytical, discussing the nature of law and of fictitious entities. However, in his method of arrangement and classification, Bentham also sought a synthesis, putting together the individual parts into a whole. The one required the other. It was only when clear ideas had been formed by logical analysis that clear codes could be drawn up to pull together those notions in a comprehensive definition.

[68] *Essay on Logic*, 248.
[69] *Chrestomathia*, 216–17. [70] *Chrestomathia*, 156–7.
[71] Discussing interpretations of the code, Bentham wrote that where general and particular provisions clashed, the particular should be preferred, since it was established on a nearer and more exact view of the subject: 'The narrower and more special the idea which is the object, the clearer and more determinate is a man's judgment with relation to it.' UC c. 90.

We should note therefore the importance of synthesis in Bentham. He chided Condillac for saying that languages were only the result of a process of analysis. Condillac had failed to see that common names were framed by a process of synthesis. The classifier made use of these synthetic words, which represented a logical whole. Thus, Linnaeus could write of 'plants' to represent a vast aggregate of objects. By synthesis were created logical wholes, which were a 'sort of fictitious *aggregate*, or *collection* of objects.' Indeed, law itself was a general proposition that applied to classes and in that sense had no real character: 'The idea of a law (in its primary sense) is the idea of an object which may be purely intellectual existing nowhere but in the mind of him who speaks of it,' he wrote; it was 'what must previously be formed in order to serve as a pattern to which the contents of a statute or any number of statutes may be reduced, and the several parts they consist of referred to the several stations they belong to in the system.'[72] Hence, it can be seen that the greater categories created in Bentham's scheme of classifications—even the most fundamental ones—were fictitious entities, and to some degree contingent on whether they represented correctly the real entities that lay beneath them.[73]

The science of law would remain conditional. That Bentham's classification would not lead to a deductive code can be seen from his empiricist epistemology. The dilemma was explained by Dugald Stewart. Those, like Leibniz, who sought a complete deductive system, presupposed it was possible for moral terms to be as precise as mathematical ones, where one could reason from definitions.[74] Stewart said that in moral science even if the deductive reasoning were perfect, all would still hinge on the presupposition of facts on which the theory was based. The only way to escape this would be to devise a set of arbitrary definitions for moral science, which need not bear any relation to facts, provided they were not directly contradicted by them. All that would matter would be the connections of the consequences with the first definitions. According to Stewart,

---

[72] *OLG* 12. Bentham was here contrasting a 'law' with a statute. Elsewhere he wrote that a statute 'does not correspond to the idea I would wish to have exclusively annexed to the word Law'. UC lxix. 98. Similarly, he contrasted a law and a regulation, in which the law was the whole single command, while the regulation was any constituent part of a law, a proposition expressing particulars. UC lxix. 147.

[73] *Chrestomathia*, 261–73.

[74] In mathematics, arguing from definitions would in effect be translating the same import into different terms.

the only area of morals in which this would be possible to achieve was law, where one could create an artificial or conventional body of knowledge, with immutable standards of right and wrong.[75] Yet this was clearly not Bentham's aim, in so far as his system did not seek to be arbitrary or conventional, but to be founded on expectations and real moral sensibilities.[76]

Bentham and the Critique of the Common Law

Bentham's critique of the common law took two forms. The first was an attack on Blackstone's jurisprudence. Blackstone's prime error was that he failed to set up a theoretical analysis that could explain the way that law worked: in that sense, Blackstone failed to explain the common law. Although he had been the first man successfully to put the whole together, necessary for the creation of guides to expectation, his analysis failed in the end to fulfil this function. This was because he had fallen into the classical trap:

Those who have undertaken to give Definitions of Legal terms seem to have had no higher ambition, nor any other aim than this: to contrive their definitions so as not to contain any thing that should be demonstrably false. To fit them to convey any instructive truth, is what they have either not cared, how to go about, or not known.[77]

This tied in with Bentham's second attack, on common law technicality. For Bentham, the common law's categories and terms of reference were entirely arbitrary and meaningless. The divisions of forms of action and the substantive categories that existed conveyed no information either to guide the conduct of individuals or to assist the litigant in his choice of forms. Law therefore had to be explained in different terms: so that Bentham's ultimate task would be a definitional one. Blackstone's error was that he had retained the technical terms.

(i) Blackstone's Misunderstandings

Blackstone's prime error, in Bentham's eyes, was that he had sought to set up first principles to explain the law, but failed to use them consistently. It was clear that Blackstone's key principles, natural

---

[75] *Elements of the Philosophy of the Human Mind*, ii. 147–53.
[76] UC c. 70.   [77] UC lxix. 116.

and divine law, did not act as clear first principles, since they did not explain what lay beneath them. Bentham argued that Blackstone's structure failed because he had had no clear and consistent definition of law, but rather used five different notions of it.[78] Nor had he possessed any clear idea of the nature of definition. In any definition, what applied to the genus must apply also to the species: so that what applied to law in general should be true of law in particular. Blackstone had given a definition of law as a rule of action prescribed by a superior to an inferior.[79] In Blackstone's case, '[t]he general character of Law was taken from that species which in truth is the only one': municipal law.[80] Yet he had applied it equally to laws of motion and gravitation, the law of nature and of nations. Thus Blackstone's definitions were none of them absolute, but were rather conditional on things which either were not, or could not be defined.[81]

Bentham's main attack seemed to be on the law of nature or reason, the apparent foundation stone of the common law. His contention was that this only boiled down to private opinion, that the individual disapproved of the action in question and assumed all others would too.[82] As a consequence, the notion of natural law gave no guides or rules to determine the law. This critique may be seen to have two aspects. First, it can be taken as a criticism of common law reasoning, assuming that judges did feel that the common law was based on the law of nature. This common law was indeterminate as a working system, since a judge could always make a ruling based on this spurious natural law. This interpretation is unconvincing, in so far as Bentham did not disapprove of flexible adjudications at case level. His objection was not that judges made varying decisions, but that they did so apparently without reason, that one could not see why decisions varied. Second, however, it can be taken as a criticism of the way to *conceive* of law. That is, those like Blackstone who invoked the law of nature as a metaphysical tool with which to explain the working of law failed to make sense of it. Bentham's task in the *Comment on the Commentaries* was hence less to expose the absurdity of the common law and seek its replacement with statute

---

[78] See Bentham's critique, *Comment/Fragment*, 8–23.
[79] 1 *Comm.* 38.
[80] *Comment/Fragment*, 283.
[81] Ibid. 13.
[82] Ibid. 159, 197–9. See also UC lxix. 102. This is discussed in Postema, 268–70.

than to show Blackstone's incompetence at explaining the law.[83]
These two interpretations link together: for only when judges had a
correct way to conceive of law could they articulate and understand
what they were doing, making adjudication more than private
opinion.

For Bentham, invoking titles like the law of nature, prerogative, or
religion as categories for classification was pointless because it
explained nothing: '[t]he disadvantage of these Titles is that opposite
and inconsistent regulations may [be] received into [them] neither of
which shall appear repugnant to this Title on the face of it'.[84]
Similarly, Blackstone's evocation of Justinian's principles meant
nothing more than that 'we should do as we ought to do'.[85] For
Bentham, the principle of utility was preferable because it fulfilled a
different function. Whereas the law of nature in Blackstone sought to
explain, the principle of utility begged questions. The uniting principle being the pursuit of happiness, the legislator, judge, and jurist
had to ask at every stage how the rule in question did this, and why
it was useful. The principle of utility in itself made a critical, and
therefore fluid, jurisprudence. Bentham talked of the principle of
utility as 'a magical wand at the touch of which every thing that is
obscure and uncertain in jurisprudence vanishes'.[86] This was so
because it was a simple *test* for each level.

Similarly, Blackstone had been unable to explain the workings of
law in one of its essential areas, that of customs and maxims. Blackstone had identified customs and maxims as being one and the same,
since the authority of maxims rested on general reception and
usage.[87] Bentham showed there was a fundamental difference
between them. First, a maxim was no more than a proposition
containing an opinion on the state of the law.[88] Anyone could make a
maxim, and its currency depended not on authority, but 'according
to the apparent truth and importance of it, or the credit of him who
utters it'.[89] However, for a legal custom, there had to be two things:
first, a custom *in pays*, that which was to be legalized, and an act on
the part of those who were to legalize it.[90] A legal custom became

---

[83] Thus, he said that while the point of an Institute of law was to 'draw aside that
curtain of mystery which fiction and formality have spread' over law, Blackstone had
merely embroidered the curtain. *Comment/Fragment* 124.
[84] UC lxiii. 86.
[85] *Comment/Fragment*, 15–16.
[86] UC xxvii. 152.
[87] 1 *Comm.* 68.
[88] *Comment/Fragment*, 185.
[89] Ibid. 191.
[90] Ibid. 183.

such not by virtue of the fact that some people were in the habit of following certain courses of conduct, but because judges threatened to punish those who violated it.[91]

This analysis revealed the incomprehensible nature of Blackstone's descriptions. The commentator had delved into the question of how one could validate a custom, and at this point in his work had descended into some of his most intriguing reasoning, saying that judges were the oracles of the law who knew what was custom, at the same time saying they should follow precedents, though they could be overruled if flatly absurd. He had further given a list of rules by which to test the validity of customs. They had to be immemorial, continued, peaceable, reasonable, compulsory, and consistent.[92] Bentham's attack showed how this made no sense. Blackstone's error lay in his failure to see that legal customs came from judicial commands, and in his view that the common law was wholly comprised of customs, and that the judicial acts which gave effect to them were only *evidence* of that law.[93] Blackstone seemed to be inverting reality; leaving him with the absurd alternative idea that it was necessary for judges to tell the people what their own customs were via the mechanism of law reports.[94]

Bentham's analysis of custom reveals a far more sensitive perception of common law adjudication than can be found in the *Commentaries*. For Bentham looked at the case as involving the question brought by the litigants, as well as the weight of legal precedent. This resulted from his reference to the principle of utility. The foundation of every act of judicial power was in every case some utility, either original or derived from expectation, the latter being grounded either on a habit or a promise.[95] On the 'occasion of every fresh case', the judge had to refer to 'future contingent utility founded upon past utility experienced'.[96] To that degree, any case could to some degree be new. This explained the reason why judges should follow the authority of precedents: not because of any deference to ancient times, but for the sake of stability, and '[t]hat men may be enabled to predict the legal consequences of an act before they do it: that public expectation may know what course it

---

[91] Comment/Fragment, 185, 191: 'who is it makes a Custom? (I mean a custom *in pays* that is become a legal one) any one? no, but the Judge who first punishes the non-observance of it after it has become a Custom *in pays*.'   [92] 1 *Comm.* 76–8.
[93] Ibid. 194.   [94] Ibid. 193.
[95] Ibid. 231.   [96] Ibid. 199.

has to take'.[97] This also explained Blackstone's words about judges mistaking the law, something which seemed to undermine their status as oracles. Bentham pointed out that so long as the judge's will had the power in court—so long as it was uncontrolled by a superior—the opinion of the judge stood as law. Hence, in talking of the judge mistaking the law, Blackstone meant either that the judge mistook what was the law in similar cases decided before (a fault of bad reporting or digesting) or that he misapplied that law to the present case.[98] It was only when one understood the position of the judges in the legal system—their issuing commands and thereby creating a law for the case—and related this to the principle of utility that one could make sense of law. It is of note that we see Bentham's theory of flexible adjudication evident in his describing of the common law. What is apparent here is that the critique of Blackstone is not a criticism of the common law *per se* but an attack on the *Commentaries* as an Institute which failed to understand how law worked. It was not that a legal system *should be* devised around the concepts of utility and expectation, but that one could only make proper sense of the system that existed if one used those terms. Otherwise, what judges did would merely look paradoxical and confusing.

(ii) The Chaos of the Common Law

Bentham wrote that the common law was 'a perfect chaos' that cried out for methodization, 'a blind inexplorable labyrinth, until a clue be given to it'.[99] The key reason for this was that it was bound up in technicalities that made no sense.[100] Firstly, technical terms lumped together all manner of disparate offences so that it was impossible to tell the distinguishing feature of the offence. This was evident for instance in the notion of felony, a classification that lumped together all sorts of crimes that had nothing in common bar their punishment. The arrangement of penal law around a category like felony was hence meaningless: one could learn nothing from it.[101] Whether it was the judge who was adjudicating, the pleader arguing, or even

---

[97] Ibid. 196, 203.   [98] Ibid. 205–6.
[99] UC lxix. 115, *Rationale of Judicial Evidence* in *Works* vii. 196.
[100] Bentham wrote that the consequence was that 'unless the nature and origin of that system were brought to view, the prevalence of the practice could not be accounted for'. Ibid. In other words, either one had to write a work like Reeves's, or make sense of the concepts that lay behind law, which itself would lead to its pruning and rationalization.   [101] UC lxix. 168.

the legislator outlining, so long as terms like felony were in use, no one would know what they were doing. This led directly to absurdities in practice: Bentham pointed out that in *R* v. *Mason*[102] counsel for the crown had argued that all acts which amounted to felony by land should amount to piracy at sea. This argument was self-evidently absurd, Bentham contended, for who would consider rape, forgery, or suicide to count as 'piracies'? Throughout the law, where classifications were based around technical terms, 'matters ever so heterogeneous to each other will often be crowded together in one and the same compartment'.[103] This had two bad effects. First, it gave birth to 'that curious learning' whereby law became a technical and complex game for its practitioners, cut off from daily life;[104] second, it threw the law into chaos even for those practitioners. Thus, '[t]he hollowness of many a piece of legal reasoning and impropriety of many a point of practise has no other source than a confused and unnatural classification'.[105] Even in statute law, legislators acted blind for want of a clear idea of what they were doing. For example, the Vagrancy laws talked of idle and disorderly persons, rogues and vagabonds and incorrigible rogues: but all these definitions supposed an idea of an offence already formed, and just pointed out that the legislator did not like these men.[106]

Second, technical terms failed to define the most important concepts, so that one was for ever in the dark. Thus, Blackstone had borrowed his definition of a title to things real from Coke's—it was the means by which a man came to the just possession of his property.[107] Bentham protested that the reader was left to figure out for himself what possession or property was, things which were as hard to define as title.[108] Bentham sought to begin with the definition of key basic ideas and develop them as workable tools. Common lawyers too often supposed men already had clear ideas of such basic terms as possession or property: 'they then go on with stating certain dispositions of Law as consequences of that relation supposing it already to be understood'.[109] In fact, all that could be assumed was collected from the those consequences. Therefore, very much of Bentham's work was devoted to a precise analysis of

---

[102] (1723) 8 Mod. 75.
[103] UC lxix. 190.   [104] UC lxiii. 98.
[105] UC lxiii. 74.   [106] UC lxiii. 93–7.
[107] *Titulus est justa causa possidendi id quod nostrum est*: 1 *Inst*. 345, quoted in 2 *Comm*. 195.   [108] UC lxix. 116.
[109] UC lxix. 116.

language and terms. He was very aware of the inability of current legal language to fulfil its function: it could not 'give any tolerably clear conception of the things it is designed to signify'. 'But let us not despair,' he concluded, 'even these dark regions, the light of philosophy may penetrate.'[110]

To do this, two things were necessary. First, one had to have a clear conception of what one was looking for; second, one needed a clear series of concepts to use. As to the first, Bentham proposed a method of parsing. According to this, the lawyer should first consider whether he was dealing with an article of real or fictitious law. If real, he should determine whether its object was to characterize an article of conduct permitted or prohibited, or the conditions in which it was commanded or prohibited, since the matter of all law concerned one of these two. If it was the first, then the lawyer should see whether this was done by definition or by modification. If the second, then the lawyer was to make a further enquiry, namely what was the command to which the article stood as a condition.[111] Thus, every operation should be set within a framework that traced the precise purport of the rule.[112] A system of definitions could not be unconnected, but there had to be a tracing of the meaning of complex ideas to simple ones. It was the common lawyers' failure to do this that rendered their law chaotic.[113] This could be done not only by creating a new system of law, but by re-examining the old. Bentham therefore spent time discussing the detail of English property law, fee-simple and fee-tail.[114]

It was in this context that Bentham asserted that the law would cease to be a science when a correct vocabulary was composed, and would become merely the issue of applying facts. Simply, those facts would be easier to find. This did not, however, simplify the function of the courts. For Bentham noted that there were almost no acts that were simply and unconditionally commanded or prohibited: the

---

[110] UC lxix. 172.

[111] UC lxix. 104. This was the same process that should be done in a suit. UC lxix. 121.

[112] This was the definitional exercise he sought for his Digest. 'To the Definitional part', he wrote, 'belongs also the Doctrine concerning Tenures: it shews the several conditions upon which that which is called property is made. By specifying the conditions annexed to the subject in question by these Tenures, &c it shews several of the ways by which that which has been a given person's property may cease to be so, viz. upon breach of any of these conditions.' UC lxix. 116.

[113] UC lxix. 135.

[114] UC lxix. 97.

majority were hedged by conditions.[115] Indeed, '[t]here are a thousand conditions annext to every Law,' he wrote, 'before the threat of it can take effect.'[116] Law was inextricably bound in with circumstance, so that the same act that was commanded under one set of circumstances would be forbidden under another set.[117] However, once it was clear what the nature of conditions were, and how they could be unravelled, the position of the law became clearer.

The analytical vocabulary was particularly important in questions of civil law, where far less depended on commands, and much more on the nature of obligations and conditions, matters where the law grew from below. Here, a key basic concept was possession, something which could be simply defined as 'in the being at liberty to exercise such acts upon a thing as other men are not left at liberty to exercise upon it'. [118] However, to have a full understanding of possession required also a knowledge of the nature of obligations, conditions, limitations, and conveyances. Bentham's analysis of legal concepts thus took him through a detailed exposition of the meaning of these terms, showing how English lawyers had confused them. For example, given a clear understanding of terms, lawyers would no longer muddle conditions and limitations in the way they currently did.[119] As a result, finding the fact in disputed cases would become easier. It should be noted that in explaining these terms of civil law jurisprudence, Bentham took for granted the current legal relations and only sought to make sense of what the effect was of a covenant, a condition, or a limitation. He was analysing current legal relations, not starting afresh.

The analytical venture could assist the problem courts had in solving difficult questions in what appeared to be new areas of law. Bentham therefore referred to the controversial line of cases over copyright, and the difficulty the courts had in conceiving of literary property. Once one had a clear notion of the nature of possession, then it could be simplified. Bentham said that the judges had been misled by their identification of possession with physical handling,

---

[115] UC lxix. 114. In fact, Bentham could only think of two: 'crimes against nature' and cruelty.

[116] UC lxix. 153.   [117] UC lxix. 138.

[118] UC lxix. 169. Bentham added, importantly, 'Now these acts it is evident are as many as are capable of a separate description.' See also *OLG* 272–82.

[119] Thus, a condition was a clause appointing an event upon which an estate would pass away from the possessor; a limitation named the person who would gain it upon the happening of the event. UC lxix. 132.

so that they could not conceive of a property right to ideas. He pointed out however that legal possession had to be defined as the absence of restraint in using something. The difference between legal possession of a thing and a copyright was simple: in the first, all men bar the possessor were restrained from using the thing; in the second, the possessor of pen and paper was partially restrained in using it for certain purposes. In other words, copyright was the case where one man was restrained in his actions for the benefit of another. This was nothing new: all trusts, restraints in trade, and partial property rights rested on the same foundation.[120] Thus, a clear concept of possession could help solve substantive problems. A clear analysis of legal terms would therefore not merely be an intellectual exercise for the jurist's amusement: it had practical applicability.

This view helps us to make sense of Bentham's civil code. In his obituary of Bentham, Mill wrote that with regard to the civil code, he had 'done least and left most to be done'.[121] Mill was right in the sense that Bentham failed to outline a code of substantive civil law rules; but Bentham's civil code writings did not aim to set out such a code for the most part.[122] Much of his work on the civil code was purely analytical, exploring the nature and meaning of possession, contract, and property.[123] Thus, in *Blackstone Familiarized*, he sought to explain the principles of civil law by following the history of a coat, beginning with its first possessor, whose right to it began with expectation and the disappointment-prevention principle, and whose possession was therefore protected by the service of a judge. Bentham then traced the coat's history to explain the nature of rights, powers, and trusts.[124] Similarly, in *Principles of the Civil Code*, he began by examining the reasons why a legislator should sanction the existence of property, and then (examining the titles which conferred property) began again by analysing possession.[125]

---

[120] UC lxix. 147, 180.

[121] In *The Collected Works of John Stuart Mill*, gen. ed. F. E. L. Priestley, vol. x. (Toronto, 1969), 497. Kelly challenges Mill's assessment in his examination of Bentham's civil law works by showing that Bentham had a sophisticated theory developed in his unpublished writings: *Utilitarianism and Distributive Justice*, p. 19.

[122] The exception was Bentham's writings on the law of real property.

[123] UC xxxi. 11–22, 32, 54–6.

[124] UC xxx. 77 ff., 133–5. Thus, the coat's history was traced as it was given to a tailor, Bentham here exploring the different circumstances in which the owner could recover possession of the coat, and those in which he could not.

[125] *Principles of the Civil Code*, 327.

P. J. Kelly has recently argued that Bentham's legislator was concerned with 'legitimate expectations', which were conceived in terms of the absence of certain categories of harm: harms against person, property, condition in life, and reputation. The legislator protected the individual from these harms, but within these bounds, the individual could pursue his own conception of good, unfettered by the legislator.[126] Kelly is right to point out that the legislator would not dictate detail to individuals at ground level, and that every man had a realm of freedom to pursue his own conception of good. However, as each individual pursued his own good, he was likely to infringe another man's interests, so that the number of acts that might fall within the fourfold division of harms (and thus offences) could be infinite. Bentham's four basic classes were in fact un-controversial classifications,[127] which did not pretend to do more than to provide a framework within which any law could be fitted. The aim of the fourfold division was the same aim Blackstone had had: to show the reasons for laws, their relations to each other, and to be formulated to be best adapted for discourse.[128] Similarly, the general titles of the civil code sought to analyse and make sense of the infinite cases that could emerge. Bentham pointed out that 'things' could be endlessly classified, divisible into natural and artificial, moveable and immoveable, employable and consumable, simple and complex, as well as in other ways.[129] Outlining his view of a civil code in the *General View*, he therefore sought to analyse all the factors that were important in understanding the right to things. The general titles of the civil code were: first, a definition of things; second, of places; third, of times; fourth, of services; fifth, of obligations; sixth, of rights; seventh, of ablative and collative events; eighth, of contracts; ninth, of the domestic and civil states; and tenth, of persons capable of contracting. Within these heads, there were not rules outlined, but an analytical framework within which the law worked. Thus, in the sixth title, he discussed the sources, objects, and subjects of rights. Discussing rights over things, he talked of seven ways in which a right of occupation could be limited.[130] In the seventh title, he discussed the ways a right began

---

[126] *Utilitarianism and Distributive Justice*, pp. 249–91. Kelly argues that this helps to explain the fact that Bentham was a liberal theorist.

[127] Compare Blackstone's three absolute rights: personal security, personal liberty, and property. The first included reputation. 1 *Comm*. 124–41.

[128] *General View*, 171.   [129] Ibid. ch. 9.

[130] Ibid. 182–4.

and ended, and went on to discuss the nature of possession. Bentham's aim in this was to analyse how disputes (and hence offences) over things could arise as men sought to pursue their own interests; and thereby to facilitate the process of adjudication. This is evident in his dismissal of existing systems of divisions:

> What shall we say of the famous division among the Romanists, of things *corporeal* and things *incorporeal*; that is to say, of things which do not exist, which are not things? It is a fiction which only serves to hide and to augment the confusion of ideas. All these incorporeal rights are only rights either to the services of men, or of real things.[131]

By a clearer analysis, courts would more easily distinguish what the rights were that were being sought.

The civil code therefore was not designed to give clear rules of action for the judge to follow in a manner analogous to the penal law.[132] Rather, when it came to substantive detail, Bentham was far too aware of the variations of circumstance that had to be taken into account. 'Reference', he therefore concluded, 'must be made to the circumstances of the parties interested, by leaving to the judge the care of pronouncing upon the cases of individuals as they present themselves.'[133] In the realm of acquisition, possession, and services, where so much depended on circumstances and the intentions of the parties, the essential thing was for the judge to have clear notions of what was being done.

Bentham's Code and the Common Law

Bentham's analytical jurisprudence casts new light on the notion that he felt he could write a code for any country for any time. Only one short work of his was published looking at the problem of local variations, the *Essay on the Influence of Time and Place in Matters of Legislation*.[134] This work may be seen to underline Bentham's ambition to create a substantive deductive code for all nations, for he stated at the outset that '[c]omplete perfection requires universal

---

[131] Ibid. 177.

[132] The exception was with regard to the rules of succession, where Bentham devised a scheme of succession based on utility. However, regarding wills, he preferred to allow complete freedom to dispose of one's goods. *Principles of the Civil Code*, chs 3–4.   [133] *Principles of the Civil Code*, 339.

[134] In *Works*, vol. I, pp. 169–94. Henceforth *Time and Place*.

accuracy: universal accuracy requires infinite detail'.[135] In this work, Bentham recognized that there were differences of local circumstance, but stated that when the legislator acknowledged the principle of utility and had arranged fundamental truths, it would be possible to form a precise notion of 'a perfect system of legislation', so that legislators would 'know as well how to make laws for one country as for another'.[136] All that the legislator would need was some knowledge of local customs. Bentham was much more sensitive to local differences than has been realized: and it is clear that what was common to all law was a system of abstract terms and concepts: the substantive detail could differ. Working on his critique of criminal jurisprudence in 1778, he therefore wrote that he was concerned much more with the affairs of the nation for which he wrote—England—than with other nations. 'Twas by the view of the particular institutions of this country that most of these general principles were suggested,' he wrote:

> To apply such of these general principles then as are applicable to the particular institutions of his own country, and to supply such other general principles as the exigencies of these particular institutions may require is a work which will probably come within the province of the Lawyers . . . of every nation in particular.[137]

Rather than Bentham joying in throwing away all existing law and starting to construct the ideal system a priori, he wrote,

> [a]n inconvenience that has been severely felt by me throughout the whole progress of this work is the want of having some particular country given (and proposed) to the particular circumstances of which the provisions I contrived should be adapted. Hence the mortification of being obliged at every step to stop short not only of my own ideas of complete perfection . . . but even of my own ideas of that moderate degree of perfect excellence which my own limited faculties seemed able to attain.[138]

Bentham's interest was hence in the arrangement and form of laws, but not in their content. He therefore argued that any system of established jurisprudence, 'how absurd soever', could be of use as a repository of cases that had occurred before and hence might

---

[135] *Time and Place*, 172.
[136] Ibid. 194, 180.
[137] UC lxix. 14. Cf. UC xxvii. 107, UC lxix. 127, UC lxx(a). 63: 'Our idea of perfection, to be a legitimate one, must be formed by abstraction of the views of the present system which we see.'   [138] UC xxvii. 130.

again.[139] More particularly, the common law was a superb source of raw materials for any legislator.[140] Bentham hence argued that what was particularly useful in the collection of cases and treatises was the variety, clarity, and comprehensiveness of the legal points covered.[141] He was therefore very cautious when it came to proposing substantive law reform. The law had to be in harmony with the times, he argued, for if new maxims were suddenly introduced, there would be a conflict between the ancient customs—which shaped people's expectations about law—and new maxims.[142] For the same substantive laws could not be applied indiscriminately to all countries. The same law could be 'good for one nation and bad for another,' Bentham wrote, 'not but that in itself it is equally proper for both, but because in one nation the people may be disposed, in another they may not be disposed to acquiesce in it.'[143] Therefore reform had to be slow and cautious: '[i]t is not well to destroy everything, upon pretence of reconstructing the whole,' he wrote; 'the fabric of the laws may be easily delapidated, but is difficult to be repaired, and its alteration ought not to be entrusted to rash and ignorant operators.'[144]

We must note that Bentham was much more sensitive to the history of the common law than is sometimes noticed. Despite his theoretical equation of law with legislation, he acknowledged the

---

[139] UC xxvii. 162.

[140] Having acknowledged the influence of Beccaria and Helvetius, Bentham said, '[f]rom the time that I understood and had learnt how to apply, I never looked into any book for principles: not even into any writer on what is called natural law: much less into any system of positive established law. The only use that I made of books was to discover *cases*.' UC xxvii. 138. Cf. UC lxix. 172: 'What *opposition* one man may lawfully give to another man's using that which is another man's own consistently with the propriety of that thing and what not may be learnt from the doctrine of Actions on the Case.'

[141] *Papers Relative to Codification*, 461: 'Traverse the whole continent of Europe,— ransack all the libraries belonging to the jurisprudential systems of the several political states,—add the contents all together,—you would not be able to compose a collection of cases equal in variety, in amplitude, in clearness of statement—in a word, all points taken together, in instructiveness—to that which may be seen to be afforded by the collection of English *Reports of adjudged cases*, on adding to them the *abridgements* and *treatises*, by which a sort of order, such as it is, has been given to their contents.'   [142] *Principles of the Civil Code*, 325.

[143] UC xxvii. 121. Cf. UC xxvii. 125: 'A model of Absolute perfection will be of use forever: practical perfection will vary according to the circumstances of persons place and time.' Cf. UC lxx(a). 19: 'Justice may truly be said to be different concerning many points among different people because among these people the expectation[s] concerning these points are different.'

[144] *Principles of the Civil Code*, 326.

growth of the common law as a system of court remedies. In *Blackstone Familiarized*, Bentham explored the early history of English law. Although the function of judges was to give execution to the body of laws, whether common or statute, in the early days there was no such body, either real or fictitious. Instead, '[w]hen one man felt himself a sufferer by the act of another he made application to a judge or all of [the] judges and asked for relief [or] satisfaction in one shape or other'.[145] Law thus began as the unconnected individual commands of judges.[146] Law evolved because lawyers took notes so that when similar cases emerged both they and the judges could save themselves the trouble of reasoning afresh each time. Judges made the law at a time when the king's edicts were imperfect and occasional. Thus, Bentham's view was not merely that the common law was the work of inference from cases, but that all law was necessarily so in the early stages of English legal history. Hence, codification and statutification was not a timeless thing, but was appropriate to a certain stage of legal development, to recast the same law. '[I]t follows not that because such was the state of things at that early stage,' Bentham wrote, 'it ought to be suffered to continue in that same state at a stage as advanced as the present.' This did not mean throwing the past away and starting from scratch: rather, Bentham spoke of putting the law into a proper state. The way of achieving this was by authoritative inference:

Generalization and arrangement are laborious and tedious processes, and require not only a more than ordinary strength of mind, but an exhaustive and variegated stock of particulars to work upon. Till comparatively of late years neither of these conditions both of which are indisputably necessary had come into existence.[147]

A reliable guide was needed both for litigants and for judges. Bentham significantly could be quite phlegmatic about the prospects of his code being complete: rather, he did foresee that judges would have to make interpretations. For he said that no method existed that would exclude all possibility of misinterpretation. The code would not serve as an 'artificial brain: all that can be expected of it is that

---

[145] UC xxx. 61.
[146] 'In the infancy of our Jurisprudence, there was no such thing as any command to men not to steal, but if a man stole, an order went out to another man to go and hang him.' UC lxix. 98.
[147] UC xxx. 66–7.

men of liberal education of sound Judgments and unruffled passions should concur in the sense which they put upon it'.[148]

As Bentham in 1775 surveyed his achievements hitherto in preparing for his Digest, and as he contemplated a system of codes, he said he had now separated his materials 'from the decayed rubbish which surrounded them'. The untempered mortar had been cleansed from the bricks: now, to compose the fabric of the new system, all that remained was to put them in their order.[149] This was an ordering of existing legal terms and concepts and legal rules. Bentham's codification ideal remained ambiguous throughout his life: but if we reject his self-proclaimed desire to create the complete new code, and focus instead on his analysis of abstract legal concepts,[150] we can make better sense of his view of adjudication, and see how it fitted the common law one. Bentham's view of the function of judges—his emphasis on their need to make adjudications that fitted popular expectation and his insistence that they follow rules—largely reflects and explains existing court practices. A rule would only go so far, and would leave cases unaccounted for: but with a clear set of concepts, the judge would be enabled to unravel the details of the case before him. In settling the substantive issue, the law would be based on expectation. If rules could shape those expectations and give certainty to law,[151] the basic grounds for decisions in many civil cases, particularly those regarding contract, lay in the expectations of the parties. In these cases, the judge might have to balance a decision on the grounds of original utility or expectation:[152] which ultimately was no clearer a guide for the judge than was offered by the common law's appeal to policy, principle, or expedience. Indeed, the fact that Bentham saw laws themselves as fictitious and foresaw the judge weighing all these considerations in each case (at least in theory)

---

[148] UC lxx(a). 126. Indeed, Bentham wrote, '[t]he herd of people must for a long time perhaps for ever be sway'd chiefly by authority: but of those who by their authority are in a way to lead them there are enough whose circumstances admitt of their being sway'd by reason.' UC xxvii. 135.   [149] UC lxx(a), 107.

[150] The contrast between Bentham's analytical thinking and his proposals for a substantive code in the *Constitutional Code* may be illustrated by the fact that whereas he allowed the latter to be amended and to develop, he noted when working on the former that the slightest alteration necessitated the entire recasting of the work; but that once sound metaphysical truth had been discovered, it was recognizable by all. UC xxvii. 141b.

[151] 'If it were not for general expectation which is fixed immoveably by a Law or a series of consistent judgments it would be as reasonable and as consonant to utility to determine such a question in one day one way and in the next another.' UC lxx(a), 19.

[152] UC lxx(a), 19–20.

shows that his view of law was in many ways as much rooted in the realm of adjudication as the common law's. But where the common law, as a result of its terms, acted in only the most imperfect way to disentangle legal concept from fact, and to organize the substantive bodies that would shape expectation, Bentham's theory could do so far better.

Judges would not usually act in direct-utilitarian ways; although they could, depending on the novelty of the case. Postema has argued that Bentham's judges could decide in this direct manner, that they could disregard the rules of the code when the balance of utilities warranted, something that would be safe given that their decisions would not act as precedents.[153] However, if we accept the above interpretation of Bentham's venture, it is evident that the judges could neither be classed as rule—or act—utilitarians in their actions. Instead, the judge would adjudicate on a case as presented to him through the pleas which he would have to 'solve'. This could be *either* directly by reference to a clear established rule which fitted the case, *or* by a reasoned application of the case at hand to a legal category with its concomitant principles, *or* in the absence of any guide, to the dictates of utility itself. The action of the judge would depend on the case: and all too often, the judge would find his rule by a combination of these methods.

[153] Postema, *Bentham and the Common Law Tradition*, 440, 447–8.

7

The Debate over Codification

THE all-important subject of Judicial Reform', declared the *Edinburgh Review* in 1830, 'has, of late years, happily occupied the almost undivided attention of thinking men, in every part of the country.'[1] Law reform was the great cause,[2] and, to many, it seemed that Bentham had initiated it, by exposing the faults of the common law.[3] As Henry Brougham put it, 'the age of law reform and the age of Jeremy Bentham are the same'.[4] The historiography of institutional and legal reform in early nineteenth-century England is dominated by the presence of Bentham and his acolytes: from Dicey[5] to the combatants in the debate on the nineteenth century 'Revolution in Government'[6] to the social history of prisons and workhouses,[7]

---

[1] *Edinburgh Review*, li. (1830), 479.

[2] As James Mill wrote in 1835, 'The change has been so great, that now the extreme badness of the law is matter of universal admission; and wonder at the long-suffering stupidity of a people who submitted to such a nuisance is the sentiment bursting from every man's lips.' *London Review*, ii (1835–6), 1.

[3] The *Edinburgh Review* wrote, 'To his master-hand we owe a picture, which, for depth of colouring, and vigour of design, has no match; it is the greatest service ever rendered to the country which he adorns, by any of her political philosophers; and its contemplation has produced, as sooner or later it was bound to produce, the resolute determination of the ablest statesmen to clear out the Augean stable.' *Edinburgh Review*, li. 481–2.

[4] Brougham, *Speeches upon Questions relating to Public Rights, Duties and Interests*, 4 vols. (Edinburgh, 1838), ii. 287.

[5] *Lectures on the Relation between Law and Public Opinion in England during the Nineteenth Century*, 2nd edn. (London, 1914).

[6] See O. MacDonough, 'The Nineteenth Century Revolution in Government: A Reappraisal', *Historical Journal*, i (1958), 52–67; H. Parris, 'The Nineteenth Century Revolution in Government: A Reappraisal Reappraised', *Historical Journal*, iii (1960–1), 17–37; D. Roberts, 'Bentham and the Administrative State', *Victorian Studies*, ii (1958–9), 193–210; Jenifer Hart, 'Nineteenth Century Social Reform: A Tory Interpretation of History', *Past and Present*, xxxi (1965), 39–61; L. J. Hume, 'Jeremy Bentham and the Nineteenth Century Revolution in Government', *Historical Journal*, x (1967), 361–75; and J. B. Brebner, 'Laissez-Faire and State Intervention in Nineteenth Century Britain', *Journal of Economic History*, vii (1948), 59–73.

[7] See, e.g., Robin Evans, *The Fabrication of Virtue: English Prison Architecture, 1750– 1840* (Cambridge, 1982).

historians have created scenes where the spirit of Benthamism presides,[8] with the master sometimes acting as the direct inspiration for reform, sometimes only as an *éminence grise*. It is a hard task to trace the influence of theoretical conjectures on practical problems, and often we are led to assume the link between Benthamite inspiration and pragmatic reform.

This is a particular problem in the history of law, for as we have seen, Bentham was unable to produce a workable substantive system, and left instead a theoretical system of analysis. None the less, many of those involved in law reform in the 1820s and 1830s were Benthamites—most notably Henry Brougham, who as Lord Chancellor presided over the most important Royal Commissions charged with reform.[9] Further, although there was no wholesale codification in England, there were serious efforts made, at the highest level, to codify centrally important aspects of the law. The challenge of codification was a serious one; and therefore it seems odder still that the most significant reforms in the common law should end in a spectacular victory for the most particularistic view of the common law, and with a total rejection of Bentham's theory of procedure. At first sight, the movement for the reform of the common law seems riddled with contradictions. However, at closer inspection, we can trace the limits of Bentham's influence.

We must divide Bentham in two: the formal analyst of legal concepts, and the substantive codifier. Then, we must trace the influence of both these areas on law reformers. Doing this, it becomes apparent that the legal disciples of Bentham tended to follow him only in the first sphere, and not in the second, so that even men like Brougham were capable of being both traditional lawyers and good Benthamites. Beyond this, however, it becomes clear that traditional common lawyers, with no axe to grind against the fee-paying system, could be good Benthamic formalists. This helps explain the dilemma of codification and how it came about that the common law system survived. Lawyers, under the influence of Bentham, were beginning to conceive of the law in Benthamic, rules-based terms, and therefore wanted a reform of the substantive law

[8] See D. Lieberman, 'From Bentham to Benthamism', *Historical Journal*, xxviii (1985), 199–224.

[9] See F. Hawes, *Henry Brougham* (London, 1957); C. New, *The Life of Henry Brougham to 1830* (Oxford, 1961); and R. Stewart, *Henry Brougham, 1778–1868: His Public Career* (London, 1985).

which would make it clearer and more capable of being comprehended in terms of rules. However, there was a fundamental separation of the spheres of theory and practice: accepting a Benthamic concept of law did not entail adopting Bentham's aims regarding the law's content, nor adopting an aim of creating a Pannomion on correct utilitarian principles which would cover all aspects of law.[10]

Bentham, as shall be seen, could have a strong influence on the way men thought about the law, without altering the way they looked at its content. One example of this is to be seen in the lectures given by Thomas Starkie to his students at the Inner Temple in 1834. Starkie began his lecture course with a definition of law expressed in Benthamic terms. 'A civil law', he said, 'prescribes the rule of conduct to be observed in a state of civil society by the different members of the community.' He added that '[t]he first and great business of the law is, to define rights and correlative duties of all kinds, whether they be public or private'.[11] If Starkie's thoughts on jurisprudence were Benthamic,[12] his thoughts on legislation similarly followed the master. Civil legislation, Starkie argued, had to provide rules of conduct 'adapted to all exigencies', and it had to be framed 'that it may embrace, in its terms, all possible combinations within its principle, and no more'.[13] These views did not lead him to reject the common law and its method, however. For at the same time, Starkie could warn his students of the danger of following principles too closely, and argue that the law in practice was infinitely varied with a vast multiplicity of sources.[14] He thus argued in favour of technical procedural rules, for the sake of certainty,[15] and pointed out that 'in our law, the extent of the right is limited and defined by the extent of the wrong'.[16] These views on the procedures and nature of the common law were quite the reverse of Bentham's, and when

---

[10] The Benthamite view of law was thus distinct from the Benthamic one. In 'Mighty Bentham', *Journal of Legal History*, ii (1981), 62–72, H. Beynon rightly argues that Bentham's direct substantive influence on the law was limited: nevertheless the Benthamites had their own influence, which was derived from the master, but more limited in its aims.

[11] *Legal Examiner and Law Chronicle*, iii. 172–3.

[12] e.g.: 'The *substantive* branch of the law has . . . for its object, the defining of all primary rights and duties in a state of society; the adjective branch is employed in the preventing or remedying violations of the substantive law.' *Legal Examiner and Law Chronicle*, iii. 173.

[13] Ibid. ii. 439.

[14] Ibid. ii. 517–20.

[15] Ibid. iii. 171 ff.

[16] Ibid. iii. 176.

Starkie came to the body of his lectures, his method was very historical, tracing the development and nature of particular statutes from the Saxons. The fact that these two approaches could sit happily together is very significant, in so far as it is evidence of the renewed separation of theory and practice, in which Bentham's theoretical views could be used to make sense of an autonomous substantive system. It is this division of thinking, between Bentham's concepts and common law content, which explains much of the impetus behind, and the nature of, law reform in the 1820s.

There remained in the 1820s and 1830s a suspicion of codification in general, particularly in response to the rise of contemporary codes, such as the Napoleonic and Louisiana Codes. The *Edinburgh Review*, reviewing Rossi's *Traité de droit pénal* in 1831,[17] hence noted that such codes were failures and needed constant elaboration since it was impossible to substitute the will and intelligence of one man for that of a whole nation. The *Law Magazine* was similarly dismissive of the Napoleonic Code, claiming it was not an entire body of novel laws. Napoleon, the journal pointed out, had taken well-established treatises and turned them into law, merely codifying what was law. In any case, the codification of existing rules had proved much more effective than starting from scratch.[18] A novel code did not dispense with the need for treatises, it was noted, but merely caused confusion: so much so, that between 1800 and 1827 there had been over 200 original compendiums and treatises published on French law, as well as hundreds of volumes of legislative decrees. In short, the perfect French code did not as yet exist.

Nevertheless, the journals which could deride the French code also despaired at the antitheoretical nature of English conceptions of law. The *Edinburgh Review* thus could also bemoan the fact that so few people read Bentham, adding, 'the existence of such a textbook as Coke upon Littleton . . . in the nineteenth century, is a national disgrace'.[19] This journal could similarly dismiss Rossi's conjectures on creating a system of criminal law built on the foundations of

---

[17] *Edinburgh Review*, liv (1831), 183–238, reviewing P. L. O. Rossi, *Traité de Droit Pénal* (Paris, 1829).

[18] *Law Magazine*, i (1828–9), 613–37. The journal commented, 'If general rules and principles were wanted, Pothier's, which must have stood the test of experience, were far more likely to be sound than any formed on the spur of the occasion; and the same may be said of the old laws that were retained' (p. 626).

[19] *Edinburgh Review*, liv. 185.

conscience, by contending that reasons in criminal law must be sought from utility. The journal thus argued for the rejection of all notions of abstract justice or rights in legislation. '[L]egislation has nothing to do with man, his nature and his destiny,' it said, 'except as a member of society. Its duty in this repect is also the measure of its right.'[20] The journal thus could draw a hard line between law and morals. In questions involving the latter, society could stand by, and leave it to spectators to judge, but in law, society had to act and speak as master, using orders, not exhortations. Hence, '[t]he lawgiver assumes, by the very fact of his solemn undertaking, that he has found out the truth, within that limited sphere, and for the special purpose, in respect of which he presumes to act'.[21] In matters of legal philosophy, Bentham was in the ascendant.

The Impetus to Reform

By the 1820s, even the most traditionally minded lawyer needed little convincing that the law was in dire need of reform. With the publication of detailed studies on particular doctrines, and the revelations of histories such as Reeves's, lawyers could see for themselves how anachronistic and senseless much of their law was. The path was set for iconoclasts even outside Bentham's circle. George Ensor was one such critic: well read, not only in Reeves's *History*, but also in the old masters and defenders of the common law from Fortescue and Hale to Blackstone and Burke, Ensor could write a critique equally scathing on the common and statute law. For him, while statute law was vast and incongruous, the common law was riddled with a confusion of jurisdictions and an absence of clear precepts. Worst of all was the vulgar prejudice of the British to revere habit, something which 'may be very pious, but [which] is very impolitic'.[22] Lawyers by the 1820s were under no illusions about any perfection of the common law wrought by time. The *Edinburgh Review* thus drew on Reeves's work to trace the rules of conveyancing: '[t]he intricacy of our modern system of real property', it concluded, 'does not proceed from any obscurity in the

---

[20] Ibid. 205.   [21] Ibid. 233.

[22] G. Ensor, *Defects of the English Laws and Tribunals* (London, 1812) 51. Ensor wrote, 'There are many in this country who seem to think that progression is helped by obstruction, and general prosperity by partialities.' Ibid. 45.

ancient doctrines of the law, for they are generally plain and intelligible enough'.[23] It proceeded from their being unsuitable to modern needs and from the fact that they had been contorted by absurd devices to evade restrictive rules. The law needed change, the journal concluded, and if the legislature recognized this, it ought in a single measure to reform this area of law, to spare conveyancers the dangerous maze of the rules they currently worked with.[24]

One of the most influential reformists in the 1820s was John Miller of Lincoln's Inn, who wrote two works urging changes.[25] Miller made numerous detailed proposals, some of which had a Benthamite flavour—he thus proposed simpler judicial procedure, public proceedings, and more accessible courts,[26] while he further supported the rationalization of the law.[27] However, Miller was not in favour of codification, and never dreamed of removing the common law. Indeed, he argued that a train of consistent cases was as useful as any legislation, and therefore urged the simplification and condensation of law reports.[28] For Miller, twenty or thirty remedial Acts, 'framed with comprehensiveness and accuracy, would tend more to facilitate the administration of justice, than all the labours of all the chancellors, chief justices, and judges, who ever sat in England'.[29] Reform for Miller was less the altering of the nature of the common law than getting it back on the right tracks. Many lawyers who deplored the idea of codification therefore believed that the law should be clarified, to produce comprehensible *rules*. John Reddie, a man who rejected codification with a passion, thus praised Miller's scheme of remedial legislation, and declared it to be the prime duty of the legislator to 'extract from the mass of existing relations, those grand leading principles which are at once the basis, and the pillars of the system,—which have been sanctioned by the consuetude of ages, and found in unison with the genius of the nation.'[30]

The legal profession thus admitted the need for reform for itself

---

[23] *Edinburgh Review*, xlvi (1827), 155.   [24] Ibid. 156.

[25] *An Inquiry into the Present State of the Statute and Criminal Law of England* (London, 1822), and *An Inquiry into the Present State of the Civil Law of England* (London, 1825).

[26] *Inquiry into the Present State of the Civil Law*, 418 ff.

[27] Ibid. 491; *Inquiry into the Present State of the Statute and Criminal Law*, 80.

[28] *Inquiry into the Present State of the Statute and Criminal Law*, 9 ff.

[29] *Inquiry into the Present State of the Civil Law*, 315.

[30] Reddie, *A Letter to the Lord High Chancellor of Great Britain on the Expediency of the Proposal for a New Civil Code for England* (London, 1828), 53.

without Bentham's help; and the sort of reform it was thinking about was conditioned by a desire to see the law simplified in terms of clear rules. This meant that the sort of reform desired was a piecemeal one, of the kind being carried out by Peel at the Home Office.[31] 'We confess,' wrote the *Quarterly Review* in 1828, 'we prefer the plan of inquiring into defects in our legal system productive of actual mischiefs, and remedying these by simple and practical corrections, to any bolder attempts at a general change of system.'[32] However, the 1820s are most associated with the Benthamites' attacks on the common law, in their campaigns for codification of all areas of law. This Benthamite attack, extending codification beyond the criminal law into all aspects of the common law, may be said to have begun in earnest in 1828, when Brougham delivered his great six-hour speech to the House of Commons, attacking an enormous range of legal practices.[33] This speech led to the creation of two Royal Commissions to examine the law of real property and the procedures and practices of the common law courts, these two subjects being in effect the cornerstones of the common law.[34] The speech created a climate of reform which would continue for more than a decade, spurred on by Brougham. The creation of the Royal Commissions

---

[31] After the Royal Commission of the Criminal Law had reported in 1824, Peel began to consolidate the criminal statutes, and, from 1825 to 1828, he replaced 278 statutes with only 8. He claimed in this to be following Bacon's aim 'to pruning and grafting the law; and not to ploughing up and planting it again.' See N. Gash, *Mr. Secretary Peel: the Life of Sir Robert Peel to 1830* (London, 1961), 332.

[32] *Quarterly Review*, xxxvii (1828), 147.

[33] *Hansard*, vol. xviii (NS) 1828, p. 241. This is not to ignore the attempts in the previous decade by Romilly and Mackintosh to reform the criminal law and urge its codification which since 1808 had achieved a large number of reforms in punishments for crimes. However, these reformist moves concentrated on clarifying the plethora of chaotic statutes rather than reforming common law procedures. Thus, when Mackintosh secured the appointment of a Select Committee to consider capital punishments in felony, he said that he did not wish to form a new criminal code or abolish 'a system of law, admirable in its principle [and] interwoven in the habits of the English people . . . [but rather] to transfer to the statute-book the improvements which the wisdom of modern times has introduced into the practice of the law'. Quoted in *Law Magazine*, xiii (1835), 3. See also Romilly, 'Bentham on Codification', *Edinburgh Review*, vol. xxix (1817–18), 217–37.

[34] Thus, Book 2 of the *Commentaries* was devoted to real property, while Book 3 concerned the activities of the courts in providing remedies. Leaving aside the criminal law (Book 4) which was relatively new as a distinct branch for treatises on the common law, these two areas represent the ambit of the law: the rules on real property being the defined aspect of the law, defining rights, and court procedures correcting wrongs. That being so, it can be seen how significant it was that there should be two commissions established to reform them.

represented the summation of a vast reforming zeal aimed at the heart of the law. The question is therefore posed: how far were the reforms under the sway of Bentham's ideas?

How Benthamic was Brougham's initial speech? When Brougham concluded by stressing 'the necessity of taking a general view of the whole system in whatever inquiries may be instituted',[35] and argued that the only safe thing to do was to reform the whole law, he was throwing out a huge challenge to the legal profession. Indeed, the speech itself was huge, for in it he covered abuses in all areas of law and proposed sweeping changes in all. It seems to have been the great Benthamic venture in action, reworking the law from anew. Brougham's speech was not what it seemed, however. It was neither a full Benthamic attack on the entire fabric and structure of law, nor a Baconian reformist approach, but rather sat some way in the middle. Brougham was taking a Benthamic broad sweep of the law, and urging men to view it as an interconnected whole, and yet his proposals in substantive terms suited the substantive ideas of common lawyers far more than Bentham's idea of the Pannomion. Brougham, the future Lord Chancellor, had no interest in the ideal, natural, and universal code: he wanted merely to reform and improve the common law he knew.

Bentham himself reviewed the speech in the *Westminster Review* where he claimed that Brougham only aspired to expose existing abuses in the law without having a clear codified alternative. 'He is not', Bentham concluded, 'the Messiah of law-reform.'[36]

Bentham had a point. Discussing the inequality of business between the three common law courts, Brougham did not aim to replace them, but only to equalize their business more; discussing the vast burden on the judges, he proposed only that their number should be swelled from 12 to 14. While the speech ran over vast areas of the law, it did not propose a reworking from first principles, but only sought the piecemeal reform so many in the profession hankered after.[37] Perhaps the acid test of his Benthamism is to be found in his views on procedure: and here, as elsewhere, Brougham only sought to reform what existed. Thus, he proposed removing obsolete procedures, such as the wager of law, and simplifying many

---

[35] *Hansard*, vol. xviii (NS) 1828, 242.

[36] *Westminster Review*, xi (1829), 448.

[37] An example of the type of reform he sought was his desire to abolish particular local customs, such as gavelkind, so that only general laws would remain.

forms and procedures which only served to swell the coffers of lawyers and to confuse everyone else.[38] His main concern was to *restore* the purity of the common law, and that included restoring the purity of pleading.[39]

Brougham's view of pleading was clearly not Bentham's.[40] In his article, Bentham reaffirmed his support for summary jurisdiction, by bringing the parties directly before the judge; yet Brougham had defended the system of written pleas, and had opposed the idea that the judge should be able to compel testimony. Why, Bentham asked, did Brougham treat written pleas with such awe—'[i]s not the whole machinery of special pleading a machinery of delay and costliness?'[41] Bentham was adamant that Brougham had missed the essentials of reform[42] and concluded that he was just another lawyer. His plan, Bentham pointed out, 'is but a ramification of the fee-gathering system, and by self-payment too: for every act performed, for every document signed—a fee'.[43] For Bentham, the key problems in law were that the substantive law was chaotic, and the adjective law was corrupt: for him, Brougham had addressed neither of these issues. All Brougham had succeeded in doing was to show up, by his overview of the law, what a chaotic system it was: '[t]he abuses which he has vainly sought to defend who shall hope to preserve?'[44]

If Bentham did not recognize Brougham's ideas as a version of his own, most lawyers rejected the speech as being too vague and abstract. C. E. Dodd, writing in the *Quarterly Review*, argued that in his proposals to set up a committee of inquiry to look into all the defects of the law, Brougham had 'proposed an inquiry too immense, too varied, and too multifarious for any human commission to grapple with promptly and effectually'.[45] The whole notion of reviewing all law was absurd: '[a]dmitting that all the subjects of his oration fall under the general denomination of "law" and "legal

---

[38] *Hansard*, vol. xviii (NS) 1828, p. 177. One of his key proposals was that the Statute of Uses should be restored; another that copyhold estates should be restored to the common law. [39] Ibid. 197–8.

[40] This difference reflects a key divergence of Bentham from the Benthamites. If Bentham lived in a world of perfect codes, perfect prisons, and perfect constitutions which he had created for himself, his followers took his approach, and applied it to the more mundane task of working in the real world.

[41] *Westminster Review*, xi. 453.

[42] For instance, against Bentham's ideas on the Quasi-Jury in the *Constitutional Code* and the *Rationale of Judicial Evidence*, Brougham supported the traditional jury, and the need for strict rules of evidence. [43] *Westminster Review*, xi. 465.

[44] Ibid. 471. [45] *Quarterly Review*, xxxviii (1828), 244.

institutions," we still can see no advantage which any of them could derive from being investigated (even if that were possible) in company with any other. What have contingent remainders to do with arrest for debt on mesne process?'[46] For the reviewer in this journal, the speech was superficial and adversarial, perversely stressing the defects in the law: the speech, Dodd pointed out, covered at least 30 topics of law, or one topic every twelve minutes.[47] While he supported many of Brougham's suggestions, Dodd could not countenance those views which sought to undermine the existing fabric of law, nor those which aimed at excessive simplicity. The law, as he pointed out, was complex: wishing it simplicity was no solution.[48]

Brougham's position was thus uncomfortably in the middle between Bentham and the lawyers. He was a lawyer, and the type of criticisms he made were those of a lawyer. Hence, it was indeed impracticable, given the nature of the task he outlined, to have a Royal Commission (as he proposed) to investigate the whole of the common law. For this would not be a committee to create a Benthamic Pannomion, but rather one to reform all the niceties of the law. The government's response to his proposals, which was the appointment of the two Royal Commissions, was hence the logical fulfilment of Brougham's aims, the closest it could get to a wholesale review of the law. As shall now be seen, these Commissions, often perceived as failures, in so far as they fell far short of codifying the law, were the appropriate response of the common lawyers' desire for a system which could be perceived in terms of rules, while still retaining the substance, content, and working of the old system.

---

[46] *Quarterly Review*, 246.

[47] Ibid. 250.

[48] Ibid. 291–2: 'we say to those who clamour for simplicity in laws regarding the modification of real property: Abolish entails—prohibit strict settlements—proscribe trusts for married women, infants creditors and widows—[etc.] . . . and you need no longer complain of the law . . . [T]he conveyancers may burn their precedents, and the judges their black letter, on your shrine of simplicity. The provisions of your code, the ten-word formulas of Mr. Bentham may be instantly adopted, and will amply accomplish every end of your system.—But if you are still to have a system which shall effect what the English land owners have always desired to do—which shall prevent their patrimonial estates from being squandered by life-owners—which shall give free usufruct to one generation and secure the unimpaired success to the next, [etc.] . . . we shall be glad to be instructed in any system of law . . . which shall not be ruled by such nicety.'

The Real Property Commission

The law of real property was vast and intricate,[49] and by the 1820s most lawyers agreed that it was in dire need of reform.[50] As a vital area of law, and as one in need of reform, it provides a good test of the climate for codification in the 1820s. By examining real property and its reform, we can see how seriously the idea of codification was canvassed, what that codification entailed, and how far it failed. This area of law is also important for producing the most important attempt at a code written by a lawyer, the real property code of James Humphreys.[51]

Humphreys was a well-known and respected property lawyer, who aimed to reform the ancient defective system to suit it to modern commercial society.[52] His intention, he said, was that 'instead of vainly seeking, by equitable inference, to adapt the crude and scanty institutions of early ages to the complicated relations of cultivated society', there should rather be 'one uniform system of laws [to] regulate the whole'.[53] His aim was to replace the fictions of real property law with a system of rules to make it more usable and accessible. If his book had a Benthamite aim, however, it did not read like a Benthamic code. It was divided into two parts, the first describing the existing system, explaining it in historical terms, the

[49] See A. W. B. Simpson, *A History of the Land Law*, 2nd edn. (Oxford, 1986), for an overview.

[50] John Miller, for instance, was one who went so far as to propose that the ancient system of seisin should be replaced by a system of registration.

[51] Humphreys' was not the only code attempted. However, previous attempts were partial or derivative. See Crofton Uniacke's *A Letter to the Lord Chancellor on the Necessity and Practicality of forming a Code of the Laws of England: to which is annexed the new Bankrupt Law: arranged in the method of Domat's Civil Law* (London, 1825); and Horace Twiss, *Inquiry into the Means of Consolidating and Digesting the Laws of England* (London, 1826). See also, A. Hammond, *The Criminal Code*, 7 vols. (London, 1828), which was a code covering simple larceny, the game laws, coining, forgery, and burglary. However, in substance, it was more like a commentary on the present law and its cases and materials than a newly defined code. Despite the rival claims by these codifiers for their works, Bentham felt that it was only with the publication of Humphreys' code that the notion of codification had been translated from theory into practice: *A Commentary on Mr. Humphreys' Real Property Code*, in *Works*, v. 387–416 at 388.

[52] See B. Rudden, 'A Code Too Soon: The 1826 Property Code of James Humphreys: English Rejection, American Reception, English Acceptance', in P. Wallington and R. M. Merkin (ed.), *Essays in Memory of F. H. Lawson* (London, 1986), 101–16.

[53] Humphreys, *Observations on the Actual State of the English Laws of Real Property with the Outlines of a Code* (London, 1826), 3–4.

second outlining the remedy to the problems in the existing law. Humphreys' analysis of the existing law was incisive, and he revealed the absurdity of many legal notions by examining their history. Often, he showed, rules had grown through judicial evasions or creations, which only went half-way to their destination.[54] The changes Humphreys proposed to this were extensive, including the removal of the system of tenures, the theoretical base of the land law, and the ending of uses and 'passive' trusts, devices intended to make the transfer of property easier by evading strict ancient rules. In their place, he proposed a code of provisions, to have fewer, but simpler and more intelligible rules. The changes he suggested were therefore radical, but this was not to propose a code on Benthamic lines, a new code designed on a *tabula rasa* based on a thorough epistemological grounding. Rather, he offered a simplification of existing law and the reduction of existing principles of law to a set of well-articulated rules, and when he came to discussing what he had in mind, he listed numerous practical changes which would rationalize the law which were often uncontentious.[55] Indeed, many of the enactments of his code were made up of equitable provisions already in use. The substance of his proposals therefore stood in the tradition of common law reformism.[56] C. E. Dodd, reviewing the code in the *Quarterly Review*, pointed out that the law of real property took years of arduous study to comprehend, and that even then much of it was unsettled, and he enthused that Humphreys' work would greatly simplify and clarify the chaos.[57] He therefore supported the reforming proposal: 'to at least a considerable extent the laws of real property may be reformed without innovating,' he commented, and 'where innovation is necessary, the proposal is sanctioned in most instances by prior changes, of the same or a greater extent, and in the rest, by justice, or obvious expediency'.[58] The *Edinburgh Review* similarly described the difficulties of learning

---

[54] On wills, he wrote, '[a]s [judges] were not prepared, however, to go the full length of holding, in cases of implied fees-simple, that the gift of the land was a gift of all the testator's property in it, they have effected their object by distinctions, so numerous and complicated, as to render their decisions of doubtful benefit'. Humphreys, *Observations*, 78.

[55] Thus, he proposed the removal of escheats, the acceptance of the half-blood in descents, as well as changes in marriage laws and the law of wills.

[56] Rudden is therefore correct to point out that one of Humphreys' main errors was to call his work a *code*, for that denomination put many lawyers off. The content of the code was not (as Rudden implies) offensive to most lawyers.

[57] *Quarterly Review*, xxxiv (1826), 571.   [58] Ibid. 576.

the current law of real property as 'insurmountable', and hence described the Humphresian code as excellent. 'If the mischiefs of tenures, uses, and *passive* trusts (as Mr. H[umphreys] designates them) could, upon his scheme, be got rid of,' the journal enthused, 'he would do more towards administering substantial relief to the sufferers in the Court of Chancery, by taking away causes of dispute, than can be effected by ten thousand contenders for the beauty and excellence of whatever they find existing.'[59] Humphreys' work was thus highly regarded by the profession for its content, and the book was very influential on the Real Property Commission.

It is noteworthy how seriously the Real Property Commission took not just the idea of reform, but the idea of codifying the law. It shows the pervasiveness and influence of a Benthamic concept of rules. However, when it came to a discussion of the code, it is clear that Bentham's influence had its limitations. The commissioners questioned James Humphreys on his proposals for a code, and this interview revealed that what he had in mind was far from the worst fears of the common lawyers. His aim, it became clear, was to create a system of rules crafted out of the content of the common law. He told the commissioners that he would begin by stating and declaring what the common law was, rather than removing what was not to be law. He would establish socage tenures as the basic tenure[60] and he would build all law around it, 'omitting parts which you find inconvenient, and forming a system, adding others which in the course of time may be rendered necessary'.[61] There were clear limits to a code. Asked if it was possible to create a code which would answer all the purposes of law, without reference to anything outside itself, Humphreys only argued that it was feasible in *theory*: in practice, such a code was never likely to be adopted in Great Britain,[62] and would take years to achieve. He preferred the idea of taking a single isolated area of law, such as descents, to see if that could be made into a simple code. As to cases not covered by the code, Humphreys proposed that they should be decided by judges sitting in the Exchequer Chamber, with these decisions being allowed to be taken as law. Evidently, he had little more in mind that

[59] *Edinburgh Review*, xlv (1827), 474.
[60] These tenures were the basic form of tenure in any case since 1660, being feudal tenures involving no service.
[61] *First Report of the Commissioners of Inquiry into the Law of England respecting Real Property*, Parliamentary Papers 1829 (263) X. Appendix, p. 248 (hereafter as, Real Property Commission, First Report).   [62] Ibid.

an authoritative digest elaborating clear rules, as became apparent in his justification for a code. 'I would keep the present technical terms,' he said, 'and as to the extent of research through different decisions, so much is done by text-writers that the task would be very much facilitated; every text-book codifies its subject to a certain extent.'[63] For Humphreys, the code would be *gradually* enacted, as he would only enact what was safe to enact. In the meantime, wherever there was not an express enactment to the contrary, the common law should remain in force.[64] In effect, this was to amend the law in a statutory way; not to create a holistic code.

The question of codification was discussed in detail by the Commissioners, but most of the lawyers they questioned opposed it, not on ideological grounds but on pragmatic ones. Henry Bellenden Ker, who was to be a leading light in the movement for codifying the criminal law, explicitly rejected a Benthamic code here, for he argued that the law was far too complex to be reworked anew. In support of this viewpoint, he quoted James Madison's reply to Bentham, in which the President had said that it would be impossible to get rid of technical terms needing precise definition. A code framed with the greatest care, Ker noted, would of necessity be imperfect and would inevitably leave much to the judges' discretion—'and then either a new technical language must be gradually invented and defined, or the old one must be adopted'.[65] In either case, he continued, great difficulties would arise for the new code: in the first case, the definitions would inevitably be imperfect; while in the second, lawyers would constantly have to refer back to the old system to explain and justify the terms used. Ker admitted the need for detailed reforms; but he did not admit the need for a code of Benthamic dimensions.

Ker was a reformist lawyer: more conservative lawyers, like John Tyrrell, were even more emphatic in rejecting the code. Tyrrell's anti-Benthamism was less ideologically motivated than practical, however. His objections pointed to the practical impossibility of uprooting the existing law. First, property rights were too entrenched to be interfered with, many estates being held under settlements which would not end for centuries. To create a code, one would either have to wait for all of them to expire or compensate those who lost out—'which it would be almost impossible to effect

---

[63] Real Property Commission, 250.   [64] Ibid. 252.   [65] Ibid. 294.

on account of the very complicated and extensive modification of rights and interests which are allowed to exist in this country'.[66] Second, to alter the law of real property would be to alter the entire system of English law, since that area of law had been the first to evolve, and since it had shaped the subsequent proceedings in the courts and had defined the boundaries between law and equity. The laws of real property, he argued, 'regulate the titles of dignity, the qualifications of members of parliament and offices of trust, the jurisdictions of the courts of hundreds and leets, the privileges of lords of manors, the rights of sporting, and a great part of our system of poor laws, and are blended with most of our civil and political institutions'.[67] Tyrrell argued that the leading rules of the law could not be altered since they were the essential fabric of society. Third, like many lawyers, he distrusted statutory laws as leading only to literal interpretations of precise words, which allowed of ambiguity not to be found in case law.[68] These objections did not, however, mean that Tyrrell was hostile to the idea that law needed reform, or that it needed formulation in terms of clear rules and guides. For he said that just as single statutes had been used in the past to reform the common law, so they should be used again: the law could be amended and consolidated, he conceded, but not *codified*. His principal objection was hence not to reform, but to the idea that the existing fabric should be destroyed. Tyrrell therefore submitted a 300-page set of proposals to the Commission, with detailed ideas on specific reforms.

These views influenced the Real Property Commission, for it was induced to reject Bentham's idea of a code, while still aiming at a system of clear rules. In their first report, the commissioners noted that it was extremely difficult to alter the law, for even incorrect rules of law involved chains of judicial consequences which would have been acted and relied upon. 'We dread the shock that would be occasioned by any precipitate attempt at emendation,' the commissioners reported, 'and we recollect that it is as impossible suddenly to change the laws as the language of any country.'[69] They declared their aim to be to interfere as little as possible with

---

[66] Ibid. 475.   [67] Ibid. 475–6.

[68] He wrote, 'It is the great advantage of those parts of our laws which are found only in adjudged cases and text books that they are not encumbered with nice distinctions regarding the meaning of words; and the only questions which can arise upon them are those which involve the principles of the rules.' Ibid. 477.

[69] Ibid. 9.

established rules, but instead to preserve the spirit and the language of the existing law. The law, they felt, could not be expected to be rendered so simple that any individual could master it, and, they wrote, 'we apprehend that disastrous effects would be produced by an experiment to construct a code by the use of terms of no defined legal import, and of known terms in a new sense'.[70]

The impetus behind the reforms in property law was therefore not in essence Benthamic. This is evident from the response of the profession to the Reports of the Real Property Commission. The *Law Magazine* for instance criticized the commissioners' methodology, arguing that they should have examined and explained how the system worked before they suggested alterations. This, the journal argued, could only be done through a historical investigation; for merely to set out the confusion of complex and intricate forms could only induce people to assume that they had been established with due deliberation and reason. Historical investigation, the reviewer argued, showed the reason behind the system—but it could also reveal where the reason had died.[71] The *Law Magazine* thus gave its own potted history of the rules of real property[72] which led the reviewer to the conclusion that there were very many areas in need of reform, which the commissioners had overlooked: it was suggested that their largely unhistorical methodology had led them to believe the law needed fewer alterations than in fact it did. Clearly, there was a vital impetus to reform from within the profession, from the detailed historical investigations of men like Reeves. Lawyers were seeking rules in the law, but rules from within the common law mine.

The recommendations of the Real Property Commission thus ended by being uncontentious reforms of specific doctrines. Thus, it simplified conveyancing in order to simplify the many rules which had evolved in a haphazard manner to evade the statutory regulations such as the Statute of Uses.[73] The commissioners also recommended changes in the rules of inheritance, their ideas being merely a compromise of proposals current in the profession since

---

[70] Real Property Commission.

[71] *Law Magazine*, ii (1829), 632 ff.

[72] This was largely culled from Reeves, a source the Royal Commission used itself.

[73] The commissioners in their second report hence recommended a reform in the use of fines and recoveries and the law of dower to facilitate the transfer of property. This was achieved by the Fines and Recoveries Act of 1833.

Blackstone.[74] The recommendations of the commission were thus piecemeal and modest in a whole range of issues, and ultimately they were extremely slow to be implemented.[75] The Real Property Commission was a key test for Benthamism, and for the idea of codification. It is an interesting case, for it reveals the priorities and thinking of the body of the profession discussing an essential area of the law. What is important is that the question of codifying the law was seriously considered, which reveals that a Benthamic formal view of law, based on defined rules and simplified sources, was becoming increasingly attractive to lawyers. Ultimately, lawyers did want a modernized, reformed law based on clear rules, not haphazard evasions; but they did not want the type of code Bentham publicly espoused. At no stage was it felt possible to begin anew with a set of definitions or notions that would satisfy all needs in a self-contained, ideal system. At best, such a code would clarify existing notions; but since those notions were bound up in history and the expectation of stability, there was no desire to uproot the system. Given what we have seen was the achievement of Bentham, this response is understandable: he had failed, after all, to produce a plausible deductive code, and he had returned to the common law as a repository of content. For lawyers in the 1820s to believe that an a priori code was an impossibility, and to hold to the needs of stability, was a logical response: for the most traditional lawyer to consider the possibility of creating a code of rules reveals the powerful influence of a Benthamic style of formal analysis by the 1820s.

[74] The Real Property Commission discussed four main rules here: first, the rule that lineal ancestors of deceased proprietors were excluded from inheriting; second, the rule that an estate, on failure of the heirs of the last proprietor on the side of the first purchaser, could not pass to the last proprietor on the other side, but escheated; third, the rule that excluded the half-blood from inheriting; and fourth, the rule tracing inheritance from the person last seised. The commissioners recommended allowing the ascending line to inherit, but only where 'the descendants of such ancestor would be entitled according to the present rules' (p. 12), which was effectively a compromise so as not to upset current rules. On the other matters, they proposed to allow the half-blood to inherit; to allow descendants of the female ancestor to inherit; and to abolish the rule tracing inheritance from the seisin of the ancestor. These ideas had been debated for decades, and aimed merely to simplify the law and render it more sensible. See, e.g.,2 *Comm*. 227–34.

[75] See A. H. Manchester, *Modern Legal History* (London, 1980), 306 ff.; A. W. B. Simpson, *A History of the Land Law*, 274–80.

The Royal Commission on the Criminal Law

The most famous attempt at codification in England, and the one which came closest to success, was made by the Royal Commission on the Criminal Law, which produced eight reports between 1833 and 1845.[76] The criminal law had been central to Bentham's concerns, seeing penal law, as he did, as the hub of the law. It was therefore the area most fit for Benthamite influence, and, as a system of commands and rules, the one most fit for codification.[77] This Royal Commission is widely perceived as being a wholly Benthamite body, but, as we shall see, while it reflected a formal view of legal theory which was heavily influenced by Bentham, its ideas on the content of law and its creation were more traditionally minded. The original Royal Commission represented all strands of legal opinion, and while it has been dubbed a Benthamite venture, its members represented a broader spectrum. The commissioners included one judge, Justice Wightman, as well as Henry Bellenden Ker, Thomas Starkie, Andrew Amos, and John Austin. The last three were all academic lawyers, but only Austin, professor of jurisprudence at London University, was a disciple of Bentham. Both Starkie and Amos lectured on the common law[78] and both were traditional common lawyers. The task of these men was to digest all the criminal statutes into one, to digest the common law crimes, and to see if they could be united into one code. The findings in the reports are therefore a good test of the pervasiveness of Benthamism, revealing how far common lawyers accepted Bentham's formal theory, and how far Benthamite reformers accepted the common law.

[76] See J. A. Hostettler, 'The Movement for Reform of the Criminal Law in England in the Nineteenth Century', unpublished London Ph.D., 1983; Sir Rupert Cross, 'The Reports of the Criminal Law Commissioners (1833–49) and the Abortive Bills of 1853', in P. R. Glazebrook, *Reshaping the Criminal Law* (London, 1978), 5–20; A. H. Manchester, 'Simplifying the Sources of Law: An Essay in Law Reform', *Anglo-American Law Review*, ii (1973), 395–413 and 527–50. On other attempts at codifying the criminal law, see S. Kadish, 'Codifiers of the Criminal Law', *Columbia Law Review*, lxxviii (1978), 1098–1144.

[77] This was also true because it was the area of law that had had the most attention since the beginning of the century. The *Law Magazine* therefore noted that nine-tenths of the 'practically operative part' of the criminal law had already been consolidated by the time the Royal Commission was appointed. *Law Magazine*, xiii (1835), 10.

[78] Their lectures, Amos as Professor at London University, and Starkie at the Inner Temple, were reproduced in the *Legal Examiner*.

The commissioners' Benthamic view of the concept of law can be seen in their early critique of the content and form of the common law, for in their first report they were highly critical of it, and proposed to merge it with the statutes. They pointed out that it was hard to derive general principles or rules out of the common law, for reported judgments and legal texts did not state rules, but left all to be extracted out of circumstance.[79] They argued that the common law emerged from changing manners and customs, and noted the fact that fluctuations in the common law often occurred because of the adoption of subtle technical distinctions. The common law offered no rules, but left all haphazard. Thus, there was (they said) no clear distinction between 'Trespass' and 'Theft': the latter was defined by its status as a felony, while the former was no felony—yet the commissioners rued that 'felonious' only meant that it was of such a nature as to constitute a theft. Not only was there no rule, but the law changed haphazardly. '[M]ost of the enlargements by construction, by means of which the Law of Theft has been extended to include cases not originally within its scope,' they contended, 'have proceeded upon principles contrary, in their spirit and objects, to those upon which the old law was founded.'[80]

The commissioners' view of law was thus shaped by Benthamic notions. 'So long as a large proportion of the penal law is merely oral, and dependent on the examination and construction of precedents,' they wrote, 'it must be, to the mass of society, inaccessible, and unintelligible in its rules and boundaries.'[81] They derided the common law, which only created the rule after the offence, and they pointed out that even a lawyer was kept in the dark as to what was law. For them, the law should be clear, a matter of rules, not inferences. They urged the need to define actions far more closely, and they argued that to be obeyed, a law had first to be known.[82] The view of law which was here put forward was one

---

[79] They quoted Hale: 'in cases of larciny [*sic*] the variety of circumstances is so great, and the complications thereof so mingled, that it is impossible to prescribe all the circumstances evidencing a felonious intention, or the contrary; but the same must be left to the due and attentive consideration of the Judge and Jury, wherein the best rule is *in dubiis* to decline either to acquit or convict'. *First Report of His Majesty's Commissioners on Criminal Law*, Parliamentary Papers, 1834 (537) XXVI (hereafter as Criminal Law Commission, First Report), p. 3.

[80] Criminal Law Commission, First Report, p. 6.   [81] Ibid. 25.

[82] This was of especial importance, it was felt, where the law was immoral but necessary for reasons of policy: '[w]ere a law to be made excessively unreasonable, as well as unreasonably severe, so much greater the necessity would there be for giving

which stressed that law was a set of commands imposed from above; where *legislation* was the heart of law. The point was that the state should protect its notion of right and wrong by legislation. Thus, '[a]nother reason for a wide diffusion of the Criminal Law is to give publicity to the moral distinctions which it ought to recognise and impress'.[83] In these concerns, we can perceive a statist notion that the law was more than a system to redress wrongs alone, that it was rather the tool with which to shape society and govern by directives. The commissioners felt it to be a vital object 'to classify crimes and apportion the punishment thereto, as to check with greater efficiency such violations as are in their tendency and consequences most dangerous to the peace and security of society'.[84] The commission's view of the function of law was therefore clearly positivist. It is notable, beyond this, how heavily the commissioners, including Starkie, Amos, and Wightman, were influenced by Benthamic jurisprudence. For at several points they discussed the nature of law, and divided law into substantive and adjective spheres. Their discussions were overtly Benthamic, which seems unexceptional given Austin's presence. What is notable is that we can find such Benthamic discussions even in the Seventh Report, issued four years after Austin had resigned from the Royal Commission in disgust at its limitations.[85] In the Fourth Report, they had written that the substantive law defined rights and obligations, while the adjective law enforced them. Considering this, they noted that the penal law was in fact adjective, being limited 'to violation of such rights and obligations as are presumed to be already defined in another department of the law'.[86] In their discussions, the commissioners went so far as to ponder the need for a Pannomion. It was shown that since the criminal law was adjective, the definition of crimes did not entail defining substantive rights *de novo*. But since the existence of a substantive right was assumed in the definition of a crime, any imperfection in those substantive laws—in the civil code—would

express notice of such a law, in order to prevent men from inadvertantly incurring penalties, by doing that which was not obviously wrong'. *Seventh Report of Her Majesty's Commissioners on Criminal Law*, Parliamentary Papers, 1843 (448), XIX, p. 4.

[83] Criminal Law Commission, Seventh Report, p. 4.

[84] Ibid. 5.

[85] See W. Rumble, *The Thought of John Austin* (London, 1985); L. and J. Hamburger, *Troubled Lives: John and Sarah Austin* (Toronto, 1985), for the biographical details.

[86] *Fourth Report of Her Majesty's Commissioners on Criminal Law*, Parliamentary Papers, 1839 (168), XIX, p. vi. This was repeated in the Seventh Report, p. 11.

make the criminal law imperfect.[87] If civil rights were uncertain, the criminal law would inevitably be so. The implication was clearly a Benthamic one, that all law needed better prior definition.

In their formal analysis of legal concepts, then, the lawyers had been convinced by Bentham. However, when they came to analysing the content of the law, they found it adequate, so that no Pannomion was needed. By the Seventh Report, they noted that in fact the civil law was much more certain than the criminal, since it had so many precedents, authorities, and legal arguments. Whereas few criminal cases had been discussed in the superior courts, most areas of civil law had had full discussion and deliberations there. The commissioners now found themselves arguing that what made the criminal law problematic was not that there were too many contradictory rulings and precedents, but that there were not enough rulings. Their view now was that out of a mass of decisions and solutions could be teased definitions which were precise. Hence, whereas in the Fourth Report they had argued that the common law was a confusion of definitions and inconsistencies, not bound by any unity but changing eternally,[88] by the Seventh Report they claimed that statutes were less clear. 'We have been better able to effect a convenient reduction of the unwritten than of the Statute Law,' the Report said, '[a]s regards the unwritten or Common Law, the rules deducible from the mass of authorities, though frequently of a conflicting nature, are yet susceptible of precise distinction and arrangement under appropriate heads; but with respect to statutory enactment, the difficulty is much greater.'[89] This was because statutes were made with specific reference to the circumstances under which they were passed, and because, out of that context, they were meaningless. The common law, on the other hand, did throw up general principles to be inferred from cases.

Ultimately, the commission shied away from creating a single code of law, uniting statute and common law. Remodelling the law, it was concluded, would be too risky, since that would involve dangerous oversimplification. What they proposed was to create a simple digest of the law: 'what was before to be collected by the aid of precedent and analogy, is now to be judged of by reference to the written rule'.[90] It would not be absolute; merely an authoritative reference. Once more, lawyers had been convinced by Bentham's

[87] Criminal Law Commission, Fourth Report, p. vii.   [88] Ibid. ix.
[89] Criminal Law Commission, Seventh Report, p. 2.   [90] Ibid. 10.

formal theory, but had rejected his substantive notions, preferring the common law system.

This Royal Commission provoked the biggest debate on codification of the era. As with real property, the profession reacted with venom against any proposal that the law could be briefly summarized. The *Law Magazine* in its review of the First Report therefore questioned the whole enterprise and argued that any legal system would inevitably lack entirely unambiguous rules.[91] What the *Law Magazine* most objected to was the desire 'to invent instead of observing, to create systems instead of regulating existing facts'.[92] Indeed, it defended a strongly traditionalist view of the common law in arguing that '[i]t is idle to suppose that people, particularly the lower orders, take their notions as to the criminality of criminal actions from books'. Rather, 'a thief knows when he is thieving without the aid of a Digest, and will be as much restrained by an unwritten as by a written law as long as punishment is equally certain under both'.[93] The *Law Magazine* espoused Hale's view that 'in truth antient lawes, especially that have common concern, are not the issues of the prudence of this or that council or senate, but they are the production of the various experiences and applications of the wisest thing in the inferior world; to wit, time, which as it discovers day after day new inconveniences, so it doth successively apply new remedies'.[94] The journal liked the Fourth Report, however, for it approved of reform and of consolidation, provided that did not involve a complete code. In its opinion, the law needed to be able to adapt and grow with society, to fulfil social needs. In its review of the Seventh Report, when it had become clear that the design was for a digest of common law rules, allowing the content of the law to continue as before, the *Law Magazine* praised the whole venture enthusiastically. While a prisoner could quibble over common law doctrines, it wrote, if there were a Digest, 'he would be compelled to grapple with written words which would be before the court'.[95] The *Law Magazine* was reconciled to a Digest simply because it was not a code: it would unite a clear concept of rules with a common law system of legal sources, in a mixture of the common law tradition and Benthamic jurisprudence. This is clear from its view of how the

[91] *Law Magazine*, xiii (1835), 56–7.
[92] Ibid. 57. This comment was taken from Rossi's work.
[93] Ibid. 43.   [94] Ibid. 58.
[95] *Law Magazine*, xxx. 17.

Digest would evolve: '[l]et a Commissioner be appointed, whose duty it shall be to watch carefully the decisions in the code, and each year offer to parliament those amendments with respect to its technical language which actual experience proves to be necessary'.[96] This was to support the idea of a well-articulated set of rules, but drawn from the method of the common law.[97]

The Debate on Procedure

Bentham's procedural ideas provided some of the greatest challenges to the common law, and his theories were debated strongly in the 1820s.[98] One of the most articulate Benthamite attacks on common law procedure was made by James Mill, writing on jurisprudence in the *Encyclopaedia Britannica* in 1825. What English lawyers called 'a strict and pure, and beautiful exemplification of the rules of logic', he argued, was in fact a 'mischievous mess, which exists in defiance of mockery and reason'.[99] Mill's article restated the classic Benthamic position, arguing that all rights had initially to be resolved, and that the legislature should define all investitive and divestitive rights, so that procedure could be entirely free.[100] This notion of natural procedure was subsequently debated in a number of journals. There were two broad responses to the Benthamic

[96] Ibid.

[97] The later history of the movement for codification reflects the balance between Bentham's formal theory and the flexibility of the common law. For, on the one hand, the judges constantly defended the common law's flexibility and its nature as a system of remedies. As Erle J put it in response to a proposed codification, 'Doubts upon the Common law, which exist after examining the authorities, are to be resolved by considerations of justice, tested by utility, whereby the law adapts itself to the changing interests of society' (Parliamentary Papers, 1854 (389), LIII, p. 7). On the other hand, however, the House of Lords accepted the principle of codification on three occasions, and gradually, the criminal code was metamorphosed into the statute law commission and ended with the Consolidation Acts of 1861. For a detailed account, see Hostettler, 'The Movement for Criminal Law Reform'.

[98] See Eldon R. Sunderland, 'The English Struggle for Procedural Reform', *Harvard Law Review*, xxxix (1925–6), 725–48.

[99] J. Mill, 'Jurisprudence', in his *Essays on Government, Jurisprudence, Liberty of the Press, and Laws of Natns [sic]* (London, n.d), p. 29.

[100] Mill argued that a system defining procedural rules before it defined substantive ones could only work in primitive societies, where community feelings vaguely established what was right. In an advanced society, with multiple cases and patterns, he urged, the only logical thing to do was to make procedure subordinate to a set of substantive rules.

position, both of which served not to undermine, but to bolster the science of pleading. The first response, as represented by the *Law Magazine*, was a downright rejection of Bentham.[101] This journal argued that while pleading was 'overloaded by perverted ingenuity', it was based on useful principles which were more workable than a system which sought the removal of rules. Mill's arguments were rejected one by one. To begin with, it was argued, even Bentham admitted in effect that a comprehensive code was impossible to achieve; but even if it were feasible, it could only work for the simplest of cases. For skill and knowledge would still be required to determine how far any given fact would be investitive or divestitive of even fully defined rights.[102] It would still take time and care in presenting the facts to the judge, to determine the relevant ones. Beyond this, the natural system would allow the litigants to state all manner of irrelevant facts before the jury, which would make a clear decision difficult to arrive at. The journal had other objections. If the natural system saved money by removing the need for fees in cases, it would multiply costs by increasing the number of courts and judges required, for where cases were currently settled before coming into the court, in future, all would need to be settled in the courtroom. In most cases, it was pointed out, only a few simple facts were involved, which were adequately covered by simple formulae. The best system, for the *Law Magazine*, was that which allowed only necessary statements to be made, which gave full proofs, and which clearly divided law and fact. This was the most telling objection: the Benthamic system would unite law and fact in such a way as to prevent points of law emerging as precedents. Without a system of precedents, the law's development would be hindered.[103] Bentham's system, it seemed, would only work with a complete code: without

---

[101] *Law Magazine*, i. 1–31.   [102] Ibid. 12–13.

[103] These views were echoed by G. J. Bell, who wrote, 'Perhaps more injustice and oppression is committed by the undue protraction of litigation, in consequence of vague, wavering, unsettled, ever-changing statements of fact in a system like the Scottish, than, upon the whole, by erroneous judgments; and nothing is more certain, than that a want of due care in the preliminary process, so as to bring out the true substantial question for judgment, is the great cause of protracted proceedings. It was on this account that the judges in early times were so watchful of the pleadings of the parties—and it was not in Scotland alone that the whole preliminary process, or statement of the pleas, proceeded in presence of the judge. It was so in England also, and their perfect system of pleading is the fruit of it.' *Examination of the Objections stated against the Bill for regulating the Forms of Process in the Courts of Law in Scotland* (Edinburgh, 1825), 16–17.

it, his procedure would undermine his desire for the law to produce rules. Thus, the defence of pleading by the *Law Magazine* is significant, for it was defended as a system capable of producing *rules*.

Therefore, while Bentham and Mill proposed the removal of pleading, the *Law Magazine* proposed making it stricter, so that the point defined would be clearer. In many forms of action, particularly assumpsit and case, there was no clear issue to divide law and fact, the journal asserted, so that the conclusion to be drawn was that the only way for clear rules of law to emerge was to have a system of special pleading. The point of pleading being to articulate the issue and cast off all superfluous matter, the allowing of the general issue to compound a wide range of unspecified facts would undermine the system. Hence, the *Law Magazine* declared, 'we would rather compel the defendant to take issue upon a single point in the declaration, or to confess the whole and confine himself to one mode of justification, than to proceed any longer in the system we are following'.[104]

The second response to Bentham came from those who were more sympathetic to his view. Yet even they did not follow the master to a natural procedure. In a series of articles on abuses in the system of pleading written by George Graham, the Benthamite *Westminster Review* constructed an ideal type and compared it with the English one. What is of note is that while Graham had a Benthamic view of rights and rules,[105] his views on procedure differed significantly from Bentham's. No system, he argued, could work without some form of pleading, since it would be uncertain, leaving both sides unable to predict what the other would say, leaving the court no point to decide, and tying up much time and money. The purpose of pleading, for Graham, was to establish whether certain indivisible facts had occurred, which invested or divested a right. Those very facts which Bentham argued could emerge in conversation with a judge Graham felt needed pleading. Hence, he proposed four principles of the ideal type: first, pleadings should be only simple statements of fact and simple denials; second, pleading should be divided into certain stages, the party pleading denying only the one

---

[104] *Law Magazine*, i. 26–7.

[105] For example, he wrote that the legislator should determine what events conferred which rights, and what events signalled their end. *Westminster Review*, iv (1825), 63–4.

indivisible fact already averred; third, the party should deny directly the occurrence of each fact contested immediately after the plea; and fourthly, all things pleaded should be true (on pain of a fine) and given orally. The latter point is Benthamic, to be sure; but the first three savour strongly of a system of special pleas. The similarity of this view to the *Law Magazine*'s is evident from this discussion of the code:

Under a good code of laws the point of law could never be doubtful. Under a bad system, if either party differed with the judge on a point of law, that is, on a question whether certain events had or had not investitive or divestitive power, he could state his reasons for such opinion, and if the judge still retained his former sentiments, and the party objecting remained unsatisfied with the decision, the question might be brought before the court in term, as is now done when difference arises at the trial as to the admission of evidence.[106]

Even a good code needed outside help.

The system outlined in the Benthamite journal was therefore akin to the existing science of pleading.[107] While Graham presumed that the legislator could define rights, his system aimed to produce rules for those areas not covered by express legislation. In effect, Graham was also espousing special pleading, for he wrote that 'where truth was regarded, seldom should more than one of those pleas at each stage be pleaded in the same cause'.[108] In the end, the Benthamite *Westminster Review* attacked the common law system for allowing a multiplicity of untrue and unnecessary pleas, and, criticizing the common law general plea, it called for a system of special pleading.[109]

Even sympathetic reviewers were hence hostile to Benthamic natural procedure. Reviewing the *Traité des preuves judiciaires* in 1824, Thomas Denman praised Bentham's ideas, but rejected his natural procedure.[110] While he agreed on the need to abandon useless

---

[106] *Westminster Review*, 66.

[107] Graham thus wrote that in disputes over land, in his ideal system, the plaintiff 'must allege that A. B. became seized of the land in question, and is since dead, and that he the plaintiff is a relation of A. B., say a son. If the plaintiff did not allege that *all* these events, or some others sufficient in law to invest him with the right, had taken place, the judge would tell him, that he had made out no claim, and the case would at once be dismissed.' Ibid. 66. The similarity with the existing theory of pleading is evident.

[108] Ibid. 69.　　　　　　　　[109] *Westminster Review*, vi (1826), 53.

[110] See W. Twining, *Theories of Evidence: Bentham and Wigmore* (London, 1985), 100–8.

formalities and technicalities, he urged the need for some rules: '[u]nless some limits be imposed,' he said, 'the judicial understanding is in danger of being bewildered and lost in the maze'.[111] Denman felt that Bentham was so keen to convict criminals that he had lost sight of the need for restraint: 'in truth, he is obviously far from familiar with the practice of the law,' he wrote, 'and his denunciations will no more persuade mankind to do without lawyers, than some proofs of pedantry and error will annul the faculty of medicine'.[112] As we have seen, Bentham was by no means unfamiliar with the intricacies of legal practice: but this was hidden beneath his sweeping rhetoric.

From these views, it is evident that special pleading was increasingly popular in the 1820s, and not just among those lawyers with a love of common law particularism. What was liked about special pleading was that unlike general pleading, which only served to settle cases before the court, special pleading produced a clear point for a rule. To that extent, special pleading, the antithesis of the ideal Benthamic procedure, was perceived to be the ideal vehicle to produce Benthamic rules.[113] The realization that the system of pleading was chaotic and unsuited to its task merely reaffirmed a belief in the special plea. Edward Lawes wrote, 'that some forms must be put upon the record is quite evident, unless it be intended to turn his majesty's superior courts of law at Westminster into courts of conscience and police offices'.[114] He therefore had no hesitation in recommending special pleading.[115] Special pleas would accomplish the main aims of pleading at the same time as causing the least possible disruptive innovation. Similarly, John Miller, who criticized the system of pleading, none the less commended it as a branch of procedure which introduced precision into adjudications.[116] Miller criticized the rules of pleading as they existed for being too complex, and he argued that the immense technicality of the system caused

---

[111] *Edinburgh Review*, xl (1824), 175.

[112] Ibid. 185.

[113] See A. Hammond, *An Analysis of the Principles of Pleading; Or Idea of a Study of that Science* (London, 1819), 40. It is important that Hammond should have written a treatise on the science of pleading since he also wrote a code of criminal law: clearly, positive rules did not entail Benthamic procedure.

[114] *Suggestions for Some Alterations of the Law, on the subjects of Practice, Pleading and Evidence* (London, 1827), 49.

[115] Ibid. 57–8.

[116] Miller, *Inquiry into the Present State of the Civil Law*, 115.

confusion: yet he also criticized the system of the general issue for concealing too much from the defendant.[117]

From these opinions it is clear why the Royal Commission on the Common Law Courts should have recommended the adoption of stricter special pleas. For while Holdsworth has argued[118] that the decision of the commissioners to recommend this change, and of the judges to adopt it with the Hilary Rules of 1834,[119] was a mistake caused largely by the undue influence on them of the author of the main treatise on pleading, Henry Stephen,[120] it seems instead that the change was wholly welcomed within the profession. The aim of the commissioners was clearly to purify the common law, for they aspired to reorder its chaotic particularism, to mould it into a system of simple rules, but without sacrificing its method of deriving substance suited to society. The commissioners were indeed reformers, and had no sentimental attachment to ancient forms. They hence proclaimed,

We shall have no hesitation in proposing the abolition, as far as practicable, of fictions, circuitous courses, and such matters of mere form, as by the progress of time have ceased to be necessary for the purposes for which they were introduced . . . We shall suggest the abridgment, in many cases, of the forms and language of pleading; some restraint upon the unlimited multiplication of counts and pleas, and an acceleration of every part of the suit, by allowing process to be returnable, pleadings to proceed, and final judgment, under certain restrictions, to be signed, not only upon default, but after verdict.[121]

The Royal Commission thus proposed a number of detailed changes to rationalize the law: thus, they recommended abolishing the original writ, replacing it with a simple and uniform system of

---

[117] The reform Miller looked for was not that of removing pleas, but of simplifying the various forms of action, since the current distinct forms required all manner of different proofs for essentially the same offences. Thus, where in cases of debt the plaintiff could currently use actions of assault, debt, covenant, and even detinue, he felt there should be a single form. Ibid. 124.

[118] *History of English Law*, ix. 325.

[119] These were reported in an appendix at the end of the fifth volume of B. & Ald. See also E. Lawes, *Rules and Orders of the Supreme Courts of Common Law from the Commencement of the Reign of William IV to Hilary Term, 8th Victoria* (London, 1845).

[120] *A Treatise on the Principles of Pleading in Civil Actions* (London, 1824).

[121] *First Report of His Majesty's Commissioners appointed to Inquire into the Practice and Proceedings of the Superior Courts of Common Law*, Parliamentary Papers, 1829 (46), XI (hereafter as Common Law Commission, First Report) 7.

summons and capias to compel appearance before the court.[122] Similarly, they proposed that all real actions save two[123] should be abolished, since real actions were rarely used, immensely technical, and little understood. In place of the various forms to recover land, they proposed a single plea of land.[124] They proposed many reforms in various personal actions, aiming to abolish all forms of action save twelve, the forms most commonly in use, which should cover all cases imaginable. The commissioners were very careful not to undermine the system, for they argued that too much innovation would disturb its foundations: but they did aim to rationalize what existed.[125]

Discussing the question of pleading, the commissioners proposed to extend special pleading. They praised the system as 'a valuable forensic invention peculiar to the common law', and admired its aim of producing a clear and single point for a ruling,[126] and they deplored the general issue, which failed to evolve such a clear point of dispute and which required a vast accumulation of proofs.[127] Answering the criticism that special pleading would involve more fees and hence greater expense, the commissioners said the costs of pleading were as nothing compared with the expense of bringing all the witnesses to court which were required by the general issue: in the end, the system of special pleas was seen to be the clearest, cheapest, and most logical way to arrive at both a decision and a rule.[128]

---

[122] The old system only led to expense, the commissioners held, and, drawing from Reeves, Madox, and Tidd, they showed that the old forms of procedure were now outdated and useless. Common Law Commission, First Report, 79. Their recommendations on this front were fulfilled by the Uniformity of Procedure Act.

[123] The actions of *Quare Impedit* and of *Dower*.

[124] *Second Report made to His Majesty by the Commissioners appointed to Inquire into the Practice and Proceedings of the Superior Courts of Common Law*, Parliamentary Papers, 1830 (123), XI, pp. 1–10.

[125] *Third Report made to His Majesty by the Commissioners appointed to Inquire into the Practice and Proceedings of the Superior Courts of Common Law*, Parliamentary Papers, 1831 (92) X. p. 7.   [126] Common Law Commission, Second Report, 45.

[127] This echoed Stephen's view, in his *Treatise*, where he had praised special pleading for separating law and fact and producing a clear issue. Stephen, *Treatise*, 460.

[128] Besides this, it was said to restore the purity of the common law, for the commissioners wrote that 'the more extensive application of the general issue is in fact a departure from the ancient and regular method, which prescribed a special plea in a great variety of cases where it is now superseded by the general issue'. Common Law Commission, Second Report, 51. The commissioners used Reeves as an authority for this assertion.

The Reports were well received by the profession.[129] The recommendations were followed by an Act of 1833 giving the judges of the Superior Courts the power to make rules for pleading in their courts,[130] which was used by the judges to make the Hilary Rules of 1834. These rules compelled the use of special pleas and made pleading a far more intricate and complex subject. To begin with, while the Uniformity of Process Act[131] reduced the number and variety of writs which could be used to begin a case, it was also designated '*to require more explicit information* to be given by such new process and memoranda'.[132] Henceforth, parties declaring needed to be much more explicit in their claim than before, with the result that many cases were liable to be lost on intricate points of detail. The Hilary Rules increased precision: thus, in actions on the case, the plea of 'not guilty' was to refer only to the precise breach of duty alleged, and was not to be taken as a denial of the plaintiff's right to the duty.[133] Anything which the defendant wanted to plead beyond the direct denial needed a special plea. Similarly, in assumpsit, the plea of *non assumpsit* was to operate only as a denial in fact of an express contract, or of the matters of fact from which a contract was implied.[134] All matters in confession and avoidance, including those which showed the contract to be void or voidable, had to be specially pleaded. According to Chitty's *Precedents in Pleading*, there were three main reasons behind the reforms in pleading. First was the need to keep a clear separation of the spheres of law and fact, in order to prevent matters of law being tried by the jury. The greatest perceived threat to the judge's function as stipulating what the law was, and hence the greatest threat to the emergence of clear rules, was the general verdict:[135] by putting all legal defences on the record, the general issue, in the words of Bosanquet J, 'may be considered as

---

[129] See, e.g., *Law Magazine*, iii (1830), 396–505, and *Fraser's Magazine*, v (1832), 422.

[130] An Act for the Further Amendment of the Law, 3 and 4 Wm. IV c. 42.

[131] 2 Wm. IV c. 39 s. 14.

[132] J. Chitty, *The Practice of the Law in all its Departments*, 3rd edn., by Robert Lush, 3 vols. (London, 1842), iii. 117.

[133] See, e.g., *Owen* v. *Knight* (1837) 4 Bing. NC 54, *M'Gregor* v. *Gregory* (1843) 11 M. & W. 287.

[134] In actions on bills of exchange and promissory notes, however, the plea of *non assumpsit* was disallowed. There, a plea in denial had to traverse some matter of fact such as the drawing, making, or indorsing of the bill.

[135] This had been Mansfield's particular concern in the contentious libel cases in the 1770s. See T. A. Green, *Verdict according to Conscience* and my 'From Seditious Libel to Unlawful Assembly: Peterloo and the Changing Face of Political Crime in England, *c.* 1770–1820'.

put an end to'.[136] This was not merely necessary to evolve clear points of law, but to allow the jury its proper function. Thus, Lord Tenterden could say in a case in 1832 that he considered special pleading 'to be founded, and to be adapted to, the peculiar mode of trial established in this country—the TRIAL BY JURY'. Because the system brought the issue to a single, simple question of fact, it was ideally suited to juries; and experience showed that this jury system could best work where all points were precisely refined.[137] Second, the clear pleading of the case by the parties would prevent the element of surprise, allowing both to be ideally prepared.[138] Finally, this would reduce the expense of trials, by making the point at issue clearer.[139]

After 1834, many lawyers enthused at the achievement of the reform. The *Legal Examiner and Law Chronicle* wrote that the rules had 'thrown us back on the original principles of pleading', reduced to a scientific form,[140] while elsewhere it wrote that the 'new rules, by disallowing the effect formerly given to the general issues . . . have made an advance towards the pristine logical beauty of pleading'.[141] 'At once,' wrote Samuel Warren, 'the study and practice of the common law, thus stripped of preliminary and extrinsic

---

[136] *Barnett* v. *Glossop* (1835) 1 Bing. NC 633 at 637. See also *Gutsole* v. *Mathers* (1836) 1 M. & W. 495. The clear separation of law and fact was particularly important in contract cases, for precise pleading allowed the judge, rather than the jury, to consider the illegality of a consideration. See *Hibblewhite* v. *M'Morine* (1839) 5 M. & W. 462. At the same time, where the defendant did not confess and avoid, but denied the promise as alleged or the matters of fact, if he attempted a special plea, it was improper as amounting to the general issue. See *Hayselden* v. *Staff* (1836) 5 A. & E. 153, *Heath* v. *Durant* (1844) 12 M. & W. 438.

[137] *Selby* v. *Bardons* (1832) 2 B. & Ad. 2 at 16.

[138] See Lord Abinger's comments in *Isaac* v. *Farrer* (1836) 1 M. & W. 65 at 69–70.

[139] Joseph Chitty thus wrote that the new rules would force practitioners to look much more carefully at the facts of their case and the law affecting it to ascertain the substance of the issue. Each fact would frame a single count, which would simplify all for judge and jury. Chitty's attitude to the reform can be seen from the title of his tract: *A Concise View of the Principles, Object and Utility of Pleadings; and of the Causes of the Abuses in Modern Practice, and the Imperative Necessity for Reformation in these Respects, and the consequent Great Importance of the New Rules* (London, 1834). The stress 'that the science of special pleading mainly consists in the appropriate delineation of *facts*' was reiterated by Charles Petersdorff in his *Practical Precedents in Pleading*.

[140] *Legal Examiner and Law Chronicle*, v. 17.

[141] *Legal Examiner and Law Chronicle*, iv. 466. Petersdorff discussing special pleading similarly praised 'its scholastic logic, its admirable distribution of the most intricate and varied facts, its masterly separation of non-essential matter from material details, its presenting reasons and giving arguments in its adroit combination of circumstances'. *Practical Precedents in Pleading*, iv, quoted in *Legal Observer*, ix (1834–5), 150.

difficulty, are become more scientific', and all pretence for ignorance had been removed.[142] Thus, after 1834, the common law entrenched its technical system of providing remedies, in the belief that it would best serve the development and flexibility of law. The reforms served a theory of law which was the reverse of Bentham's, reflecting an ancient theory reformulated at the end of the eighteenth century. As we shall see, however, the judges, obsessed with form,[143] soon began to miss the wood for the trees, allowing the law to develop haphazardly at case level, losing sight of both justice and policy.

As a result of these reforms, pleading became far more technical, and many more cases were lost due to technicalities, with judges focusing much more closely on technical accuracy than ever before. '[T]hese new requirements have occasioned so great an increase of trifling motions and summonses to set aside proceedings for really unimportant irregularities,' one textbook related, 'that more inconvenience than benefit has arisen from the requisition of so much particularity.'[144] In hindsight, the inconvenience of such an obsession with technical details became obvious.[145] Since parties were increasingly required to give a special plea in actions of case, assumpsit, and trespass, there was after 1834 a rise in the number of special demurrers on technical points unconnected with the merits.[146] Too often, the law appeared to be frustrated because of minor technical points, leading to public outrage. 'When a court has become so destitute of judicial astuteness', the *Law Magazine* wrote in 1851, 'as to be unable to know that "the year 1845" meant the year of the Christian era, and has compelled the parties to incur all the

---

[142] Warren, *A Popular and Practical Introduction to Law Studies*, 18. The enduring appeal of special pleading for students is evidenced by Joseph Philips's *Letters on Special Pleading, being an Introduction to the Study of that Branch of the Law*, which came out in a second edition in 1850.

[143] See, e.g., *Yardley v. Jones* (1835) 4 Dowl. 45, *Roberts v. Wedderburne* (1834) 4 Moo. & Sc. 488.

[144] Chitty, *The Practice of the Law*, iii. 120–3.

[145] See Holdsworth, 'The New Rules of Pleading' and *First Report of Her Majesty's Commissioners for Inquiring into the Process, Practice and System of Pleading in the Superior Courts of Common Law* (henceforth Common Law Procedure Commission), 1851 (1389) XXII 567, p. 20.

[146] Hence, parties without a good substantial defence could put in special demurrers to obtain delays or simply on the chance that they would win on a technicality. This was a major reason for the recommendation of the Royal Commission of 1851 to abolish the need to allege fictitious and unnecessary statements in the pleas—such as the words *contra pacem* or *vi et armis*—and to remove altogether the need to state a form of action. See Common Law Procedure Commission, 20–3.

expense of pleading and argument afresh because of the omission of the words "of our Lord"', it was high time for reform.[147]

Probably the most spectacular case of a party winning on a technicality, apparently against the merits, came in 1843, with the trial of Feargus O'Connor and 58 fellow Chartists for a seditious conspiracy in the aftermath of the Plug Plot Strikes in the North-West in 1842. The main counts against the defendants were the fourth, which was aimed against the violent leaders, charging them with aiding and abetting the gathering of unlawful assemblies, to force men out of work, and to incite hatred of the constitution, and the fifth, aimed at the peaceable leaders, charging a conspiracy to induce men to strike. When the case was argued before the Queen's Bench the defence claimed that the indictments drawn against the accused were inadequate since they did not specify the venue of the offences adequately. Since it was not specified where the offence had been committed, as far as the court could tell from the record, it could have occurred anywhere in the world, so that it was not shown the court had jurisdiction to try the case. In the fifth count, a venue had been laid, but only in the margin of the indictment.[148] This line of reasoning succeeded, the court conceding that the offences charged could have happened in France or anywhere else.[149] Hence, the fifth count was held invalid since the court was not shown to have had a jurisdiction.[150] As for the fourth count, it did not state where the unlawful assemblies had taken place, though it had charged the defendants with aiding and

[147] *Law Magazine*, New Series, xv (1851), 127.

[148] *State Trials. New Series*, iv. 1231 ff.

[149] Dundas told the court that all the authorities confirmed that every material fact had to be laid with time and place on the record. Here, he said, the unlawful assemblies charged 'might be any where in the world; they were not laid as being within the county of Lancaster, but at certain times and certain places; no man could say where'. *The Times*, 5 May 1843. Lord Denman agreed: 'No venue is stated in the fifth count,' he said, 'and it is plain that at common law the count on that ground is bad. Every material fact must be stated, with time and place, in order that it may be known whence the petty jury are to come who are to try the case.' *The Times*, 8 June 1843. The stress on the origin of the petty jury reveals that it was still considered important that the judgment should be shaped by local people, forming the judgment from below.

[150] The prosecution had attempted to argue that the error could be corrected by the court, by the statute 7 Geo. IV c. 29 s. 20 which corrected formal defects on the record. However, the judge rejected even this line, by holding firmly to technicalities. For he said, '[t]o bear any analogy to these statutes [of jeofails] the 7th of George IV should have cured the defects of venue where the case was tried by jury of the county in which the indictment was preferred'. He added, 'the venue in the margin may shew

abetting in the parish of Manchester. This was held by the court to be an imperfect venue which could be corrected by the statute; but judgment was never given on this count, for the arguments continued on the sufficiency of the charge. The defence had argued that since the defendants were charged as accessories, the act of the principals had to be laid with a correct venue to make the count valid; now they claimed that the offence they were charged as abetting—of unlawful assembly and intimidation to prevent work—was too vaguely stated and failed adequately to outline a crime. Lord Denman inclined to their views on this, but judgment was never given.[151] This was an important result, and one which outraged public opinion. That O'Connor and his associates did create chaos in Lancashire in 1842 was a fact so notorious, fumed *The Times*, that 'no one can entertain the remotest shadow of a doubt upon [it], unless he happens to be one of the Justices of HER MAJESTY'S COURT of QUEEN'S BENCH . . . [T]heir judicial understandings are so oppressed by "technical niceties"', it continued, 'that they are of necessity unable to conceive it, unless stated to them in some form of words totally incapable of being twisted, with the assistance of the absurdest suppositions, into meaning something else.'[152]

It was clear that particularly after 1834, the courts took very seriously their duties to reason on precise points disputed by litigants, and to explore in detail the substantive matter charged. Hence, in another major political trial of the 1840s, that against Daniel O'Connell and 17 others, the leaders of the Irish Repeal

---

this, but certainly does not make the indictment shew that the Court had jurisdiction to try the offence unless specifically referred to in the body of the indictment'. The jurisdiction of the court did not appear on the record, and therefore the defect was too deep-rooted to be cured. *The Times* 8 June 1843. See the report of the case in 5 QB 16. This supported the defence cases that the statute could only cure imperfect venues, and could not supply one where none was laid. See *R v. Hart* (1833) 6 C. & P. 123.

[151] *State Trials. New Series*, v. 1247 n.

[152] *The Times*, 29 May 1843. The reaction and the nature of the discharge shows that the release of the Chartists was not something connived at by a government keen not to produce martyrs, as has sometimes been imagined. Sir James Graham, the Home Secretary, had been convinced in 1842 that there existed a massive treasonable conspiracy, and the Attorney General, Sir Frederick Pollock, had sought throughout to 'bend in one accusation the Head and the Hands,—the bludgeon and the pen, and let the jury and public see in one case the whole crime, it's commencement and it's consequences'. Pollock to Graham, 9 Oct. 1842, Graham Papers, Cambridge University Library, Reel 32.

movement, for conspiracy, the court threw out four of the six counts charged as finding three conspiracies where only one was charged, and threw out a count for a conspiracy to intimidate on the grounds that intimidation was not necessarily unlawful.[153] After a verdict was given on the remaining count, the House of Lords had to decide whether judgment could be given, by presuming that the jury had convicted only on the grounds of the good count. The defence won the point, it being held that no such presumption could be made. Lord Denman's comments reveal the judges' interest in precision, and their desire for a precise differentiation between the judge's and the jury's role in law:

[A] criminal charge ought to be distinct, clear, and intelligible in itself, and free from all matter of imputation that does not belong to the offence. The subject is so far from being merely technical, that it may involve the greatest injustice, because you may inflict the heaviest punishment for the lightest offence, or indeed for that which may turn out to be no subject for punishment at all.[154]

Thus, at the time of Bentham's greatest influence, the law of procedure was reformed on lines wholly anti-Benthamite, re-inforcing those areas of law that he detested most. This seems a dilemma: a dilemma resolved when it is borne in mind that Bentham's greatest influence was theoretical, not practical. Lawyers agreed on the need for rules and clear laws, and to that end they sought to rationalize the law. But they did not want a deductive code, but instead a system drawing its rules from society, in a remedial way. Reformulating the common law was their solution.

The Defence of Common Law Reasoning

The debate over codification and Benthamic procedure induced many lawyers to reformulate defences of common law theory in the 1820s. James Humphreys' contention that laws should 'flow as natural deductions, each from the preceeding one',[155] and his

---

[153] *State Trials. New Series*, v. Tindal CJ (at 778) pointed out that 'intimidation' was not a technical word, adding that charging intimidation did not necessarily imply an offence, since (here) all it implied was that there were many people involved. Erle had referred to *O'Connell v. The Queen* 1 Cox. C. C. 462 to support his arguments as to the vagueness of the fourth count in O'Connor's case.

[154] Ibid. 881.   [155] Quoted in *Law Magazine*, i (1828–9), 617.

invocation of Bacon provoked a large response from common lawyers. The biggest attack was made by John Joseph Park,[156] who criticized the 'mechanical analysis' of the law put forward by all codifiers, which he claimed was rooted in 'that German school of synoptical arrangement in natural history and science' which sought to reduce all things to subdivisions and named species in a clinical manner. The natural sciences, Park argued, were wholly different from law: 'the former being learnt principally by induction, classification and arrangement are the first stages to the successful prosecution of the science . . . In law, however, the classification and arrangement of digested indexes has no other value whatever than as it enables the searcher to find what he wants.'[157] The law, by this token, could not be defined by first principles: it could only be described by systematization. This was an important point, and it reveals a belief pervasive among common lawyers that jurisprudence was useful for describing and clarifying the common law, but not for defining the law a priori.

Park described the common law as a reasoning process, a system using precedent and analogy for 'substituting argumentative corollary or inference for arbitrary and pre-constituted rule'.[158] Human transactions being infinite, it was impossible to set forth a finite series of preconceived propositions, as in a code, for an infinite series of rights. The common law process allowed all these circumstances to be covered, he argued, in typical common lawyers' fashion. However, Park's view of the common law was none the less a rule-oriented one, to a significant degree: 'It has in so far the semblance of a mathematical science,' he said, 'though without its capability of *positive* demonstration. Every proposition once decided becomes a datum from which to reason to the conclusion upon a new combination.'[159] The law thus created its own system of rules:

This is the process of adjudication which has been very naturally and unavoidably going on for centuries; and while it has been going on, the law, as an aggregate result of it, and of the publicity which is given to the decisions, has grown up into a dialectic system, boundless in the extent and variety of its propositions and reasonings; and, as a whole, infinitely beyond the grasp of any one human mind; but still preserving its original

---

[156] *A Contre-Projet to the Humphresian Code* (London, 1827).
[157] Ibid. 61.   [158] Ibid. 21.
[159] Ibid.

characteristic, that every part of that whole fits into some number of other parts, like the pieces of a child's puzzle map.[160]

Out of the reasoning process of the common law came this system of rules. The system of rules, however, was combined with the fact that law grew from below. 'Every decision not growing out of pre-conceived rules, is *in the first instance*, a rule of supposed convenience, justice, or policy,' he wrote; '[i]n the absence of analogy the whole common law of England has no other origin.'[161] This made the common law flexible and suited to people's needs, for it 'moulded the law to the general purposes and general sentiments of mankind'.[162] The idea of codification was attacked therefore for undermining the flexibility of law and its attachment to society by attempting to withdraw 'the plastic power of the law from the hands of the men daily conversant in the business of jurisprudence, and daily experiencing its practical workings and defects'.[163] It was indeed a common argument against codification that it was despotic and authoritarian, a law imposed from the outside.[164] Thus, in the late 1820s, many common lawyers defended their system as one which was animated by the genius of the people,[165] as is evidenced by Reddie's contention that 'the Legislature, the Judges and the Lawyers, are but the organs of the nation; they merely fix the limits, and connexion between, the various principles and rules which have thus arisen'.[166] The common law was the people's law, a living law. 'Putting a stop to further amelioration and advancement', Reddie claimed, 'will teach the nation, that the law is a dead letter, a mere engine of state, a rule of conduct prescribed to the people, not voluntarily adopted *by* them from a conviction of expediency and justice.'[167]

The notion that the common law was a flexible science, drawing its rules from all manner of sciences, was hence still a strong one by

---

[160] Ibid. 25.
[161] Ibid. 31.
[162] Ibid. 155.
[163] Ibid. 156.

[164] This point was made not only by Park, but by John Reddie, a Göttingen-trained lawyer under the influence of Savigny. See his *A Letter to the Lord High Chancellor of Great Britain on the Expediency of the Proposal to form a new Civil Code for England* (London, 1828).

[165] A key influence behind this was the argument of Savigny's *Vom Beruf unserer Zeit für Gesetzgebung und Rechtswissenschaft*, which argued that law lay in the popular consciousness in the same way that language did. This work was translated into English in 1832.

[166] Reddie, *Letter*, 7.
[167] Ibid. 61.

the 1830s. When Samuel Warren wrote his highly influential *Popular and Practical Introduction to Law Studies* in 1835, he therefore told the student to begin his study of the law with the study of pleading, but also to study history, geography, and political economy.[168] More importantly, he advised the student to study logic, and pursue an abstract and analytical method in his researches. He therefore recommended him to read both Whately on Logic and Dugald Stewart's *Elements of the Philosophy of the Human Mind*. In an implicit critique of Blackstone and Bentham, he quoted Stewart's words:

> In order to proceed with safety in the use of general principles, much caution and address are necessary, both in establishing their truth, and in applying them to practice. Without a proper attention to the circumstances by which their application to particular areas may be modified, they will be a perpetual source of mistake and of disappointment, in the conduct of affairs, however rigidly just they may seem in themselves, and however accurately we may reason from them.[169]

Warren reiterated that the lawyer had to begin with an examination of individual events in an analytic way. Only later could one speak of principle. With Warren, we can see the ideas expressed by the common lawyers after Blackstone reiterated. The law was no self-contained science, but grew from particular cases through particular pleas. Nor did the science stand alone: it had to be seen in the context of, and alongside, all the others.

Thus, by the 1830s, the Benthamic idea of the Pannomion had failed to take root. In the sphere of substantive law, Bentham's positive proposals failed to make the impact he desired. Most common lawyers still saw their law as a growing body, flexible and responsive to the needs of society, but growing through the mechanism of pleading. However, they did take on board Bentham's ideas on the nature and form of the law, seeing law as a set of rules. In terms of formal theory, not even the most traditionally minded common lawyer now saw the law as an infinite series of unconnected forms. There had, in a sense, been a meeting of minds between Bentham and the common lawyers, based on the recognition that formal theory did not dictate the content of substantive law. This meeting of minds was to be encapsulated in the work of John Austin.

---

[168] Warren, *A Popular and Practical Introduction to Law Studies*, 124–51.

[169] Stewart, *Elements of the Philosophy of the Human Mind*, i (Edinburgh, 1792), 214–15. Quoted by Warren, 230.

8

John Austin's Analytical Jurisprudence

JOHN Austin is usually seen as the man who took on Bentham's ideas on legal definitions, and presented them to the public in a workmanlike manner which lacked the subtlety and sophistication seen in the master's work;[1] and indeed this view was reinforced by Austin's own words in a letter to Bentham in which he said that if he had enough means to support himself, he would 'feel no violent desire for any other object than that of disseminating your doctrines'.[2] It is rare, however, to examine how Austin differed from Bentham, or to look at how he adapted Benthamic notions to fit different ends. The two men seemed to have fundamentally different attitudes towards the common law, and different aspirations for their work. For whereas Bentham was celebrated as the great codifier and reformer, the prince of the Pannomion, Austin was to be seen as an educationalist and expositor, who had no desire to transform the substantive legal order, but who was engaged in a definitional and jurisprudential exercise. It is significant that Bentham's most celebrated jurisprudential disciple should have taken up his analytical concerns, and attempted to put them into a more complete and coherent workable structure of legal concepts, without attempting the political exercise of creating complete codes of substantive and constitutional law.

If much of Austin's interest in the importance of analytical jurisprudence derived from Bentham, its execution owed a great deal to the German Jurists he encountered in the 1820s. Developments in

---

[1] See, e.g., H. L. A. Hart, *Essays on Bentham*, 108. For a discussion on Austin's debts to Bentham, see W. L. Morison, *John Austin* (London, 1982), *passim*.

[2] Quoted by W. E. Rumble, 'Divine Law, Utilitarian Ethics and Positivist Jurisprudence: A Study of the Legal Philosophy of John Austin', *American Journal of Jurisprudence*, xxiv (1979), 139–80, at 146. See also, A. D. E. Lewis, 'John Austin (1790–1859): Pupil of Bentham', *Bentham Newsletter*, no. ii (1979), 18–29.

German jurisprudence since Kant and Hugo had led to a rejection of attempts to build complete mathematical deductive systems and had focused attention more on the systematic study of concepts.[3] German methodology coloured most of Austin's work: it explained how he was not interested in defining *all* strands of law (like Bentham) but how instead he came to realize that legal entities had so many facets that they could not be defined in a priori terms. It also helps to explain how and why Austin was not hostile to the common law and its forms. For Austin, the system of substantive law would allow for change and development from below, through cases, pleas, and judicial reasonings: law was a social phenomenon that could not be defined through theoretical constructs. It further explains his attitudes to codification, which were markedly different from Bentham's. As such, Austin represents an important shift in English jurisprudence away from the attempts to create deductive substantive legal structures.

This location of Austin's jurisprudence helps shed light on recent debates over Austin, which question how far he was engaged in a conceptual or an empirical pursuit. On the one hand, Julius Stone has argued that he was not attempting to describe any real law, but was only setting up definitions of concepts which lay behind the law, in order to understand the law which existed as a separate entity.[4]

---

[3] For German influences on Austin, see A. B. Schwarz, 'John Austin and the German Jurisprudence of his Time', *Politica*, i (1934), 178–99; W. L. Morison, *John Austin*, 60–3; and A. Agnelli, *John Austin alle origini del positivismo giuridico* (Turin, 1959), 22–34. Most writers note that there was a German influence on Austin, without explaining its significance or influence on the body of his works, which are usually taken to be wholly Benthamic in character. For instance, Schwarz wrote that 'German influence on Austin's *work* should not be regarded as too important' (at 180), while Lotte and Joseph Hamburger (*Troubled Lives: John and Sarah Austin* (Toronto, 1985), 47) write that the German 'influence, such as it was, minimally affected only the most general context and a few subordinate parts of his theory of law, but barely touched the main features of Austinian theory'. Austin's Romanism (which he saw through the German prism) has received more attention from historians and critics: see, for example, M. H. Hoeflich, 'John Austin and Joseph Story: Two Nineteenth Century Perspectives on the Utility of the Civil Law for the Common Lawyer', *American Journal of Legal History*, xxix (1985), 36–77, and J. L. Montrose, 'Return to Austin's College', *Current Legal Problems*, xiii (1960), 1–21.

[4] J. Stone, *The Province and Function of Law* (London, 1947), 59–72, and *Legal System and Lawyers' Reasonings* (London, 1964), 66–92. He writes (*Legal System*, 88) '[w]hat Austin terms principles and distinctions "common to all systems of law" should better have been called "principles useful for analysing and understanding actual systems of law" '. Gerber has suggested a similar view, arguing that Austin did not seek to describe, but to set up an analytical vocabulary of terms: '[t]hey are not correct or incorrect, but are useful or not'. D. Gerber, 'A Note on Woody on Dewey on Austin',

Stone's view has been criticized, however, for describing Austin as a deductivist, who felt that the law was a closed legal system where the judges arrived at decisions from the premises in a deductive way.[5] Robert Moles has recently restated the 'conceptualist' interpretation, in a way to reinterpret traditional assumptions about Austin's positivism. For Moles, Austin's greater concern was with the organic unity of positive law, positive morals, and ethics, and his definitions of law in the *Province of Jurisprudence Determined* were stipulative definitions to mark out the boundaries of the minimum content of the legal realm. It was useful to divide the moral, legal, and political world into three spheres, since this gave a clearer perspective on the world: but for Austin, the three were different perspectives on the same world.[6] On the other hand, W. L. Morison argues that Austin's science was an inductivist one, built on observed facts, and not rational abstractions. Austin's definitions of 'sovereign' and 'command' were hence not mere logical premises, but 'a connotation of the word "law" in terms of empirical facts'. Thus, when Austin discussed 'necessary notions', he was only making the 'matter-of-fact proposition that any system of law is susceptible of classification under certain categories'.[7] For Morison, if Austin's theory were empirically false, it would be useless.[8]

Ethics, lxxix (1968–9), 303–8 at 306. For other discussions of Austin's analytical jurisprudence, see Alan R. White, 'Austin as a Philosophical Analyst', *Archiv für Rechts- und Sozialphilosophie*, lxiv (1978), 379–99; Gerard Maher, 'Analytical Philosophy and Austin's Philosophy of Law', *Archiv für Rechts- und Sozialphilosophie*, lxiv (1978), 401–16; and Herbert Morris, 'Verbal Disputes and the Legal Philosophy of John Austin', *UCLA Law Review*, vii (1959–60), 27–56.

[5] This derives from Stone's comment (*Province*, 138), '[a] system such as Austin's is purporting to expose the premises from which each particular rule may follow as a conclusion, and to ascertain how far all such premises may be ultimately found to stand together consistently with one supreme set of premises like the definition of 'law' and 'sovereign' or of the necessary legal conceptions'. See H. L. A. Hart, 'Positivism and the Separation of Law and Morals', *Harvard Law Review*, lxxi (1957–8), 593–629 at 608 n.; W. L. Morison, 'Some Myth about Positivism', *Yale Law Journal*, lxviii (1958–9), 212–33 at 218. See also Austin's comments on logic in *Lectures*, 1885, 1013.

[6] Robert N. Moles, *Definition and Rule in Legal Theory: A Reassessment of H. L. A. Hart and the Positivist Tradition* (Oxford, 1987).

[7] Morison adds that 'Austin's notion of general jurisprudence as an exposition of principles of law is inconsistent with the empirical foundations upon which the predominant part of his theory is based'. 'Some Myth', 229–30. Compare R. S. Summers's view of the 'old' analytical jurists' tendency to convert conceptual questions into questions of fact, thus, beginning with the question of what constituted an obligation, the analytical jurist engaged in empirical research to discover what did, as a

[*See page 226 for n. 7 cont. and n. 8*].

It will be argued here that Austin's structure was concerned with formal theory, and his aims were purely analytical in the sense that he never sought any deduction of real rules nor a description of real entities, but only abstractions out of legal materials which existed beyond.[9] He was creating constructs with which to understand the workings of a legal system, and thereby to clarify what judges and legislators should look for in their deliberations. The fact that Austin's conceptual apparatus owed so much to German writing on Roman Law shows that his conceptual framework was not derived from empirical fact in the common law; nor did he engage in the epistemological explorations of Bentham to found his system in the facts of human nature. However, the system was designed to fit the common law as it existed. His attempt was thus to create a systematic view of legal concepts which would be more integrated and rational than the ones that Bentham had attempted. This helps explain his rigid division of law and morals: Bentham, to a large degree, had been unable to create a rational and coherent analytic structure because his codes always bore in mind the end in view as an integral part. There is hence a clear difference between his view of the content and substance of legal systems, and his formal analysis of terms in use in developed systems. This interpretation must colour our view of the Austinian sovereign. Austin's positivism was a conceptual tool for seeing law as rules, and in his legal system, the sovereign stood as a shorthand for the 'source of law' or 'legal system' as a whole.[10] His positivism was in a sense a legal truism: nothing was law which was not enforced as law. In Austin's analytical structure, then, the sovereign could not be seen as a normative proposition discussing the nature of legislation or the

matter of fact, constitute an obligation, and from here derived his simple (but inadequate) notion of sanctions. 'The *New* Analytical Jurists', *New York University Law Review*, xli (1966), 861–96 at 879.

[8] The empiricist thesis has most recently been restated by Wilfrid Rumble in 'John Austin and his Nineteenth Century Critics: the Case of Sir Henry Sumner Maine', *Northern Ireland Legal Quarterly*, xxxix (1988), 119–49.

[9] As Mill said, Austin's aim was 'the clearing up of the puzzles arising from complex combinations of ideas confusedly apprehended, and not analysed into their elements.' For Austin, jurisprudence was a lexicon of legal concepts, which did not pre-exist, but needed derivation by abstraction. J. S. Mill, 'Austin on Jurisprudence', *Edinburgh Review*, cxviii (1863), 439–82 at 440.

[10] Moles, *Definition and Rule*, p. 71 makes a similar point that Austin's sovereign was an abstraction, not an empirical entity. However, Moles does not explore the issue of why Austin had so much difficulty in his attempts to locate the sovereign.

content of legal systems: as a result, his disquisitions on where to locate the sovereign, those ideas which have often been seen as undermining his venture, were, like his discussions of utility, beside the point.

The German Influence

It is significant that when Austin was appointed to the chair of Jurisprudence at University College, he should have gone to Bonn to prepare his lectures. For although he was already familiar with Roman law, having taught J. S. Mill in the 1820s,[11] it was in Germany that he encountered the great enthusiasm for systematization and classification that would so influence him. Austin's library was well stocked with German textbooks, and he had clearly devoted much attention to Hugo's *Lehrbuch des Naturrechts*, Falck's *Encyclopaedie*, Savigny's *Possession*, and Thibaut's Essays, as well as the Institutes of Haubold and Mackeldey, when he came to compose his lectures.[12] Austin was exposed to both the philosophical and historical schools of German legal thought, and sought to adapt their notions to a Benthamic concept of sovereignty and law in general. If we put together his English and German influences, we can see his work in the *Province of Jurisprudence Determined* and his *Lectures on Jurisprudence* as a unity, rather than as separate works written under separate influences. We can similarly see how this hybrid of ideas allowed him to create a view of law that was different from Bentham's.

At the time that Austin was in Germany, German jurists were divided into two groups: the historical school, with Savigny at its head and the philosophical school, associated with Thibaut. Austin was clearly influenced by the latter, with its attempt to create a system of legal dogmatics, but at first it seems as if he either ignored or misunderstood the historical approach. While Austin took the subtitle of his lectures—*The Philosophy of Positive Law*—from Gustav Hugo's *Lehrbuch*,[13] Hugo's use of the term seemed very different

[11] Mill, *Autobiography*, in *Collected Works of John Stuart Mill*, i, ed. John M. Robson and Jack Stillinger (Toronto, 1981), 67, and E. M. Campbell, 'John Austin and Jurisprudence in Nineteenth Century England', 24.

[12] See Schwarz, 190 ff. For the contents of Austin's Library, see his *Lectures*, ix-xiii.

[13] Hugo's *Lehrbuch des Naturrechts, als einer Philosophie des positiven Rechts* (Berlin, 1819 edn.). Austin borrowed the title in subtitling his work *The Philosophy of Positive*

from Austin's. For Hugo, the term 'positive law' was used to describe a concept of law antithetical to the mathematical deductive natural law systems. He was particularly concerned to fight the rationalistic a priorism of Christian Wolff and his followers, pointing out that any complete system of law that aimed to be rational also had to explain the rationality of particular judicial decisions and positive laws.[14] Hugo's attacks on natural law therefore came from an explicitly empiricist base, showing that law did not build on abstract truths, but on historical reality.[15] Hugo was particularly concerned with private law and custom and he felt that instead of constructing abstract systems, the modern jurist should examine the history of law, in order to trace its intrinsic life and development. This concept of positive law served by the end of the eighteenth century to discredit a Wolffian view of law. The idea that law was a social institution was accepted equally by those who remained loyal to natural law, like Thibaut and Hufeland, who treated natural law not as an abstract standard of judgment, but as a standard derived from an empirical examination of the nature of legal relations, constructed into a system, with which to criticize positive law.

One central feature of Hugo's historical thought seems to contradict Austin. For Hugo, the source of law was the people, and so he wrote in 1812, 'die Gesetze sind nicht die einzige Quelle der juristischen Wahrheiten'.[16] There was a clear distinction between *Recht* and *Gesetz*, the former being much more extensive and important than the latter. Hugo was hence suspicious of legislation, seeing the people as the primary source of laws, which developed by chance out of concrete situations. The classic critique of Austin, from Maine onwards, has, on the other hand, shown a theorist who was wholly insensitive to the subtleties of history, and whose focus of all law deriving from a determinate sovereign, which apparently contradicted history, was plainly wrong.[17] Yet, as has

---

Law, but noted that Hugo's work blended ethics and jurisprudence in a way he considered undesirable. *Lectures*, 32.

[14] For the undermining of the Wolffian approach in the mid-eighteenth century, see P. H. Reill, *The German Enlightenment and the Rise of Historicism* (Berkeley, Los Angeles, and London, 1975).

[15] See G. Marini, *L'opera di Gustav Hugo nella crisi del giusnaturali tedesco* (Milan, 1969). [16] Quoted by Marini, *L'opera di Gustav Hugo*, 35.

[17] See H. S. Maine, *The Early History of Institutions* (London, 1875), 355; F. Harrison, 'The English School of Jurisprudence', *Fortnightly Review*, xxiv (New Series) (1878), 475–92; and J. Bryce, *Studies in History and Jurisprudence*, 2 vols. (Oxford, 1901), ii. 96.

recently been argued, Austin did allow for judicial legislation: which was a form of turning custom into law. To some degree, his arguments on custom are therefore a half-way house between Bentham and the historical approach. For Austin rejected both the argument that custom existed as law by spontaneous adoption, and the opposite Benthamic view that all judicial legislation was usurpation.[18] In his argument that judges transform customs— positive morality—into the law of the sovereign, we can see both a Benthamic view of custom,[19] and a historically inspired notion that customs were important sources for the content of law. The point that apparently contradictory approaches to law could sit together in Austin's work is confirmed not only by the fact that he smudged over any differences between Savigny and Thibaut,[20] but also by his comments on Bentham and the historical school, which sought to forestall any distinction between the historical and the analytical school. The proper sense of the 'historical' approach, he said, was that the law could not be spun out from a priori principles, but had to be founded on the experience of subjects. Bentham, said Austin, clearly belonged to this school: so that a 'fitter name for [the historical school] would be the *inductive* and *utilitarian* school'.[21] In this discussion, he clearly characterized Thibaut as one of the historical school, dismissing Savigny's and Hugo's objections to codification by enlisting Thibaut's support. This was an uncomfortable welding of different approaches: but it reveals how his modification of the Benthamic urge for legislation may be said to have been influenced by German customary notions.[22]

More important than the history of the 'external law' or

---

[18] *Province*, Hart, 30–2. Austin's judicial legislation has attracted recent important attention. See W. Rumble, 'John Austin, Judicial Legislation and Legal Positivism', *University of Western Australia Law Review*, xiii (1977–8), 77–109; his *The Thought of John Austin* (London, 1985); and Moles, *Definition and Rule*.

[19] See the discussion in Ch. 6.

[20] Austin did not seem particularly sensitive to the differences and divergences in the German writers he read: thus, he praised Thibaut as a writer, 'who, for penetrating acuteness, rectitude of judgment, depth of learning and vigour, and elegance of exposition, may be placed by the side of Von Savigny, at the head of all leading Civilians', *Lectures*, 72, and quoted in his work equally from historical and philosophical jurists.   [21] *Lectures*, 679.

[22] There are two reasons why it was *German* notions he was drawing on, rather than English. First, eighteenth-century German writers were more explicit in their formulation of a customary theory of law than Blackstone had been, and were more unequivocal than Blackstone. Second, Austin's references were to Germans. *The Province of Jurisprudence Determined*, ed. H. L. A. Hart (London, 1954), 30.

Rechtsgeschichte was the 'internal history', the *Rechtsaltertümer*, the detailed historical study of juristic concepts. This was something engaged in by the historical jurists (for it was through those theoretical constructs that customs were seen to become law), but it was the philosophical jurists who most sought to create systems of dogma. At the same time that Hugo was researching into the history of Romanist legal thought, jurists like A. D. Weber and K. S. Zachariae, influenced by a Kantian methodology, sought to progress towards a systematization of the modern use of Roman law. Two important assumptions lay behind their attempts. First was their view of a system, influenced by Kant, seen not as a fixed doctrinal structure, but as a tool to explore a variety of causal relations. Second was their attitude to Roman law, and their desire to distil from its principles a general theoretical system which could be used to determine the most scientific organization of the positive law of a state. For Weber, this involved distinguishing Roman law from its dogma. Weber saw that the Pandects could not be used uncritically like evidence of facts, but that Roman law had to be theorized to provide the link between its principles and contemporary German needs, which were distinct from Roman ones. The jurist should therefore not treat the Roman code as a source of laws, but see it as containing a system of all law. Legal dogmatics could be used to trace back law and its meaning, and a legislator's law could be fitted into the system, but the Pandectist science was essentially the development of a systematized dogma. Roman law contained the characteristic forms, which could be applied to single cases arising in society.[23] The Pandectists therefore separated theory and practice, seeking to create a philosophy of positive law which would submit the data of history and daily experience to determinate general principles. This systematizing approach was most associated in the early nineteenth century with the philosophical school (the new natural lawyers) rather than the historical school: and it is evident that Austin was very familiar with the system building of Thibaut, Mühlenbruch, and Mackeldey. The two German approaches, moreover, came together to some degree in the 1840s in Savigny's *System des Heutigen Römischen Rechts*,[24] where historical investiga-

---

[23] For a history of this trend and its influences, see P. Capellini, *Systema Iuris*. 2 vols. (Milan, 1984–5). See 108–73 for Weber and Zachariae.

[24] F. C. von Savigny, *System des Heutigen Römischen Rechts*, 8 vols. (Berlin, 1840). Austin had a copy of the first volume of this work, though it was published too late to influence his lectures.

tion of the 'internal' history of law aided in discovering its principles, and in perfecting the law as a system, allowing the jurist to see the unity and interdependence of the law in a way that old dogmatic works failed to do. This theoretical concern was the one that most influenced Austin, and it was this approach that most influenced his *Lectures*. The Romanist bias in the *Lectures* has long been recognized: yet commentators on Austin have been slower to realize its larger significance for the analytical nature of his work. Austin's course of lectures followed a typically Pandectist structure, beginning with a general discussion of the notions of law and jurisprudence and then discussing in detail the ordering of persons, things, and actions.[25] Similarly, the division of general and particular jurisprudence that Austin talked of in his definitions paralleled Pandectist scholarship.[26] By examining Austin's jurisprudence through German lenses, we can see that his was a conceptual venture, not an empirical one.[27]

The German debate on codification also reveals Austin's distance from the Pannomion, and his acceptance of many of the assumptions of German jurisprudence. As became apparent in the famous dispute between Savigny and Thibaut in 1814, what most divided the

[25] See, e.g., the work of Austin's Bonn contemporary, Ferdinand Mackeldey, *Handbook of the Roman Law*, trans. Moses A. Dropsie (Philadelphia, 1883).

[26] Thibaut, for example, wrote, 'A system of Law, founded on logical principles, should consist of two parts; viz, a *general part* in which the great leading ideas and principles of law are brought together, and a *special part* in which the nature of each law is separately examined and its application to individual cases correctly determined.' N. Lindley, *An Introduction to the Study of Jurisprudence; being a translation of the General Part of Thibaut's System des Pandekten Rechts* (London, 1885).

[27] This is to challenge Morison's view that Austin's jurisprudence was aimed to be a 'logically systematic science', analogous to political economy. Morison argues that the key influences on Austin were James Mill's *Elements of Political Economy* and J. S. Mill's ideas on logic, and that Austin used these influences in attempting 'to define the species law by its genus and its differentia, and to investigate what propria were exhibited by all systems of the legal species'. *John Austin*, 1. By this means, he could take facts from the real world and fit them into logical and ordered patterns. Morison's argument is intriguing and suggestive. However, not only is it questionable how far Austin was in fact influenced by the writings of Mill (the *System of Logic* was published, as Morison admits, 12 years after Mill was in Austin's class), but the substantive body of Austin's *Lectures* do not use a discourse of Aristotelian logic. Similarly, any reference to Mill's *Logic* as influencing Austin is highly problematic. The 'traditional logic associated with Aristotle' at the time Austin was writing was Whately's: Mill's *Logic* was an innovative marrying of inductivist logic and the Aristotelian system. One might expect a Benthamite like Austin to take a more Benthamic classificatory view of logic than this one. For that reason, it is more useful to look in detail at the German influence than the Mills'; which in turn enables us to evaluate Austin's empiricism differently from Morison. For a critique of Morison's ideas, see Rumble, *The Thought of John Austin*, 93–7.

approaches was their attitude to codification,[28] a question which reflected their attitudes towards the sources and nature of law. In this debate, neither side favoured the type of a priori codification associated with Bentham, nor a mathematical deductive system of law; and neither side rejected the need for empirical and historical investigation. However, where Savigny and his followers felt that the law was as yet insufficiently known to be codified—the Roman sources of German law needed further exploration and systematization—Thibaut felt that enough was known to create a system that would maintain the good and cut away the bad parts of the law.

Austin failed to see why Savigny was so opposed to codification. First of all, Savigny admired the Roman law, which itself had been codified and was treated as a code of laws. Secondly, Savigny admitted that a code would be acceptable if it did not claim to anticipate future cases.[29] Yet Austin admitted that no code could anticipate future cases which did not resemble past ones.[30] Austin's view of codification was therefore not an ideological exercise, but a technical one which aimed at a better expression of the law. He never aimed at the rational deductivism to be found in Bentham's visions of a code.[31] His view of codification owed as much to Thibaut as to Bentham. First, Austin felt that while a code was the ideal form of law, the question of codification was a matter of time and place.[32] It was therefore related both to the development of the law and to

---

[28] Thibaut's treatise *Über die Nothwendigkeit eines allgemeines bürgerliches Rechts für Deutschland* (Heidelberg, 1814) proposed a code for all Germany, and elicited Savigny's *Vom Beruf unserer Zeit für Gesetzgebung und Rechtswissenschaft* which was translated into English in 1832.

[29] By the time of the publication of Savigny's *System*, the codification debate in Germany had been won by the historical school. This work may be seen as the resolution of the historians' emphasis on private law, their distrust of legislation, and their notion of law growing with the people, for it sought to elaborate a unified systematic view of the principles and concepts of the modern Roman law in Germany, in a way analogous to a code. Konrad Zweigert and Hein Kötz write that Savigny and his disciples had the 'thoroughly unhistorical view that the legal forms and institutions created by the Romans belonged to a higher and purer conceptual world and possessed a sort of eternal validity . . . For them the legal system was a closed order of institutions, ideas and principles developed from the Roman law.' *Introduction to Comparative Law*, 2nd edn., 2 vols. (Oxford, 1987), i. 144.

[30] No system could hope to cover every eventuality: '[i]t would be endless': *Lectures*, 665.

[31] As Agnelli has written, 'La codificazione non ha per Austin nessuna qualità taumaturgica: è solo uno strumento che può conferire agli uomini vantaggi in numero maggiore di quelli assicurati dal complesso delle disposizioni di diritto giudiziario.' *John Austin*, 238.

[32] *Lectures*, 662.

the development of juridical science. The whole notion of codification was seen as a modern one, for Austin felt that the ancient 'codes' were not complete bodies of law, but mere collections of the societies' laws.[33] Second, it required the talents of many experts in the law to accomplish the task.[34] Austin was insistent on the role of the jurist above the legislator, for it was only the former who could accurately represent the law. The code would be 'merely an exposition sanctioned by the supreme legislator and by his will converted into law'.[35] Sovereign legislators were incapable of legislating in detail. Austin recognized the objections to codification—that it would be too bulky, that it might be arbitrary, and that it would fail to cover all cases—but his answer to these objections—that the existing law already had these faults and that an authoritative statement of the law would do no harm—revealed that he was aiming at an improvement of the existing method, not at an instant panacea. The first step to codification would be a digest. Austin's code did not aim to be the perfect system of a perfect content, but a methodological re-expression of current law. He declared that 'codification does not involve any innovation in the *matter* of the existing law. It is clear that the law of England might change its shape completely, although the rights and duties which it confers and imposes remain substantially the same.'[36] A code would therefore extract the *ratio decidendi* from various cases, and give these embodiment:[37] but the rules would be drawn from society through the courts.[38] Austin never had the same rage for codification to be found in Bentham, and indeed the only detailed discussion of

---

[33] *Lectures*, 636. Justinian's code could therefore not be seen as a modern code.

[34] *Lectures*, 1093.

[35] *Lectures*, 680. Austin further argued that the '[b]usiness of legislation ought to be performed by persons who are at once thoroughly versed in the science of jurisprudence and legislation, and in the particular system of the given community: The sovereign legislature merely authorizing and checking, and not affecting to legislate itself.' *Lectures*, 613.

[36] *Lectures*, 663.   [37] *Lectures*, 666.

[38] Austin favoured a system whereby judicial rules would be incorporated into the code periodically, in a way similar to Bentham's views in the *Constitutional Code*: 'there should . . . be a perpetual provision for [the code's] amendment, on suggestions from the judges who are engaged in applying it, and who are in the best of all situations for observing its defects. By this means the growth of judiciary law explanatory of, and supplementary to, the code, cannot indeed be prevented altogether, but may be kept within a moderate bulk.' *Lectures*, 675. What Austin most favoured was a system where judge-made law could be promulgated in the form of statute law as a rule for the future, in the manner of the Roman Praetors. *Lectures*, 613.

the merits of a code in his work came at the end of his analysis of the sources of law. The difference was that for Austin, codification was largely a technical exercise, a way of re-expressing the law, whereas for Bentham it involved a total reformulation of substance. It will be seen that Austin's prime concern was refining the concepts of law, and that this allowed him to develop a view of the evolution of substantive rules that grew out of society. His conceptual apparatus was more flexible and sensitive to variations at ground level than has usually been acknowledged. This contradicts a prevalent view of the sovereign in Austin, which will be discussed in the final section.

Austin's System of Concepts

Austin's structure of legal concepts in the *Lectures* sought to make sense of legal relations as they existed in society: conceptual definitions in Austin were not absolutes, but were tools with which to understand a flexible and variegated reality. This is apparent in his analysis of property. The key Romanist distinction he began with was that between *dominium*—the power to use a subject in an unlimited and undefined way—and *servitus*—where there were limitations on the right of use one had, as in a right of way. Having drawn this conceptual distinction, however, Austin showed that it was not absolute, for he acknowledged that in practice property was susceptible of various modes and limitations, while still being capable of being defined as *dominium*. In England, there were limitations on tenancies by curtesy or in dower, yet there was no general limit to the use which could be made of them. They were still seen as *dominium*, being freeholds distinctly different from copy-holds, which came more clearly under the class of *servitus*. Austin thus realized that there was no simple twofold division, but an infinity of degrees, and thence arrived at a vague definition dependent on circumstance:

though the possible *modes* of property are infinite, and though the indefinite power of user is always restricted more or less, there is in every system of law, some one mode of property in which the restrictions to the power of user are fewer than in others . . . And to this mode of property, the term dominion, property or ownership is pre-eminently and emphatically applied.[39]

<hr/>

[39] *Lectures*, 796–7.

Austin thus had a *concept* of property: but exactly what the types of property were varied in each society according to local rules. There was no rigid definition and no absolutes, but all related to the system prevalent on the ground. Hence, in England, the 'purest' form of property was that held in fee-simple: estates for life, less pure, were none the less still to be classed as *dominium*. Ultimately, Austin admitted that 'property' was an indeterminate concept, which could not be defined in substantive terms; for if *dominium* was a right to unlimited use, then it could only be defined in a negative way, by elaborating every right or duty contained in the *corpus juris*. No thinker had successfully defined property, Austin pointed out, but had only described certain aspects of it. This was an admission that key concepts could not be defined clearly in terms of rules: all that could be achieved was a guide in skeletal terms to what was meant by an idea, whose application and nature varied in practice.[40]

The fact that Austin's conceptual apparatus was a set of tools with which to understand real law, and not a deductive set of concepts with which to create or describe a system, is seen in the way in which he drew on the law of England, and how far he accepted it without criticizing its rules or workings. In his discussion of *dominium* and *servitus*, he pointed out that ultimately they were distinguished in terms of their duration, so that before one could understand what was meant by a right of unlimited duration, one had to know 'the nature of *descent* or of succession *ab intestato*',[41] and the modes of alienation. To be a right of unlimited duration, the right had to be capable of devolving *ab intestato* from the party entitled to an infinity of descendants: hence, Austin was drawn into a discussion of the various modes of tenure in England. Austin's definition self-consciously accorded with Blackstone's, revealing how far he distilled his distinctions by reference to the existing common law in its most complex area, the law of tenure. He even discussed the detailed rules of feudal descent, pointing out that 'feuds and the feudal system are really an exceedingly specific and purely historical notion, not to be got at by scientific speculation, but by diligent reading of the history of the middle ages'.[42] Austin was clearly reconciled to the intricacies and peculiarities of English law, seeking to build a system in order to understand it, but not to replace it.

---

[40] *Lectures*, 799–800.   [41] *Lectures*, 830.   [42] *Lectures*, 850.

It is therefore clear that Austin was not attempting to create a deductive structure, but that his theorizing depended on the content of real systems. These had their own contents, which were not the subject of his concerns. Thus, when discussing property, Austin had said that titles to property were necessary to signify when rights began: but like Blackstone,[43] he argued that it did not matter what *facts* were taken to perform the function of a title, as long as there was a mark.[44] The content of structures thus depended on circumstance, and was largely a matter of indifference. This helps us to pinpoint the nature of Austin's task: he did not seek simple definitions from which others developed, but rather explained the concepts behind real systems. These systems were complicated, and the jurist could only pick out single strands from the complex whole. Thus, he noted, 'such is the ultimate connection between the various departments of every legal system, that . . . reference forward to matter yet unexplained, is an inconvenience which cannot be avoided by any expositor of law, although by long and assiduous reflection it might be considerably reduced'.[45] The job of jurisprudence was to help understand what happened in legal systems; and because jurisprudential concepts presented a two-dimensional view of a three-dimensional problem, the concepts had to be flexible and adaptive.

This is evident in Austin's discussion of the structure of law considered with reference to its purposes. His key division built on the Romanist division of the Law of Things and of Persons. However, the Law of Things was not the law of property or the law relating to things, but signified the entire body of the law, excluding certain portions of the law affecting particular classes of persons. The latter constituted the Law of Persons, which was excluded from the main body for the sake of convenience, since it was easier to specify rules pertaining to certain classes separately than to include them in the general mass.[46] This, Austin realized, was very close to

[43] Austin cited Blackstone's comments on the inability of the half-blood to inherit by descent, at 2 *Comm.* 228 ff. He claimed that Blackstone had held it 'a matter of indifference, because every right is a creature of law, which is as much as to say that, because all legal rights are created by law, it matters not one rush what rights the law creates'. This was assuredly an Austinian opinion. *Lectures,* 881.

[44] 'There are', he wrote, 'no common reasons applying to all titles alike. The reasons why property is conferred by occupancy are not the same as the reasons why it is conferred by alienation.' *Lectures,* 882.   [45] *Lectures,* 830.

[46] Austin rejected the notion that the Rights of Things covered non-human entities and that the Rights of Persons covered human ones, for he said that both related to

the Benthamic division of general and particular codes;[47] however, he derived his ideas on the redefinition of the division of Person and Thing from the theorizing to be found in Thibaut's essays.[48] For Austin, the Law of Persons was the law of status, or conditions. Status was no inherent quality in a man, but was rather a label used to sum up certain rights and duties that he possessed.[49] Thus, a right of action which seemed to come from a certain status was not the legal consequence of that status, but the consequence of the relations and rights from which that status arose.'Status' was therefore only a tag: it was clear what the notion of status was, but one could not define a priori the contents of rights appertaining to any status, since the status only acted as a label to connote those rights. The division between the Law of Persons and Things was therefore not a necessary division, nor one that could be absolutely defined, for it depended on the subjective way in which one classified various rights under the variable heading of status. Hence, he wrote that '[t]here are [. . .] reasons in every system for adopting the distinction [between the Law of Persons and Things], although it may not be described precisely alike in any two systems'.[50] The Law of Persons hence concerned certain anomalies and exceptions. In his overall analysis, it therefore contained the law relating to private, political, and anomalous conditions.[51] However, since these rights were only a modification of the *jus rerum*, the lawyer needed knowledge of the whole law modified in the exception.

In discussing status, Austin modified both civilian and Benthamic positions. First, against Heineccius' notion that status was an inherent quality, he affirmed that it consisted not of the fact or event

rights and duties incumbent on men. This was a challenge to the Blackstonian division: 'Many rights and duties treated of in the Law of Persons relate to things properly so called; as for instance, an estate in land belonging to a married woman: and many rights and duties treated of in the Law of Things have no regard to *things* proper: as, for instance, the right arising from an obligation to *forbear* under a contract'. *Lectures*, 687.

[47] *Lectures*, 692.

[48] A. F. J. Thibaut, *Versuche über einzele Theile der Theorie des Rechts*, 2 vols. (Jena, 1817), ii. 6–7.

[49] *Lectures*, 700 ff.   [50] *Lectures*, 723.

[51] Austin explained the distinction: 'Whenever a set of rights and duties capacities and incapacities regards specially and constantly one class of persons, every person of that class has a *status* or condition, composed of those special rights and duties, capacities and incapacities. But those rights and duties, capacities and incapacities which have no particular regard to any particular class, are matter for the Law of Things.' *Lectures*, 689.

(for example a marriage) which was the cause of certain rights and duties but rather of the peculiar rights or duties relating to a condition. Against Bentham's notion that these rights or duties were the consequences of one investitive fact or title of acquisition, Austin argued that this definition was no test of the character of status, since it would not distinguish status from the rights and duties which were a matter for the Law of Things, since the same could be said of all complex sets of rights or duties.[52] His view thus was that status and the Law of Persons was subordinate to the Law of Things: the jurist had to be aware of things before examining status, since the rights pertaining to certain statuses 'have such a coherency with the bulk of the legal system, that if they were detached from it, the requisite continuity in the statement or exposition of it would be lost'.[53]

Having established this notion of status, Austin pointed out that public law relating to the sovereign should in fact be inserted in the Law of Persons. He noted the extreme difficulty of pointing to a precise distinction between private and public law, for the powers of a master or a father were often set up for the same purposes as those of a judge.[54] The distinction was no more than the vague one that when the condition was private, the powers were vested in a person with regard to specifically determined persons, whereas when it was public, the powers regarded the public in general. From here, Austin argued that it made no sense to divide public and private law as types, for there was scarcely any provision of law that did not affect the public as well as private individuals of whom the public was composed. Public law, as regards the political superiors, should therefore be seen as part of the Law of Persons: for while it could be detached easily from the general part of the law, it was nevertheless linked into it. Thus, no one could fully understand English kingship without understanding the rules of descent. There was, in short, no more reason for opposing the rights which grew out of a political status to all other rights than there was for so selecting any other particular status for special treatment.[55]

Austin's main body of rights, the Law of Things, was divided into

---

[52] Thus, Austin pointed out that the right of ownership, though deemed singular, was in fact a collection of a large number of rights. These also came together from one investitive fact. *Lectures*, 703–4.

[53] *Lectures*, 720.   [54] *Lectures*, 747.

[55] *Lectures*, 757–8. Austin hence praised Hale and Blackstone for treating public and private law together (in the first book of the *Commentaries*).

primary and sanctioning rights. This seems to parallel Bentham's division of substantive and adjective law, for in Austin's terms 'I should divide the Law of Things, or the bulk of the legal system, into law conversant about rights and duties which are *not* means or instruments for rendering others available; and law conversant about rights and duties which are merely means or instruments for rendering others available'.[56] However, Austin's division was more specifically that between rights and duties arising from delicts and those not arising from delicts: it did not therefore reflect any division between positive and procedural law. Austin pointed out that there was no clear division between the two types of *law*: 'though secondary rights and duties are merely adjective or instrumental' to primary rights, he said, 'many of the rights and duties which I style primary are also of the same character: E.g. The rights and duties of Guardians are merely subservient to those of the ward'.[57] The division was not therefore referable to any difference of purpose for which the rights were given. The real division arose from the *events* from which the rights or duties arose.

Austin argued that in fact there was no logical distinction between primary and secondary rights and duties, for neither could in practice exist without the other. In most systems of law, the two concepts were not distinguished, for instead of legislating a set of primary rights, legislatures rather declared that certain acts or omissions would amount to an injury, for which the injured party could obtain redress, or simply legislated for punishments which implied primary rights. Indeed,

the law which gives the remedy, or which determines the punishment, is the only one that is absolutely necessary. For the remedy or punishment implies a foregone injury, and a foregone injury implies that a primary right or duty has been violated. And, further, the primary right or duty owes its existence as such to the injunction or prohibition of certain acts, and to the remedy or punishment to be applied in the event of disobedience.[58]

One needed to bear in mind both the right and the remedy at the same time: 'the definition of primary rights cannot be made complete (not even approximately) without reference to the acts which are violations of them'.[59] For Austin, then, the division between primary and secondary rights was one of convenience, because many rights

---

[56] *Lectures*, 762.
[58] *Lectures*, 767.
[57] *Lectures*, 762.
[59] *Lectures*, 772.

had the same remedy. Everything was interconnected in Austin's vision: if one attached to the description of each primary right a description of the rights and obligations which grew out of its breach, it would also be necessary to describe the acts which were violations of it; as well as the procedures by which it was to be enforced. This would lead to huge and repetitious descriptions and would preclude classing together all violations which were susceptible of the same description although they were violations of different or complex primary rights. It was preferable for convenience to class together similar rights *ex delicto*, even though they grew out of different delicts. This was evidently an exercise in convenient classification, and not one of logical separation. Most importantly, it revealed the link between rights and their violation, what was recognized by law, and what arose from society.

The interconnection of primary and secondary rights and duties, and the facts which determined what constituted a breach, also extended to procedure. Since Austin was far less confident about the possibility of defining the content of rights than Bentham had been, he favoured a stricter system of procedure than was associated with Bentham. This point has important ramifications for Austin's status as a common law theorist, and for the nature of his positivism. Austin's notion of sovereignty and of the nature of law as commands was far less important for his view of practice than is often realized: instead, his analysis of the sources of law reflected much more closely the common lawyers' notion of law growing out of society through procedural remedies. His positivism influenced how one thought about rules once they had been acknowledged by the courts—but the rules were to be developed from below.

For Austin, the institutional separation of the *Jus Actionum* from the *Jus Rerum* and *Jus Personarum* was senseless. For him, the law of actions should rather be distributed under the two main heads of Things and Persons, all general matter falling under the former, all specific under the latter.[60] This reorganization was important in reestablishing the primacy of procedure in determining rights, and it revealed how far Austin felt that rights and the procedures used to secure those rights were bound in together. This was a clear rejection of the Benthamic scheme of dividing substance and procedure. Austin pointed out that the law regarding substantive rights needed

[60] *Lectures*, 726–7.

enforcement by tribunals with complex procedural rules which could not be violated since 'it is manifest that much of procedure consists of rights and duties, and that all of it relates to the manner in which secondary rights and duties are exercised or enforced'.[61] Substantive rights and procedure were so closely intertwined as to be inseparable. It was, he said, 'impossible to distinguish completely a *right of action* from the action or procedure which enforces it. For much of the right of action consists of rights to take those very steps by which the end of the action is accomplished.'[62] All secondary rights, or rights arising from delicts, were in effect instrumental or adjective: and he thence argued that in defining them as substantive rights, Bentham had failed to notice the close union between procedure and substance.

Austin significantly acknowledged the centrality of pleading as a way to define wrongs:

So long as law and fact shall continue uncertain, questions will frequently arise as to whether a wrong has been really committed or not. To determine this very question is manifestly the purpose of the process which is styled pleading.[63]

This was a view classic to the common law: law could not define wrongs absolutely, since so much of what was wrong depended upon fact. The job of the court was to refine the uncertainties in the system, to help determine whether a wrong had occurred: the wrong existed outside the definition of the law, and the court merely gave the remedy which reinforced the right. The base of law could thus be seen to be the idea of a wrong.

In this context, we should note the importance Austin accorded to judicial legislation. He was clearly fond of it, calling it 'highly beneficial and even absolutely necessary', and arguing that the part of the law made by the judges was more satisfactory than the statute law.[64] There is an obvious clash between Austin's positivist conception of law and his acknowledgement that the law could grow through the decisions of judges, a contradiction that appears to be resolved only by seeing judges as subordinate legislators whose

---

[61] *Lectures*, 765. [62] Ibid.

[63] *Lectures*, 766. Austin rejected Bentham's idea that the courts should be able to decide prospective cases before any wrong had been committed.

[64] *Province*, Hart ed. 191. Austin did not share Blackstone's fictitious contention that the judges 'found' the law. Instead, he noted that in every judicial decision, 'the *ratio decidendi* is a *new* ground or principle *not previously law*'. *Lectures*, 628.

powers came from the sovereign.[65] Austin noted that any command of the sovereign could be tacit, so that when customs were turned into legal rules by judicial decisions, the rules which emerged were tacit commands. The rules which the judge made thus derived their force from the authority given by the state by way of acquiescence.[66] This analysis explained the position of the judges as part of a rule-making process, and sought to define in what senses their pronouncements were law, but it cannot be taken as a descriptive account of the judicial function. For Austin did not conceive of the judges making any rules in a legislative sense. His discussion of judicial legislation reveals a profound understanding of the way that judges worked in the common law, arriving at rules only through the details of particular cases.[67] All new cases were retroactive:

It must be observed that a judicial decision *primae impressionis*, or a judgment by which a new point of law is for the first time decided, is always an *ex post facto* law with respect to the particular case on which the point first arose, and on which the decision was given.[68]

This view accorded with the common law position that the law could correct wrongs as they arose in society without their being predetermined. From this, it was clear that the law was not *made* by the judge, but *inferred* later, as the case became a precedent in retrospect:

If the new rule obtains as law thereafter, it does not obtain directly, but because the decision passes into a precedent: that is to say, is considered as evidence of the previous state of the law; and the new rule, thus disguised under the garb of an old one, is applied as law to new cases.[69]

The judicial process was therefore one of settling cases, in such a manner that the *ratio decidendi* could in future act as a form of rule to guide future conduct. The case which established the rule only in fact settled the case: the decision became a rule only in retrospect. The command came from the *ratio decidendi* of the case, but that was not something which could be pinpointed easily or defined in

---

[65] Rumble, following Maine, points out that Austin's contention that judges were delegates of the sovereign was little more than a trick to smooth over his problematic conception of sovereignty. 'John Austin, Judicial Legislation and Legal Positivism', 82.

[66] *Province*, Hart ed. 31–2.

[67] As he put it, the judge 'legislates *as properly judging*, and ,not *as properly legislating*'. *Lectures*, 621.

[68] *Lectures*, 487.   [69] *Lectures*, 531.

words.[70] The process of deriving rules from cases was a method of induction, which could not be tied to the specific words of the judge pronouncing in the first case.[71] Since no two cases were precisely alike, the rule had to be an abstraction of a general reason from the case, something which was difficult to do, and which was incapable of producing absolute certainty.[72] Austin was thus clearly aware of the nature of common law adjudication and its method of abstracting rules from circumstance.

Indeed, while Austin desired a rule-based system of law, he remained sceptical about the ability of rules to solve all problems. This can be seen from his discussion of Paley's notion of the competition of opposite analogies. Austin maintained that every decided case held only one *ratio decidendi*, so that in determining what the reason of the case was, only one rule would be found. Problems arose, however, which necessitated a competition of analogies when it came to applying the rule to specific cases, which were made up of peculiar circumstances, some of which would resemble one case, some another. New rules for new cases were crafted through analogy: the judge in the new case 'derives the new rule, by a consequence built on analogy, from a rule or rules actually part of the system'. Austin's discussion was a subtle analysis of the process of legal reasonings, where rules could be tailored to particular cases, and where there could be no deduction of rules in a Benthamic sense:

The new rule is formed by consequence from the anterior rule. The subjects of the new rule are analogous to those of the old one. But, by reason of the

---

[70] 'Though not a rule in form, it is tantamount to a general command proceeding from the sovereign or state, or from any of its authorised subordinates. For, since it is its known will that the general reason of a decision on a particular or specific case shall govern decisions on future resembling cases, the subjects receive from the state (on the occasion of such a decision) an expression or intimation of its sovereign will, that they shall shape their conduct to the reason or principle thereof.' *Lectures*, 627–8.

[71] 'As the general propositions which the decision contains are not commonly expressed with much premeditation, and as they must be taken in connection with all the peculiarities of the case, it follows that the very terms in which those propositions are clothed are not the main index to the *ratio decidendi*.' *Lectures*, 630.

[72] 'Since no two cases are precisely alike, the decision of a specific case may partly turn upon reasons which are suggested to the judge by its specific peculiarities or differences. And that part of the decision which turns on those differences (or that part of the decision which consists of those special reasons), cannot serve as a *precedent* for subsequent decisions, and cannot serve as a rule or guide of conduct.' *Lectures*, 627.

specific difference of the species or sort which its peculiar subjects belong to, the new rule is different from, as well as like, the old one.

However, where the new rule is formed from an old rule regarding the genus generally, the new rule is not co-ordinate with the old one, but is included under it, as the minor of a syllogism is included under the major. But where the new rule is derived from an old rule specifically regarding a species or sort, the new rule is merely co-ordinate with the old and is not included in it as a consequence.[73]

Every case before a court thus had circumstances which rendered it unique and which might require a new or unique rule. Interpretation was needed, and a competition of analogies was required, because no system of law could provide perfectly definite rules for every case.[74] What was significant in Austin's discussion of this was that he applied the arguments equally to rules derived from statutes. Since the problem lay in the *application* of rules to specific cases, owing to the variety of cases and the inspecificity of rules, the judge could be faced with two contradictory rules, or two rules neither of which applied directly to the case at hand.[75] We must therefore notice how much of a sceptic Austin was when it came to rules: he never believed that it was possible to define perfect rules and held rather that new rules would constantly have to be made for individual cases, by analogy from previous ones, in the process of adjudicating unique disputes. The *ratio decidendi* would act as an imperfect form of rule for guiding conduct; but that rule could never cover all situations and all conduct. This seems a startling position for the positivist jurist to take, for it was to suggest that rules grew, rather than being imposed. However, by placing Austin's theory of adjudication alongside his positivist conception of subordinate judicial legislators, it can be seen that the latter was designed not to be descriptive but formally conceptual.[76] If this is so, the function and nature of Austin's sovereign must be explained.

---

[73] *Lectures*, 640.   [74] *Lectures*, 997–8.

[75] Austin criticized Romilly's position (in 'Bentham on Codification') that the common law solved its rules problem by the competition of analogies. He pointed out Romilly's error in assuming the problem would disappear if there was a code, adding, 'Sir Samuel Romilly supposes that the competition of opposite analogies is a means of surmounting this difficulty. It is, in truth, the difficulty to be surmounted. He falls into the mistake of confounding the competition incident to the application, with the competition incident to the creation, of law. This arose from his assuming unconsciously at the moment (against what he had shewn in the text) that common or judiciary law, when virtually made, is only administered or applied.' *Lectures*, 641.

[76] Thus, Austin's discussion of judicial legislation is not problematic, nor an

Austin's Sovereign

Austin's positivist definition of law—the command of a sovereign backed by sanctions—is usually related to its Hobbesian and Benthamic origins,[77] and it is assumed that in putting forward this definition, Austin was putting forward a normative proposition, or an empirically verifiable one.[78] Indeed, given his theoretical stance, and his separation of law and morals, it is easy to see Austin as the perfect jurist for a conservative era of repression, the years of the legal onslaught on Radicalism and Chartism, the era of the New Poor Law.[79] It has been argued that his theory of sovereignty must be related to his political writings, which were conservative, defending the constitution from radical ideas in favour of universal franchise.[80] If, however, we put Austin's ideas into a European context, it can be seen that he was not making normative statements about the content of actual systems, but that his definition of the sovereign was in essence a purely conceptual one which did not entail any comment

exception to his theory. Rumble has written, '[Austin's] reconciliation of judicial legislation with his concept of positive law is not notable for its success.' ('John Austin, Judicial Legislation and Legal Positivism', 109.) This view is only true if we take Austin's positivism as descriptive of the way in which judges behaved.

[77] See, e.g., F. Harrison, 'The English School of Jurisprudence', *Fortnightly Review*, 475–92; and H. S. Maine, *The Early History of Institutions* (London, 1875), 355.

[78] See J. Raz, *The Concept of a Legal System*, 2nd edn. (Oxford, 1980), ch. 1; and S. M. Woody, 'The Theory of Sovereignty: Dewey versus Austin', *Ethics*, lxxviii (1967–8), 313–18.

[79] Mark Francis writes, 'it is the concept of personal and supreme authority, ostensibly borrowed from Hobbes, that eventually corrupts Austin's attempt to create a science of government or positive law which would not depend on a government's ethical content, its goals or its form. His hostility to libertarian and democratic sentiments eventually overcame his attempt at political neutrality.' 'The Nineteenth Century Theory of Sovereignty and Thomas Hobbes', *History of Political Thought*, i (1980), 517–40 at 530.

[80] See E. Rubin, 'Austin's Political Pamphlets', in E. Attwoll, *Perspectives in Jurisprudence* (Glasgow, 1977), 20–41. Any political interpretations of Austin's jurisprudence which focus on his concept of the sovereign must be handled with care. Firstly, the political opinions in the *Province* (written in the 1820s) are different from Austin's later conservative writings of the 1840s: the utilitarianism he expresses, as well as his enthusiasm for Malthus and the doctrines of the political economists, are quite different from his later Toryism. Secondly, even the most ardent Tory in the 1840s would not have accepted the draconian authoritarianism implicit in his sovereign, if it is to be taken as a normative proposition. For a study which stresses the changes in Austin's political opinions, see L. and J. Hamburger, *Troubled Lives*. For a critique of Rubin, see Morison, *John Austin*, 122–32.

about particular types of government.[81] Austin was not the high priest of despotism, but was suggesting a philosophical concept about the nature and sources of law. Second, it will be seen that although Austin was a utilitarian, his separation of law from morals was convincing: Maine was correct to argue that his definitions were consistent with any ethical theory.[82] Austin created confusion by spending much time in the *Province of Jurisprudence Determined* discussing utilitarian theory. Yet this was irrelevant to *jurisprudence*: jurisprudence was a realm of pure theory and abstract concepts, whereas utilitarian theory addressed the question of what should be the content of law. We must be careful to distinguish Austin's utilitarianism from his jurisprudence, for they show fundamentally different methodologies and attitudes to the task he was engaged in. As shall be seen, his utilitarian disquisitions were political and normative; but his jurisprudential ones, including the sovereign, were not. The *Province* should therefore not be seen as separate and distinct from the *Lectures* it precedes:[83] what should be seen as distinct are the chapters on utilitarianism.

In setting up an analytical system of legal concepts, Austin needed a theoretical postulate to stand at the head of his series of definitions. The concept of the sovereign as the source of laws thus played this role: and the *Province* was to stand as 'a merely prefatory though necessary and inevitable part.'[84] A definition of the concept of law clearly involved the notion of coercion as its defining characteristic, as distinct from moral rules. The identification of law with coercion was something of a commonplace by the early nineteenth century, being as much a part of Kant's idealist concept as of Bentham's utilitarian one.[85] The view of law as a coercive apparatus involved

---

[81] See Enid Campbell, 'John Austin and Jurisprudence in Nineteenth Century England', unpublished Duke University Ph.D., 1958, ch. 3, for an argument which holds that the existence of a sovereign is an assumption underlying an Austinian theory of law, an assumption which need not have application in the realm of social science.   [82] Maine, *Early History*, 368.

[83] Usually, the lectures are seen as wholly distinct from the *Province*, the former being Romanist, the latter Benthamic. See C. A. W. Manning, 'Austin Today: or "The Province of Jurisprudence" Re-examined', *Modern Theories of Law* (1933), 18–21.

[84] See *Province*, Hart ed. ix.

[85] Kant wrote that when one said a creditor had a right to demand the repayment of a debt, 'this does not mean that he can persuade the debtor that his own reason itself obligates him to this performance; on the contrary, to say that he has such a right means only that the use of coercion to make anyone do this is entirely compatible with everyone's freedom, including the freedom of the debtor'. *The Metaphysical Elements of Justice*, trans. J. Ladd (Indianapolis, 1965), 37.

some separation of law and morals. Hence, a description of positive law similar to Austin's could be found in Thibaut:

Positive law which is by far the most important of all the sources of law, may arise either from commands proceeding directly from the supreme power of a state, or from the concurring views either of the judicial authorities or of the individual members of the state by virtue of a sort of lawgiving power entrusted to or left with them by the supreme authority. Law of the first description, whether it be actually written or not, is usually called *Jus scriptum*, law of the two last descriptions *Jus non scriptum*.

Thibaut also noted that it was the common modern opinion that the moral law left everything to conscience, and that a judge should only take note of moral duties if they were also recognized by positive law.[86] Moral laws were not coercive in the manner that positive laws were.[87]

For Austin, the definition of law as the sovereign's command was no empirical statement but a purely abstract concept, the starting point in a series of conceptual relations in which the idea of command explained what was meant by law and which allowed a consequent explanation of the ideas of rights and duties.[88] The sovereign was the 'source of laws'. It is useful to compare Austin's concept with Kant's, for it may be seen that both men sought to define the sovereign that underlay the law, but both had difficulties locating the sovereign. For Kant, it was only possible to have external things as one's property in a juridical condition of society— in civil society. Rights could not be guaranteed by individual wills: only a will binding everyone else, a collective and universal will, could provide the guarantee. Kant's civil society guaranteed property by conferring legality on it: '[a] civil constitution only

[86] Lindley, *Introduction*, 9–10. Kant also distinguished legal and moral duties, arguing that the mere agreement of an action with the law without regarding the motives or incentives to the action, was called its legality. *Metaphysical Elements of Justice*, 19.

[87] See Mackeldey, *Handbook of the Roman Law*, 1: 'Compulsory laws or laws of right are those which the government of the state can by force compel the people therein to observe. Moral laws in their narrow sense are those in which no external force is permitted to compel their observance.'

[88] See his 'Analysis of Pervading Notions' section in the *Lectures*, 343–507. Thibaut similarly discussed rights and duties as consequences of laws and used an initial positivist definition to explain what was meant by rights, e.g.: 'As a right is neither more nor less than a legal power to compel, everything done in exercise of a right is juridically speaking lawful, even if another be hurt thereby.' Lindley, *Introduction*, section 58, p. 52.

provides the juridical condition under which each person's property is secured and guaranteed to him, but it does not actually stipulate and determine what that property shall be'.[89] Whatever it was, however, it was only provisional until it was determined by a public, legal, distributive justice and guaranteed by an authority executing the law.[90] Central to this concept was that of the sovereign. Kant divided the state into three authorities—the sovereign legislature, the executive ruler, and the judiciary, but argued that they were co-ordinates in the constitution. This attempt to divide up functionaries threatened to make it confusing to locate a sovereign, but Kant's comments showed that, for him, sovereignty was not the same as the ruler or the person exercising sovereignty. This can be seen in two areas.

First, Kant argued that there was no right to resist:

The reason for this is that resistance to the supreme legislation can itself only be unlawful; indeed it must be conceived as destroying the entire lawful constitution, because, in order for it to be authorized, there would have to be a public law that would permit the resistance. That is, the supreme legislation would have to contain a stipulation that it is not supreme and that in one and the same judgment the people as subjects should be made sovereign over him to whom they are subject; this is self-contradictory.[91]

Kant abhorred the formal execution of monarchs as being a subversion of the principles governing the relationship of sovereign and people, for it made the people master over that to which they owed their existence. However, he did feel the sovereign legislature could depose the ruler, and argued for the progressive modification of constitutions towards a democratic form. The second area of importance is Kant's attitude towards taxation, and the position of the sovereign as supreme proprietor of land. Kant said that the supreme commander could have no private estates, since if he did, he could appropriate all to himself. In one sense, then, he possessed nothing; in another, he possessed everything, for he had the right to command the people and to settle the rules of distribution. Ultimately,

This supreme proprietorship is . . . only an Idea of the civil union that serves the purpose of representing the necessary unification of the private property of all the people under a public general possessor, so that the determination

---

[89] *Metaphysical Elements of Justice*, 65.
[90] Ibid. 77.   [91] Ibid. 86.

of particular owners is in accordance with the necessary formal principle of division (division of the land) in terms of concepts of justice, rather than by principles of aggregation (which proceed empirically from part to whole.)[92]

The sovereign was to an important degree an abstract that represented the total legal rules of society: it did not stand for a particular individual with superior special rights. The holder of sovereign power might be removed, but he could not be punished for what he did as sovereign, nor could he be deposed *qua* sovereign.

Austin argued that the sovereign could have no legal rights against its own subjects: since every right was the creature of a positive law which also imposed a relative duty, every legal right involved three parties: the sovereign, the right-bearer, and the obliged.[93] Unless the party burdened with the duty were subject to the author of the law, he could suffer no punishment by which the right was enforced. The command of the sovereign therefore held together the legal system: in the abstract sense, a right was confirmed when a sovereign expressly or tacitly commanded subjects to do or forbear from certain acts towards the right-bearer. The command was an abstract generalization: in rights *in rem*, which availed against persons generally, the command was a negative command against all persons in general not to do something, such as interfering in property.[94] Thus, any right and duty to exist as such required a mediating sovereign. For this reason also, the sovereign was incapable of legal limitation, since any such limitation would constitute a duty, which would imply a superior sovereign. Conceptually, the notion was impossible.[95] Austin's concept of sovereignty is enlightened by his examination of natural rights and absolute and relative duties. 'Natural or inborn rights', he wrote, 'are those which reside in a party merely as living under the protection of the state, or as being within the jurisdiction of the state.'[96] They were rights which arose without a special title, which did not need to be annexed by the law to any particular investitive event. From here, absolute duties were general legal obligations which came from the sovereign generally, while relative duties arose from commands of acts to be done or forborne from with respect to determinate parties.[97] The sovereign in this analysis is seen as an abstract source of laws. Austin thus made it clear that ideas such as 'absolute' and

[92] Ibid. 90.
[93] *Province*, Hart ed. 278–85.
[94] *Lectures*, 370–1, 397–8.
[95] *Province*, Hart ed. 254.
[96] *Lectures*, 728.
[97] *Lectures*, 400–3.

'relative' rights bore no relation to their substantive content or purpose. Nor (as we have seen) did he seek to distinguish spheres of public and private law: the sovereign was above law because it was the source of laws.

Austin's sovereign, as a postulate in the legal system, thus played a role analogous to Kant's. However, Austin did not agree with Kant's ideas on the origin of the state, nor with his idealist epistemology. The utilitarian Englishman rejected any notion of the categorical imperative, and with it any idea that the state was formed by a contract of citizens driven by an imperative to form that civil union. For Kant, men were impelled by the quest for justice to enter society: in a state of nature, there were no legal rights, no competent judge to resolve disputes.[98] Austin dismissed any Kantian notion of 'the extension over the earth . . . of the empire of right or justice'. This justice being anterior to law, and its measure, could be no more than 'general utility darkly conceived and expressed'.[99] Austin concentrated then on the contract as a real thing, not as a conceptual idea to explain justice and legality, and rejected the notion.[100] If one took it as a contract between a sovereign and a society, it could not work, since any contract was a creature of positive law, which implied a superior.[101] Austin's rejection of the contract theory, rehearsing by now familiar arguments,[102] thus rested on the idea that a contract theory could not explain legality, but begged the question. For Austin, the only explanation of sovereignty lay in the fact that the bulk of a given society were in a habit of obedience to a determinate and common superior. This definition made it difficult to say precisely what was a sovereign society, since it depended on what was meant by bulk;[103] but that hardly undermined the use of the definition, given the fact that '[i]n most societies political and independent, the constitution of the supreme government has *grown*'.[104] The point was that a sovereign state was not a necessary or inevitable thing: for that reason, it was determined and bounded not by rules of positive law, but of positive morality. The question whether the subjects actually obeyed the sovereign was determined

---

[98] *Metaphysical Elements of Justice*, 72.   [99] *Province*, Hart ed. 310.

[100] He recognized that German Idealist philosophers claimed that the contract was not a historical fact, but that it was nevertheless the basis of civil society: but he argued that this still failed to explain the question. *Province*, Hart ed. 341–2.

[101] *Province*, Hart ed. 315–16.

[102] In particular, the arguments of Hume and Bentham.

[103] *Province*, Hart ed. 202, 210.   [104] *Province*, Hart ed. 337.

by positive morality, not by law. Ultimately, the analytical construct had to rest on a given assumption: in Austin, this assumption was that of the habit of obedience, not an idealist concept of justice. To this degree, the habit of obedience in Austin played the same part as that played by the categorical imperative in Kant: the final assumption.

If the notion of the sovereign was only the basic abstract definition from which his analytical system grew, why did Austin spend so much time seeking to locate the sovereign? As Hart has argued, Austin erred in seeking to reduce to commands and the determinate sovereign what should be seen rather as rules and the 'ultimate *test* in accordance with which the laws to be obeyed are identified'.[105] In discussing the habit of obedience and the system of justice, Austin looked to define *who* was being obeyed, not *what* was being obeyed. Hence, in looking for what held a sovereign system together, he looked for the people whose commands were obeyed, rather than for any concept of validity or a rule of recognition that might otherwise explain it. As a result, he treated the separate notions of government and sovereignty as being the same thing, using the terms as virtually interchangeable.[106] For his theory, it was only necessary to argue that government was the instrument by which sovereignty was exercised, an instrument which was the removable agent of the sovereign. There are hints that Austin perceived this, in his arguments that the powers of the House of Commons were held in trust from the electorate: 'the commons exercise through representatives the whole of their sovereign powers . . . excepting the power of electing and appointing their representatives'. This meant that 'if the commons were sovereign without the king and the peers, not a single sovereign power, save that which I have now specified, would be exercised by the sovereign directly'.[107] In this lay the notion that governments were distinct from the sovereign, and that disobedience to a government might take away its mandate without destroying the sovereignty.

The Benthamic definition of the sovereign as a given *superior* who was habitually obeyed cast the sovereign into a human mould which

---

[105] *Province*, Introduction, xii. See also Hart's modifications in *The Concept of Law* (Oxford, 1961), ch. 6.

[106] For this reason, many commentators have discussed Austin's problems with defining an active sovereign, and have used this as the starting point for criticisms of the Austinian theory. See, e.g., H. L. A. Hart, *The Concept of Law*, chs. 2–4.

[107] *Province*, Hart ed. 228.

did not fit.[108] In arguing that the sovereign had to be subject to no other and had to be permanent, Austin was adopting notions relevant to the power of governments, but ones which could not be used to 'test' sovereigns: for the sovereign had these attributes by definition, not by test. Explaining the position of government was notoriously difficult, since it exercised sovereignty but was itself subject to it. Austin revealed his confusion in discussing particular cases. He contended, for example, that the allied armies which occupied France in 1815, whose commands were obeyed by the French government and people, were not strictly sovereigns: 'since the commands and the obedience were comparatively rare and transient, they were not sufficient to constitute the relation of sovereignty and subjection between the allied sovereigns and the members of the invaded nation'.[109] Because there was no *habit*, there was no sovereignty. This is a clear instance of the confusion of the two ideas. First, the question of transience and habit could only become apparent in retrospect, for had the allies remained longer, they might have become sovereigns. Should a Frenchman in 1815 have regarded them as sovereigns or not? In fact, the question of sovereignty was irrelevant: the armies may have exercised governmental and legislative powers, but the fact that they were ruling as a government in a France with its own laws shows that the sovereign state remained, albeit with a new crew at the helm. Sovereignty could only change if the whole state and its legal system disbanded. Second, the French government and constitution collapsed and reformed itself on innumerable occasions between the Revolution and the publication of the *Province*: but even with this instability, the sovereign state remained intact.

Austin's attempts to locate the sovereign, for instance in federal states like the United States, revealed how distant and abstract the concept of sovereignty could be, and how far removed from the daily exercise of power.[110] His confusion of sovereignty and government is understandable: governments exercised sovereignty, and could change the system, and they issued rules which had to be obeyed. Ultimately, the questions of who exercised sovereignty and why

[108] Austin's sovereign in democracies was defined to be the electorate. As Hart has shown, this definition revealed certain strains in his theory: by this definition, the sovereign superior which was habitually obeyed by the bulk of the community was the bulk of the community itself. Hart, 'Positivism', 604.

[109] *Province*, Hart ed. 196.   [110] See *Province*, Hart ed. 251 and n.

people obeyed it were questions that went beyond his analysis of law: whether legal rules were obeyed because they were acknowledged to come from a legitimate superior or whether they were acknowledged through a rule of recognition were in the end questions of fact or of positive morality.[111] All that Austin's analytical system of definitions needed was the concept of sovereignty as representing the *legal* order to explain and act as a reference for the other definitions. The notions of the sovereign and of commands were not normative propositions. First, Austin's notion of command was an abstraction, as can be seen from his discussion of rights *in rem*. Second, since many (if not most) of the commands were adopted (out of contracts or judgments), it was irrelevant to a large degree who exercised sovereignty at governmental level.

In his analysis of legal concepts, Austin was seeking to resolve fundamental ideas to their most basic definitions: the idea of the sovereign in the *Province* thus stands as a working back of basic concepts. The Pandectists, after all, while discussing the ordering of concepts, did not take the further step of defining the sovereign and source of laws in the way that Austin did. The analysis of the sovereign was hence an extension of the exercise in the *Lectures*, not the factual presupposition from which all else flowed.

Austin's difficulties in the *Province* show the gap between his work and that of Bentham's. Bentham's sovereign was not an analytic construct, but was to be a real ruler whose governmental system worked in a regimented and controlled manner. Not only did Bentham seek to argue that his vision of a sovereign *in fact* existed everywhere, but in the *Constitutional Code* he wrote at great length about the limitations exercised on the sovereign through the Public Opinion Tribunal and a host of regulations which controlled and influenced those holding office.[112] Austin's concepts of the habit of

[111] In his analysis of the position of the sovereign resting on a habit of obedience or on positive morality, Austin realized that he was dealing with a complex and subtle process. He wrote that, with the law regarding the sovereign, he was dealing with a situation where law and morals were very closely intertwined, and had to be seen together: 'A description, therefore, of the law which regards the constitution of the State, and which determines the ends or modes to and in which the Sovereign exercises the sovereign powers, is an essential part of a complete *corpus juris*, although, properly speaking, that so-called law is not positive law.' *Lectures*, 746.

[112] See F. Rosen, *Bentham and Representative Democracy* (Oxford, 1983), J. H. Burns, 'Bentham on Sovereignty: An Exploration'.

obedience and the moral influences on government were less subtle and complete, because they did not fit his system in the way he desired. The same can be said of his discussion of utilitarianism in the *Province*. This discussion of utility lacked the sophistication of Bentham, and equally lacked its rigorous application in practice, playing no part in the *Lectures*. Moles has argued that Austin's project was not limited to jurisprudence, but that he promised a far greater analysis of the organic whole of positive law, positive morals, and ethics. As a consequence, Moles contends that Austin's separation of law and morals was heuristic, not ontological, and that, as a result, questions of morality and ethics did play a large part in the legal sphere.[113] Austin certainly promised works to unite law and ethics, yet it is significant that he did not get any further than the chapters in the *Province* on this subject. For the combination was clearly a Benthamic one, which went against the route he was pursuing.

Austin's chapters on utility are an odd intrusion. Firstly, utility was clearly part of the science of ethics, and had nothing to do with law *as* law. Austin's discussions of utility were a discussion of what *should* be the content of law.[114] As such, they were out of place in a treatise that was seeking to define the minimum conceptual content of law. If the chapters on utility were to stand as a disquisition on the reasons why people were in the habit of obedience, they would still be out of place in going beyond the sphere of law. However, since he treated them as Divine Laws, they did not fulfil this function, but stood uncomfortably as potential tests for the validity of positive law. Secondly, Austin's conception of moral philosophy presented a stark contrast to his jurisprudence. In contrast to his flexible view of law, he had an inflexible view of the sciences of ethics and political economy. For Austin, ethics was a science capable of demonstration,

---

[113] Moles, *Definition and Rule*. Interestingly, Moles attempts to draw parallels between Austin and Aquinas, rather than looking to Bentham.

[114] This follows the traditional view of Austin's utilitarianism as extraneous. See, e.g., Wolfgang Friedmann, *Legal Theory* (London, 1967), 258. It contrasts with the view put forward by Wilfrid E. Rumble, *The Thought of John Austin*, 60–108. Rumble interestingly suggests that since many notions in jurisprudence could not be explained without reference to ethical notions, utility could be seen as a basis for evaluating concepts of jurisprudence. However, Austin did not develop his notion of utility as an evaluative legal concept in the way Bentham did. Furthermore, his clear separation of matters of jurisprudence and legislation, and the relative lack of sophistication of his chapters on utility, suggest that he did not seek to use the concept of utility in this way.

ethical knowledge coming from long reflection and observation on the tendency of acts.[115] This suggested that ultimately it would be possible to construct a legislative system upon the basis of a complete and correct ethical system. This, however, merely raised once more the Benthamic dilemma: if there was a coherent organic whole, with incontrovertible ethical principles, then it should be possible to create a deductive substantive code based on those principles. This would contradict his flexible and variable view of the judicial function and of legal concepts.

One way to avoid this inflexibility would be to abandon the rigid view of the science of ethics and argue that an ethical science based on utility would not be strictly deductive, but that the principle of utility could be used (as Bentham did) as an analytic key to the system, so that the question of utility would play a large part in judicial determinations. However, Austin did not do this, but instead sought to attach utility to clear rules applicable to classes of actions.[116] Moreover, his analysis of ethics was rigid and dogmatic. In these chapters, we find him abandoning the careful, close reasoning of his jurisprudence and preaching a moralizing sermon to the poor, convinced that the science of political economy had found undeniable truths. Austin's comments here were far more inflexible and dogmatic than Bentham's economic views, for he felt that many of the social ills of the day were due to the fact that the poor did not understand and broke the rules. While, he said, it took expertise to understand fully the details of ethical science, the multitude could at least comprehend the leading principles, and if they were imbued

---

[115] *Province*, Hart ed. 63 ff. especially at 79.

[116] *Province*, Hart ed. 38. Austin said (40) that God's commands were rules which were commonly inflexible. Austin's discussion here sees rules in a much more normative sense than Moles's interpretation suggests. Moles argues that for Austin, rules were inferences or abstractions from individual actions (*Definition and Rule*, 108–9). As we have seen, this point is confirmed by his jurisprudence. However, in his writings on utility, Austin makes it clear that the rules would act in a normative manner. For he argues that 'our conduct would conform to *rules* inferred from the tendencies of actions' (*Province*, 47). Equally, his contention that utility is the index to a Divine Law, coupled with his view of ethics being a science that was demonstrable, suggest that the pursuit was one of finding complete rules. Austin does, as Moles points out, allow a direct resort to principle of utility beyond the rule where the case dictates it (p. 53): but this is rather an exception, where the consequences of following the rule would be worse than breaking it. This is compatible with his discussion of the objection to utility (p. 80) that since utility is an imperfect guide to the Divine Law, there is room for error. Austin countered that as ethical science progressed, the room for error would diminish.

with those principles, 'they would be docile to the voice of reason, and armed against sophistry and error'.[117] In practice, this meant accepting the principles of political economy and particularly the principle of population, and recognizing that the welfare of the poor was in their own hands. 'Want and labour', he wrote, 'spring from the niggardliness of nature, and not from the inequality which is consequent on the institution of property.' Property and capital lightened the burdens of nature. If only the poor realized this,

They would scarcely break machinery, or fire barns and corn-ricks, to the end of raising wages, or the rate of parish relief. They would see that violations of property are mischievous to *themselves*: that such violations weaken the motives to accumulation, and, therefore, diminish the fund which yields the labourer his subsistence.[118]

Austin's middle chapters in the *Province* indeed read like the authoritarian ruminations of a devotee of the school of Malthus, Chadwick, and Senior. If there were two Benthams, then, there were equally two Austins, one of whom took up the analytical jurisprudential concerns of the master and refined them and reordered them with the help of a foreign theoretical structure denied to Bentham, while the other inherited the aspiration that it would be possible to build a perfect science of ethics. The latter side of Austin lacked the sophistication of Bentham, perhaps because Austin, the jurist, devoted far less time to moral philosophy, and was happy to borrow commonplace prejudices of the 1820s and 1830s and turn them into eternal truths. Austin, of course, never finished his jurisprudence, let alone his whole project, leaving only his detailed jurisprudential ideas. These were significant for two reasons: first, for showing that law grew out of social relations and problems presented to courts; and secondly, for showing that one had to think of law in terms of rules and commands, in order to make sense of it.

---

[117] *Province*, Hart ed. 65.
[118] Ibid. 68–9.

9

Rules and Remedies in Early Nineteenth-Century Law

WE are now in a position to assess the relationship between theory and practice in the common law of our period more clearly. By the 1830s, both in the jurisprudence of John Austin and in the triumph of special pleading, it was clear that the essential view of the common law remained the one which saw it as a system of remedies, deriving the substantive content of law from below largely out of cases presented by litigants. The rule-based models aspired to by Blackstone and Bentham had failed to alter the way that the common law worked, so that after 1834 it remained apparently particularistic and irrational, showing little of the unity which the theorists had sought. By the 1830s, the common law had resisted the attempts of theorists to turn it into a system of defined rules: most significantly, it had resisted codification. However, in Austin, it had found a theorist who combined the formal jurisprudential notions of a rule-based science with a remedy-based explanation of how the common law created its substance. It was Austin, rather than the largely unpublished Bentham, who came to be seen as the founder of jurisprudence, particularly when his *Lectures* became widely known after 1863.[1]

---

[1] For Austin as the founder of jurisprudence, see Frederic Harrison, 'The English School of Jurisprudence', 475. Sheldon Amos, in his *The Science of Law* (London, 1874), argued that Austin had created a strict science of law by his rigid separation of law and morals, which Bentham had confounded. Interestingly, two years earlier, in *A Systematic View of the Science of Jurisprudence*, he had written that 'Modern Jurisprudence is essentially a German creation' (p. 505). Most commentators from Mill ('Austin on Jurisprudence', *Edinburgh Review*, cxviii (1863)) to Maine ('Sovereignty' in his *Lectures on the Early History of Institutions*) noted the distinction that whereas Bentham wrote on legislation, Austin confined his thinking to pure jurisprudence. The 'English School' of analytical jurists therefore often attacked Bentham's division of 'censorial' and 'expository' jurisprudence for not being an examination of terms (but of substance, desired or real) and praised Austin's method: see, e.g., T. E. Holland, *Jurisprudence*, 13th edn. 1924 (1st edn. 1880), 5–6.

Many areas of law did come to be systematized in the nineteenth century, yet this was done not via legislation but through the works of treatise writers summarizing areas of the law. Lawyers were still dominated by the 'common law frame of mind', which assumed that although the law looked chaotic and haphazard, nevertheless a set of principles and concepts could be teased out of it if one thought hard enough.[2] Clear analytical concepts and definitions helped uncover the principle, but the motor for change and development remained case law. The era of the growth of legal education and the 'textbook tradition' was the era of the analytical jurists; it largely had to await the second half of the nineteenth century.

The type of analytical jurisprudence developed by Bentham and Austin could elaborate concepts and definitions to show the lawyer and the judge what he should be looking for, and thereby enable judges to look beyond the narrow boundaries of forms of action. However, we must note that in a large degree a focus on forms of action and the quest for clarity went together. When judges towards the end of the eighteenth century began to look ever more closely at forms of declarations and pleas, it was not simply that they were wedded to an irrational and over-technical form of proceeding. Rather, it was through strict forms of procedure that precise questions could be elaborated. In the absence of a set of complete rules (which many lawyers did not want), a rigorous system of pleading could elaborate complex points. If analytical theorizing could elaborate large concepts, such as contract, precise deliberations on the pleas could help pinpoint what judges meant by those concepts. At least until the Common Law Procedure Act of 1852, the intricacies of pleading were more important than the larger substantive categories being evolved. An understanding of the nature of common law thinking and its use of new and larger categories helps us to understand some of the important developments in the law in our period; and it is useful, in conclusion, to examine how substantive law grew in a haphazard way determined by technical reasoning in the key era of the industrial revolution.

One area where we can trace the influence of this technical reasoning most clearly is that of contract law, where the mid-nineteenth century saw the ascendancy of the notion of the freedom

---

[2] See David Sugarman, 'Legal Theory, the Common Law Mind and the Making of the Textbook Tradition', in W. Twining (ed.), *Legal Theory and the Common Law* (Oxford, 1986), 26–61.

of contract. This was very important for an industrial society: the free contract was the legal encapsulation of *laissez-faire* and the backbone of industrialization. In the realm of contract law, the nineteenth century therefore saw a number of new emphases: most importantly, the contract was seen as an exchange of mutual promises, governed by the will and intention of the parties, rather than the substantive merit or fairness of what they agreed to. Therefore, the parties to the contract alone were seen as fit to determine its adequacy, without the courts seeking to uphold fair relations between them in a paternalistic way.

In general, by the mid-nineteenth century, lawyers and jurists had begun to conceive of the law of contract in terms of a large conceptual category, under the influence of theoretical writers; and these influences have been seen to have been both doctrinal and political. Thus, A. W. B. Simpson has noted the influence of the civilian notions of contract on English law;[3] while P. S. Atiyah has related the change in thinking about the law of contract to changes in broader economic and political theories of *laissez-faire* and utilitarianism.[4] Less attention has been paid, however, to the influence of changing forms of plea on the definition of the modern notion of contract. By looking at contract law in the early nineteenth century, we can see how influential close reasoning on pleas was for the development of substantive law, and how it intertwined with thinking in larger, substantive terms. For as judges and lawyers from the late eighteenth century on began to look ever more closely at the different forms of action and the declarations and pleadings necessary for them with a view to rationalize them, so they began to examine in much greater detail questions which would determine the nature of contracts. The same urge for an analytical view of law to be found in Bentham and Austin had an impact on judges: but their analytical thoughts on such things as offer and acceptance were made within a structure dominated by the traditional forms of pleas. Not only were judges looking ever more closely at what they meant by a contract: they were examining ever more closely the forms and pleas being used; which in turn helped them settle the first question.

Although lawyers began to explore the concept of contract with greater sophistication after the publication of Pothier's treatise in

---

[3] See A. W. B. Simpson, 'Innovation in Nineteenth Century Contract Law', *Law Quarterly Review* (1975). xci. 247–78.

[4] See P. S. Atiyah, *The Rise and Fall of Freedom of Contract*, *passim*.

English, early treatises on contract served to provide general principles which would help clarify what judges and pleaders had to look
for, rather than defining contract in clear substantive terms. This is
apparent in Powell's discussion of the disability of lunatics and idiots
to contract. He pointed out that such contracts had usually been seen
as voidable rather than void, on the notion that *non est factum* could
not be pleaded to them, since they had the form and appearance of
deeds. Because of that, it had been assumed that they were not void
as not being deeds unless the parties could show the special matter
which made them ineffective. Powell countered this on principle:
such imbecility went, he said, to the gist of the action, showing the
contract a nullity from the start, which could be taken advantage of
on the general issue.[5] Clear ideas about terms would therefore
instruct the lawyer what to look for in the pleas. Precision in
pleading and the search for clear analytical terms went hand in hand.

The grand age of the English analytical treatise on contract had to
await the mid-century. From the mid-century on, we can see increasingly the influence of a jurisprudential viewpoint: thus, Leake's *Elements of the Law of Contracts* in 1867 began with a discussion of the
differences of *jura in rem* and *jura in personam*, and of wrongs *ex
contractu* and *ex delicto*.[6] While earlier writers looked for general
principles to unite cases, it was largely after the publication of
Austin's *Lectures* that a more philosophic view of concepts was put
forward.[7] The key change in the mid-nineteenth century which saw
the triumph of the more theoretical view of contract occurred in
1852, when the Common Law Procedure Act abolished the require-
ment of parties to state the form of action they relied on in the
declaration, and hence allowed the joinder of different causes of
action for the first time. Henceforward, the statement of causes was
arranged in two classes—on contract and wrongs independent of
contract—and for that reason, close reasoning on precise forms of
pleas began to diminish in importance.[8] However, this should not

[5] John Joseph Powell, *Essay upon the Law of Contracts and Agreements*, 2 vols.
(London, 1790), i. 11–12.

[6] S. M. Leake, *The Elements of the Law of Contracts* (London, 1867), Introduction.

[7] Leake therefore drew on Austin, Mackeldey's *Lehrbuch* and Warnkönig's
Commentarii Juris Romani Privati, while Pollock and Anson both relied on Savigny's
System for their definitions.

[8] Nevertheless, the distinctions rooted in the precise forms of plea were still seen
even after the Judicature Acts to be important for explaining substantive issues in law.
In its entry on *Cutter* v. *Powell*, the 1887 edition of *Smith's Leading Cases* noted 'that the

blind us to the real importance of close reasoning on the pleas for the development of substantive law before the mid-century.

Pleading in Contracts

The nineteenth-century paradigm contract, according to Atiyah, was the forward-looking executory contract, where the essential ground of obligation was the promise, and not the consideration. By contrast, in the eighteenth century, a promise was not seen to be conclusive evidence of an obligation, but there were other ways in which obligations were seen to emerge, so that '[i]t was the consideration which was the principal ground for the creation of the obligation; the promise played a subordinate role'.[9] It may be argued, however, that what Atiyah portrays as two different approaches to contract in fact reflected different types of promises, which had different rules of pleading governing them, so that the changing focus on promise and consideration thus reflected thinking about different forms of pleas.

The distinction to be made is that between special and general assumpsits.[10] Where the plaintiff set out the language or effect of the contract, it was a special assumpsit, the special count usually containing the inducement explaining the foundation of the contract, the statement of the contract itself (including the promise and consideration), an allegation of the plaintiff's performance of his part, and a statement of the defendant's breach, as well as the damage to the plaintiff.[11] Where the plaintiff declared by a promise implied by law, it was general—as in the *indebitatus* or *quantum meruit* counts. Here, the plaintiff declared that the defendant was indebted to him, showing an executed consideration as evidence of this, that the defendant had promised to pay in consideration of that, and that he had failed to do so. There was therefore a clear

pleading test which has been adopted as the basis of the present note, resting as it does upon a logical analysis of the cause of action in each case, is not only the simplest and most exact that can be applied, but must still, under a looser system of pleading, be as practically useful, as it has been heretofore'. *Smith's Leading Cases*, 9th edn., ed. R. H. Collins and R. G. Arbuthnot, 2 vols. (London, 1887), ii. 20.

[9] Atiyah, *The Rise and Fall of Freedom of Contract*, 140, 146, 154–67.

[10] For a fuller examination of the form of action, see A. W. B. Simpson, *A History of the Common Law of Contract. The Rise of the Action of Assumpsit* (Oxford, 1975).

[11] Joseph Chitty, *Precedents in Pleading*, 2nd edn., ed. H. Pearson (London, 1847), 216–21.

distinction between the way to view consideration in *indebitatus* counts, and in special agreements, which reflects on the nature of the promise in both. In the latter, the consideration underscored the mutuality of (real) promises, in the former, it linked an existing debt to the implied promise. In effect, the promise was more important in special assumpsits, while the consideration was more important in general ones. Therefore, the essential difference between eighteenth- and nineteenth-century cases is to be found less in a changing view of contract *per se* than in the changing nature of the actions most commonly brought.[12]

The function of consideration was to act as an explanation for the promise, to show it was not all one-sided.[13] The key concern of the courts seems to have been to show the relation of mutuality between the parties and their intention. As early as 1810 therefore, the traditionally minded Edward Lawes could write that a book on pleading in assumpsit could not look at the question of the sufficiency of a consideration: this was not a matter for pleading.[14] In effect, the consideration had the technical role in special contract pleading of providing the link between the parties. Thus, where in one case, the plaintiff had declared that one J.S. at the time of his death was indebted to him, and in consideration that the plaintiff, at the defendant's request, would forbear to sue on the debt, and that the defendant would pay, this was held bad for want of averring from whom the debt was due at the time of making the promise or that there was anyone liable to pay it.[15] The case failed for want of connecting the parties together, which was the function of the consideration.[16] Hence, we can point to numerous cases involving special contracts where the common law courts held that 'the smallness of a consideration is not material, if there be any'.[17] There

---

[12] It will be seen that what Atiyah sees as the nineteenth-century view of consideration was that associated with the special count, and that the eighteenth century 'fair contract' view was that of the *indebitatus* count.

[13] In the view of later nineteenth-century writers, a consideration was needed as 'a test that the parties have the intention of making a binding engagement, and are not using promissory expressions without any serious intention of engaging themselves to a contract'. Leake, *Contract*, 10.

[14] E. Lawes, *A Practical Treatise of Pleading in Assumpsit* (London, 1810), 49.

[15] *Jones* v. *Ashburnham* (1804) 4 East 455.

[16] See also *Lee* v. *Mynne* (1606) Cro. Jac. 110.

[17] *Knight* v. *Rushworth* (1596) Cro. El. 469, quoted in Atiyah, *The Rise and Fall of Freedom of Contract*, 170. Atiyah (169–77) argues that in the eighteenth century, judges under the influence of a more paternalistic view of economics were still disposed (particularly in equity) to refuse to sanction unfair bargains. Yet John Fonblanque

had to be some benefit to the defendant and some detriment to the plaintiff, in order to make the contract;[18] and the question of *sufficiency* could therefore often be reduced to the question of the ultimate existence of any benefit or detriment. Hence, it was ruled in an Elizabethan case that 'when a thing is to be done by the plaintiff, be it never so small, this is a sufficient consideration to ground an action'.[19] An inequality between the parties was not something that could annul a contract.[20] In *Thornborow v. Whitacre*,[21] where the defendant promised for a specified sum to supply the plaintiff with an amount of corn throughout the year that would increase in arithmetical progression, so that the promise would ultimately be impossible to perform, it was held that while the contract was foolish, the defendant should pay damages for his folly. However, some tangible benefit and detriment had to exist. Thus, it had been held in the Elizabethan case of *Philips v. Sackford*[22] that a promise to forbear from taking a suit against the defendant without specifying the time-span of the forbearance was an insufficient consideration since the forbearance might last only 15 minutes.[23] In this case, clearly there might very well be no consideration, once the agreement had been made.[24] However, it was well established that a mere promise could act as a sufficient consideration for another promise,

could write at the time in his edition of the *Treatise of Equity*, 'I have not been able to find a single case, in which it has been held that mere inadequacy of price is a ground for the court to annul an agreement, though executory, if the same appear to have been fairly entered into, and understood by the parties, and capable of being specifically performed' (i. 127 n). He pointed to *Keen v. Stuckley* (1721) Gilb. Rep. 155 in support; but more important cases were *Floyer v. Sherard* (1743) Amb. 18; *Griffith v. Spratley* 1 Cox 383; *Stephens v. Bateman* (1778) 1 Bro. CC 22; *Bullock v. Saddlier* (1776) Amb. 764; *Low v. Barchard* (1803) 8 Ves. 133; *Underhill v. Horwood* (1804) 10 Ves. 209. These cases show that, in the absence of fraud (which seems to be the distinguishing feature of *Heathcote v. Paignton* (1787) 2 Bro. CC 167), a meagre consideration was not taken into account by the court.

[18] See *Barber v. Fox* (1770) 1 Vent. 159.
[19] *Sir Anthony Sturlyn v. Albany* (1587) Cro. El. 67.
[20] It could, however, mitigate damages. In *James v. Morgan* (1664) 1 Lev. 111, 1 Keb. 569, the defendant agreed to buy the plaintiff's horse, paying a certain amount of barley-corn for however many nails there were in the horse's shoes. Although this amounted to some 500 quarters of barley, Hyde J directed the jury only to find damages equivalent to the value of the horse. See Hardwicke's comments on this case in *Chesterfield v. Jansen* (1750) 1 Wils. 286.
[21] (1706) 2 Ld. Raym. 1164.   [22] (1594) Cro. El. 455.
[23] Cf. *Ross v. Moss* (1597) Cro. El. 560. By contrast, in *Dell v. Fereby* (1601) Cro. El. 868, the court allowed as a sufficient consideration for paying the charges of a suit, a promise to stay *ab ulteriori prosecutione sectae praedictae*.
[24] Cf. *Anon* (1581) Godbolt 13.

without it being averred that the promise on the one side had been perfomed.[25] Mutual promises to perform specified acts linked the parties together sufficiently. It had to be apparent that there were two promises, and no gratuity; but once that was clear, the adequacy of the promise was not important.

After the reforms in pleading, we can see that the courts' attitude to consideration in special contracts remained a very formal one that built on the rule that a consideration had to exist on the face of the record and be that agreed between the parties. In *Chanter* v. *Leese*,[26] the plaintiff and three others had given a licence to the defendants to use patents of theirs, and the defendants had then failed to pay. In their defence, they pleaded that there was no consideration for the promise, since the plaintiff's patent—one of several that was contracted for—was not for a new invention, so that the grant of the patent was void. The plea therefore impeached the consideration, and, according to Lord Abinger, avoided the contract.[27] Abinger here looked closely at what consideration the defendant had to accept, and his substantive arguments were built on reasonings taken from the pleas. Hence, he stated that if the plaintiff was unable to perform that which was the consideration for the promise, then the contract was ended. 'The party contracting to pay his money is under no obligation to pay for a less consideration than that for which he has stipulated.' If the defendants had accepted partial performance, then it could be a question whether they would be liable on an implied contract to pay for what they had received, to see if the consideration could be divided: but then the declaration had to allege that they had so enjoyed the *parts* and not the *whole*. In this case, the declaration did not allege that the defendant had enjoyed the other five patents. In substance, therefore, the defendants might have enjoyed great benefits from the patents they had used: but according to the pleas, the consideration could not be divided, but had to be taken as what was set down. Since this was imperfect, the case failed.

There hence existed a distinction between the adequacy and the

---

[25] See *Gower* v. *Capper* (1596) Cro. El. 543, *Wichals* v. *Johns* (1599) Cro. El. 703, *Nichols* v. *Raynbred* (1615) Hob. 88, *Hebden* v. *Rutter* (1663) 1 Sid. 180. See Simpson, *A History of the Common Law of Contract*, 461.   [26] (1838) 4 M. & W. 295.

[27] It may be argued that the plea should have been *non assumpsit*, in so far as there was no patent to be granted from the outset, there was no consideration *ab initio*. However, the principle for allowing a plea in confession and avoidance here was that at the time of the contract, it did not appear that there was no consideration, but was later discovered.

sufficiency of a consideration. What was an adequate consideration would always be hard for the court to tell, if only because it was often not specified.[28] There was clearly a problem for judges to weigh up the adequacy of a consideration in cases where not every precise fact regarding the nature of the consideration was set on the record: in such situations, either the question would be left for the jury to decide, or the judge would usurp matters of fact. Nevertheless, the freest contract needed a consideration. In *Wade* v. *Simeon*,[29] the two parties had agreed that if the plaintiff would forbear from prosecuting the defendant for certain sums, he would pay them by a certain date with interests and costs. When the defendant failed to pay, the plaintiff sued, but the defendant pleaded that the plaintiff had had no cause of action for the money, which he well knew, and that there was hence no consideration. Tindal CJ here held that since the plaintiff demurred to the plea, he admitted the fact that there had been no cause of action: and hence there was no consideration. The court here ignored the argument that since the promise was for a forbearance to sue, the defendant might have accepted that for whatever reasons of his own as might have existed, since there was no consideration.

It is clear that there were a number of decisions in the mid-nineteenth century which upheld contracts that were virtually worthless for one side, on the grounds that they were supported by mere promises. Such was *Haigh* v. *Brooks*,[30] where the defendant was liable to pay over £9000 for the return of a guarantee of his that turned out not to be binding. In upholding this, Lord Denman CJ ruled, 'how can the defendant be justified in breaking this promise, by discovering afterwards that the thing in consideration of which he gave it did not possess that value which he supposed to belong to it?'[31] This was clearly a decision that seemed to take the sanctity of promises to its ultimate conclusion: however, as the parties were linked by the promise, and since there might be other reasons why the defendant would want the document back beyond his legal liability, the promise was held sufficient.[32] In special contracts, therefore, the fairness of the consideration had a minor role.[33]

---

[28] See *Thomas* v. *Thomas* (1842) 2 QB 851, *Hitchcock* v. *Coker* (1837) 6 A. & E. 438.
[29] (1846) 2 CB 548.   [30] (1839) 10 Ad. & E. 309.   [31] 10 Ad. & E. 321.
[32] At first sight, this case seems analogous to the cases involving a forbearance to sue, where the court held that since one side (in effect) promised nothing, there was no contract. In this case, the plaintiff did promise something—a piece of paper—and the defendant accepted it in exchange for a fortune, for whatever reason.
[33] Against this interpretation, it might be argued that in contracts involving

In the *indebitatus* count, however, the consideration had a more important function since the promise was implied. In cases of collateral promises, where the promise was not raised by the law, the court could only work from what was formally stated on the record, and could not extend that beyond what was set down. However, where the law implied the promise, it could not assume that the parties intended themselves bound by *any* consideration set on the record, for it was the court which made the contract. Where the law raised the promise, it was intended that the promise was made in consideration of the debt, which meant that the consideration need not be strictly alleged.[34] Hence, we can see that in the *indebitatus* count, the foundation of the contract was the debt, which was seen as a consideration for an implied promise.[35] The recovery was for what was owed.[36] This meant that in general counts, the nature of

restraint of trade, one can perceive a clear change in attitude, centred on *Hitchcock* v. *Coker* (1837) 6 Ad. & E. 438, from the courts seeing their role as one of weighing the adequacy of a consideration in a contract that involved such a restraint, to their holding that the adequacy of consideration was a question for the parties alone. See Atiyah, *The Rise and Fall of Freedom of Contract*, 451. However, a closer examination of these cases reveals less of a change in attitude than seems at first glance to be the case. The key issue is that the courts were handling two distinct issues—sufficiency of consideration and the question of restraint of trade as a question of public policy. The two issues intertwined closely, yet they had separate functions. The key point in cases such as *Horner* v. *Graves* (1831) 7 Bing. 735 where the court commented on the small-ness of the consideration and held an agreement in restraint of trade to be void, was less that of the consideration itself, but 'whether there is a reasonable restraint of trade', that is, so large as to affect the public. This was to focus on the distinction articulated in *Mitchell* v. *Reynolds* (1711) 1 P. Wms. 181, 10 Mod. 27, 85, 130, between particular and local restraints. In this case, Tindal CJ said that whatever restraint was larger than the parties needed was of no benefit to either, and was hence unreason-able. This was a policy decision beyond the issue of consideration. It may therefore be said that making contracts void as being in restraint of trade was similar to making them void as being immoral or illegal: the wider principle acted as a trump to the intention of the parties. The courts thus looked at the extent of the restraint, not the price given for it. Of course, a determination of how far a restraint was *necessary* might reflect on the nature of the contract and its consideration: but nevertheless it was, and was treated, as a distinct issue. See also *Archer* v. *Marsh* (1837) 6 Ad. & E. 959, *Leighton* v. *Wales* (1838) 3 M. & W. 545 and *Gale* v. *Reed* (1806) 8 East 80 and *Young* v. *Timmins* (1831) 1 C. & J. 330.

[34] *Tyler* v. *Bendlowe* (1673) 2 Sho. 180.

[35] See *Slade's Case* (1602) 4 Co. Rep. 92b.

[36] Nevertheless, the cause of the action was the implied promise and not the debt: thus, in *Lee* v. *Welch* (1727) 2 Stra. 793, 2 Ld. Raym. 1516, the plaintiff had declared that the defendant was indebted for goods sold and delivered, and being so indebted 'would' pay, without averring that he had faithfully promised in consideration thereof: for this omission, the case was lost. Also *Blackhead* v. *Cock* (1615) 1 Rol. Rep. 43. With executory contracts, the plaintiff had to wait until they were executed to recover. In

the consideration which linked the debt to the promise was one whose substance the court could examine.[37] The fairness of the contract was essential, since the court had to judge whether the debt charged was large enough to warrant the promise sought to be implied.

The different forms of declaration also had an important bearing on the distinction between executory and executed contracts. A key question concerning executory contracts was the issue of when a plaintiff could sue on the contract without having first performed his part of the agreement. It was certainly possible to sue on executory contracts in the eighteenth century,[38] though clearly not on an *indebitatus* count since that count raised an implied duty based on what had been done by the plaintiff. However, executory contracts could be sued on in an action of covenant and on special assumpsits.

The fact that there was no novelty in suing on executory contracts can be seen from a case where Holt CJ had ruled, in an action on the case, that where there were mutual promises, if the one thing to be done was in consideration of the other, then a performance had to be averred, but '[i]f a day be appointed for the payment of the money and the day is to happen before the thing can be performed' an action could be brought for the payment before the thing was done.[39] The courts began to grapple with this problem in a more systematic way at the end of the eighteenth century, when judicial attention was focused strongly on sorting out a rational system of pleading. It is therefore no coincidence that the first systematic examination of the rules on this matter should have been in a note by Williams in his

actions on the general counts, for executed contracts, the defendant could not traverse the consideration, for to do so was to plead the general issue and in effect deny the promise, since without the consideration, there would be no promise. *Smith* v. *Hitchcock* (1590) 1 Leon. 252.

[37] Similarly, where the defendant, in debt to the plaintiff, had promised to pay, in consideration that the plaintiff would give him a certain time, it was held that the declaration need not show why the defendant was in debt: for the debt was not in question, and the day given for payment was the consideration of the promise. The court held that there had to be a debt seen for there was an express promise to pay it, while the debt was also found by implication in the verdict. *Woolaston* v. *Webb* (1611) Hob. 18. Thus, in cases of forbearance, the debt that lay behind the whole case was still of the essence.

[38] The clearest cases were those of wagers and breaches of promise to marry. See *Da Costa* v. *Jones* (1778) 2 Cowp. 729 at 735; *Good* v. *Elliott* (1790) 3 TR 693; *Hebden* v. *Rutter* (1663) 1 Sid. 180. See also Simpson, *A History of the Common Law of Contract*, 534–5, 537–8, and the text at n. 25 above.

[39] *Thorpe* v. *Thorpe* (1701) Salk. 171.

edition of Saunders' Reports.[40] Williams's first two rules, which sought to determine when the plaintiff had to show performance of his side of the agreement, said that if the day for payment could or was to occur before the thing which was the consideration was to be performed, then an action could be brought before performance, since the performance was not a condition precedent. However, where the day appointed for payment was after the consideration was to be performed, then there could be no action before performance. It is important to note that these were points developed out of an examination of pleading, rather than a general view of contract.

These principles were used from the 1790s on to guide judges in decisions allowing actions on purely executory contracts. In *Campbell* v. *Jones*,[41] therefore, the plaintiff, in consideration of £250 paid and £250 to be paid by the defendant, had covenanted to teach the defendant how to bleach linen in a way he had the patent of; and the defendant had covenanted to pay him by a certain date. In this case, Lord Kenyon held that the plaintiff could recover, although he had not shown he had taught the defendant: the grounds for the decision were that the defendant's covenant was to pay by a certain date, while there was no duty on the plaintiff to teach by that date.

By contrast, in *Glazebrook* v. *Woodrow*,[42] the plaintiff had covenanted to sell a schoolhouse to the defendant, to hand over possession by a certain time and make a conveyance of it by a later date, by which second date the defendant would pay. Here, the plaintiff failed to recover the money, because he had not shown a conveyance. In this case, the covenants were said to be dependent, so that the plaintiff could not recover without having performed his part. The key question, Kenyon said here, was the intention of the parties, for 'every man's agreement is to be performed according to his intent'.[43] Here, the substance of the consideration was the making of the conveyance, which had not been done. The discussion in these cases turned on what were dependent and independent covenants. The distinction is difficult to pinpoint: however, it may be suggested that in these cases, the court held covenants independent when the promise that was the consideration could still be

---

[40] *Pordage* v. *Cole* (1669) 1 Wms. Saund. 319.
[41] (1796) 8 TR 570. See also *Morton* v. *Lamb* (1797) 7 TR 125.
[42] (1799) 8 TR 366.
[43] 8 TR 370. This follows *Thomas* v. *Cadwaller* (1744) Willes 496.

performed in future, according to the agreement, but dependent, when it could not.[44] These rules on conditions precedent and how they affected the consideration were easily applied in cases brought on special assumpsits. Thus, in *Wilks* v. *Smith* in 1842, the court allowed a plaintiff to recover in assumpsit on an agreement to sell a building for £120, to be paid with 5 per cent interest within four years. The four years were not expired, but the court held that the plaintiff could recover the interest due, although he did not aver either that he had delivered the possession of the land, or that he was willing to convey. Alderson B ruled that since one of the acts was not fixed in time, it could not be a condition precedent. The court similarly upheld the contention that it was the promise that was the consideration.[45] The key questions for executory contracts of when one could sue for their breach, before performance, were thus being explored through close technical reasoning.[46]

It can be seen that from the late eighteenth century judges, faced with more precise declarations and pleas, began to develop points that would shape later nineteenth-century contract law. Thus, the first cases that considered what constituted an acceptance were addressing issues of consideration in special assumpsits, on issues arising on the record. Discussing what constituted an acceptance, the judges looked not to the principles of contract in general, but the precise points before them on the pleas.[47] It is clear that in coming to

[44] In *Glazebrook* v. *Woodrow*, Le Blanc J pointed out that where the defendant had received the advantages of the material parts of the agreement, the other side could sue for the consideration, although not everything had literally been performed. See *Boone* v. *Eyre* (1779) 2 W. Bl. 1312, 1 H. Bl. 1270.

[45] 1842 10 M. & W. 355. Parke B ruled (at 360) that 'the rule as laid down in the notes to *Pordage* v. *Cole*, applies directly to this case'. See also *Mattock* v. *Kinglake* (1839) 10 A. & E. 48.

[46] See also *Ikin* v. *Brook* (1830) 1 B. & Ad. 124. Here the defendant was the assignee of a deceased bankrupt, who promised an indemnity for the plaintiff against all future claims against him 'in consideration of the money so secured' by his giving two promissory notes. The plaintiff sued when the defendant failed to indemnify him against an action for a debt for which he was liable on account of the deceased bankrupt. In defending this, it was claimed that the condition precedent had not been fulfilled, since the defendant had only the notes, not the money. However, Lord Tenterden ruled against this. 'By the terms of the guarantee, the indemnity is to begin immediately,' he said. Though it did not appear when the notes were to be made payable, 'the fact of giving securities, instead of paying down the money, clearly shows that a future payment of money was intended'. (1 B. & Ad. 127–8) See also *Irving* v. *King* (1830) 4 C. & P. 309.

[47] *Payne* v. *Cave* (1789) 3 TR 148; *Cooke* v. *Oxley* (1790) 3 TR 653; *Humphries* v. *Carvalho* (1812) 16 East 45.

conclusions as to what would constitute an acceptance, the judges were influenced by treatise writers like Pothier[48] and by considerations of public policy:[49] nevertheless the questions on which the judges had to adjudicate were raised by the pleas on the special count.

Problems of Pleading in the Contract of Employment

By the second half of the nineteenth century, as Atiyah has shown, the standard view of contract was that of the governing of future promises.[50] In this section, we will examine how the closer examination of declarations and pleas by the courts in the early nineteenth century made it ever harder to use the *indebitatus* count in contracts of service, and how the courts began to develop more substantive ideas of contract beyond the pleas.

In *indebitatus* counts, as has been seen, there could be no action where the plaintiff had not performed his part of the contract. This form of general assumpsit only lay where there was a debt due to the plaintiff from the defendant: it did not lie where there were mutual promises or a collateral undertaking.[51] The consideration in these cases was hence the debt that existed, so that it had to be shown that the plaintiff had done all that was necessary to establish the debt. Thus, where the special agreement remained unperformed, the plaintiff failed in his action. While the contract remained open, the plaintiff had to sue on the contract, or else wait until the end of the contract period. This principle is evident in a number of cases involving contracts of service, where it was held that the contract was

---

[48] *Raper* v. *Birkbeck* (1812) 15 East 17; *Cox* v. *Troy* (1822) 5 B. & Ald. 474.

[49] See *Adams* v. *Lindsell* (1818) 1 B. & Ald. 681, which held that offers by letter remained open until the answer was due to be sent, for otherwise no contract could ever be made by the post. The court however observed the strictness of pleas here, holding that the fact that the offer was sent by mail implied its continuance until receipt.

[50] See Pollock, *Principles of Contract at Law and in Equity* (London, 1876), 5.

[51] See *Hard's Case* (1696) 1 Salk. 23, *Anon* (1675) 1 Vent. 258. Mansfield's decision in *Moses* v. *Macferlan* (1760) 2 Burr. 1005 seems to contradict this, for he encouraged the use of the general assumpsit seeing it as 'very beneficial'. This case may be seen as one way in which Mansfield attempted to extend the moral consideration idea, for he said, 'If the Defendant be under an Obligation, from the ties of natural justice, to refund; the Law implies a Debt and gives this action' (at 1008). However, for our purposes, it should be noted that this was a count for money had and received, where money could be recovered without alleging a formal debt.

entire and not divisible.[52] Thus, in *Hulle* v. *Heightman*,[53] a seaman who had a contract to serve on a voyage from Altona to London and back, payment being due at the end of the trip, was denied food by the captain half-way through the journey, at London. Leaving the service of the ship, the plaintiff sued on an *indebitatus assumpsit* for his wages, but was refused damages. The court held that in spite of the wrongful dismissal, the plaintiff could not sue on this form of action, but should take an action in tort against the captain, for preventing him from earning his wages. In this case, the judges were misled by associating it with other cases involving the rescinding of contracts, here holding that the defendant's act had not rescinded it.[54] A rescinding of the contract would have allowed a *quantum meruit*: but, more importantly, the plaintiff should have sued on the special contract, alleging its breach by the defendant.[55] In *Spain* v. *Arnott*,[56] it was held that if a servant hired for a year refused to obey his orders, he could be dismissed before the end of the year, and could not recover his wages, for the year must be completed before there was any entitlement to payment.[57] Therefore, if the servant was fairly dismissed, he could not recover any wages for the whole year since the contract was unperformed and unperformable.[58]

The employee who was unfairly dismissed had the problem of trying to recover both past wages and damages for breach of contract, which required different forms of declaration. At first, in

[52] See *Cutter* v. *Powell* (1795) 6 TR 320 at 326, and *Bates* v. *Hudson* (1825) 6 Dowl. & Ry. KB 3. The question of whether a contract was entire, needing complete performance, or divisible, was one of construction; in *Cutter* v. *Powell* the contract between a sailor who had died and his employer was construed as entire, and it was held that his wages could not be apportioned, and no part could be recovered by his estate. On this question, see S. J. Stoljar, 'The Great Case of *Cutter* v. *Powell*', *Canadian Bar Review*, xxxiv (1956), 288–307, and M. R. Freedland, *The Contract of Employment* (Oxford, 1976), 126–9. As Freedland shows, the presumption against apportionment was not universal: see *Pangani* v. *Gandolfi* (1826) 2 C. & P. 370.

[53] (1802) 2 East 145.

[54] See the note to *Cutter* v. *Powell* in *Smith's Leading Cases* 9th edn., ed. R. H. Collins and R. G. Arbuthnot, 2 vols. (London, 1887), ii. 20, where it is argued that the plaintiff here could have rescinded, and thence recovered.

[55] See E. Lawes, *Pleading in Assumpsit*, 24.

[56] (1817) 2 Stark. 256.

[57] See *Plymouth* v. *Throgmorton* (1688) 1 Salk. 65, *Lilly* v. *Elwyn* (1848) 11 Law Times 151.

[58] B. W. Napier, 'The Contract of Service: the Concept and its Application' (unpublished Cambridge Ph.D., 1975), 83–7. By contrast, in *Bayley* v. *Rimmell* (1836) 1 M. & W. 506, an assistant surgeon who had served for half a year before falling ill was allowed to recover his salary on a *quantum meruit* since there was no evidence of hiring for a year. In higher forms of employment, the contract period was not implied.

Gandell v. *Pontigny* in 1816,[59] the courts tried to solve the problem by using the *indebitatus* count. In this case, the plaintiff was a servant hired by the quarter who was dismissed in the middle of a quarter. Lord Ellenborough held here that since he was unfairly dismissed, and since he showed he was willing to serve the rest of the period, he could recover on an *indebitatus assumpsit* both for the time he had served and for the rest of the quarter's work.[60] Ellenborough was in effect ruling for breach of contract; but this attempt failed since later cases showed this was a stretching of the common count beyond its bounds. Thus, in *Archard* v. *Horner*,[61] the court ruled that on a general count, the employee could only recover for the time he had actually served: there could be no prospective debt. This case also revealed, however, the difficulty of suing for breach of the special contract. Lord Tenterden CJ ruled that the ordinary contract with servants was for a year, 'but to entitle you to recover, you must declare properly upon that contract, and not declare as if your contract was for a year absolute'.[62] The dilemma for servants was the fact that the *law* implied that the contract of service was for a year. This meant that the employee had to wait until the end of the year to recover what he was due, but since there was no exact special contract for the whole year, he could not recover for breach of it for that period.

The importance of the form used in unfair dismissals was pointed out three years after the Hilary Rules, in *Smith* v. *Hayward*,[63] a case whose facts resembled *Gandell* v. *Pontigny*. Here Lord Denman CJ ruled that the plaintiff could not recover prospective wages under an *indebitatus assumpsit*. 'There is obviously a great difference between suing for a breach of contract in dismissing the plaintiff, and for work and labour which, by reason of the dismissal, has not been performed,' he said. 'The defence in the last case would be the non-performance of the work; in the other, some excuse for breaking off the contract'.[64] To recover for prospective losses, the party had to sue on the special count.

Dismissed servants were often therefore caught uncomfortably between the Scylla of the special contract and the Charybdis of the *indebitatus assumpsit*. This was equally true where there were notice

---

[59] 4 Camp. 375.
[60] Cf. *Collins* v. *Price* (1828) 5 Bing. 132.
[61] (1828) 3 C. & P. 349.   [62] 3 C. & P. 349.
[63] (1837) 7 Ad. & E. 543.   [64] 7 Ad. & E. 548.

periods. In *Hartley* v. *Harman*,[65] the plaintiff's job as superintendent of works could be ended by either side with one month's notice. After 18 months, Hartley was dismissed, and sued one month later, having neither been paid his 18 months' salary, nor the notice pay. However, as he sued on a breach of the contract for the dismissal without the month's notice, it was held that he could not recover the past wages due, but had to bring a separate common count for work and labour. On the other side of the coin, in *Flewings* v. *Tisdal*,[66] the court held that when a servant was dismissed without one month's notice, the action for the money could not be sustained on a common count but needed a special one. However, where there was no proof of any hiring, but only of service and payments without any reference to any definite period, and the servant left in the middle of the year without being asked to return, he could recover on a *quantum* meruit.[67]

The dilemma of the wrongfully dismissed employee caught between forms of declaration was finally adressed in *Goodman* v. *Pocock* in 1850,[68] when the problem was solved by focusing on the breach of the special contract. The plaintiff, a commercial traveller engaged on a salary of £200 per annum paid quarterly, was dismissed in the middle of a quarter, and sued, with both a special count for the wrongful dismissal, and a general count for work and labour. In the trial before Erle J, the judge ruled that in the action on the special count, the jury in assessing damages could not take into account services that had actually been rendered in the broken quarter, but that for this a separate *indebitatus* case had to be brought. Therefore, the plaintiff brought a second case of *indebitatus assumpsit*; but now the court held that the action was not maintainable because the plaintiff in his action on the special contract had treated it as an open contract, and could not therefore later treat it as rescinded, which was what he required to recover in an *indebitatus* count. 'In a case like this, the servant may either treat the contract as rescinded and bring *indebitatus assumpsit*, or he may sue on the contract,' Coleridge J ruled, 'but he cannot do both; and, if he has two counts, he must take his verdict on one only.'[69] Since he had been given damages for completed service in previous quarters and

[65] (1840) 11 A. & E. 798.
[66] (1847) 10 Law Times 166.
[67] *Bayley* v. *Rimmell* (1837) 1 M. & W. 506.
[68] 15 QB 576.   [69] 15 QB 583.

£50 for breach of contract, he could not recover on a *quantum meruit*. Therefore, in the first case, the jury should have been directed to take into account the services rendered during the broken quarter, in awarding damages for the wrongful dismissal. In his ruling on this case, Erle J commented that the servant could not wait until the end of the period for which he was hired, and sue for constructive service on an *indebitatus* count:[70] the solution to the dilemma of the wrongfully dismissed servant was therefore to be found for breach of the special contract. Lord Campbell CJ dismissed the objection that to allow the plaintiff to recover for the incomplete term would leave the defendant without a plea, for he said *non assumpsit* would suffice: 'it obliges the plaintiff to shew a debt due; and that could be only by shewing what work was done for which payment could be claimed under the common count'.[71] Thus the special count proved triumphant over the *indebitatus*.

The Ascendancy of a General View of Contract

As the courts puzzled over which form of action to use, so they began to evolve answers to substantive questions over the nature of executory contracts. The only way that a plaintiff could recover on a special contract that had not been completed by using an *indebitatus* count was where something had been done under it, but not in accordance with its precise terms,[72] or where one party had refused to perform or made the performance impossible.[73] The development of these rules led judges to think in broader terms about the nature of contract. Thus, in *Planche* v. *Colburn*,[74] the defendants, publishers of the 'Juvenile Library', had engaged the plaintiff to compose a work for this library; but before he had finished, they abandoned the venture. It was held in this case that the plaintiff could sue on a *quantum meruit* for compensation, even though he did not tender the treatise, for Tindal CJ held that by abandoning the work, the special contract had been ended, and the plaintiff could therefore sue. The

[70] 15 QB 583.
[71] 15 QB 580. He distinguished *Hartley* v. *Harman* by arguing that that case was not for wrongful dismissal but for notice payment, and that the contract was not for a fixed period but for a rate of annual pay in the latter case.
[72] See *Basten* v. *Butter* (1806) 7 East 479, *Farnsworth* v. *Garrard* (1807) 1 Camp. 38.
[73] *Withers* v. *Reynolds* (1831) 2 B. & Ad. 882, *Franklin* v. *Miller* (1836) 4 A. & E. 599.
[74] (1831) 8 Bing. 14.

principle of ending contracts can be seen in two cases involving the sale of horses. In *Weston* v. *Downes*,[75] the plaintiff bought horses from the defendant, and being dissatisfied with them, exchanged them twice for new ones. Returning his final set, he sued on an action for money had and received, but failed, since it was held that the contract was still subsisting, since he had previously accepted exchanges. But in *Towers* v. *Barrett*,[76] the plaintiff had bought a one-horse chaise and harness for ten guineas from the defendant, on condition that his wife approved of it. If she did not, he would return it and pay a sum per day for the hire of the equipment. The plaintiff's wife disliking it, he returned it with a hire fee, but the defendant refused to accept it. Nevertheless, the court allowed an action for money had and received, by holding that the contract was at an end, and that the defendant held plaintiff's money without conscience. 'It is admitted that if the defendant had actually accepted the chaise, the action would lie', Buller J said, adding that the contention was that he did not receive it. 'Then let us see', he added, 'whether there be not something equivalent to an acceptance?' Since the defendant left it in the power of the plaintiff to end the contract, by the very terms of it, it was not now in his power to refuse acceptance of the goods— 'he was bound to receive it; and therefore it is the same as if he had accepted it'.[77] Hence the contract was no longer open, and he could use a general assumpsit. What is of note in these cases involving the nature of the action is how judges are addressing questions of the nature of acceptance and intent in contracts, before the publication of larger English treatises on the principles of contract. The principles evolved in these cases would prove influential in the rise of the executory view.

The effect of the 1834 reforms in pleading was double-edged, as we have seen. However, despite the frustration of special demurrers, a focus on the different requirements of the forms of action continued to shape substantive ideas. In *Alexander* v. *Gardner*,[78] the plaintiff sold to the defendant a quantity of butter to be shipped from Sligo to London in October and paid for by a bill at two months from the date of the landing. The butter was shipped in November, but the defendants waived the objection to it, and accepted an invoice and a bill of lading. However, the butter was lost in a shipwreck. On these facts, the plaintiffs sued in an action for goods bargained and

[75] (1778) Dougl. 23.   [76] (1786) 1 TR 133.
[77] 1 TR 136.   [78] (1835) 1 Bing NC 671.

sold, to which the defendants argued that the declaration should have been a special one. They gave three reasons: first, the butter was not in the possession of the defendants at the time of the contract; second, that the butter was not shipped in November as it should have been; and third, that since payment was due two months after landing, the landing was a condition precedent that had never been fulfilled. However, the court held that the contract had been executed, and that the form of declaration sufficed. To get there, however, they had to unravel the meaning of possession and conditions precedent here. Tindal CJ held that the goods had been ascertained and accepted before the action was brought.[79] Bosanquet J supported this: 'It is not necessary for the support of such an action that the goods should be actually in the possession of the vendor', he said, since here he had done all that was required to obtain the possession. Legal possession began when the goods had been dispatched.[80] As for the second point, since the defendant had waived the condition precedent in a parol contract, it was no longer necessary. More controversially, Tindal CJ ruled as to the third that the landing time was only a time fixed for payment, so that landing was not a condition precedent.[81] Thus, substantive questions on the nature of legal possession and the rights and duties attached thereto were raised and resolved in the process of considering questions concerning the correct forms of action.

By the mid-century, we can find a growing number of cases involving employees suing on executory contracts. It can be seen that some of the cases that seem most to demonstrate the ideology of freedom of contract and *laissez-faire* economics built on doctrines on the nature of the special contract developed over the preceding half-century. The most striking case was *Hochster* v. *De la Tour*,[82] where it was held that the plaintiff could sue for the breach of a contract after it had been repudiated but before the time fixed for performance. The plaintiff here had been engaged for a three-month period to be a courier for the defendant. He had averred his willingness to perform his part of the contract until the time of its repudiation, and this was held by the court to be a sufficient performance of the condition

---

[79] He drew on *Rohde* v. *Thwaites* (1827) 6 B. & C. 388.

[80] Cf. *Fragano* v. *Long* (1825) 4 B. & C. 219.

[81] He drew on *Fragano* v. *Long* for this, but in that case, the decision rested on the fact that the vendor had had insurance taken out in his name in case the goods did not arrive.   [82] (1853) 2 E. & B. 678.

precedent to recover damages. It can be seen how the court mixed policy and precedent to arrive at this conclusion. This case is the apotheosis of special assumpsit reasoning, for much of the reasoning of Lord Campbell CJ drew on earlier cases of repudiations, where one side had made the performance by the other side impossible.[83] The most important precedent here was *Ford* v. *Tiley*,[84] where the defendant, having agreed to execute the lease to a public house by a certain time to the plaintiff, made a lease with another person before the time due for his lease with the plaintiff. The court held that the plaintiff was entitled to his action 'before such day arrives' not because the defendant had made it impossible to perform his part of the agreement (because he might get a surrender of the new lease before the due time) but because he had made an inconsistent conveyance, and had therefore broken his stipulation. The contract was clearly broken. The question for *Hochster* v. *De la Tour* was therefore not whether the plaintiff could recover damages before the time of performance, but that of whether the repudiation amounted to a breach of the contract. This was decided on the grounds of convenience—that to decide the other way would both prevent the plaintiff looking for other work in the meantime, and require him to spend money in preparations for his prospective job, and also that in the meantime, the defendant could disappear on his travels, leaving the plaintiff without remedy. In addition it is clear that the court, in looking at what was a breach of contract, was influenced by theoretical ideas on the nature of contracts as being agreements: ending the agreement ended the contract.

The mid-century is important in showing the transfer from an obsession with correct pleas to a greater interest in substantive questions of contract. In *Aspdin* v. *Austin* in 1844,[85] the defendant agreed to pay the plaintiff a certain weekly rate of wages for three years and then to take him as a partner, for which the plaintiff would manufacture cement for the defendant, and instruct him in the trade. Both were bound in a penal sum to fulfil the agreement. However, the defendant dismissed the plaintiff, who sued for breach of contract. There was no stipulation here that the defendant was bound to employ the plaintiff for three years: but the plaintiff claimed it was implied from the stipulation for weekly wages.

---

[83] Thus, he drew on *Planche* v. *Colburn*, *Bowdell* v. *Parsons* (1808) 10 East 359.

[84] (1827) 6 B. & C. 325.

[85] 5 QB 671; see also *Dunn* v. *Sayles* (1844) 5 QB 685.

Against this, it was held that where parties had made express agreements, the court could not extend them by implication to cover what would have been a fitting intention. Here, the court ruled, the defendant did not covenant to continue his business for three years: 'he covenanted only to pay weekly sums for three years to the plaintiff in consideration of his performing what on his part he has made a condition precedent'.[86] The court here strictly followed what it saw to be the intentions of the parties in the case: and that was determined by the precise import of the special agreement as laid before the court.[87]

This case contrasted with *Emmens* v. *Elderton*,[88] where it was held that the executory contract of employment was binding for both sides, covering a fixed period, so that the dismissed employee could recover damages for what he expected to gain from the contract, as well as recovering for what he had done. This case comes at an interesting juncture, for the 1848 decision of the Exchequer Chamber was upheld in 1853 by the House of Lords. In between, parliament passed the Common Law Procedure Act in 1852, which rendered it unnecessary to mention the form of action used in the writ of summons, and which gave power to the plaintiff 'of joining in one action all his claims, of whatever nature, against the same defendant, provided these claims are in the same right'.[89] This legislation similarly abolished the need to mention fictitious promises which needed no proof. It was highly significant for the types of contract cases we have been examining. 'The combined effect of these enactments is that the substance of the cause of action in all cases is considered irrespectively of the form in which the action is framed,' Leake commented, 'and the doctrine of implied promises has no longer any practical application'.[90] *Emmens* v. *Elderton* is therefore interesting in that it straddled two eras.

In this case, E. M. Elderton had agreed to act as the attorney of the company of which William Emmens was the secretary for the period of one year, being paid a £100 retainer. By the agreement, he was to

[86] 5 QB 671 at 685.

[87] Lord Denman CJ said, 'Where parties have entered into written engagements with expressed stipulations, it is manifestly not desirable to extend them by any implications: the presumption is that, having expressed some, they have expressed all the conditions by which they intend to be bound.' 5 QB 684.

[88] 13 CB 495, affirming the decision on the Exchequer Chamber *Elderton* v. *Emmens* (1848) 6 CB 160 which overturned the case in the Common Pleas (1847) 4 CB 479. For a discussion of this case, see M. R. Freedland, *The Contract of Employment*, 22–3.

[89] 15 & 16 Vic. c. 76 s. 41.   [90] Leake, *Contract*, 40.

act for the company in all matters and attend the secretary of the company and the board of directors when required. After four months, having paid £50, the company said they would no longer retain him, and terminated the agreement. Elderton sued for a breach of the contract, claiming to suffer a loss of business worth £5000 as a consequence. When the case was heard in the Common Pleas, it was held that the consideration of the contract was exhausted by the mutual promises, so that there was no consideration to sustain a promise by the company to employ the plaintiff: the promise was a promise to pay in return for the promise to work, not a promise to retain and employ till the end of the year.[91] However, this was overruled by the Exchequer Chamber and House of Lords. The ruling of the Lords reveals an interesting mixture of pleading and policy. Crompton J ruled that this was not a contract for payment at a certain rate, but that the contract was for the sum specified to be paid at the end of the year. The court had to consider whether the words 'retain and employ' were to be construed as meaning anything more than was to be found in the terms of the agreement, and implied by it—in other words, whether they did or did not import a new consideration. This was resolved by finding that the word 'employ' did not mean that the company was bound to give actual employment to the attorney, but that the word only amplified the terms of the contract, that is that 'the company engage to retain and employ the plaintiff according to the agreement, and no further'.[92]

The judges considered also the argument that the plaintiff should have waited until the end of the year, averring readiness to perform, and then sued for a certain sum. The court rejected this, Crompton J pointing to the inconvenience of requiring the employee not to look for work but to wait until the time due for every instalment of the salary and then sue on that. If that were the case, the plaintiff could not look for any other work while the contract subsisted.[93] This case has been seen as being innovative in its view of the contract of employment: but we can see how specific the questions were that

[91] This was seen to be in line with the principle of *Aspdin* v. *Austin* 5 QB 671, *Dunn* v. *Sayles* 5 QB 685, and *Williamson* v. *Taylor* 5 QB 175.

[92] 13 CB 504. Crompton J argued that the words 'retain and employ' were superfluous, and merely put in by overzealous special pleaders trying in a dangerous way to escape the regulation of 1834 that pleaders could not declare in one count on the agreement as set out in the mutual promises and another on their legal effect.

[93] 13 CB 507–8.

were considered by the judges. First, Elderton was suing for the loss of what he might have *expected* to earn from the continuing employment—thus, the jury awarded damages of £1000 on the first two counts. Yet the court treated this as a case for the recovery of the £100 fee, and they expressly said that the contract did not require the company actually to *employ* him.[94] Second, the judges did not see themselves overruling *Aspdin* v. *Austin*: rather, in this case, the contract was for the single sum of £100. The contract was one for retaining, not employing the plaintiff, and the retainer could not be apportioned. The question of expected earnings beyond that stipulated by the contract therefore came in, as it were, through the back door.[95] Lord Truro therefore explained the special damage by saying that the pleader only inserted it to show that the plaintiff lost the probable chance of employment that he would have enjoyed, 'and that the jury were warranted in adding to the balance due in respect of his salary, some damages by way of indemnity for the loss of that contingent employ which was incidental to his character of attorney for the company'.[96] However, if the cause of the action was the loss of actual earnings he expected, then the meaning of 'employ' would (as counsel claimed) be different from the one accepted by the court.

The question of the nature of the employment contract was also considered in a number of cases where the question of a restraint of trade was raised. Two cases illustrate the development of thinking towards a more general view of contract after the mid-century. In *Pilkington* v. *Scott*,[97] the plaintiffs had agreed with one Joseph Leigh that he would work for them as a crown glass maker for seven years, the contract specifying the wage rate he was to be paid, the fact that he need not be paid when he was sick, and that he could be dismissed with one month's notice. When Leigh left them and went to the defendants, they were sued for unlawfully harbouring him, but pleaded that the contract was void as being in restraint of trade, since there was no stipulation in the contract actually to employ him, but only to pay him when employed. The court rejected this

[94] Crompton J expressly pointed out that the question of special damage alleged was irrelevant to the breach in hand, and that it did not alter the meaning of 'employ' in the declaration, which did not refer to actual use. 13 CB 505. See also Parke B, 13 CB 535.

[95] Thus, Erle J talked of 'the general law relating to contracts' and said that 'the measure of damage is, an indemnity to the plaintiff for his loss by the breach'. 13 CB 518–19.

[96] 13 CB 541.

[97] (1846) 15 M. & W. 657.

however, and held that the provision as to notice showed that they agreed to employ him for the seven years at the given rates.[98]

However, after the mid-century, broader, general notions of contract were undermining the precision previously used. This is evident in *Whittle* v. *Frankland*,[99] where the appellant, a collier, had absented himself from the respondent's employment. His contract of employment gave a fortnightly wage and stipulated a 28-day notice period, but counsel claimed the contract lacked mutuality and was in restraint of trade. '[T]his contract neither specifies the kind of work nor the rate of wages,' Mellish contended. 'The contract may mean that the workman is to be provided with piece work; and if so, what would be the case supposing by a rise of water, the colliery were stopped for a month?'[100] The court held that there was an implication that the employers would find work, and that the usage of the trade would determine how workers would be employed during quiet times. Yet there was nothing concrete in the contract to merit that assumption.[101]

Thus, we can see that the promise-based special contract in service agreements had triumphed by the mid-nineteenth century, largely thanks to problems involved with what was required in the general counts. It was with this triumph that courts began to turn increasingly to general concepts of contract and to construct rules that broke away from the strictness of case allegation into vaguer ideas about what was a contract. In some cases (as in the last case discussed), this perhaps involved judges playing a more important part in the substantive merits of contract than before, by their assumptions that there was a reason for the contract that was not stated on the record. If the doctrine of free contract was implicit in the special assumpsit, it could grow into a larger ideology after the mid-century as the pleading shackles of the action of assumpsit were loosened: for the judge was allowed, even encouraged, to assume all was well between the parties.

---

[98] See also *Hartley* v. *Cummings* (1847) 5 CB 247. In this case, as in *Pilkington* v. *Scott*, there were stipulations about rates of pay and service in trade depressions.

[99] (1862) 2 B. & S. 49.

[100] 2 B. & S. 49.

[101] Contrast *Williamson* v. *Taylor* (1843) 5 QB 175.

Irrationality and the Law

The era of the expansion of the industrial revolution thus saw the survival of a system of law that was 'irrational.'[102] The rules that emerged came through a tortuous and often contradictory form of reasoning on the pleas, and the law was often unable to provide clear guides for acceptable conduct in an industrializing society. The function of law in the early nineteenth century was far from what Bentham would have desired: it was adjudicative and responded to the wrongs which had occurred in the intercourse of the wider society, as seen through the prism of pleading. The courts tended to limit themselves to the precise dispute at hand and its precise formulation: an attitude which could only restrict the impact of their decisions on guiding future conduct.

The question of how far law in the industrial revolution was influenced by policy considerations and the prejudices of the judges is a contentious one. By understanding the nature of legal reasoning, we can see how far the judges were manipulating the law for policy, and how far they were working within confined frameworks, without attempting to shape society. The irrationality of the law in the industrial revolution can be seen in its working as a system of forms to correct wrongs as defined by the antagonists. As has been shown, in the system of pleading, the plaintiff had to claim his right correctly: thus in many areas involving torts which seemed to involve policy choices by the judge, the plaintiff lost his case merely because he was unable to prove the defendant responsible. Most cases involved straightforward resolutions of pleas; but where there was a balance between both sides, both plaintiff and defendant having made plausible claims for the existence of the right or the wrong, then policy came into play. This explains the inconsistency of cases where rights were infringed: where the wrong was sufficiently alleged, the right was upheld; where it was in doubt, the judge had a choice to make. A key problem was that in these years new forms of corporate activity emerged which were often wholly new to the common law and for which no law existed.

[102] See Max Weber, *Economy and Society: An Outline of Interpretive Sociology*, 3 vols. (New York, 1968), ii. 641–900. See also W. Schluchter, *The Rise of Western Rationalism: Max Weber's Developmental History*, trans. G. Roth (Berkeley, Los Angeles, and London, 1981), 82–105, and Bryan S. Turner, *For Weber: Essays on the Sociology of Fate* (Boston, London, and Henley, 1981), 320–51.

What is discernible in many of the decisions of the early nineteenth century is the strictness of judges in their interpretations of the declarations and pleas. Because the judges were looking so closely for the correct presentation of rights and legal justifications for wrongs, they often missed the public interest in their concern for the case at hand. In *Brown* v. *Mallett*,[103] the defendant's ship had sunk by accident in the Thames, and the plaintiff's ship had collided with it, because there had been no warning buoy placed to show the underwater obstruction. Brown claimed that when Mallett's ship sank, it became his duty to prevent such accidents; but the court ruled that this declaration was bad, since the plaintiff had failed to show that a duty existed. The judges held that it merely stated that a duty existed without showing the facts which created the duty, and they doubted that the facts existed here which would allow them to infer a duty. While a man might have a duty of care if his ship sank, that duty could not last forever. Since such a duty had to end when the owner of a sunken vessel abandoned it, the duty could only exist if the plaintiff had averred that the defendant had maintained possession of the ship; which he failed to do here. As far as the facts in the declaration went, in which the ship sank without Mallett being at fault, the defendant was in the same position as any other member of the public, with the only difference being that he had also suffered a private calamity—'and this difference does not appear to be any reason for throwing on him the cost of remedying or mitigating the evil'.[104] The facts alleged were all true, Brown had suffered, but there was no duty on the defendant.[105]

The plaintiff in *Chadwick* v. *Trower*[106] similarly failed to allege a duty. Here, Trower had pulled down his vaults without warning his neighbour, Chadwick, with the result that the latter's vaults had also collapsed. In this case, the court held that the mere juxtaposition of the walls created no obligation, particularly since the declaration did not aver specifically that Trower knew of the existence of Chadwick's vault. 'How is the defendant to ascertain the precise degree of

---

[103] (1848) 5 CB 599.   [104] 5 CB 619.

[105] Contrast *Parnaby* v. *the Company and Proprietors of the Lancaster Canal Company* (1839) 11 A. & E. 223, where the defendants' statute allowed them to collect up tolls and to weigh up sunken barges if the owners failed to do so. In this case, where the plaintiff's barge collided with an underwater wreck, the court said that the facts of the case did allow them to infer a duty, since the company operated the canal for profit and charged people to use it. Those facts implied a duty on their part to keep it reasonably clear.   [106] (1839) 6 Bing. NC 1.

care and caution required of him, if he has no notice of the existence of the nature of the structure?' asked Rolfe B.[107] Hence the judge could conclude that no duty existed.

Judges showed increasing formality in requiring a strict allegation of responsibility.[108] This was especially true where there were statutes involved. In 1852, there was a case where in a cotton mill, the machinery was driven by vertical shafts, connected to a horizontal shaft powering them, which all had by statute to be fenced while the machines were at work. When one shaft was disconnected from its machines for repair, and left unfenced, but continued to revolve with the other working shafts, a nine-year-old girl, ordered to sweep the floor by it, became entangled in the revolving shaft and was severely injured.[109] In the case for negligence, Alderson B ruled that there was no common law negligence here, since 'the defendant has taken all the precautions which, but for the special provisions of the statute as to fencing the mill gearing, would be required from cautious men'.[110] He then ruled that there was no statutory liability, since the statute referred to *working* machinery, and while the shaft was revolving, it was not actually driving any machinery. Thus, an extremely close reading of statute linked up with a casual view of the duty of mill owners to deny the girl compensation.

Policy choices are to be found at the secondary level. This is evident in *Blyth* v. *the Birmingham Waterworks Company*[111] where the plaintiff's house was flooded after water escaped through a valve attached to underground pipes when it had frozen in a severe winter. The court had to decide if the company was guilty of negligence in allowing the valve to freeze, and whether a wrong was therefore correctly alleged. Here, the court found for the company, arguing that negligence was the omission to do something a reasonable man would do, and that this accident was so exceptional that an ordinary man could not have been expected to foresee it. Since the company had provided against such frosts as a reasonable man

---

[107] 6 Bing. NC 10.

[108] See *M'Kinnon* v. *Penson* (1855) 9 Ex. 609. In this case, it was ruled that no action lay against the county surveyor for damage resulting from a failure to repair the county bridge. Coleridge J ruled that there would be an injustice in giving compensation to the injured party, for the men of the county sued in the name of their surveyor would be liable well into the future for any damage done, and 'being a fluctuating body, individuals coming into the county three or four years after the cause of action accrued might be compellable to pay for acts of commissions in which they had taken no part'.   [109] *Coe* v. *Platt* (1852) 7 Ex. 923.

[110] 7 Ex. 926.   [111] (1856) 11 Ex. 781.

might expect, they could not be held responsible for the effects of such a severe and exceptional winter as that of 1855. Here, the court was given a choice, after the pleadings, to say whether the harm to the plaintiff's house was the responsibility of the company which acted for profit, or whether the company should not be expected to take excessive precautions. The fact that they chose to see the company as a set of ordinary individuals, rather than as experts who should have foreseen more than a reasonable man, reveals that the judges made a choice which had economic ramifications and which reflected their economic world-view. The judges' notion of reasonableness reflected a choice: they could equally have taken the view that the standard of ordinary reasonableness was inappropriate here: but that would have reflected a different view of what was efficient and desirable for society.[112]

Much nineteenth-century tort law was haphazard because judges were looking so closely at the precise allegations and precise justifications that it was hard to find a clear principle running through the cases. This can be seen, for instance, in the area of nuisance,[113] where many of the contradictory cases reflected less a neglect by the judges of industrial pollution than the fact that the cases presented to them differed greatly.[114] The need for strict

---

[112] Contrast *Rylands* v. *Fletcher* (1865) L.R. 1 Ex. 265. See also, *Holden* v. *the Liverpool New Gaslight Company* (1846) 15 LJCP 301. See A. W. B. Simpson, 'Legal Liability for Bursting Reservoirs: The Historical Context of *Rylands* v. *Fletcher*', *Journal of Legal Studies*, xiii (1984), 209—64, on the historical background to that case and the policy reasons that lay behind it.

[113] See J. F. Brenner, 'Nuisance Law and the Industrial Revolution', *Journal of Legal Studies*, iii (1973), 403–33 and J. P. S. McLaren, 'Nuisance Law and the Industrial Revolution: Some lessons from Social History', *Oxford Journal of Legal Studies*, iii (1983), 155–221.

[114] Judges usually allowed nuisances where there was an authorizing statute involved, even if the statute did not allow the specific nuisance, but gave damages where there was no statute. Compare *R* v. *Pease* (1832) 4 B. & Ald. 30 and *R* v. *Morris* (1830) 1 B. & Ad. 440. See also the judges' comments in *Broadbent* v. *the Imperial Gas Company* (1856–7) 7 De G. M. & G. 736; *Reg.* v. *the Longton Gas Company (Ltd.)* (1860) 29 LJNSMC 118 at 124; *Reg.* v. *Train* (1862) 31 LJNSMC, 169 at 173; and *Reg.* v. *the United Kingdom Electric Telegraph Company Ltd.* (1862) 31 LJNSMC 166. In the apparently contradictory brick-burning cases of *Hole* v. *Barlow* (1858) 4 CBNS 334 and *Bamford* v. *Turnley* (1862) 3 B. & S. 62, the first court ruled that the plaintiffs could only win if their lives were rendered less comfortable by the brick burning and found that given the industrial area in which the nuisance occurred, this was not the case, while the second found a tangible nuisance caused by the defendant. There were obvious policy statements made by judges in these cases, but first the litigants had to show precise damage to their property for which the defendant was to blame. In many cases of industrial pollution, it was difficult to show either that the defendant was

allegations of responsibility underlies some of the most contentious areas of nineteenth-century tort law. It can be seen at work, for instance, in the case of *Priestley* v. *Fowler*, the notorious father of an infamous line of precedents.[115] In this case, it was ruled that the employer, who had ordered his servant to deliver goods in a van which collapsed and which caused the servant to break his thigh, was not liable in an action for negligence. This case is remembered for Lord Abinger's biased remarks on the desirable relationship between a master and a servant, yet it should be noted that the case for the defence rested not on policy questions but on the precision required for the action to succeed. Serjeant Adams argued that for the action to be successful, three things had to be shown, which had not been: first, it should have been alleged that the cart was over-loaded with the defendant's knowledge or at his bidding; second, the plaintiff had to be shown to have been ignorant of the overloading; and third, it had to be shown that the defendant had ordered the plaintiff to use the van. In addition, it was argued that since there was a master and servant relationship, any liability arising from the circumstances of the case would not be a common law one, but one arising from a contract: and that the plaintiff should therefore have sued in assumpsit and not in case.

This is a clear example of a judge turning to policy to resolve the case, in the absence of legal precedents. Lord Abinger commented on the absence of precedents, and observed, '[w]e are therefore to decide the question upon general principles, and in doing so we are at liberty to look at the consequences of a decision'.[116] He found that the mere relationship of master and servant implied no contractual duty[117] and that it was undesirable to make masters so liable.

---

specifically to blame for the pollution or to determine how far responsible he should be held (see e.g, *St Helens Smelting Company* v. *Tipping* (1865) 11 H.L.C. 642. However, where the damage caused was tangible and clear, as in *The Stockport Waterworks Company* v. *Potter* (1861) 7 H. & N. 160, where the defendants discharged arsenic into a brook used as a water supply, the courts had no room for policy deliberations. For problems of allegation, see also *Mumford* v. *the Oxford, Worcester and Wolverhampton Railway Company* (1856) 1 H. & N. 34.

[115] (1837) 3 M. & W. 1. See T. Ingman, 'The Rise and Fall of the Doctrine of Common Employment', *Juridical Review* (1978), 106–25 and his 'A History of the Defence of Volenti non fit Injuria', *Juridical Review* (1981), 1–28.

[116] 3 M. & W. 5.

[117] The servant could refuse to perform any acts which he saw would injure him. 3 M. & W. 6.

By comparing the nature of the reasoning in cases involving workmen's compensation with the reasoning in other cases, it can be seen why it was often almost impossible for injured workers to obtain compensation. This is seen in cases respecting the rule that masters were liable for the negligence of their servants which caused damage to third parties. In *Quarman* v. *Burnett*,[118] two elderly ladies who had hired a coachman to take them for regular rides were sued for damages resulting from the horses bolting while the coachman was in their house taking off the uniform they had supplied him with. The court held the ladies were not liable, since the driver was not their permanent employee, but was hired from a contractor. For the ladies to be liable, they had to be seen to have had full powers over the driver. Since they did not control his actions, they were not liable. Similar notions prevented improvement commissioners from being liable for the acts of their subcontractors, since they did not direct the precise acts of the contracted workers.[119] This need for precise allegations of responsibility, control, and supervision explains the legal thinking which resulted in the rule expressed in *Hutchinson* v. *the York, Newcastle and Berwick Railway Company*[120] that masters were not liable for injuries done to workmen in their employ caused by the negligence of their fellow workmen. This case led to a series of judgments in which it was held that a worker, on entering into employment, implicitly accepted all the risks of a job which were not created by the negligence of the employer.

The line of cases is long and controversial;[121] but what should be noted in them is how far the judges expressed their policy choices through the requirements of correct allegation. For instance, in *Bartonshill Coal Company* v. *McGuire*[122] Lord Cranworth ruled that where the accident was caused by the negligence of a fellow-workman and a third party—the employer—was sued, the injured person would have to show such circumstances as would make that third party liable. If a man in 'common employment' with the injured man was guilty of negligence, but was appointed in good faith by the employer, who had no reason to suspect him of being incapable,

---

[118] (1840) 6 M. & W. 499. See also *Laugher* v. *Pointer* (1826) 5 B. & C. 547.

[119] See *Humphreys* v. *Mears* (1827) 1 Man. & Ry. 130 and *Allen* v. *Hayward* (1845) 7 QB 960.   [120] (1850) 3 Ex. 343.

[121] See P. J. W. Bartrip and S. B. Burman, *The Wounded Soldiers of Industry: Industrial Compensation Policy, 1833–1897* (Oxford, 1983).

[122] (1858) 3 Macq. H. L. Sc. 300.

then the employer was not liable.[123] In these cases, the courts took an exceptionally narrow view of what constituted responsibility. Given that the injured workmen were unable to prove specifically that the employer was himself negligent—for instance in appointing bad workers[124]—it was for the court to decide whether they should be: and they in effect made a policy choice in ruling that workers must be presumed to accept the risks of being harmed by the negligence of their fellow workers.[125] This extended not merely to industrial accidents caused by the negligence of fellow workmen: it extended equally to the use of faulty machinery, where it was not shown that the master knew of the fault.[126]

As legal education developed, and as more treatises were written which drew out the principles of the law, so the law could appear more integrated and rational. By 1883, Dicey could urge upon his students 'the habit of looking upon law as a series of rules',[127] as a way to make sense of the mass of legal materials. The jurisprudence of Bentham and Austin allowed lawyers to conceive of law in that way; their analytical approach helped identify the materials to be seen as rules. None the less, it should not be forgotten that until after

---

[123] This was taken to its ultimate conclusion in *Wislon* v. *Merry* (1868) LR 1 Sc. & Div. 326. Here Lord Cairns ruled, 'if an accident occurs to a workman to-day in consequence of the negligence of another workman, skilful and competent, who was formerly, but is no longer, in the employment of the master, the master is, in my opinion, not liable, though the two workmen cannot technically be described as fellow workmen'.

[124] See *Tarrant* v. *Webb* (1856) 18 CB 797, *Potts* v. *Port Carlisle Dock and Railway Company* (1860) 8 WR 524. In *Wilson* v. *Merry* (1868) LR 1 Sc. & Div. 326 Lord Cairns said, '[n]egligence cannot exist if the master does his best to employ competent persons; he cannot warrant the competency of his servants'.

[125] See also *Degg* v. *the Midland Railway Company* (1857) 1 H. & N. 773. This case extended the 'common employment' rule to those individuals who were not employees, but who assisted the employers' servants voluntarily. Here, the plaintiff's husband was killed while helping railway workers to turn a truck. Bramwell B ruled that the plaintiff had failed to show the defendants were liable: 'it may be,' he said, 'that had the mischief here resulted from the personal act of the master, he knowing that the deceased was here, the master would have been liable; and that as the defendants' servant knew the deceased was on the railway, and because they knew that, were guilty of a wrong to him, they are liable to an action; but on what reason or principle should the defendants be?' On the narrowest interpretation of common law pleading, he felt that the company was not liable; and on policy, he did not see why it should be.

[126] See *Paterson* v. *Wallace* (1854) 1 Macq. 748, *Hall* v. *Johnson* (1865) 3 H. & C. 589, *Ashworth* v. *Stanwix* (1861) 3 E. & E. 708, *Mellors* v. *Shaw* (1861) 1 B. & S. 444, *Skipp* v. *Eastern Counties Railway Company* (1853) 9 Ex. 223, and *Dynen* v. *Leach* (1857) 26 LJ Ex. 221.

[127] *Can English Law be Taught at the Universities?*, 21.

after the mid-century, most judges still saw the law as a system of remedies for individual cases. As judges sought to refine pleading, to develop it from being the senseless technical confusion that Bentham berated, into a logical system to get to the kernel of the dispute, so they developed a more analytical way of looking at the law. Yet it was still seen through the adjudication of the common law system of remedies.

Bibliography

PRIMARY WORKS

(i) Parliamentary Papers

Hansard

First Report of His Majesty's Commissioners appointed to Inquire into the Practice and Proceedings of the Superior Courts of Common Law, 1829 (46) IX.

Second Report made to His Majesty by the Commissioners appointed to Inquire into the Practice and Proceedings of the Superior Courts of Common Law, 1830 (123) XI.

Third Report made to His Majesty by the Commissioners appointed to Inquire into the Practice and Proceedings of the Superior Courts of Common Law, 1831 (92) X.

Fourth Report made to His Majesty by the Commissioners appointed to Inquire into the Practice and Proceedings of the Superior Courts of Common Law, 1831–2 (239) XXV.

Fifth Report made to His Majesty by the Commissioners appointed to Inquire into the Practice and Proceedings of the Superior Courts of Common Law, 1833 (247) XXII.

Sixth Report made to His Majesty by the Commissioners appointed to Inquire into the Practice and Proceedings of the Superior Courts of Common Law, 1834 (263) XXVI.

First Report of His Majesty's Commissioners on Criminal Law, 1834 (537) XXVI.

Second Report of His Majesty's Commissioners on Criminal Law, 1836 (343) XXXVI.

Third Report of Her Majesty's Commissioners on Criminal Law, 1837 (79) XXXI.

Fourth Report of Her Majesty's Commissioners on Criminal Law, 1839 (168) XIX.

Fifth Report of Her Majesty's Commissioners on Criminal Law, 1840 (242) XX.

Sixth Report of Her Majesty's Commissioners on Criminal Law, 1841 (316) X.

Seventh Report of Her Majesty's Commissioners on Criminal Law, 1843 (448) XIX.

Eighth Report of Her Majesty's Commissioners on Criminal Law, 1845 (656) XIV.

First Report of the Commissioners of Inquiry into the Law of England respecting Real Property, 1829 (263) X.

Second Report of the Commissioners of Inquiry into the Law of England respecting Real Property, 1830 (575) XI.

Third Report of the Commissioners of Inquiry into the Law of England respecting Real Property, 1831–2 (484) XXIII.

Fourth Report of the Commissioners of Inquiry into the Law of England respecting Real Property, 1833 (226) XXII.

First Report of Her Majesty's Commissioners for Inquiring into the Process, Practice and System of Pleading in the Superior Courts of Common Law, 1851 (1389) XXII 567.

Copies of the Lord Chancellor's Letters to the Judges and of their Answers, respecting the Criminal Law Bills of the last Session, 1854 (389) LIII.

(ii) Periodicals

Edinburgh Review
Fraser's Magazine
Law Journal
Law Magazine
Legal Examiner and Law Chronicle
London Review
Northern Star
Quarterly Review
The Times
Westminster Review

(iii) Books

[Anon.] *The Pleader's Assistant* (London, 1786).

[Anon.] *The English Pleader* (Dublin, 1783).

[Anon.] *A Treatise on the Study of Law* (London, 1797).

Aston, Richard, *Placite Latine Rediviva* (London, 1661).

Austin, John, *Lectures on Jurisprudence, or the Philosophy of Positive Law*, ed. R. Campbell, 3rd edn., 2 vols. (London, 1869).

Ayliffe, John, *A New Pandect of the Roman Civil Law* (London, 1734).

Bacon, Francis, *Of the Advancement and Proficience of Learning, or the Partitions of the Sciences* (Oxford, 1640).

Barrington, Daines, *Observations on the Statutes*, 2nd edn. (London, 1766).

Barton, Charles, *The Grounds and Maxims and also an Analysis of the English Laws* (London, 1794).

Bell, George Joseph, *An Examination of the Objections stated against the Bill for regulating the Forms of Process in the Courts of Law in Scotland* (Edinburgh, 1825).

Bellers, Fettiplace, *A Delineation of Universal Law* (London, 1754).

Bentham, George, *Outline of a New System of Logic, with a Critical Examination of Dr. Whately's Elements of Logic* (London, 1827).

Bentham, Jeremy, *Chrestomathia*, ed. M. J. Smith and W. H. Burston (Oxford, 1983).

—— *A Comment on the Commentaries and A Fragment on Government*, ed. J. H. Burns and H. L. A. Hart (London, 1977).

—— *Constitutional Code. Volume I*, ed. F. Rosen and J. H. Burns (Oxford, 1983).

Bentham, Jeremy, *An Introduction to the Principles of Morals and Legislation*, ed. J. H. Burns and H. L. A. Hart (London, 1970).

—— *Of Laws in General*, ed. H. L. A. Hart (London, 1970).

—— *The Theory of Fictions*, ed. C. K. Ogden (London, 1932).

—— *The Works of Jeremy Bentham*, ed. J. Bowring, 11 vols. (Edinburgh, 1838–43).

—— *Anarchical Fallacies*, in *Works*, ii. 489–534.

—— *Codification Proposal*, in *Works*, iv. 535–94.

—— *A Commentary on Mr. Humphreys' Real Property Code*, in *Works*, v. 387–416.

—— *Constitutional Code*, in *Works*, ix.

—— *Essay on Logic*, viii. 213–93.

—— *A General View of a Complete Code of Laws*, in *Works*, iii. 155–210.

—— *Justice and Codification Petitions*, in *Works*, v. 437–548.

—— *Nomography; or the Art of Inditing Laws*, in *Works*, iii. 231–83.

—— *Pannomial Fragments*, in *Works*, iii. 211–30.

—— *Papers relative to Codification and Public Instruction*, in *Works*, iv. 451–533.

—— *Principles of the Civil Code*, in *Works*, i. 297–364.

—— *Principles of Judicial Procedure*, in *Works*, ii. 1–188.

—— *Rationale of Judicial Evidence*, in *Works*, vi and vii.

—— *Scotch Reform*, in *Works*, v. 1–53.

—— *Truth v. Ashhurst*, in *Works*, v. 231–7.

—— *The Correspondence of Jeremy Bentham*, ii, 1777–80, ed. T. L. S. Sprigge (London, 1968).

Bever, Thomas, *A Discourse on the Study of Jurisprudence and the Civil Law* (Oxford, 1766).

Blackstone, William, *An Analysis of the Laws of England*, 3rd edn. (Oxford, 1758).

—— *Commentaries on the Laws of England*, 4 vols. (Oxford, 1765–9).

Blount, Thomas, *A Law Dictionary*, 3rd edn. ed. W. Nelson (London, 1717).

Bohun, William, *The English Lawyer* (London, 1732).

—— *Institutio Legalis* (London, 1724).

Boote, Richard, *An Historical Treatise of an Action or Suit at Law* (London, 1766).

Bridgman, R. W., *A Short View of Legal Bibliography* (London, 1807).

Brougham, Henry, *Speeches upon Questions relating to Public Rights, Duties and Interests*, 4 vols. (Edinburgh, 1838).

Burke, Edmund, *The Works of the Right Honourable Edmund Burke*, ed. W. King and F. Laurence, 16 vols. (London, 1826–7).

Burn, Richard, *The Justice of the Peace and Parish Officer*, 4th edn., 3 vols. (London, 1757).

Burnet, Gilbert, *The Life and Death of Sir Matthew Hale, Kt.* (London, 1682).

Cay, John, *An Abridgment of the Publick Statutes in Force*, 2 vols. (London, 1739).

Chambers, Ephraim, *Cyclopaedia; Or, an Universal Dictionary of Arts and Sciences*, 7th edn., 2 vols. (London, 1751; 1st edn. 1728).

Chambers, Richard, *A Course of Lectures on the English Law delivered at the University of Oxford 1767–73*, ed. T. M. Curley, 2 vols. (Oxford, 1986).

Chitty, Joseph, *A Concise View of the Principles, Object and Utility of Pleadings* (London, 1834).

—— *A Practical Treatise on Bills of Exchange*, 5th edn. (London, 1818).

—— *The Practice of the Law in all its Departments*, ed. R. Lush, 3 vols. (London, 1842).

—— *Reports of Cases Principally on Practice and Pleading determined in the Court of King's Bench*, 2 vols. (London, 1820–3).

Chitty, Joseph (junior), *A Practical Treatise of the Law of Contracts*, 2nd edn. (London, 1834).

—— *Precedents in Pleading*, 2nd edn. ed. H. Pearson (London, 1847).

Clift, Henry, *A New Book of Declarations, Pleadings, Verdicts, etc.* (London, 1719).

Coke, Edward, *A Booke of Entries* (London, 1614).

—— *The First Part of the Institutes of the Laws of England; Or, a Commentary on Littleton*, 17th edn., ed. F. Hargrave and C. Butler, 2 vols. (London, 1817).

Comyn, Samuel, *The Law of Contracts and Promises upon various Subjects*, 2nd edn. (London, 1824).

Comyns, John, *A Digest of the Laws of England*, 5 vols. (London, 1762–76).

Condillac, Etienne de, *La Logique* (Paris, 1780).

Cowell, John, *Institutiones Iuris Anglicani ad Methodum et Seriem Institutionum Imperialium Compositae et Digestae* (London, 1605).

Crompton, G., *Practice Common-Placed: Or the Rules and Cases of Practice in the Courts of King's Bench and Common Pleas Methodically Arranged*, 2 vols. (London, 1780).

Cunningham, Timothy, *The History and Antiquities of the Four Inns of Court* (London, 1780).

—— *A History of Taxes* (London, 1783).

—— *The Law of Simony* (London, 1784).

D'Alembert, Jean le Rond, *Mélanges de littérature, d'histoire et de philosophie*, 4th edn., 5 vols. (Amsterdam, 1767).

Dalrymple, John, *An Essay towards a General History of Feudal Property in Great Britain* (London, 1757).

Dawes, Manasseh, *Epitome of the Law of Landed Property* (London, 1818).

Dodderidge, John, *The Lawyer's Light: or a Due Direction for the Study of the Law* (London, 1629).

Dogherty, Thomas (ed.), *The Crown Circuit Companion*, 7th edn. (London, 1799).

Domat, Jean, *The Civil Law in its Natural Order: Together with the Publick Law*, trans. W. Strahan, 2 vols. (London, 1722).

Encyclopédie, ou Dictionnaire raisonné des sciences, des arts et des métiers, par une société de gens de lettres, 17 vols. (Paris, 1751–65).

Ensor, George, *Defects of the English Laws and Tribunals* (London, 1812).

Espinasse, Isaac, *A Digest of the Law of Actions and Trials at Nisi Prius*, 2nd edn. (London, 1792).

Euer, Samson, *A System of Pleading* (London, 1677; Dublin, 1791).

Finch, Henry, *A Description of the Common Law of England* (London, 1759).

—— *Law, or a Discourse thereof*.

Fonblanque, John (ed.), *A Treatise of Equity, with the additions of Marginal References and Notes*, 5th edn., 2 vols. (London, 1820).

Fortescue, John, *De Laudibus Legum Angliae*, ed. A. Amos (Cambridge, 1825).

Fox, William, *A Treatise on Simple Contracts and the Action of Assumpsit* (London, 1842).

Fraunce, Abraham, *The Lawiers Logicke* (London, 1588).

Fulbecke, William, *A Directive, or Preparation to the Study of the Law*, 2nd edn., ed. T. H. Stirling (London, 1829).

Furneaux, Philip, *Letters to the Hon. Mr. Justice Blackstone, concerning his Exposition of the Act of Toleration . . . in his celebrated Commentaries on the Laws of England*, 2nd edn. (London, 1771).

Gardiner, Robert, *The Doctrine of Demurrers* (London, 1706).

—— *The English Pleader* (London, 1734).

—— *Instructor Clericalis* (London, 1693).

Gilbert, Jeffrey, *The Law of Evidence*, ed. C. Lofft, 3 vols. (London, 1791).

—— *An Historical View of the Court of Exchequer, and of the King's Revenues There Answered* (London, 1738).

—— *The History and Practice of Civil Actions*, 3rd edn. (London, 1779).

Hale, Matthew, *The Analysis of the Law; Being a Scheme, or Abstract, of the Titles and Partitions of the Law of England, Digested into a Method* (London, 1713).

—— *History of the Common Law*, 5th edn., ed. C. Runnington (London, 1794).

—— *Reflections by the Lrd. Cheife Justice Hale on Mr. Hobbes his Dialogue of the Lawe*, in W. S. Holdsworth, *History of English Law*, v. 500–13.

Hallifax, Samuel, *An Analysis of the Roman Civil Law*, 2nd edn. (Cambridge, 1775).

Hammond, Anthony, *An Analysis of the Principles of Pleading; Or Idea of a Study of that Science* (London, 1819).

—— *The Criminal Code*, 7 vols. (London, 1828).

Harris, George, *D. Justiniani Institutionum*, 2nd edn. (London, 1761).

Hobbes, Thomas, *A Dialogue between a Philosopher and a Student of the Common Laws of England*, ed. J. Cropsey, (Chicago and London, 1971).

Holliday, John, *The Life of William late Earl of Mansfield* (London, 1797).

Holloway, William (ed.), *System of the Modern Roman Law* (Madras, 1867).

Hugo, Gustav, *Lehrbuch des Naturrechts als einer Philosophie des positiven Rechts* (Berlin, 1819).

Humphreys, James, *Observations on the Actual State of the English Laws of Real Property with the outlines of a Code* (London, 1826).

Impey, John, *The Modern Pleader* (London, 1794).

Jacob, Giles, *The Student's Companion* (London, 1725).

Jones, William, *An Essay on the Law of Bailments*, 2nd edn. (London, 1798).

—— *The Works of Sir William Jones*, 16 vols. (London, 1799).

Kames, Henry Home, Lord, *Sketches of the History of Man*, 2 vols. (Edinburgh, 1774).

Kant, Immanuel, *The Metaphysical Elements of Justice*, trans. J. Ladd (Indianapolis, 1965).

Lawes, Edward, *A Practical Treatise of Pleading in Assumpsit* (London, 1810).

—— *Rules and Orders of the Supreme Courts of Common Law, from the Commencement of the Reign of William IV to Hilary Term, 8th Victoria* (London, 1845).

—— *Suggestions for Some Alterations of the Law, on the Subjects of Practice, Pleading and Evidence* (London, 1827).

Leake, S. M., *The Elements of the Law of Contract* (London, 1867).

Lindley, Nathaniel, *An Introduction to the Study of Jurisprudence* (London, 1855).

Mackeldey, Ferdinand, *Handbook of the Roman Law*, trans. Moses A. Dropsie (Philadelphia, 1883).

Mackintosh, James, *A Discourse on the Study of the Law of Nature and Nations* (London, 1799).

Madox, Thomas, *The History and Antiquities of the Exchequer*, 2nd edn. (London, 1769).

Mallory, John, *Modern Entries in English* (London, 1734).

Maugham, Robert, *A Treatise on the Law of Attornies, Solicitors and Agents* (London, 1825).

Mill, James, *Elements of Political Economy* (London, 1826).

—— *Essays on Government, Jurisprudence, Liberty of the Press, and Law of Natns* (London, n.d.).

Mill, John Stuart, *A System of Logic*, ed. J. M. Robson and R. P. McRae (Toronto, 1973).

—— *The Collected Works of John Stuart Mill*, gen. ed. F. E. L. Priestley (Toronto, 1963).

Miller, John, *An Inquiry into the Present State of the Civil Law of England* (London, 1825).

—— *An Inquiry into the Present State of the Statute and Criminal Law of England* (London, 1822).

Montesquieu, Charles de Secondat, Baron, *The Spirit of Laws*, trans. T. Nugent, 2 vols. (London, 1763).

Nelson, William, *Lex Maneriorum: Or, the Law and Customs of England Relating to Manors and Lords of Manors*, 2nd edn. (London, 1733).

Ollyffe, Thomas, *The Young Clerk's Tutor Enlarged: Being a most useful collection of the best precedents of recognizances, obligations, conditions, acquittances, bills of sale, warrants of attorney, etc.*, 16th edn. (London, 1717).

Paley, William, *The Principles of Moral Philosophy* (London, 1785).

Park, John James, *A Contre-Projet to the Humphresian Code* (London, 1827).

Philips, Joseph, *Letters on Special Pleading, being an Introduction to the Study of that Branch of the Law*, 2nd edn. (1850).

Plowden, Edmund, *The Commentaries or Reports of Edmund Plowden* (London, 1779).

Pollock, Frederick, *Principles of Contract at Law and in Equity* (London, 1876).

Pothier, Robert Joseph, *A Treatise on the Law of Obligations or Contracts*, trans. W. D. Evans, 2 vols. (London, 1806).

Powell, John Joseph, *An Essay upon the Law of Contracts and Agreements*, 2 vols. (London, 1790).

—— *An Essay on Devises*, ed. T. Jarman, 2 vols. (London, 1827).

Pufendorf, Samuel, *On the Law of Nature and Nations*, ed. J. Barbeyrac, trans. B. Kennet, 3rd edn. (London, 1717).

Rastall, William, *The New Natura Brevium of the Most Reverend Judge Mr. Anthony Fitzherbert* (London, 1652).

Reddie, John, *Inquiries Elementary and Historical into the Science of Law* (London, 1840).

—— *A Letter to the Lord High Chancellor of Great Britain on the Expediency of the Proposal to form a new Civil Code for England* (London, 1828).

—— *Historical Notices of the Roman Law and of the recent progress of its study in Germany* (Edinburgh, 1826).

Reeve, Thomas, *Lord Chief Justice Reeve's Instructions to his Nephew concerning the Study of Law* (London, 1791).

Reeves, John, *History of the English Law from the time of the Saxons to the End of the Reign of Philip and Mary*, 4 vols. (London, 1787).

Ritso, Frederick, *An Introduction to the Science of Law* (London, 1815).

Rossi, P. L. O., *Traité de droit pénal* (Paris, 1829).

Rowe, W. H., *Observations on the Rules of Descent* (London, 1803).

Rutherforth, Thomas, *Institutes of Natural Law*, 3rd edn. (London, 1754).

Sanderson, Robert, *Logicae Artis Compendium*, 11th edn. (Oxford, 1741; 1st edn. 1618).

Savigny, F. C., *System des Heutigen Römischen Rechts*, 8 vols. (Berlin, 1840).

—— *Vom Beruf unserer Zeit für Gesetzgebung und Rechtswissenschaft* (Heidelberg, 1814).

Schiefer, J. F., *An Explanation of the Practice of Law* (London, 1792).

Sedgwick, James, *Remarks Critical and Miscellaneous on the Commentaries of Sir William Blackstone* (London, 1800).

Selden, John, *De Jure Naturali et Gentium* (London, 1640).

Smith, Adam, *An Inquiry into the Nature and Causes of the Wealth of Nations*, 2 vols., ed. R. H. Campbell, A. S. Skinner, and W. B. Todd (Oxford, 1976).

—— *Lectures on Jurisprudence*, ed. R. Meek, D. D. Raphael, and P. G. Stein (Oxford, 1976).

Stair, James Dalrymple, Viscount, *The Institutes of the Law of Scotland* (Edinburgh, 1681).

Stephen, H. J., *A Treatise on the Principles of Pleading in Civil Actions* (London, 1824).

Stewart, Dugald, *Elements of the Philosophy of the Human Mind*, vol. i (Edinburgh, 1792), vol. ii (1814).

Sullivan, F. S., *Lectures on the Constitution and Laws of England*, 2dn edn. (London, 1776).

Taylor, John, *Elements of the Civil Law*, 4th edn. (London, 1828).

Theloall, Simon, *Le Digest des Briefs et des Choses concernant eux* (London, 1687).

Thibaut, A. F. J., *System des Pandekten Rechts*, 2 vols. (Jena, 1846).

—— *Versuche einzele Theile der Theorie des Rechts*, 2 vols. (Jena, 1817).

—— *Über die Nothwendigkeit eines allgemeines bürgerliches Rechts für Deutschland* (Berlin, 1814).

Thomas, J. H., *A Systematic Arrangement of Lord Coke's First Institute*, 3 vols. (London, 1818).

Twiss, Horace, *An Inquiry into the Means of Consolidating and Digesting the Laws of England* (London, 1826).

Uniacke, Crofton, *A Letter to the Lord Chancellor on the necessity and practicality of forming a code of the Laws of England: Arranged in the method of Domat's Civil Law* (London, 1825).

Warren, Samuel, *A Popular and Practical Introduction to Law Studies* (London, 1835).

Watts, Isaac, *Logic, or the Right Use of Reason in the Inquiry after Truth* (London, 1792; 1st edn. 1725).

Wentworth, John, *A Complete System of Pleading*, 10 vols. (London, 1797–9).

Wilkins, David, *Leges Anglo-Saxonicae* (London, 1721).

Wood, Thomas, *An Institute of the Laws of England: Or the Laws of England in Natural Order according to common use*, 2 vols. (London, 1720).

—— *A New Institute of the Imperial or Civil Laws* (London, 1730).

—— *Some Thoughts concerning the Study of the Laws of England, particularly in the two universities* 2nd edn. (London, 1727).

Wooddeson, Richard, *Elements of Jurispudence* (London, 1783).

—— *A Systematical View of the Laws of England*, 3 vols. (London, 1792–3).

Wright, Martin, *An Introduction to the Law of Tenures* (London, 1730).

Wright, William, *Advice on the Study and Practice of Law*, 3rd edn. (London, 1824).

Wynne, Edward, *Eunomus: Or Dialogues concerning the Law and Constitution of England*, 3rd edn., 2 vols. (London, 1809).

—— *Miscellany containing several Law Tracts* (London, 1765).

Secondary Works

(i) Books

Allen, C. K., *Law in the Making*, 6th edn. (Oxford, 1958).

Amos, Sheldon, *A Systematic View of the Science of Jurisprudence* (London, 1872).

—— *The Science of Law* (London, 1874).

Atiyah, P. S., *The Rise and Fall of Freedom of Contract* (Oxford, 1979).

Baker, Ernest, *Traditions of Civility* (London, 1948).

Baker, J. H., *The Reports of Sir John Spelman*, Selden Society, vol. 94 (London, 1978).

Baumgardt, David, *Bentham and the Ethics of Today* (Princeton, 1952).

Boorstin, Daniel J., *The Mysterious Science of the Law* (Cambridge, Mass., 1941).

Boralevi, Lea Campos, *Bentham and the Oppressed* (Berlin, 1984).

Bryce, James, *Studies in History and Jurisprudence*, 2 vols. (Oxford, 1901).

Capellini, Paolo, *Systema Iuris*, 2 vols. (Milan, 1984–5).

Collins, R. H., and Arbuthnot, R. G. (ed.), *Smith's Leading Cases*, 9th edn., 2 vols. (1887).

Cross, R. A., *Precedent in English Law*, 3rd edn. (Oxford, 1977).

Dawson, J. P., *The Oracles of the Law* (Ann Arbor, 1968).

Dicey, Albert Venn, *Lectures on the Relation between Law and Public Opinion in England during the Nineteenth Century*, 2nd edn. (London, 1914).

Dickinson, H. T., *Liberty and Property: Political Ideology in Eighteenth Century Britain* (London, 1977).

Dowrick, F. E., *Justice according to the English Common Lawyers* (London, 1961).

Dworkin, Ronald, *Law's Empire* (London, 1986).

—— *Taking Rights Seriously* (London, 1977).

Evans, Robin, *The Fabrication of Virtue: English Prison Architecture, 1750–1840* (Cambridge, 1982).

Fifoot, C. H. S., *English Law and its Background* (London, 1932).

—— *The History and Sources of the Common Law: Tort and Contract* (London, 1949).

—— *Judge and Jurist in the Reign of Queen Victoria* (London, 1959).

—— *Lord Mansfield* (Oxford, 1936).

Freedland, M. R., *The Contract of Employment* (Oxford, 1976).

Friedmann, Wolfgang, *Legal Theory* (London, 1967).

Fryer, B., Hunt, A., McBarnet, D., and Moorhouse, B. (ed.), *Law, State and Society* (London, 1981).

Gash, Norman, *Mr Secretary Peel: The Life of Sir Robert Peel to 1830* (London, 1961).

Gray, John Chipman, *The Nature and Sources of Law* (New York, 1909).

Green, Thomas A., *Verdict according to Conscience. Perspectives on the English Criminal Trial Jury 1200–1800* (London, 1985).

Grimsley, R., *Jean d'Alembert* (Oxford, 1963).

Halévy, Elie, *The Growth of Philosophic Radicalism* (London, 1928).

Hamburger, Lotte and Joseph, *Troubled Lives: John and Sarah Austin* (Toronto, 1985).

Hanbury, H. G., *The Vinerian Chair and Legal Education* (Oxford, 1958).

Harrison, Ross, *Bentham* (London, 1983).

Hart, H. L. A., *Essays on Bentham: Studies in Jurisprudence and Political Theory* (Oxford, 1982).

—— *The Concept of Law* (Oxford, 1961).

Hawes, Frances, *Henry Brougham* (London, 1957).

Heward, Edmund, *Lord Mansfield* (Chichester and London, 1979).

Holdsworth, W. S., *A History of English Law*, 17 vols. (London, 1922–72).

Holland, T. E., *Jurisprudence*, 13th edn. (London, 1924).

Hont, Istvan, and Ignatieff, Michael (ed.), *Wealth and Virtue: The Shaping of Political Economy in the Scottish Enlightenment* (Cambridge, 1983).

Horwitz, Morton J., *The Transformation of American Law* (London, 1977).

Howell, W. S., *Eighteenth Century British Logic and Rhetoric* (Princeton, 1971).

Hume, L. J., *Bentham and Bureaucracy* (Cambridge, 1981).

Kelly, P. J., *Utilitarianism and Distributive Justice: Jeremy Bentham and the Civil Law* (Oxford, 1990).

Kelsen, Hans, *Pure Theory of Law*, trans. M. Knight (Berkeley, Los Angeles, and London, 1978).

Kenyon, J. P., *Revolution Principles: The Politics of Party, 1689–1720* (Cambridge, 1977).

Letwin, Shirley R., *The Pursuit of Certainty: David Hume, Jeremy Bentham, John Stuart Mill, Beatrice Webb* (Cambridge, 1965).

Levack, Brian P., *The Civil Lawyers in England: A Political Study* (Oxford, 1973).

Lieberman, David, *The Province of Legislation Determined: Legal Theory in Eighteenth Century Britain* (Cambridge, 1989).

Long, Douglas G., *Bentham on Liberty: Jeremy Bentham's Idea of Liberty in relation to his Utilitarianism* (Toronto, 1977).

Lyons, David, *In the Interests of the Governed* (Oxford, 1973).

McAdam, E. L., *Dr. Johnson and the English Law* (Syracuse, 1951).

Mack, Mary, *Jeremy Bentham: An Odyssey of Ideas, 1748–1792* (London, 1962).

Maine, Henry Sumner, *Ancient Law: Its Connection with the Early History of Society and its Relation to Modern Ideas* (London, 1861).

—— *The Early History of Institutions* (London, 1875).

Maitland, F. W., *Equity. Also the Forms of Action at Common Law. Two Courses of Lectures*, ed. A. H. Chaytor and W. J. Whittaker (Cambridge, 1909).

Manchester, A. H., *Modern Legal History* (London, 1980).

Marini, Giuliano, *L'opera di Gustav Hugo nella crisi del giusnaturali tedesco* (Milan, 1969).

Milsom, S. F. C., *Historical Foundations of the Common Law*, 2nd edn. (Cambridge, 1981).

Moles, Robert N., *Definition and Rule in Legal Theory: A Reassessment of H. L. A. Hart and the Positivist Tradition* (Oxford, 1987).

Morison, W. L., *John Austin* (London, 1982).

New, Chester W., *The Life of Henry Brougham to 1830* (Oxford 1961).

Ong, Walter J., *Ramus, Method and the Decay of Dialogue* (Cambridge, Mass., 1958).

Parekh, Bhikhu, *Jeremy Bentham: Ten Critical Essays* (London, 1974).

Pocock, J. G. A., *The Ancient Constitution and the Feudal Law* (Cambridge, 1957).

—— *Politics, Language and Time: Essays on Political Thought and History* (London, 1972).

Postema, Gerald J., *Bentham and the Common Law Tradition* (Oxford, 1986).

Pound, Roscoe, *Essays in Jurisprudence from the Columbia Law Review* (New York, 1963).

Prest, Wilfrid R., *The Inns of Court under Elizabeth I and the Early Stuarts, 1590–1640* (London, 1972).

Radzinowicz, Leon, *A History of English Criminal Law and its Administration from 1750*, 4 vols. (London, 1948–68).

Raz, Joseph, *The Concept of a Legal System*, 2nd edn. (Oxford, 1980).

Reill, P. H., *The German Enlightenment and the Rise of Historicism* (Berkeley, Los Angeles, and London, 1975).

Rosenblum, Nancy, *Bentham's Theory of the Modern State* (Cambridge, Mass., 1978).

Ross, Janet, *Three Generations of Englishwomen*, 2 vols. (London, 1888).

Rubin, G. R., and Sugarman, David (ed.), *Law, Economy and Society, 1750–1914: Essays in the History of English Law* (Abingdon, 1984).

Rumble, Wilfrid, *The Thought of John Austin* (London, 1985).

Salmond, J. W., *Jurisprudence*, 11th edn., ed. Glanville Williams (London, 1957).

Schluchter, Wolfgang, *The Rise of Western Rationalism: Max Weber's Developmental History*, trans. G. Roth (Berkeley, Los Angeles, and London, 1981).

Schumpeter, J. A., *History of Economic Analysis* (London, 1955).

Simpson, A. W. B., *A History of the Common Law of Contract. The Rise of the Action of Assumpsit* (Oxford, 1975).

—— *A History of the Land Law*, 2nd edn. (Oxford, 1986).

Steintrager, James, *Bentham* (Ithaca, NY, 1977).

Stewart, Robert, *Henry Brougham, 1778–1868: His Public Career* (London, 1985).

Stone, Julius, *Legal System and Lawyers' Reasonings* (London, 1964).
—— *The Province and Function of Law* (London, 1947).
Stourzh, Gerald, *Alexander Hamilton and the Idea of Republican Government* (Stanford, 1970).
Sugarman, David (ed.) *Legality, Ideology and the State* (London, 1983).
Tuck, Richard, *Natural Rights Theories: Their Origin and Development* (Cambridge, 1979).
Turner, B. S., *For Weber: Essays on the Sociology of Fate* (Boston, London, and Henley, 1981).
Twining, William, *Theories of Evidence: Bentham and Wigmore* (London, 1985).
Watson, Alan, *The Making of the Civil Law* (Cambridge, Mass. 1981).
Webb, Sidney and Beatrice, *English Local Government: Statutory Authority for Special Purposes* (London, 1922).
Weber, Max, *Economy and Society: An Outline of Interpretive Sociology*, 3 vols. (New York, 1968).
Welsby, W. N., *The General Turnpike Road Acts*, 4th edn. (London, 1854).
Williford, Miriam, *Jeremy Bentham on Spanish America* (Baton Rouge, 1980).
Zweigert, Konrad, and Kötz, Hein, *An Introduction to Comparative Law*, trans. T. Weir, 2nd edn. 2 vols. (Oxford, 1987).

(ii) Articles

Alfange, Dean, 'Bentham and the Codification of Law', *Cornell Law Review*, lv (1969), 58–77.
Allen, T. R. S., 'Legislative Supremacy and the Rule of Law', *Cambridge Law Journal*, xliv (1985), 111–43.
Annette, John, 'Bentham's Fear of Hobgoblins: Law, Political Economy and Social Discipline', in Bob Fine *et al.* (eds.), *Capitalism and the Rule of Law: From Deviancy Theory to Marxism* (London, 1979), 65–75.
Atiyah, P. S., 'Common Law and Statute Law', *Modern Law Review*, xlviii (1985), 1–28.
Berger, Michel, 'Codification', in E. Attwoll (ed.), *Perspectives in Jurisprudence* (Glasgow, 1977), 142–59.
Beynon, Helen, 'Mighty Bentham', *Journal of Legal History*, ii (1981), 62–72.
Bland, D. S., 'Rhetoric and the Law Student in Sixteenth-Century England', *Studies in Philology*, liv (1957), 498–508.
Brebner, J. B., 'Laissez-faire and State Intervention in Nineteenth Century Britain', *Journal of Economic History*, vii (1948), 59–73.
Brenner, J. F., 'Nuisance Law and the Industrial Revolution', *Journal of Legal Studies*, iii (1973), 403–33.
Brooks, Christopher, and Sharpe, Kevin, 'History, English Law and the Renaissance', *Past and Present*, no. lxxii (1976), 133–42.
Burns, J. H., 'Bentham on Sovereignty: An Exploration', *Northern Ireland Legal Quarterly*, xxiv (1973), 399–416.

Burns, J. H., 'Bentham and Blackstone: A Lifetime's Dialectic', *Utilitas*, i (1989), 22–40.

—— *The Fabric of Felicity: The Legislator and the Human Condition* (London, 1967).

Burns, Robert P., 'Blackstone's Theory of the "Absolute" Rights of Property', *University of Cincinnati Law Review* liv (1985), 67–86.

Cairns, J. W., 'Blackstone, an English Institutist: Legal Literature and the Rise of the Nation-State', *Oxford Journal of Legal Studies*, iv (1984), 318–60.

—— 'Eighteenth Century Professorial Classification of the English Common Law', *McGill Law Journal*, xxxiii (1987), 225–44.

Campbell, Enid, 'German Influences in English Legal Education and Jurisprudence in the Nineteenth Century', *University of Western Australia Annual Law Review*, iv (1957–9), 357–90.

Chloros, A. G., 'Some Aspects of the Social and Ethical Elements in Analytical Jurisprudence', *Juridical Review*, lxvii (1955), 79–102.

Cross, R. A., 'Blackstone v. Bentham', *Law Quarterly Review*, xcii (1976), 516–27.

—— 'The Reports of the Criminal Law Commissioners (1833–49) and the Abortive Bills of 1853', in P. R. Glazebrook (ed.), *Reshaping the Criminal Law: Essays in Honour of Glanville Williams* (London, 1978, 5–20).

David, Helene, 'Deux Contemporains: Stair et Domat', *Juridical Review* (1982), 68–85.

Dicey, A. V., *Can English Law be Taught at the Universities?* (London, 1883).

DiFilippo, Terry, 'Jeremy Bentham's Codification Proposals and some Remarks on their Place in History', *Buffalo Law Review*, xxii (1972–3), 239–51.

Dinwiddy, J. R., 'Adjudication under Bentham's Pannomion', *Utilitas*, i (1989), 283–9.

—— 'Bentham's Transition to Political Radicalism, 1809–10', *Journal of the History of Ideas*, xxxvi (1975), 683–700.

Doolittle, I. G., 'Sir William Blackstone and his *Commentaries on the Laws of England* (1765–9): A Biographical Approach', *Oxford Journal of Legal Studies*, iii (1983), 99–112.

Finnis, J. M., 'Blackstone's Theoretical Intentions', *Natural Law Forum*, xii (1967), 163–83.

Fletcher, George P., 'Two Modes of Legal Thought', *Yale Law Journal*, xc (1980–1), 970–1003.

Francis, Mark, 'The Nineteenth Century Theory of Sovereignty and Thomas Hobbes', *History of Political Thought*, i (1980), 517–40.

Fried, Charles, 'The Artificial Reason of the Law, or: What Lawyers Know', *Texas Law Review*, lx (1981–2), 35–58.

Fuller, Lon L., 'The Forms and Limits of Adjudication', in K. I. Winston (ed.), *The Principles of Social Order: Selected Essays of Lon L. Fuller*, (Durham, NC, 1981), 86–124.

Gerber, D., 'A Note on Woody on Dewey on Austin', *Ethics*, lxxix (1968–9), 303–8.

Giuliani, A., 'The Influence of Rhetoric on the Law of Evidence and Pleading', *Juridical Review*, vii (NS) (1962), 216–51.

Goodhart, A. L., 'Determining the Ratio Decidendi of a Case', in A. L. Goodhart, *Essays in Jurisprudence and the Common Law* (Cambridge, 1931), 1–26.

Gordon, Robert W., 'Critical Legal Histories', *Stanford Law Review*, xxxvi (1984), 57–125.

Griffiths, John, 'Is Law Important?', *New York University Law Review*, liv (1979), 339–74.

Harrison, Frederic, 'The English School of Jurisprudence', *Fortnightly Review*, xxiv (NS) (1878), 475–92.

Hart, H. L. A., 'Blackstone's Use of the Law of Nature', *Butterworth's South African Law Review* (1956), 169–74.

—— 'Positivism and the Separation of Law and Morals', *Harvard Law Review*, lxxi (1957–8), 593–629.

Hart, Jenifer, 'Nineteenth Century Social Reform: A Tory Interpretation of History', *Past and Present*, no. xxxi (1965), 39–61.

Himmelfarb, Gertrude, 'The Haunted House of Jeremy Bentham', in G. Himmelfarb, *Victorian Minds* (London, 1968), 32–81.

Hoeflich, M. H., 'John Austin and Joseph Story: Two Nineteenth Century Perspectives on the Utility of the Civil Law for the Common Lawyer', *American Journal of Legal History*, xxxix (1985), 36–77.

Holdsworth, W. S., 'The New Rules of Pleading of the Hilary Term 1834', *Cambridge Law Journal*, i (1921–3), 261–78.

Hume, L. J., 'Jeremy Bentham and the Nineteenth Century Revolution in Government', *Historical Journal*, x (1967), pp. 361–75.

Ingman, Terence, 'The Rise and Fall of the Doctrine of Common Employment', *Juridical Review* (1978), 106–25.

—— 'A History of the Defence of Volenti non fit Injuria', *Juridical Review* (1981), 1–28.

James, M. H., 'Bentham on the Individuation of Laws', *Northern Ireland Legal Quarterly*, xxiv (1973), 357–82.

Jones, G. H., 'Per Quod Servitium Amisit', *Law Quarterly Review*, lxxiv (1958), 39–58.

Kadish, Sanford H., 'Codifiers of the Criminal Law', *Columbia Law Review*, lxxviii (1978), 1098–1144.

Keeton, G. W., and Marshall, O. R., 'Bentham's Influence on the Law of Evidence', in G. W. Keeton and G. Schwarzenberger (ed.), *Jeremy Bentham and the Law* (London, 1948), 79–100.

Kelley, Donald R., 'History, English Law and the Renaissance', *Past and Present*, no. lxv (1974), 24–51.

Kennedy, Duncan, 'The Structure of Blackstone's Commentaries', *Buffalo Law Review*, xxviii (1979), 205–382.

King, Peter, 'Gleaners, Farmers and the Failure of Legal Sanctions in England 1750–1850', *Past and Present*, no. cxxv (1989), 116–50.

Knafla, Louis A., 'Law Studies of an Elizabethan Student', *Huntington Library Quarterly*, xxxii (1968–9), 221–40.

—— 'The Matriculation Revolution and Education at the Inns of Court in Renaissance England', in A. J. Slavin (ed.), *Tudor Men and Institutions: Studies in English Law and Government* (Baton Rouge, 1972), 232–64.

Lewis, A. D. E., 'John Austin: Pupil of Bentham', *Bentham Newsletter*, no. ii (1979), 18–29.

Lieberman, David, 'From Bentham to Benthamism', *Historical Journal*, xxviii (1985), 119–24.

Lobban, Michael, 'From Seditious Libel to Unlawful Assembly: Peterloo and the Changing Face of Political Crime in England, *c.*1770–1820', *Oxford Journal of Legal Studies*, x (1990), 307–52.

Long, Douglas, 'Censorial Jurisprudence and Political Radicalism: A Reconsideration of the Early Bentham', *Bentham Newsletter*, no. xii (1988), 4–23.

Lucas, Paul, 'Blackstone and the Reform of the Legal Profession', *English Historical Review*, lxxvii (1962), 456–89.

Luig, Klaus, 'The Institutes of National Law in the Seventeenth and Eighteenth Centuries', *Juridical Review*, xvii (1972), 193–226.

Lysaght, L. J., 'Bentham on the Aspects of a Law', *Northern Ireland Legal Quarterly*, xxiv (1973), 383–98.

MacCormick, Neil, 'The Rational Discipline of Law', *Juridical Review*, xxvi (NS) (1981), 146–60.

MacDonough, Oliver, 'The Nineteenth Century Revolution in Government: A Reappraisal', *Historical Journal*, i (1958), 52–67.

McKnight, Joseph W., 'Blackstone, Quasi-Jurisprudent', *Southwestern Law Journal*, xiii (1959), 399–411.

McLaren, J. P. S., 'Nuisance Law and the Industrial Revolution—Some Lessons from Social History', *Oxford Journal of Legal Studies*, iii (1983), 155–222.

McRae, R., 'The Unity of the Sciences: Bacon, Descartes and Leibniz', *Journal of the History of Ideas*, xviii (1957), 27–48.

Maher, Gerard, 'Analytical Philosophy and Austin's Philosophy of Law, *Archiv für Sozial- und Rechtsphilosophie*, lxiv (1978), 401–16.

Manchester, A. H., 'Simplifying the Sources of Law: An Essay in Law Reform', *Anglo-American Law Review*, ii (1973), 395–413 and 527–50.

Manning, C. A. W., 'Austin To-day: Or, the "Province of Jurisprudence" Revisited', in *Modern Theories of Law*, (London, 1933), 180–226.

Menlowe, Michael A., 'Bentham, Self-Incrimination and the Law of Evidence', *Law Quarterly Review*, civ (1988), 286–307.

Mill, John Stuart, 'Austin on Jurisprudence', *Edinburgh Review*, cxviii (1863), 439–82.

—— 'Bentham,' in B. Parekh (ed.), *Jeremy Bentham: Ten Critical Essays* (London, 1974), 1–40.

Milsom, S. F. C., 'The Nature of Blackstone's Achievement', *Oxford Journal of Legal Studies*, i (1981), 1–12.

—— 'Reason in the Development of the Common Law', *Law Quarterly Review*, lxxxi (1965), 496–517.

Montrose, J. L., 'Return to Austin's College', *Current Legal Problems*, xiii (1960), 1–21.

Morison, W. L., 'Some Myth about Positivism', *Yale Law Journal*, lxviii (1958–9), 212–33.

Morris, Herbert, 'Verbal Disputes and the Legal Philosophy of John Austin', *UCLA Law Review*, vii (1959–60), 27–56.

Olivecrona, Karl, 'The Will of the Sovereign: Some Reflections on Bentham's Concept of "a Law"', *American Journal of Jurisprudence*, xx (1975), 95–110.

Parris, Henry, 'The Nineteenth Century Revolution in Government: A Reappraisal Reappraised', *Historical Journal*, iii (1960), 17–37.

Perry, Stephen R., 'Judicial Precedent, Obligation and the Common Law', *Oxford Journal of Legal Studies*, vii (1987), 215–57.

Plucknett, T. F. T., 'John Reeves: Printer', *Columbia Law Review* (1961), 1201–9.

Postema, Gerald J., 'Bentham on the Public Character of Law', *Utilitas*, i (1989), 41–61.

—— 'Co-ordination and Convention at the Foundations of Law', *Journal of Legal Studies*, xi (1982), 165–203.

—— 'The Expositor, the Censor and the Common Law', *Canadian Journal of Philosophy*, ix (1979), 643–70.

—— 'The Principle of Utility and the Law of Procedure: Bentham's Theory of Adjudication', *Georgia Law Review*, xi (1977), 1393–1424.

Prest, Wilfrid, 'The Dialectical Origins of Finch's *Law*', *Cambridge Law Journal*, xxxvi (1977), 326–52.

Prichard, M. J., 'Trespass, Case and the Rule in *Williams* v. *Holland*', *Cambridge Law Journal* (1964), 234–53.

—— *Scott* v. *Shepherd (1773) and the Emergence of the Tort of Negligence*, Selden Society (London, 1976).

Rinck, Hans-Justus, 'Blackstone and the Law of Nature', *Ratio*, ii (1960), 162–80.

Roberts, David, 'Jeremy Bentham and the Victorian Administrative State', *Victorian Studies*, ii (1958–9), 193–210.

Rodgers, C. P., 'Humanism, History and the Common Law', *Journal of Legal History*, vi (1985), 129–56.

Romilly, Samuel, 'Bentham on Codification', *Edinburgh Review*, xxix (1817–18), 217–37.

Ruben, Eira, 'Austin's Political Pamphlets', in E. Attwoll (ed.), *Perspectives in Jurisprudence* (Glasgow, 1977), 20–41.

Rudden, Bernard, 'A Code Too Soon: The 1826 Property Code of James Humphreys: English Rejection, American Reception, English Acceptance', in P. Wallington and R. M. Merkin (ed.), *Essays in Memory of Professor F. H. Lawson* (London, 1986), 101–16.

Rumble, Wilfrid, 'Divine Law, Utilitarian Ethics and Positivist Jurisprudence: A Study of the Legal Philosophy of John Austin', *American Journal of Jurisprudence*, xxi (1979), 139–80.

—— 'John Austin and his Nineteenth Century Critics: The Case of Sir Henry Sumner Maine', *Northern Ireland Legal Quarterly*, xxxix (1988), 119–49.

—— 'John Austin, Judicial Legislation and Legal Positivism', *University of Western Australia Law Review*, xiii (1977–8), 77–109.

Schoek, R. J., 'Rhetoric and Law in Sixteenth Century England, *Studies in Philology*, l (1953) 110–27.

Schwarz, Andreas B., 'John Austin and the German Jurisprudence of his Time', *Politics*, i (1934), 178–99.

Shapiro, Barbara, 'Law and Science in Seventeenth Century England', *Stanford Law Review*, xxi (1968–9), 727–66.

Simpson, A. W. B., 'The Common Law and Legal Theory', in A. W. B. Simpson (ed.), *Oxford Essays in Jurisprudence*, 2nd series (Oxford, 1973), 77–99.

—— 'Innovation in Nineteenth Century Contract Law', *Law Quarterly Review*, xci (1975), 247–76.

—— 'The Rise and Fall of the Legal Treatise: Legal Principles and Forms of Legal Literature', *University of Chicago Law Review*, xlviii (1981), 632–79.

—— 'The *Ratio Decidendi* of a Case and the Doctrine of Binding Precedent', A. E. Guest (ed.), *Oxford Essays in Jurisprudence* (Oxford, 1961), 148–75.

Stein, Peter, 'Nineteenth Century English Company Law and Theories of Legal Personality', *Quaderni Fiorentini per la storia del pensiero giuridico moderno*, xi–xii (1982–3), 503–19.

—— 'The Procedural Models of the Sixteenth Century', *Juridical Review* (1982), 186–97.

Stumpf, S. E., 'Austin's Theory of the Separation of Laws and Morals', *Vanderbilt Law Review*, xiv (1960), 117–49.

Sugarman, David, 'Legal Theory, the Common Law Mind and the Making of the Textbook Tradition', in W. Twining (ed.), *Legal Theory and the Common Law* (Oxford, 1986), 26–61.

Summers, Robert S., 'The *New* Analytical Jurists', *New York University Law Review*, xli (1966), 861–96.

Sunderland, Eldon R., 'The English Struggle for Procedural Reform', *Harvard Law Review*, xxxix (1925–6), 725–48.

Terrill' Richard J., 'Humanism and Rhetoric in Legal Education: the Contribution of Sir John Dodderidge (1555–1628)', *Journal of Legal History*, ii (1981), 30–44.

Watson, Alan, 'The Structure of Blackstone's Commentaries', *Yale Law Journal*, xcvii (1988), 795–821.

White, Alan R., 'Austin as a Philosophical Analyst', *Archiv für Rechts- und Sozialphilosophie*, lxiv (1978), 379–99.

Willman, Robert, 'Blackstone and the Theoretical Perfection of English Law in the Reign of Charles II'. *Historical Journal*, xxvi (1983), 39–70.

Winfield, P. H., 'The History of Negligence and the Law of Torts', *Law Quarterly Review*, xlii (1926), 184–201.

—— and Goodhart, A. L., 'Trespass and Negligence', *Law Quarterly Review*, xlix (1933), 359–78.

Woody, S. M., 'The Theory of Sovereignty: Dewey versus Austin', *Ethics*, lxxviii (1967–8), 313–18.

Yale, D. E. C., 'Hale and Hobbes on Law, Legislation and the Sovereign', *Cambridge Law Journal*, xxxi (1972), 121–56.

Zagday, M. I., 'Bentham on Civil Procedure', in G. W. Keeton and G. Schwarzenberger (ed.), *Jeremy Bentham and the Law* (London, 1948), 68–78.

(iii) Theses

Campbell, E. M., 'John Austin and Jurisprudence in Nineteenth Century England' (Duke University Ph.D., 1958).

Hostettler, J. A., 'The Movement for Reform of the Criminal Law in England in the Nineteenth Century' (University of London Ph.D., 1983).

Napier, B. W., 'The Contract of Service: The Concept and its Application' (Cambridge University Ph.D., 1975).

Reibman, J. E., 'Dr. Johnson and the Law' (Edinburgh University Ph.D., 1979).

Index